The Data Warehouse Challenge
Taming Data Chaos

Michael H. Brackett

WILEY COMPUTER PUBLISHING

John Wiley & Sons, Inc.
New York • Chichester • Brisbane • Toronto • Singapore

Publisher: Katherine Schowalter
Editor: Theresa Hudson
Managing Editor: Susan Curtin
Text Design & Composition: Publishers' Design and Production Services, Inc.

Designations used by companies to distinguish their products are often claimed as trademarks. In all instances where John Wiley & Sons, Inc. is aware of a claim, the product names appear in initial capital or all capital letters. Readers, however, should contact the appropriate companies for more complete information regarding trademarks and registration.

This publication is designed to provide accurate and authoritative information in regard to the subject matter covered. It is sold with the understanding that the publisher is not engaged in rendering legal, accounting, or other professional service. If legal advice or other expert assistance is required, the services of a competent professional person should be sought.

Library of Congress Cataloging-in-Publication Data:
Brackett, Michael H.
    The data warehouse challenge : taming data chaos / Michael H. Brackett.
      p.   cm.
    Includes index.
    ISBN 0–471–12744–2 (paper : alk. paper)
    1. Database management. 2. Data structures (Computer science).
    I. Title.
    QA76.9.D3B683   1996
    005.74—dc20   96–14608
                                                  CIP

Printed in the United States of America
10 9 8 7 6 5 4 3 2

To Jeanne

About the Author

Mr. Brackett was the Data Resource Coordinator for the State of Washington with the Department of Information Services. He has been in the data processing field 35 years and has worked for the state for 30 years in a variety of agencies, including the Department of Natural Resources, Department of Fisheries, Employment Security Department, and Washington State University. He recently retired from state service and is now a consulting data architect.

Mr. Brackett has developed many innovative concepts and techniques for designing applications and managing a data resource. He developed a common data architecture for the state that includes state agencies, cities, counties, Indian tribes, public utilities, and Federal agencies. That common data architecture covers large multijurisdictional areas, such as water resource, growth management, criminal justice, and health care.

Mr. Brackett has a B.S. in Forestry and an M.S. in Forestry (Botany) from the University of Washington, and an M.S. in Soils (Geology) from Washington State University. He has written and published four previous books on application and data design. He has also written many articles and given numerous presentations at local, national, and international conferences on the topic of application design, data design, and data refining.

Mr. Brackett is a member of the Seattle chapter of the Data Resource Management Association (a chapter of DAMA International), was a past board member of that organization, and is currently on the DAMA International Board. He taught Data Modeling and Design in the Data Resource Management Certificate Program at the University of Washington. He also teaches Data Architecture classes and consults with public and private organizations about development of an integrated data resource within a common data architecture. He is listed in *Who's Who in the West* and *Who's Who in Education*.

Foreword

by William H. Inmon

Spock has just arrived from a long trip to the outer regions of nebula QIIU1-190 in the year 2525. The trip through the nether lands of outer space has been long. It has been a while since Spock has touched the green/blue terrestrial orb called by some the planet "Earth." Spock's arrival on the humble planet is reenergizing. The stretches of time Spock has had in the cold emptiness of deep space have sparked new questions and insights.

One of the marvels Spock has made note of in his travels throughout the galaxy is that organizations on Earth in 2525 are spectacularly adaptable and at the same time are self-regenerating. The efficiency and the effectiveness of the modern Earth-bound organization of 2525 is an amazement to Spock. Spock's interest is piqued in that modern organizations are at the same time highly adaptable, quickly responsive to change, globally uniform and locally autonomous, and stable and self-regenerative.

Spock is fascinated at the ability of the organization to fulfill these seemingly contradictory goals all at the same time and with no apparent conflict. At the heart of the organization's power to satisfy diverse and complex organizational goals at the same time is the ability of the organization to use information effectively. The wise and effective use of information is the key that unlocks the true potential of the organization.

Spock, being a scientist, is curious as to how the earthling organizations came to this powerful and incongruous ability to use information so effectively. All history of the usage of information points to a year long ago—2000—as the turning point where organizations began to be effective in their understanding and usage of information. Just what intersection of ideas and opportunity has occurred in the year 2000 that has spawned this wondrous facility?

Looking further into the subject, Spock discovers some early clues to the transformation of the organization that was made in the year 2000. In the ancient 1960s there were some primitive notions about the need to organize and manage programming code by early, venerated information adventurers Yourdon and deMarco. Then in the 1970s came some larger notions about the structure and scope of applications from a pioneer named Martin. In the 1980s Spock discovers the ideas about databases that led to a formalized approach by Codd and Date. And in the 1990s, Spock finds that maverick architects Zachman and Inmon expressed some interesting ideas about the larger structure of information systems and entire environments. But nowhere does Spock find a complete unified discussion of exactly what happened in the 1995–2000 time frame that transformed the corporate ability to use information effectively. Spock—now fully determined and spurred on by ever mounting curiosity—presses on with the search in the archives of 2525.

Almost by accident, on a late October night while the meteor showers were lighting the sky, Spock stumbles upon the work by Brackett. In the back of a dusty shelf—with crinkled pages yellowed by the centuries—lay the answer Spock was looking for. Picking up the work by Brackett, Spock read—page by page, concept by concept, detail by detail—how it was that the technician and the businessman who controlled the organization in 1995–2000 achieved the uplift of the corporation. Now that the secret was revealed, and Spock's intellectual curiosity can rest.

This book by Michael Brackett is the definitive source for understanding modern data architecture. Other books have bits and pieces of architecture described, but nowhere else is there a single source that has all the components of modern data architecture in one place in an organized and readable manner.

There are many reasons to put Michael Brackett's book in a prominent and prized place on your computer reference bookshelf. The two most prominent reasons are his insight and his completeness. I hope you enjoy and find as much use for this book as I have. And I hope you highlight the most important places that you find for future reference for the space explorers like Spock that are sure to come one day. They will appreciate your guidance and instruction across the sands of time.

William H. Inmon
December 1995

Acknowledgments

The author thanks Susan Garza for her input about data integrity and Denise Prowse for her interest and comments about the practical side of data management. The author also thanks Tom Crawford for his continued personal and professional support. Thanks also go to Janet Voorhies for her constant encouragement to move ahead into uncharted territory, to Carlene Covey for her interest and guidance, to Chris Larkin for his continued encouragement, and to Billie Lasater for her excellent copy editing, and to Shelagh Bury for her support in the final stages of editing and proofing.

The author also thanks the students in his classes, the conference attendees, and the project team members he has worked with for their thoughts and comments about approaches to understanding and managing disparate data and about developing an integrated data resource. Their input helped make this book a success.

Special thanks go to Carey Clark and Scott Denkers for the time they spent discussing current data problems that organizations face and for their comprehensive reviews of the manuscript for this book. Without their professional thoughts and candid comments, many of the concepts and techniques presented in this book would not be available. The author also extends special thanks to John Zachman for his continued efforts with the Framework for Information Systems, thoughts and comments about managing a data resource, and his professional encouragement. His input is most appreciated.

Special thanks also go to Marc Brackett, Sean Brackett, and Kevin Brackett who tolerated, encouraged, and supported their father while he wrote this book. Their help really made the book possible. Extra special thanks go to Jeanne Brackett, to whom this book is dedicated, for the unwavering support she provides her big brother.

Finally, with great respect, the author thanks Bill Inmon for the work he has done on developing and implementing data warehouses and for his insight into understanding and resolving many of the data problems that organizations face today. The author also thanks Bill Inmon for his foreword; it is a classic that will be long remembered.

Preface

Data chaos crisis exists in almost every organization. Many organizations are not aware they have data chaos. A few organizations know a chaos exists, but will not, or do not want to, admit it. Data chaos is the result of many years' accumulation of disparate data; data that are not part of any common or consistent architecture. Organizations are on the threshold of losing control over their data resource because of these disparate data—and that's the good news. The bad news is that disparate data are being produced faster than they have ever been produced before. The really bad news is that few organizations are doing anything about this chaotic situation.

The rapidly increasing quantities of disparate data do not meet the need for rapid data integration to support constantly changing business activities. The need for information to support the business, often on short notice, is not being met. Organizations need to learn at the speed of change just to keep up, but they need to learn faster than the speed of change to move ahead. Disparate data are blocking the learning process and preventing organizations from keeping up and moving ahead. Organizations are literally data-rich with disparate data and information-poor for integrated data.

Disparate data create a real dilemma for organizations because integrated data are needed for survival, yet the continued production of disparate data is often ignored in favor of information system development and hardware acquisition. Developing client/server applications, building data warehouse systems, implementing geographic information systems, and distributing data over networks without control over the data result in data problems several orders of magnitude greater than problems that already exist. The fragmentation of data and the loss of data heritage and data lineage could be disastrous to the organization's business.

A real shock comes when organizations realize that their existing disparate data resource does not, will not, and cannot support dynamic business needs. This book is about the stark realization that disparate data are the rule, not the exception. It is about the challenge of building a robust data warehouse—a single integrated data resource—that supports the organization's business needs from disparate data.

Identifying, understanding, and transforming disparate data into an integrated data resource to meet the constantly changing demand for information is the key to stopping the development of disparate data and eliminating existing disparate data. Increasing the awareness of existing disparate data, understanding the content and meaning of disparate data so they can be readily shared and reused within an organization and across organizational boundaries is mandatory for developing an integrated data resource.

The Data Warehouse Challenge explains the current disparate data situation and how organizations can develop an integrated data resource that supports the dynamic need for information. The book is about building a stable, integrated data resource that survives changing business activities, changing hardware and system software, and changing applications. It is about taking the opportunity to be successful at providing information to support business activities.

The Data Warehouse Challenge builds on the author's two most recent books, *Practical Data Design* and *Data Sharing Using A Common Data Architecture*. It extends the concepts and techniques to build an integrated data resource within a common data architecture, design new data within that integrated data resource, and refine disparate data to that integrated data resource. It presents new concepts and techniques, such as integrating massive quantities of disparate data, managing disparate metadata, managing data warehouse systems, geographic information systems, and distributed data.

The Data Warehouse Challenge begins with an explanation of the data dilemma that most organizations face today and the disparate data cycle that creates that dilemma. It describes what organizations must go through when they realize their data resource is not meeting their information demand. The book goes on to explain how to develop an integrated data resource within a common data architecture to meet the business information demand.

The common data architecture provides a common context within which all data can be defined to understand their content and meaning. This book describes how to develop an integrated data resource within a common data architecture through formal data names, comprehensive data definitions, and a data structure that is technically correct and culturally acceptable. It also describes the steps necessary to determine data quality, including data integrity, data accuracy, and data completeness, and to ensure that data quality is at the level necessary to meet the information demand.

Metadata, the data needed to understand and manage the data resource, become critically important as the integrated data resource grows. This book explains the techniques to design, manage, integrate, store, and retrieve metadata, and presents the concept of a robust metadata warehouse to make metadata readily available to anyone interested in using the data resource. An integrated data resource is only as good as the metadata about that data resource and the availability of those metadata.

The Data Warehouse Challenge also explains the concepts and techniques to refine massive quantities of disparate data and transform them into the integrated data resource. The techniques for identifying and resolving data redundancy and variability, and designating official data sources and data variations to reduce the redundancy and variability of data are also described.

Data warehouse systems are extremely important for the analysis of time-variant data for trends and projections. This book presents techniques for transforming disparate data into a data warehouse system and managing multiple levels of summary data. Geographic information systems are useful for integrating tabular and geospatial data and developing maps electronically. This book presents techniques for managing spatial data in geographic information systems and for creating references between tabular and spatial data. Rapidly increasing quantities of historical data, both tabular and spatial, are available for the analysis of trends, projections, and alternatives. This book describes techniques for controlling these time-variant data in order to evaluate business opportunities.

The *Data Warehouse Challenge* presents techniques for distributing data within an organization, in a client/server environment, or on a network, and to other organizations. It describes ways to document the dynamic distribution of both data and metadata. It also presents methods of determining the primary source of data, managing data replication, assuring concurrency of replicated data, and identifying data versions.

New technologies, such as data warehouse systems, geographic information systems, and client/server applications require more robust data models. This book describes concepts and techniques for developing common data models within a common data architecture, including strategic, tactical, and detailed data models. A new five-schema approach is presented for modeling data from business needs to physical data files. This book explains techniques for including tabular and nontabular data in the same data model.

Finally, the book presents guidelines for resolving the data dilemma and overcoming data chaos. It explains methods for managing conflicting data standards, managing purchased applications, creating common client data, dismantling legacy systems, and supporting business transformation and business improvement. Cultural issues for surviving on disparate data until an integrated data resource is developed are described as well.

Organizations must recognize that data chaos exists, realize that they are losing control of their critical data resource, and take corrective action to stop the development of disparate data and build an integrated data resource within a common data architecture. They must realize that the situation is bad and will continue to get worse before it gets better. Organizations need to manage their data before their disparate data manage them. Slimmer budgets, limited personnel, higher workload, rapid changes, and increased competition demand a stable, integrated data resource. Organizations must develop an integrated data resource to meet today's information needs without compromising future information needs.

The only way an organization can gain a competitive advantage and remain competitive is to take action now to understand and survive on disparate data while developing an integrated data resource for the future.

Olympia, Washington
December 15, 1995

Contents

CHAPTER 1

Data Crisis

A data dilemma prevents many organizations from fully utilizing their data resource to meet current and future information needs.

The data crisis that most organizations face today is rapidly increasing quantities of disparate data that conflict with an urgent need to integrate current, accurate data to support changing business needs. These rapidly increasing quantities of disparate data result from an orientation toward the rapid development of independent information systems to meet current, critical business needs without regard for future business needs. The changing business needs result from an ever-increasing rate and magnitude of change in the business environment.

Some organizations recognize this data crisis and others do not. Many organizations are aware of the data crisis, but refuse to admit it is happening in their organizations. To use a term from environmental management, organizations are thinking locally rather than globally about their data resource. As a result, they are losing control of the very resource on which they depend for survival. They are actively, and often knowingly, compromising future flexibility to meet current needs.

The high demand for current, accurate, integrated information, often on short notice, is not being met because of the large quantities of disparate data, yet organizations are continuing to manufacture disparate data faster than ever before. Organizations are caught in a cycle that perpetuates the creation of disparate data. Current technology trends are making the cycle worse.

This chapter begins with a brief explanation of the dynamic business environment and the ever-changing demand for new information to survive in that environment. This chapter describes prominent trends in information technology and concludes with an explanation of the metadata demand and the need to produce an integrated data resource.

INFORMATION DEMAND

The business situation today is characterized by an increasingly dynamic business environment, an emphasis toward changing the business to survive in that dynamic environment, and a high demand for current, accurate, integrated information to support business activities. The only real competitive advantage an organization has is to be able to learn and to respond to changes faster than their competitors. Most people know this situation all too well.

With respect to data, an organization must be able to learn what data exist, what those data represent in the real world, and how those data can be readily integrated and used to strengthen its competitive advantage. The ability to learn what data exist and to integrate those data will not solve all the problems an organization faces today. It will, however, stabilize one of the variables and allow an organization to concentrate on other critical issues.

Dynamic Environment

The business environment today is changing rapidly, and both the rate and magnitude of change are constantly increasing. In the 1960s and early 1970s, the only constant was change. Then, in the late 1970s and 1980s, the only constant was the increasing rate of change. Now, in the 1990s, the only constant is the increasing rate and magnitude of change. Constant change is here to stay and organizations must manage that change to remain competitive.

> The business environment is becoming increasingly dynamic as both the rate and magnitude of change increases.

This *change-is-the-name-of-the-game* culture is difficult for many people to deal with even though they are aware it exists. There is little time to assimilate one wave of change before the next wave hits. Not enough time is available to understand, evaluate, and completely implement one wave of change before the next wave arrives. The dynamic business environment forces many organizations to position themselves for change, but finding the time to position themselves for future changes is difficult when so much time is spent making current changes.

Analogy: The analogy about the difficulty of draining the swamp while being waist-deep in alligators has been around a long time, but it is still so very true.

Business Changes

Organizations are evaluating their businesses and making changes to position themselves for change. They are analyzing what lines of business they want, or are required, to have and what activities are needed to support those lines of business effectively and efficiently. They are changing and improving their existing business activities to add value to these lines of business. Any business activity that does not add value is either changed so that it adds value or is eliminated.

> Few organizations, government, quasi-public, or private, are immune from business change.

Business, as used here, includes both goods and services. It includes public, quasi-public, and private sector business, as well as services to both citizens and to customers. For-profit and not-for-profit organizations are included because all organizations are operating in the same dynamic business environment. Few organizations are immune from budget constraints, human resource constraints, time constraints, or rapid changes.

Changing the business requires the ability to understand and integrate disparate data from within and without the organization and to deploy those data so they adequately support business needs. Changing the business also requires the ability to quickly adjust information systems to eliminate old business activities and support new business activities. A major problem arises when organizations cannot easily adjust their information systems because they are tightly linked to legacy databases.

> Business change is severely constrained by the growing quantities of disparate data.

The underlying problem is that organizations tend to change and improve their information systems rather than their data resource because information systems are more visible than data. However, organizations cannot make substantial business changes if the supporting information systems are based on legacy databases that cannot be changed to support the business changes. This inability to improve business activities is holding organizations back and courting disaster.[1]

Business Information Demand

The need for new information changes rapidly. More information is needed to support an organization's business activities, it is needed on shorter notice, and it must be current and accurate. The survival of many organizations depends on having more and better information quicker than competitors. This demand for business information is well-known to most organizations.

The *business information demand* is an organization's continuously increasing, constantly changing need for current, accurate, integrated information, often on short notice, to support its business activities. The business information demand changes the philosophy about a data resource from supply-driven to demand-driven. The data resource must meet the critical needs of the organization as defined by senior management, not the desires of data administration.

An integrated, sharable data resource containing current, accurate data is mandatory to meet the business information demand. A successful organization is one that is able to find the data it needs to thoroughly understand those data, and to use them to its advantage. Such an organization learns how to use disparate data in order to survive today and how to develop an integrated data resource in order to survive in the future.

DATA SITUATION

The data resource in many organizations does not support the business information demand. It contains large quantities of disparate data, and the rate of disparate data is increasing rapidly. Many information sys-

---

[1]The approach to managing legacy systems is explained in more detail in Chapter 15.

tems are being designed and developed to meet today's business needs rather than to provide for future flexibility. This current-need orientation perpetuates the development of disparate data. The result is a dilemma where integrated data are needed for survival, yet disparate data continue to be created.

Disparate Data

Most organizations have large quantities of disparate data.

Disparate data are data that are essentially not alike, or are distinctly different in kind, quality, or character. They are unequal and cannot be readily integrated to adequately meet the business information demand. Disparate data are ambiguous and unclear and are often referred to as *heterogeneous data*.

Most organizations have large and growing quantities of disparate data.

Example: An item in a data file is named *City*, which had meaning to the person who originally defined that data item. That meaning has been lost over time because it was not properly documented. It is not readily known whether the contents are the nominal name of the city, such as *Seattle*, the legal name of the city, such as *City of Seattle*, the city and state, such as *Seattle, Washington*, or the airline abbreviation of the city, such as *SEA*. Even a name like City Name does not help because it fails to provide complete understanding of the content and meaning of the data item. A more formal name like City Name Legal, City Name Nominal, or City Name Abbreviation Airline would be more meaningful.

Example: A name like Birth Date is not meaningful because dates come in many forms of dates, such as month/day/year or year/month/day. In addition, a birth date of *10/12/11* has no explicit meaning because people are alive today that were born in the early part of this century. Any selects, searches, or analyses on these data will not find the desired data, may find the wrong data, and may produce the wrong results. The wrong business decisions could be made, and business opportunities could be missed. A more formal name like Employee Birth Date CYMD provides more meaning.

Example: Confusion between ethnicity, representing cultural decendency, and race, representing biological decendency, could result in incorrect affirmative action summaries and possible lawsuits. Improper use of the terms gender and sex, and disability and handicap could have similar consequences. Formal names that represent current cultural trends, such as Race Code, Ethnicity Code, Gender Code, and Disability Code, will prevent these situations. Comprehensive definitions of the meaning and purpose of such terminology further avoids detrimental situations from occurring.

Example: A name like First Name and Last Name for a student may be meaningless because a student may come from a culture where the student's first name is really the student's last name and the student's last name is really the student's first name. Using a convention like Christian Name and Surname could cause problems with certain religions. A convention like Given Name and Surname is not explicit because a person's middle name is usually a given name. Formal names like Student Name Individual, Student Name Middle, and Student Name Family are more explicit and avoid most problems.

Disparate data are not identified, named, defined, structured, or maintained by a uniform set of rules. They are inconsistently named, poorly defined, improperly structured, and incompletely documented. Their meaning, content, and format are highly variable, and the meaning is often hidden in cryptic codes. Their values are often generated by elusive business rules, and their meanings may change with time. They have low integrity and unknown accuracy and are often not current.

Disparate data are fragmented in different locations, on different databases, with different structures. They are often stored redundantly and the redundant versions are frequently inconsistent. They are often in a raw, unorganized state, and frequently do not exist in electronic form. They are generally unreliable, incompatible, incomplete, and inaccurate. They are difficult to understand, identify, and access, and they are expensive to maintain.

The existence of large quantities of disparate data within a large organization or across many organizations involved in similar business activities, such as growth management, water resources, health care, and criminal justice, results in *massively disparate data*. Thousands of data items exist in hundreds of databases in dozens of organizations for which the true content and meaning are not known. These data have different levels of accuracy and represent different time periods. The greater the number of organizations involved, the greater the degree of disparity. Decisions that often involve the welfare of people are often made based on these massively disparate data.

That's the good news!

Disparate Data Cycle

Disparate data are being produced faster than they have ever been produced before. The ready availability and use of CASE tools, rapid application development tools, application and code generators, database products, spreadsheets, and other client-friendly products give everyone the capability to create disparate data. It is a continuing trend that began with flat files, proceeded through database management systems, and is continuing with current technology.

That's the bad news!

The active production of disparate data results from a hidden cycle. The *disparate data cycle* is a self-perpetuating cycle where disparate data are continuing to be produced at an ever-increasing rate because people either do not know about existing data or do not want to use existing data. The cycle continues because of the client-friendly products mentioned above, but it also continues because people do not know about the cycle.

In some situations, people do not know the data already exist and duplicate the data for their use. In other situations, people know the data exist, but the data are in such poor form or require so much time to understand that they cannot be easily used and new data are created. Sometimes people just want control over their own data and do what they want to do with minimal concern for the business as a whole. All of these situations create additional disparate data.

> Disparate data are created as much from disregard as from ignorance.

The disparate data cycle often continues without organizations knowing it even exists. It evolves so slowly and incrementally that organizations either do not know what is happening, know what is happening and believe that new technology can resolve or prevent it, know what is happening and do not care, or know what is happening but are not aware of its disastrous impact.

Analogy: If a frog is put in boiling water, it immediately jumps out safely. However, if a frog is put in cold water that is heated slowly, the frog is boiled alive. In the first situation, the frog is immediately aware of the dangerous environment and immediately takes corrective action. In the second situation, the incremental change is so slight that the frog is not aware of the change until it is too late.

The same situation is true with disparate data today. Organizations are being "boiled alive" by incrementally increasing quantities of disparate data. They cannot take action because they are not aware of the incremental changes until it is too late. Their failure is inevitable.

Analogy: People do not realize their eyesight is incrementally failing until they are unable to read or see things at a distance. During their eye exam, corrective lenses are dropped in front of their eyes, and they are surprised, often shocked, at how bad their eyesight has become. Once they understand the situation, and see the value of corrective lenses, they take action by wearing glasses or contact lenses.

The difference between responding to the situation by taking corrective action, and not responding to the situation is the rate of change. When the rate of change from a comfortable situation to an uncomfortable situation is rapid, people recognize the situation and take corrective action. When the rate of change is slight, people do not recognize the change and allow the condition to continue until it becomes painful or disastrous. The latter situation is happening with the disparate data cycle.

Data Dilemma

Very little is being done about the disparate data cycle in most organizations. Organizations concentrate on developing hardware for application processing and on developing communications for accessing and moving data. They concentrate on changing the business and on application development. Client/server networks, data warehouse systems, geographic information systems, imaging systems, and a variety of other technologies are implemented. But organizations are not concentrating on controlling their disparate data in spite of many new techniques and tools for data management.

That's the really bad news!

A real *data dilemma* exists in organizations today. A *dilemma* is a situation that requires a choice between two or more options that are, or appear to be, unfavorable or mutually exclusive. It is a situation that seems to defy any resolution. The *data dilemma* is the situation where a critical need for current, accurate data, often on short notice, to meet the business information demand is being compromised by the active development of large quantities of disparate data. This situation seems to require a choice between meeting the current business information demand at the expense of future flexibility or ensuring future flexibility at the expense of meeting the current information demand.

> The data dilemma perpetuates the disparate data cycle.

About seven years ago, resources began to be constrained, and the three T's, training, travel, and temporaries, were cut. However, attitude about the management of the data resource changed very little. As resources became more constrained, cuts were made in the meat of an organization. Still, very little changed in attitude about the management of data. Recently, resource constraints have cut to the heart of the organization and are painful.

Two trends are now emerging. First, a need to understand and integrate the data resource to support rapidly changing business needs is emerging. Organizations are becoming aware of their current disparate data situation and are beginning to plan for the integration of data. Second, with the information demand up and resources down, more people are creating local data faster to support current business activities. The result is the rapid creation of additional disparate data.

Organizations are caught in the disparate data cycle. Unable to break the cycle, they hide in new technology to avoid the issue of disparate data, look for silver bullets to resolve disparate data, and hope technology will solve the problem. Organizations find excuses to concentrate on issues other than building an integrated data resource and are often very creative at finding new ways not to survive.

TECHNOLOGY TRENDS

Many different information technologies are evolving. Each of these technologies promises tremendous benefits if it is implemented properly. If the technologies are not implemented properly, or they are not based on an integrated data resource, they can create disasters far greater than the problems that result from the existing disparate data.

Client/Server Architecture

The client/server architecture offers a strategy for the distribution of data to support the business information demand. It provides the opportunity to share data within and between organizations. Client/ server technology is growing about five-fold each year because of its capability to fit computing into the business process. However, there are two problems with data in the client/server technology.

First, client/server technology appears to resolve the disparate data problem by providing transparent access to a variety of different databases. It appears to integrate disparate data to meet the business information demand. However, simply providing access to databases does not resolve the disparate data problem because it does not integrate the data.

Second, current implementation of client/server technology usually creates more disparate data. It perpetuates the disparate data problem by allowing smaller information systems to be developed with less rigor. Databases are designed independently to meet specific needs and are frequently changed as the need changes.

> Successful client/server requires an integrated data resource.

If client/server technology is not properly implemented with sound data management practices, it will enable the disintegration of data. The true client/server model strongly implies an integrated data resource where data are integrated and shared across business activities and organizational boundaries. It implies forcing the integration of data to meet the business information demand.[2]

Data Warehouse Systems

Data warehouse systems are becoming popular for the management of time-variant data in order to analyze business trends and make projections. They provide an opportunity to bring large quantities of data together and the ability to summarize data to higher levels of generalization or to drill down to lower levels of detail. Data warehouse systems provide the primary support for on-line analytical processing, decision support systems, and executive information systems. However, the data in data warehouse systems present two problems.

First, simply moving disparate data from operational databases to a

---

[2]The management of distributed data is explained in more detail in Chapter 13.

data warehouse system does not resolve the disparate data problem. Second, not many people use the proper techniques for managing multiple levels of summary data. Data that are selected and summarized to meet a specific need are often stored long after the algorithm that created the data is forgotten. These data may never be used again, or they may be used for the wrong purpose because their content and meaning are not known.

> A successful data warehouse system requires an integrated data resource.

A data warehouse system offers tremendous opportunities for an organization to become and remain competitive. However, the data placed in a data warehouse system must be consistent, and the organization must use formal techniques for managing and documenting summary data. An organization building a data warehouse system on disparate data is staking its business on the analysis of those disparate data. Data warehouse systems are a strong technology for understanding the business, but if they are not based on an integrated data resource, they are ineffective and can be disastrous.[3]

Geographic Information Systems

Geographic information systems are becoming popular for storing both spatial and tabular data and for producing maps and reports based on spatial analysis. There will likely be a proliferation of desktop computer mapping within the next five years as the technology becomes less expensive, has more capability, and becomes more client-friendly. However, the data in geographic information systems have three problems.

First, the techniques for designing the data in geographic information systems within an integrated data resource are not well known. Data layers are often created independently for specific purposes, and the data are often redundant and inconsistent between mapping layers.

Second, the data in geographic information systems are not easily integrated with the massive quantities of tabular data in database management systems. The inability to integrate the data in geographic information systems and the data in database management systems limits the usefulness of both spatial and tabular data.

Third, the spatial data in geographic information systems is time-

---

[3]The management of the data in data warehouse systems is explained in more detail in Chapters 10 and 11.

variant and can be saved for the analysis of trends and projections similar to tabular data. Data warehouse systems may be developed for the analysis of time-variant spatial data, just like data warehouse systems are used for the analysis of time-variant tabular data. The problem is that most geographic information system plans do not include the maintenance of time-variant data.

> Successful geographic information system need an integrated data resource.

Geographic information systems offer tremendous opportunities for many organizations, particularly local and state governments. The data in these systems, however, are on the verge of becoming as disparate as tabular data within a few years unless they are managed as part of an integrated data resource.[4]

Other Trends

In recent years emphasis on voice data, textual data, and image data has increased. Users can search textbases in document retrieval systems or text information management systems for keywords, conclusions, and themes. Voice data can be converted to textbases for similar processing, and image bases can be scanned for a variety information. These data are becoming popular, and their volume is growing at an alarming rate. They will contribute substantially to the disparate data problem unless they are managed as part of an integrated data resource.

> All data must be managed as part of an integrated data resource.

Object-oriented programming is a technology where both data and processes are encapsulated. It offers promise for the development of information systems that can be easily adjusted to meet the business information demand. However, object-oriented technology has as much difficulty with disparate data as traditional information systems. It is difficult to determine which disparate data should be encapsulated with the processes, and what those data mean. The result is often the

---

[4]The management of data in geographic information systems is explained in more detail in Chapter 12.

definition of new data independent of existing data, which makes the disparate data problem worse. Object-oriented technology will be successful only if it is based on an integrated data resource.

Document image systems, text information management systems, voice systems, multimedia, electronic data interchange, executive information systems, expert systems, neural nets, and a variety of other technologies are also contributing to the disparate data situation. They, like the technologies mentioned above, will be more successful if they are based on an integrated data resource. The boundaries between these technologies are steadily blurring, and the quicker they can be based on an integrated data resource, the quicker data can be readily shared between technologies to meet the business information demand.[5]

METADATA DEMAND

Metadata management is becoming more important as the volume and complexity of data grows. Good, readily available metadata are mandatory to be able to locate and understand the data needed to meet the business information demand. Individuals who develop an information system and its databases understand the data. That understanding leaves as those individuals retire or move on to other jobs. The result is no explicit understanding of the data in information systems.

This continuing trend of metadata loss is only part of the problem. The other part is that the metadata that do exist are as disparate as the real data. In addition, metadata are becoming more disparate as data are documented in different places, in different forms, and in different degrees of detail. People are documenting data in CASE tools, data dictionaries, repositories, text processors, spreadsheets, and a variety of other products. It is difficult to find all the metadata and to integrate those metadata for a consistent understanding of the real data.

> Good metadata are mandatory to support the business information demand.

Organizations need to know as much as possible about the real data so that they can use the data to meet the business information demand. The *metadata demand* is an organization's need for complete,

---

[5]The integration of different types of data is explained in more detail in Chapter 14.

accurate data about its data resource that is easily understandable and readily available to anyone using, or planning to use, that data resource. To meet this metadata demand, metadata must be managed as part of an integrated data resource just like financial data, personnel data, or customer data.[6]

SUMMARY

The data situation in most organizations today is bad. It is worse than most organizations want to believe. The current situation, however, is mild compared to what it will be if disparate data are not brought under control or organizations do not learn to survive on their disparate data.

The volume of tabular data is doubling about every two years, meaning that the problems with tabular data alone will increase by an order of magnitude in four to five years. Moving tabular data to either a client/server environment or to a data warehouse system will increase data problems by another order of magnitude in about five years. The volume of nontabular data is increasing rapidly and will follow the same pattern as tabular data, increasing the data problems by another order of magnitude. Putting the nontabular data in a client/server environment or in a data warehouse system increases the problems again. Implementing object-oriented technology on disparate data could increase the problems yet again.

That's four to five orders of magnitude increase in an organization's data problems in the next five years! And that estimate may be conservative! That's 10,000 to 100,000 times the data problems that exist today, and today's data problems are unmanageable.

Organizations are leaping into the unknown with new technology without knowing what they are really doing. They are trying to understand technology before they understand the business. Business is being shaped to new technology rather than applying new technology to the business. People cannot wait to try the latest technology, yet they are not using the full features of current technology to support the business. Maybe it is easier to learn new technology than to understand the business. Perhaps an emphasis on new technology is the easiest way to hide from the current problems.

However, an organization cannot hide from the disparate data problem very long and still expect to survive. If the situation goes unchecked, an organization may drown in its own sea of unorganized data without having any information to support the business informa-

---

[6]The management of metadata is explained in more detail in Chapter 8.

tion demand. Survival depends on the ability to understand existing data, start integrating those data, and use those data to meet the business information demand.

QUESTIONS

The following questions are provided as a review of the chapter and to stimulate thought about the data dilemma that exists in most organizations and how that dilemma can be resolved.

1. What is the data crisis that most organizations face today?
2. What is the business situation in most organizations today?
3. How are business changes being hampered by disparate data?
4. What is the business information demand?
5. How did data become disparate?
6. What is the disparate data cycle?
7. What is the data dilemma?
8. How is client/server technology affecting the disparate data problem?
9. How are data warehouse systems affecting the disparate data problem?
10. How are geographic information systems affecting the disparate data problem?
11. Why doesn't object-oriented programming solve the disparate data problem?
12. Why is metadata management becoming important?

## CHAPTER 2

Data Challenge

The challenge is to stop the active creation of disparate data and create an integrated data resource to meet the business information demand.

The challenge for most organizations is to develop a new order for managing data. The challenge is the proactive prevention of any further data disparity by breaking the disparate data cycle. The challenge is the transformation of data into an integrated data resource that supports both the current and future business information demand. The challenge is the development of good metadata so people know what data exist, what they mean, where they are located, and how to access them.

The real challenge, however, is learning to survive on disparate data while developing an integrated data resource. Disparate data cannot be resolved overnight, but the trend of continued disparate data development can be slowed, and even stopped, if an organization takes the initiative. The organization must be able to survive on disparate data while their continued development is stopped and the existing data are transformed into an integrated data resource, however long that may take.

Meeting the challenge means that an organization begins to control its data, rather than the data controlling the organization. Data no longer constrain the business opportunities of the organization, but support the existing business activities as well as new business opportunities. Meeting the challenge means using an integrated data resource as the linchpin to provide a solid foundation for survival in a dynamic business environment.

Chapter 2 begins with an explanation of the realities faced today and the hidden resource that often exists in disparate data. This chapter describes what happens when an organization realizes the disparate data situation and understands that tools and standards are not solving the problem. This chapter then presents an initiative and supporting strategies for developing an integrated data resource that meets the business information demand. The chapter concludes with an explanation of possible approaches and justifications for developing an integrated data resource.

THE REALITIES

The realities of disparate data are often shocking in both negative and positive ways. The negative aspect is that disparate data do exist, often in massive quantities, and are continuing to be developed at an alarming rate. Tools and standards cannot help solve the existing problem, and provide little support for preventing the creation of disparate data. The positive aspect is that often a valuable resource is hidden in disparate data that can help meet the business information demand if properly used.

Basic Problem

All the problems with disparate data, including those described in Chapter 1, can be grouped into four basic categories: awareness, understanding, variability, and redundancy. Meeting the challenge to survive on disparate data while resolving the situation begins with an understanding of these four basic problem categories.

Data Awareness

People are not aware of all the data that exist in an organization's data resource or are available to the organization. They often know of data that exist in their organizational unit or that support their specific business activity, but they are not aware of all the data that are available within and outside the organization to meet the business information demand.

People are not aware of the data that already exist.

Example: The people in marketing are not aware of all the data available from the sale of products and are unable to use those data to develop successful marketing strategies.

Not being aware of all the data that are available results in additional data being captured and stored, which further increases the quantity of disparate data.

Example: The people in marketing may conduct their own customer surveys to determine the products that are purchased by various types of customers at specific times of the month or year.

Not being aware of all the data that are available also results in the data not being fully utilized to meet the business information demand.

Example: These new customer survey data are stored for use by the marketing people but are largely undocumented, so the existence of those data are not known throughout the organization. Manufacturing, in turn, does not know about the data available from sales or from marketing and cannot adjust their schedules accordingly.

Data Understanding

If, and when, the existence of data is known and documented, the real content and meaning of those data are seldom thoroughly understood. The lack of good information about disparate data severely limits both the understanding and the use of those data.

People do not understand the existing data.

Example: An existing database has short mnemonic names, such as EMP_BD, CUST_NM, and STDT_STAT, with definitions like *employee birth date, customer name, and student status*. Although these definitions explain what the mnemonic names mean, they provide little insight into the content and meaning, such as the form of the employee's birth date, what is included in the customer's name, and what the student's status represents.

Example: Does EMP_ETHN really mean an employee's ethnicity, an employee's race, or a mixture of both ethnicity and race?

This limited understanding of the existing data creates an uncertainty about those data. People often avoid using existing data because of this uncertainty and create new data that they do understand. The new data, however, are not thoroughly documented because the creators of those data understand the data, are comfortable with the data, and do not need the documentation. This limited documentation creates additional uncertainty in other people, which causes the creation of more disparate data, and the cycle continues.

Data Variability

Disparate data are highly variable in both content and meaning. The format of data frequently changes from one data item to the next in different data files and may change within the same data item from one record to the next in the same data file.

> Existing disparate data are highly variable.

Example: A student's name may be in the normal sequence in one data file and in the inverted sequence in another data file, such as *Susie Smith* and *Jones, John J*. The student's name may even be in different forms within the same data file.

The meaning of data values with respect to the real world also frequently changes from one data item to the next.

Example: The accuracy of a well depth cannot be determined from a data item named Well_Depth and defined as the depth of a well. The units of measurement are not known, the accuracy is not known, and even the meaning of depth is not known, such as drilled depth, total depth, water depth, or casing depth.

The high variability of disparate data makes those data extremely difficult to use. The analysis of highly variable data may lead to erroneous, and often disastrous, results. Identifying and documenting the variability and designating official forms of data is critical to the successful use of those data to meet business needs.

Data Redundancy

Disparate data are highly redundant; data often are repeated 10 or more times within the organization. It is often unclear which of these redundant data sources contains the most appropriate data, which most accurately reflects the real world, and which is most current.

> The existing disparate data are highly redundant.

Example: Is a student's address in the payroll file, the training file, or the affirmative action file the most current or the most accurate address? Is the product price most current and accurate in the manufacturing database, the sales database, or the marketing database?

The redundant data values are usually inconsistent because they are seldom maintained consistently.

Example: A customer sends a address change notice to an organization. The notice gets routed to one organizational unit, such as sales, because that was the customer's last contact. The people in sales update their address and usually discard the change notice. It is seldom routed to all other organizational units that maintain addresses.

The high redundancy of disparate data makes it extremely difficult to determine which data should be used as the official record of reference. The result of not having official data sources is confusion within the organization and frustration for people that deal with that organization. Understanding all locations of redundant data and designating official sources is also critical to the successful use of data.

> Redundant data values are seldom maintained consistently.

All four of these basic problems must be resolved to stop the development of disparate data and begin development of an integrated data resource. Solving these basic problems starts the process of surviving on disparate data. There are, however, approaches to solving these basic problems that really work and approaches that only appear to work.

Data Access

The two types of data disparity are disparate data and disparate databases. Disparate data, as described above and in Chapter 1, are disparate by reason of their content, meaning, variability, and redundancy. *Disparate databases* are databases or database management systems that are not electronically or operationally compatible. The data in one database management system cannot be readily accessed by another database management system. Disparate databases are also known as *heterogeneous databases*.

Data access is the process of entering a database to store or retrieve data. Many tools today provide electronic and operational access to a wide variety of database management systems and data file formats. Many of these tools provide conversion routines for moving data from one database management system to another. Some even provide conversion routines for data values. Having access to database management systems and providing the ability to move data between database management systems, however, does not solve the disparate data problem. Having data access, such as through open database connectivity, only resolves the disparate database problem. It does not provide the understanding necessary to resolve the disparate data problem.

Data merging is the process of moving a set of data from one database and adding it to another database, such as the merging of data from several databases into a single database. Merging data from disparate databases through open database connectivity does not solve data disparity any more than data access solves data disparity. Merging data may even make the problem worse because any inherent meaning in the data is lost when the data from separate databases are merged. It becomes extremely difficult to track the merged data back to their original source to determine their content and meaning.

Analogy: To build on the environmental management analogy from Chapter 1, disparate data are locally useful and globally junk. They usually have local meaning within a specific information system at the time they were developed, but they have minimal meaning when combined with other local data.

Accessing and merging data solve only a relatively trivial connectivity problem.

The two aspects of *data sharing* are commonly referred to as the medium and the message. The *data sharing medium* is the mechanism by which data are shared; it is the how of data sharing. The *data sharing message* is the actual data being shared; it is the what of data sharing. Most emphasis today is on the data sharing medium, which includes data access and data merging, rather than the data sharing message. The result is only apparent data sharing. True data sharing requires a thorough understanding of the data being shared.

Tools

Tools cannot, have not, and will not, solve the disparate data problem because tools cannot understand data! People understand data! Client-friendly development tools, data documentors, CASE tools, data access tools, data mining and integration tools all sound good, but people must understand the data to properly use those data. The biggest problem with resolving disparate data is understanding the content and meaning of the data. Only people understand data, and people know that only people understand data, yet people are relying on tools as an easy way out of the disparate data problem.

Tools do not understand data; people understand data.

Tools can support people by showing where data are used and stored, determining the existence of the same data name within and between applications and databases, displaying the range of data values, and documenting the data that exist in applications and databases. But tools cannot document the content and meaning of data, resolve homonyms and synonyms, or show intended integrity rules, accuracy, or currentness.

Organizations must face the reality that no easy solution to the disparate data situation exists. They must face the reality that technology alone cannot solve the data dilemma. The apparent solutions to disparate data, such as integration tools and data standards, are not solutions at all. Only when organizations realize that the apparent solutions do not, will not, and cannot resolve disparate data can they get on with the task of breaking the disparate data cycle and resolving the data dilemma.

Technology alone will not solve the disparate data problem.

A traditional perception is that technology can resolve the disparate data situation. Organizations, influenced by a little vendor hype, believe that they can use technology to identify their data, determine the redundancy and variability of that data, and understand the data's content and meaning. Many organizations hope that new technology will resolve the disparity and create an integrated data resource. Organizations even use rapidly evolving technology to hide from the real problem of cleaning up their disparate data. But technology will not solve data disparity.

Quote: Albert Einstein once said, "We cannot solve problems with the same thinking we used when we created the problem."

Only the thought, analysis, and reasoning of people can resolve disparate data. People rely on tools because they do not understand the real problems with disparate data and they hope the tools will understand. Until people recognize the real problems with disparate data and begin to understand the content and meaning of data, there will be no resolution to disparate data, and there will be no integrated data resource. The orientation must be toward increasing people's understanding of the data.

Increasing data understanding helps people build an integrated data resource that meets the business information demand. Increasing data understanding also prevents useful data from being discarded, a critical problem in many organizations.

Analogy: There is an old saying that junk is something you keep for years and then discard the day before you need it. The same situation is often true for data. Data are often kept for years and then discarded because their real value is not known.

Organizations need to take the initiative to resolve data disparity by using knowledgeable people, not tools, to understand the content and meaning of data and build an integrated data resource.

Standards

Developing data standards does not solve the disparate data problem, and the rapid creation of new data standards only makes the situation worse. Many organizations create data standards in an attempt to prevent the creation of disparate data, but they are really creating disparate data standards. Most of these organizations feel it is within their authority, or their duty, to develop data standards and have lost sight of what they are trying to accomplish with data standards.[1]

An organization cannot resolve data disparity through data standards.

An organization cannot mandate the understanding of existing disparate data, however, through data standards. Good data standards provide a framework for preventing data disparity, but the development of conflicting data standards only means that there is no data standard.

Hidden Resource

Many organizations have a hidden resource in their disparate data. The *hidden data resource* is the large quantities of data maintained by an organization that are largely unknown, unavailable, and unused because people are either not aware of the data or do not understand the data. The data just sit in databases or filing cabinets waiting to be useful. If their existence were known and their content and meaning were understood, the data would be readily available to meet the business information demand. This hidden data resource is a welcome surprise to many organizations and is a strong motivator for developing an integrated data resource.

Disparate Data Shock

The disparate data cycle will continue until an organization either goes out of business or goes through the shock of realizing that their existing data resource is not supporting the rapidly changing information needs. *Disparate data shock* is the realization that the data dilemma really exists and is severely affecting an organization's ability to be responsive to changes in the business environment. It is the panic that an organization has about the sad state of its data resource.

Disparate data shock is the wake-up call.

---

[1]The management of data standards is presented in Chapter 5.

When an organization goes through this shock, action can be taken to break the cycle, resolve the dilemma, and create an integrated data resource that adequately supports both their current and future business needs. Organizations often find they are at a crossroads where they need to decide whether they will take the initiative to break the disparate data cycle and begin developing an integrated data resource or continue developing a deluge of disparate data.

Analogy: Disparate data are a lot like the weather. People recognize the situation, talk about it, complain about it, make jokes about it, and learn to live with it. Few people do anything about the disparate data situation; they just learn to live with it. However, unlike the weather, something can be done about disparate data.

The disparate data cycle can be broken and existing disparate data can be cleaned up and placed in an integrated data resource to meet the business information demand. Organizations need to face the challenge and take the initiative to develop an integrated data resource.

MEETING THE CHALLENGE

The *data resource challenge* is an organization's determination to resolve the data dilemma by breaking the disparate data cycle and transforming data to an integrated data resource that meets the business information demand. Meeting this challenge is the only way that an organization can stop creating disparate data, clean up existing disparate data, and then integrate and manage all data to meet the widest range of normal or emergency situations.

> The challenge is to meet the business information demand with an integrated data resource.

Data Resource Initiative

The challenge to develop an integrated data resource is met with a data resource initiative and supporting strategies. The *data resource initiative* provides the incentive for developing an integrated data resource. The data resource initiative is:

To resolve the data dilemma by breaking the disparate data cycle and developing an integrated data resource so it can meet both the current and future business information demand of an organization.

Data Resource Strategies

An organization meets the data resource initiative through five supporting strategies. Carrying out these strategies breaks the disparate data cycle, resolves the data dilemma, and creates an integrated data resource that meets both the current and future business information demand.

Identify Data

The primary strategy for meeting the data resource initiative is:

To identify all data that currently exist in the organization's data resource or are readily available to an organization so that they can be understood and used to support the current and future business information demand.

Data awareness is the knowledge about all the data that are available to the organization and where those data are located. When people know what data are available to them, within or without the organization, they can readily use those data to support business activities. They can also identify the data needed to support the business that are not currently available to the organization and make plans to acquire those data. Data awareness often uncovers the hidden data resource that organizations did not know existed. Increasing the data awareness is the first major step to developing an integrated data resource and resolving the disparate data situation.

Understand Data

The next strategy for meeting the data resource initiative is:

To thoroughly understand the content and meaning of all data so they can be fully utilized to support the current and future business information demand.

Data understanding is the process of learning the full content and meaning of the data and what those data represent in the real world. When people understand the content and meaning of all data in the data resource and what the data represent in the real world, the use of those data to support the current and future business needs is limited only by people's imagination. Increasing the understanding of data through development of good metadata is a key step resolving disparate data and fully utilizing the data resource.

Integrate Data

The third strategy for meeting the data resource initiative is:

> To transform all important and critical data to an integrated data resource so that it can support the current and future business information demand.

Transforming disparate data into an integrated data resource is more than just connecting a few databases and merging their data, building bridges between information systems, or sending electronic messages over a network. It is a precise, detailed, rigorous process.

Aggregate Data

The fourth strategy for meeting the data resource initiative is:

> To conscientiously save and properly aggregate the detailed operational data for the analysis of trends, patterns, and projections in order to evaluate the current business and future business alternatives.

Aggregation is used here in the broad sense to mean aggregating data horizontally, vertically, and chronologically. Horizontal data aggregation is the edge-matching of data between different sets of data. Vertical data aggregation is the summarization of data to higher levels of generalization. Chronological data aggregation is the historical continuity of data between different time periods.[2]

Deploy Data

The fifth strategy for meeting the data resource initiative is:

> To deploy both the data resource and information about the content and meaning of that data resource to locations where they can most appropriately support the current and future business information demand.

---

[2]The different types of aggregation will be explained in more detail in subsequent chapters.

Deployment is used here in the broad sense to mean placing data and metadata in a product at one or more data sites where they can most appropriately support the business activities. Deployment is more than just moving data around a network or determining where the data reside on a large network. It is determining the products and the sites where both data and metadata can best be placed to support the organization.

Opportunity for Change

Organizations still have an opportunity to break the disparate data cycle and develop an integrated data resource. The cycle is broken by first recognizing its existence and going through the data shock. An organization cannot avoid going through the data shock. However, the impact of going through the data shock can be reduced the sooner an organization realizes that the existing data resource is not supporting the business information demand.

The longer an organization waits, the more severe the disparate data problem becomes, and the greater the impact of going through the shock. An organization also recovers from the shock more quickly if it is aware of the techniques available for breaking the disparate data cycle and developing an integrated data resource.

> The guiding principle for developing an integrated data resource is to think globally and act locally.

The guiding principle for meeting the data resource challenge is, using the environmental analogy again, to think globally and act locally. An organization must think in terms of an integrated data resource within a common data architecture that will meet its current and future business information demand (thinking globally), and then develop applications that maintain and use that data resource according to current, localized needs (acting locally).

Approaches

There are four basic approaches to managing the data resource. The first approach is to allow disparate data to be developed without any controls. This approach usually meets the current business information demand for specific functional areas. However, it compromises the development of an integrated data resource that provides the flexibility to meet the future business information demand. This approach is a *locally useful–globally junk* approach.

The second approach is to slow the development of disparate data on a priority basis with appropriate controls on the development of critical data. Any data that are critical to the current or known future business activities are developed within the integrated data resource. The appropriate controls must, of course, not compromise the current business information demand. This proactive approach considers both the current needs and the future flexibility of data. The degree of control is up to each individual organization.

The third approach is to begin resolving the existing disparate data by transforming them to an integrated data resource that meets both the current and future business information demand. This proactive approach usually follows, or occurs in conjunction with, the second approach. An organization usually does not start transforming existing disparate data while allowing the uncontrolled creation of new disparate data.

The fourth approach is to stop the development of disparate data and begin the transformation of existing disparate data into an integrated data resource. This approach is valid, but it is a massive frontal approach that requires tremendous resources and coordination. It is usually not a good approach unless an organization has the resources and the commitment to use those resources to transform their disparate data.

There are many variations to these four approaches, but the orientation is generally towards resolving the four basic problems: increasing the awareness of data, increasing the understanding of data, reducing the variability of data, and decreasing the redundancy of data. Most approaches are phased approaches based on priorities established by the crucialness of the data. The orientation is also toward using a rigorous construct that provides a new order for developing and managing the data resource.

Justification

There are many different ways to justify the development of an integrated data resource and the transformation of disparate data to that integrated data resource. Specific justifications are up to each organization based on their current and future business information demand. Most justifications are based, in one form or another, on the cost to develop an integrated data resource, the risks of allocating resources to developing an integrated data resource rather than to other critical problems, the risk of not allocating resources to development of an integrated data resource, and the return on the investment.

There is a cost to building and maintaining an integrated data resource. The costs to develop an integrated data resource include the cost of identifying and understanding disparate data, the cost of transforming data to an integrated data resource, the cost of altering applications to use that new integrated data resource, the cost of designing and managing data in an integrated data resource environment, and the cost of developing new applications to use the integrated data resource.

There are risks in allocating resources to the development of an integrated data resource. The risks include an effort that failed because it was not done properly and may have made the disparate data situation worse. The effort may have created an excellent integrated data resource that existing legacy applications cannot access. The effort may have diverted critical resources from another problem that became more critical than the data resource problem.

There is also a risk in not stopping the development of disparate data and creating an integrated data resource. The production of disparate data will continue at an increased rate. Legacy systems will continue to be developed. Employees that have knowledge about the existing data will continue to leave the organization. The problems will increase by orders of magnitude in the next few years and will be increasingly difficult to correct.

The benefits of developing an integrated data resource include the benefit of knowing what data exist and are available to the organization, knowing the quality of data, reducing redundancy and variability, reducing uncertainty about the data, being able to allow clients to access the data resource for analysis and reporting, and having faster application development from a data resource that already exists. The disparate data problem is larger in larger organizations, the cost to develop an integrated data resource is larger too, but the benefits are also greater. The bottom-line benefit is being able to respond to changing situations faster than competitors.

Not all data need to be transformed to an integrated data resource. There is a point of diminishing returns where the additional investment in transforming disparate data does not produce a corresponding return on that investment. A decision needs to be made about taking a prospective approach for new data only, a retrospective approach for existing disparate data, or an approach based on critical priorities including both existing disparate data and new data. The best approach is one that creates a pathway for surviving on disparate data while an integrated data resource is developed on a priority basis.

It is very easy to save useless data and throw away valuable data. All data in an integrated data resource should be routinely put through a justification process to determine whether they have a valid purpose for meeting either the current or future business information demand. Data that have no valid purpose should be removed from the data resource; data that do have a valid purpose should be retained.

Quote: Saint-Exupe'ry said, "In anything at all, perfection is finally attained not when there is no longer anything to add, but when there is no longer anything to take away."

Organizations have many problems to face and limited resources to allocate to those problems. The resolution of disparate data and development of an integrated data resource must be considered as only one of the problems and it should go through a prioritization for the use of limited resources the same as any other problem. An organization must consider both the return on the investment and the risk of not investing in an integrated data resource.

SUMMARY

The real data management challenge for most organizations is to survive on disparate data while developing an integrated data resource. The way to survive is to establish a new order for identifying and understanding disparate data so they can be fully utilized. The new order is based on solving the four basic problems with disparate data: data awareness, data understanding, data variability, and data redundancy. Resolving these four basic problems gives an organization the opportunity to stop or slow the continued development of disparate data, fully utilize those data until they can be transformed to an integrated data resource, and ultimately resolve the disparate data problem by actually transforming critical data into an integrated data resource.

The challenge is met first by realizing that the disparate data situation is increasing at an alarming rate and that data access tools, data merging tools, and data standards cannot solve the problem. Only people can solve the problem! When an organization goes through the shock of understanding that there are no silver bullets and that there is a large hidden resource at their disposal, they can start meeting the challenge.

The challenge is met by establishing a data resource initiative and five supporting strategies that resolve the basic problems with disparate data. The initiative addresses the issue of developing an integrated data resource to meet the current and future business information demand. The strategies address the four basic problems with disparate data. Four different approaches can be used to implement the data resource initiative, with variations on those approaches depending on the specific situation within an organization.

An organization can use a variety of justifications to support the effort, including the costs involved in developing an integrated data resource, the risks of developing an integrated data resource, the risks of not developing an integrated data resource, and the return on investment. Each organization needs to weigh the future cost of continuing to produce disparate data against the current cost of stopping the development of disparate data and transforming critical data to an integrated data resource.

Organizations can break the disparate data cycle and resolve the data dilemma by taking the opportunity to understand the content and meaning of their data and develop an integrated data resource They need to take the opportunity, recognize the disparate data situation, go through the shock, and justify the initiative and supporting strategies to support the current and future business information demand.

Seize the opportunity! Learn to survive on disparate data while developing an integrated data resource.

QUESTIONS

The following questions are provided as a review of the chapter and to stimulate thought about the challenge that exists for organizations to develop an integrated data resource.

1. What is the real challenge to managing disparate data?
2. What are the four basic problems with disparate data?
3. What is the difference between data awareness and data understanding?
4. Why won't data access and data merging solve the disparate data problem?
5. Why won't tools solve the disparate data problem?
6. Why won't data standards solve the disparate data problem?
7. What is the hidden data resource?
8. What is the disparate data shock?
9. What is the data resource initiative?
10. How do the data resource strategies resolve the basic problems with disparate data?
11. What are the best approaches for resolving disparate data?
12. What should be considered when justifying development of an integrated data resource?

CHAPTER 3

Data Vision

An integrated data resource provides the data needed to meet the current and future business information demand.

An integrated data resource that contains all the data needed to support the rapid development of information systems is the ultimate goal for data resource management. It is developed by implementing the data resource initiative and supporting strategies to break the disparate data cycle and resolve the data dilemma. An integrated data resource stops the production of disparate data and corrects the current disparate data problem. It also provides the data necessary to meet an organization's business information demand.

An integrated data resource, however, cannot be developed in one step, and all disparate data cannot be transformed into an integrated resource in a short period of time. An integrated data resource must be developed incrementally based on priorities established by critical data needs. Incremental development of a fully integrated data resource is supported by an interim formal data resource that begins to bring disparate data under control. This formal data resource is the means by which an organization can begin surviving on disparate data while a fully integrated data resource is developed.

Successfully developing an integrated data resource begins with a vision that describes what an integrated data resource will be like when it is developed. The vision is clarified by several basic principles that ensure the integrated data resource supports both the current and future business information demand. This *preferred-future* approach helps an organization define and incrementally develop an integrated data resource.

Chapter 3 begins with the definition of an integrated data resource followed by an explanation of the basic principles supporting an integrated data resource. The chapter then describes incremental development of an integrated data resource through an interim formal data resource and presents the concept of a data resource library containing both the interim formal data resource and the fully integrated data resource. The chapter concludes with an explanation of the support that a data resource library provides for information engineering and how the data engineering discipline develops and maintains the data resource library.

INTEGRATED DATA RESOURCE

A *integrated data resource* is a data resource where all data are integrated within a common context and are appropriately deployed for maximum use in supporting the business information demand.[1] Both data awareness and data understanding are increased in an integrated data resource. Data variability is at a minimum, and data redundancy is reduced to a known and manageable level. The data are formally named, comprehensively defined, well-structured, and properly documented. Data accuracy is known and is at the desired level. All the data necessary to meet the current and future business information demand are available and are as current as the organization needs to conduct its business. High-quality metadata adequately describe the data resource and are readily available to clients so they can easily identify and readily access any data needed to perform their business activities.

An integrated data resource includes all data available to an organization regardless of the form or location of those data. It is not just the electronic data in an organization's databases. Only 10 to 20 percent of an organization's data are in electronic form, and most of those data are disparate. The remainder of an organization's data are in the form of drawings, documents, charts, graphs, maps, and photographs scattered throughout the organization. All of these data need to be integrated to provide support for business activities.

PRINCIPLES

An integrated data resource is based on five basic principles that ensure the data resource meets the business information demand. Each of these principles must be considered when an integrated data resource is developed.

---

[1]The term mature data resource was used in Brackett, 1994.

Subject-Oriented

An integrated data resource cannot be organized by business activities because data cross business activity boundaries and business activities frequently change. Organizing data by one business activity limits that data's use for other business activities and frequently results in redundant data. One major cause of disparate data is the independent development of databases that support single business activities.

An integrated data resource must be subject-oriented. A *subject-oriented data resource* is a data resource that is organized by data subjects based on the identification and definition of objects and events that are of interest to an organization. These objects and events include any person, place, thing, or concept in the real world. Each object and event is represented by a data subject in the integrated data resource.

Example: Customers and employees are persons, cities and countries are places, buildings and rivers are things, fires and earthquakes are events, and accounts and budgets are concepts. Each is defined as a data subject in an integrated data resource.

All features about a particular object or event belong to the data subject representing that object or event, regardless of the business activities using the data. Data subjects cross business activities, and data are reusable by many different business activities. Data subjects contain all the features about an object or event that any business activity might need.

> An integrated data resource must be subject-oriented.

The design of a subject-oriented data resource is often referred to as a relational design. A relational design, however, only applies when data are converted from a logical data model to a physical data model for implementation into a relational database management system.[2] It does not apply to the design of an integrated data resource representing objects and events in the real world.

---

[2]The process of designing a logical data resource and adjusting that logical design for a specific operating environment is explained in more detail in Chapter 14.

Business Survival-Oriented

Developers of an integrated data resource must consider the business if the data resource is to meet the business information demand. The *business-driven* approach is the process of identifying the data needed to support business activities, acquiring or capturing those data, and maintaining them in the data resource. The problem with traditional business-driven approaches is their orientation toward current business needs without regard for future business needs. This short-term business focus contributes substantially to the disparate data situation.

A new orientation that ensures both current and future business success is needed. The new orientation must consider both the short-term and the long-term data needs of an organization to improve the chances for survival. A *business survival* orientation is the process of identifying the data needed to support both current and future business needs, acquiring or capturing those data, and maintaining them in an integrated data resource so they are readily available to information systems. It is a process that takes a business perspective of the long-term mission of an organization and its survival in a dynamic business environment.

> An integrated data resource must have a business survival orientation.

A business survival orientation requires the direct involvement of *business experts* who thoroughly understand the business and the data needed to support the business. These business experts must be knowledgeable about past, present, and future business activities and the data needed to support those activities. They must be knowledgeable about the changes in business activities and the changing data needed to support those changing business activities. If people do not thoroughly understand the business, they cannot understand the data needed to support the business.

The best approach is to form a partnership between business experts, *domain experts* who thoroughly understand a particular discipline, such as finance, engineering, or water resources, and *data experts* who thoroughly understand the development of an integrated data resource. This partnership encourages knowledgeable experts to combine and exploit their knowledge to develop an integrated data resource.

Real-World Perspective

The business survival orientation requires a thorough understanding of the real world in which the business operates. It requires an understanding of the way an organization views the real world, identifies and defines objects and events in the real world, and interacts with those objects and events. The business survival orientation also requires an understanding of the organization's perspective of real-world objects and events.

Like the short-sighted, business-driven approach explained previously, organizations often take a short-sighted perspective of the real world. They concentrate on today and the near future, but they fail to consider the past and the future. They usually fail to understand that the real world is changing, and the organization's perspective of the changing real world is also changing.

Organizations need to take a broader perspective of the real world. An *extended business perspective* is a perspective of the real world that includes both how the real world changes over time and how an organization's perspective of that real world changes over time. It is a chronological perspective that includes the past, present, and future.

> An integrated data resource has both extended and expanded business perspectives.

Different organizations often have different perspectives of the real world. These different perspectives often result in the identification and definition of different objects and events. Integrating these different perspectives within large organizations, across many organizations, and across different disciplines can be difficult.

Example: Different organizations may see the same people as patients, drivers, students, home owners, or employees. Different organizations may look at vehicles as motorized and unmotorized, as commercial and noncommercial, or as licensed and unlicensed.

An integrated data resource must include many different perspectives of the real world. An *expanded business perspective* is an overall perspective of the real world that includes all the individual perspectives by many different organizations in many different disciplines. The expanded business perspective ensures that data in the data resource are reusable by different business activities supporting different business perspectives.

Analogy: Some people use rivers as a source for domestic or livestock water, others use rivers as recreational areas for fishing, swimming, rafting, and water skiing. Still others use rivers as a source of hydro-electric power, commercial fishing, or scenic beauty. A few people use rivers as a dumping ground for waste.

Robust Resource

An integrated data resource is a robust resource where the data values are constantly changing and the size is steadily increasing through the addition of more detailed data or the addition of new business areas. Although some data and some business areas may occasionally be dropped from the data resource, the size of the data resource usually increases steadily.

> An integrated data resource is continuously enhanced, expanded, and extended.

An integrated data resource is continuously enhanced with new data values to represent changes in the real world. *Data resource enhancement* is the process of constantly changing data values in the data resource to reflect changes in the real world. These data value changes must be made as frequently as necessary to ensure that the organization has data as current and as accurate as necessary to adequately support its business activities.

Example: People continue to move their offices and residences resulting in address changes. Products, product prices, and vendors are constantly changing. New educational curriculums are offered every year.

An integrated data resource can be expanded to include new data within the business areas already included in the data resource. *Data resource expansion* is vertical enlargement of the data resource to encompass detailed data not previously included within the current scope. These additional detail data are usually added to support new or expanded business activities, or to prepare for future business activities.

Example: A sporting goods store decides to expand its product lines to include more options for skis, bicycles, and roller blades. A grocery store expands the varieties of canned goods to include additional brand names.

An integrated data resource can be extended into new business areas. *Data resource extension* is horizontal enlargement of the data resource to encompass business areas not previously included. These new business areas may already be part of the organization that are being included in the data resource, or they may be newly acquired business areas.

Example: A department store decides to extend its business to include prepackaged seasonal food items and seasonal decorations. A grocery store decides to extend its business by adding a pharmacy.

Sharable Resource

An integrated data resource is a shareable resource that supports a formal *data sharing concept*, as shown in Figure 3.1. Official data variations are shared over a data sharing medium, such as a network, tape, or diskette. If the data source does not maintain the official data variation, it must translate its nonofficial data variation to an official data variation by accepted data translation schemes prior to sharing. If the data target does not use the official data variation, it must translate the official data variation to its nonofficial data variation by using accepted data translation schemes.

Example: The official data variation for dates is century, year, month, and day, such as 19951022. An organization has data in the form of month, day, year, such as 102295, so it must convert the data to the century, year, month, day form prior to data sharing. The receiving

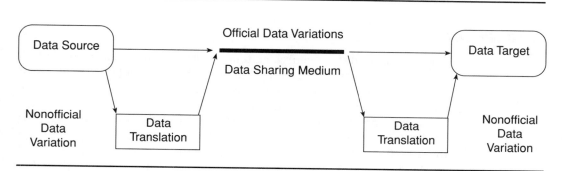

Figure 3.1   The data sharing concept.

organization uses data in the form of month/day/year, such as 10/22/95, so it must convert data to that form after they are received.

This data sharing concept is better than *traditional data sharing* where individual physical files and independent translation schemes are only useful as long as the source and target databases retain the same content and structure. Whenever the content or structure changes, the physical files and/or translation schemes must be changed. Traditional data sharing results in a proliferation of data sharing files that often require high maintenance and may block the resolution of disparate data. The new data sharing concept promotes the use of official data variations and allows each organization to change its data resource without affecting another organization's data resource or the data sharing process.

Data sharing is not the same as data access!

Data sharing and data access are not the same thing! *Data sharing* is the process of understanding the content and meaning of data, identifying and selecting the appropriate data to meet business needs, and sharing those data according to the data sharing concept. Data access, as explained in Chapter 2, is the process of entering a database to store or retrieve data. Many tools are available that provide transparent access to heterogeneous databases and allow data to be moved between heterogeneous databases. Providing access to heterogeneous databases does not help people understand those data, identify and select the appropriate data, or share data according to the data sharing concept.

DEVELOPMENT

An integrated data resource cannot be developed in one step, and all disparate data cannot be transformed to an integrated data resource at the same time. An integrated data resource must be developed incrementally based on the identification of data critical to operation of the business. One of an organization's goals is to be able to build and adjust applications quickly to meet changing business needs. The priority for incrementally developing an integrated data resource should be based on the data that support the applications that will most likely need to be changed on short notice.

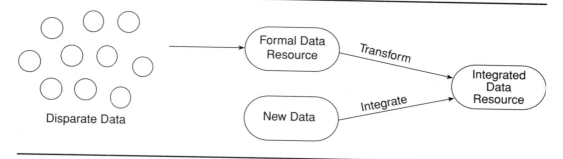

Figure 3.2   The formal data resource concept.

A Formal Data Resource

An integrated data resource must be developed incrementally through a formal data resource, as shown in Figure 3.2. Disparate data are first identified and defined within a formal data resource and then transformed to an integrated data resource. At the same time, new data are integrated directly into the integrated data resource.

A *formal data resource* is an interim step between disparate data and an integrated data resource where disparate data are identified and defined within a common context. Data awareness and understanding are increased, and data variability and redundancy are identified but not resolved. The accuracy is known but has not been adjusted to the desired level. Metadata about the disparate data are captured, enhanced, and stored where they can be readily accessed.[3]

> The formal data resource is an initial step to integrating disparate data.

The formal data resource allows an organization to begin surviving on disparate data while correcting the disparate data situation. It is an interim step that begins to formalize disparate data. The extent of data disparity and the disparate data are understood within a common context. There is not, however, any attempt to resolve the data variability or data redundancy. The data variability and redundancy are resolved during transformation to the integrated data resource.

[3]The process for defining disparate data within a common context is explained in Chapter 9.

Data Resource Library

A library is a resource of works organized by subject independent of how people will use those works to obtain information. People go to the library and check the indexes to find the information they need. In most cases, people need only part of the information they find about one subject. They take only the information that is meaningful to them and ignore the rest. The library contains information for everyone, but a person does not use all the information in a library.

The *data resource library* is a library of data for an organization that contains both the formal data resource and the integrated data resource, as shown in Figure 3.3. The data are organized by subject independent of their use, just like the books in a library are organized by subject independent of their use. The location of all the data in the data resource library, like the location of all the works in a library, must be known so data can be readily accessed. A comprehensive metadata warehouse provides an index to the data in the data resource library just like a card catalog provides an index to the works in a library.[4]

Information Engineering Support

The data resource library supports information engineering. Information systems go to the data resource library, just like people go to a library, to find the data needed to prepare a message, as shown in Figure 3.4. Information systems usually do not need all the data available in the data resource to prepare a message. They take only what they need and ignore the rest. The data are still available for the next information system.

Information engineering is the discipline for identifying information needs and developing information systems that produce messages that provide information to a recipient. It is a manufacturing process that uses data as the raw material to construct and transmit a message to a recipient. Information engineering is also a filtering process that reduces masses of data to a message that provides information. A simple *information engineering objective* is to get the right data, to the right people, in the right place, at the right time, in the right form, and at the right cost, so they can make the right decisions and take the right actions.

Information engineering ensures that a message maximizes information to the recipient and minimizes noise. A *message* is a communi-

---

[4]The metadata warehouse is explained in Chapter 8.

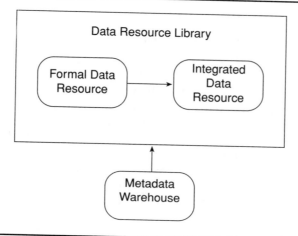

Figure 3.3   The data resource library concept.

cation containing a collection of data in some order and format. If that message is relevant to the recipient, it contains information. If the message is not relevant to the recipient, it does not contain information and is useless or less than fully useful. Only the recipient, not the sender, determines whether the message contains information.

Information is a collection of data that is relevant to one or more recipients at a point in time. It must be meaningful and useful to the recipient at a specific time for a specific purpose. Information is data in context—data that have meaning, relevance, and purpose. Data that are out of context, known as *contextless data*, are nearly useless; they are noise. Contextless data are a major reason why organizations have more and more data and less and less information.

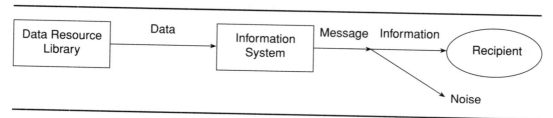

Figure 3.4   The information engineering concept.

> Information is data in context, with meaning, relevance, and purpose.

Information exists only when uncertainty exists. The rapidly changing business environment causes uncertainty, which creates a need for information to resolve or reduce the uncertainty. The more dynamic a business environment is, the more rapid the change, the greater the uncertainty, and the greater the need for information. The current trend is accelerated change that requires an accelerated need for new information. Information engineering can meet the accelerated need for new information only if the data resource library contains data that are in context.

Generally, information overload does not occur because information resolves uncertainty. However, data overload occurs when a recipient receives a deluge of data that does not resolve any uncertainty.

Example: A person wants to take a train trip through western Canada during a vacation in June. The person's travel agent provides all the train schedules for North America for the entire year. The result is data overload because the person's uncertainty is only train schedules for western Canada in June.

Information overload can exist when information is provided that is only partially relevant to resolving a recipient's uncertainty. It is the situation where more information is provided than is necessary to resolve the uncertainty. The additional information is not noise, as described previously, but it is not fully useful information. The degree of relevance to the uncertainty at hand determines the extent of the overload. Information systems should strive to provide information that is fully relevant to a specific uncertainty.

Data

It may be startling in the information age, but many people do not know the difference between data and information. In an age where information is a major commodity, people do not know what is the resource and what is the product. The terms *information* and *data* are often used interchangeably without definition.

Data are individual facts with specific meaning at a point in time or for a period of time. Data include both primitive data and derived data. *Primitive data* are data that are obtained by measurement or observation of an object or event in the real world. *Derived data* are data that are obtained from other data, not by the measurement or observation of an object or event.

Example: A person's birth date is primitive data because it is obtained directly from the person. A person's age is derived data because it is developed from the person's birth date and the current date. Even though the person's age is derived, it is still data, not information because it has not yet been used to resolve uncertainty.

Data remain data until they are relevant to a recipient at a point in time.

Data are often viewed as primitive facts, and information is often viewed as anything derived from those facts. This viewpoint is not true in an integrated data resource. A fact, whether primitive or derived, is considered data. Information is only packaged data in the form of a message that is useful to the recipient. Data are stored in the data resource library; information is not stored in the data resource library.

Example: A customer's bank transactions, account balance, and monthly interest are viewed as data in the data resource library. They are not information until they are placed in a message that is relevant to a person at a point in time.

Data include both elemental and combined data. *Elemental data* are individual facts that cannot be subdivided and retain any meaning. *Combined data* are a concatenation of individual facts. The combination of individual facts does not make that combination information.

Example: A date is not information just because it is a concatenation of elemental data. A person's birth date is combined data consisting of four pieces of elemental data: century, year, month, and day. A person's complete name is combined data consisting of that person's individual name, middle name, and family name.

Data Engineering

Data engineering is the discipline that designs, builds, and maintains the data resource library shown in Figure 3.5. It is a structured process for developing both the formal data resource and the integrated data resource in the data resource library and the metadata warehouse that documents the data resource library. The primary objective of data engineering is to build and maintain the data resource library to support information engineering and the development of information systems.

Data engineering supplies the raw materials to information engineering for producing messages that resolve uncertainty. It is not the responsibility of information engineering to find the appropriate data.

Analogy: Data are the building blocks used to develop information, like Lego blocks are the building blocks for children's toys. The information built from data is limited only by the need and imagination of the business client, like the toys built by Lego blocks are limited only by the need and imagination of children.

Data engineering provides the data for information engineering.

Data engineering is largely undefined and unsupported by automated tools. Most techniques and tools, including CASE tools, concen-

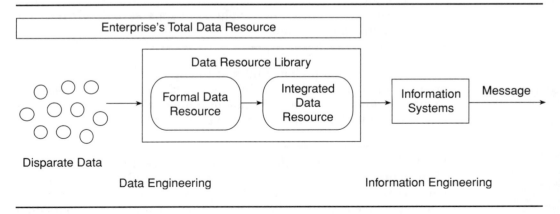

Figure 3.5   Data engineering.

trate on information engineering rather than data engineering because it is relatively easy to work with new data and produce good results at a project level. It is also easier to define and automate the information engineering process.

Data engineering is much more difficult and cannot be fully automated. It is a discovery process that relies largely on people to determine the content and meaning of disparate data. Data engineering takes real thought, analysis, intuition, and consensus by knowledgeable people to understand disparate data. Automated tools can support people by identifying and documenting data by name and location, but they cannot perform the discovery process or gain consensus for understanding data. A new class of *ccmputer-aided data engineering* (CADE) tools needs to be developed to support data engineering and the resolution of disparate data.

Considerable hype and misinformation surround data engineering and the development of an integrated data resource. Numerous products and methods are promoted to resolve the disparate data problems. But there are no quick fixes, no magic formulas, no silver bullets, no tools to develop an integrated data resource overnight. In spite of the current level of vendor hype, there is no panacea for resolving data disparity and developing an integrated data resource.

SUMMARY

The future belongs to organizations that can search massive quantities of disparate data. Organizations that can quickly search disparate data, understand their content and meaning, and tap the hidden data resource are the ones that will survive in a dynamic business environment. Organizations that can build a data resource library, and ultimately a fully integrated data resource, will break the disparate data cycle, resolve the data dilemma, and begin meeting current and future business information demand.

Taking control of the data resource begins with the vision of an integrated data resource where all data are integrated within a common context and are appropriately deployed for maximum use in supporting the business information demand. The vision is supported by five principles that ensure the data resource is subject-oriented, business survival–oriented, based on real-world perspectives, robust enough to meet changing business needs, and sharable across business activities and organizational boundaries.

A fully integrated data resource is developed incrementally by developing a data resource library that contains a formal data resource and the integrated data resource. The formal data resource begins the process of understanding and transforming disparate data to the fully integrated data resource. It represents disparate data that have been identified and understood within a common context. The variability and redundancy of the disparate data, however, have not been resolved. When the disparate data are transformed to the fully integrated data resource, their variability and redundancy are resolved.

The data resource library supports information engineering and its objective to provide information to recipients that resolve uncertainty. It provides the means by which an organization can begin surviving on disparate data. Data engineering is the emerging discipline that is responsible for developing and maintaining the data resource library. It is data engineering's responsibility, not information engineering's responsibility, to sort out the data disparity, develop an integrated data resource, and ensure that all new data are part of the new integrated data resource that supports the business information demand.

QUESTIONS

The following questions are provided as a review of the chapter and to stimulate thought about the vision for an integrated data resource.

1. What is the vision for an integrated data resource?
2. What does subject-oriented mean?
3. Why should an integrated data resource be subject-oriented?
4. Why should an integrated data resource be business survival–oriented?
5. Why do organizations have different perspectives of the real world?
6. What is an expanded business perspective?
7. What is an extended business perspective?
8. What is data resource enhancement?
9. What is the difference between data resource expansion and data resource extension?
10. How is the data sharing concept different from traditional data sharing?
11. What is the difference between data sharing and data access?
12. What is the purpose of a formal data resource?
13. What does the data resource library contain?
14. How do information and data differ?
15. What is the difference between information engineering and data engineering?
16. What is the objective of data engineering?

CHAPTER 4

Data Architecture

A common data architecture provides the common context within which an integrated data resource is developed.

Developing an integrated data resource requires a common context within which all data can be identified and understood. A comprehensive data architecture that encompasses the formal data resource, the integrated data resource, information systems, and the messages produced by information systems provides that common context. The development of a comprehensive data architecture begins with the concept of a total infrastructure for information technology, the establishment of a data resource framework within that infrastructure, and the definition of a formal data architecture within that framework.

A formal data architecture provides the common context for understanding the content and meaning of data, structuring data, identifying and adjusting data quality, and defining metadata. It provides uniformity not only within an organization, but across different organizations and across different disciplines. It provides a way to easily identify and understand all data so they can be readily shared. A formal approach provides new perspectives about the management of data and implementation of an integrated data resource within a formal data architecture.

Chapter 4 begins with a description of the information technology infrastructure, the data resource framework within that infrastructure, and a formal data architecture within that framework. This chapter presents the formal approach to developing an integrated data resource, a new architectural perspective, and a new data model perspective. The chapter concludes with an explanation of the data units used in each of the data models and the concept of data megatypes.

FORMAL ARCHITECTURE

A formal data architecture provides the construct for building and maintaining data resource library to meet the business information demand. Development of a formal data architecture begins with a definition of the information technology infrastructure, followed by the definition of a data resource framework representing the data resource component of the information technology infrastructure, and the definition of a data architecture within the data resource framework.

Information Technology Infrastructure

An *infrastructure* is an underlying foundation or framework for a system or an organization. This term generally refers to the basic installations and facilities for community development or military operations.

Example: Roads, schools, power, transportation, and communication are part of a community infrastructure.

The concept of an infrastructure can also be applied to the information technology discipline. The *information technology infrastructure* is an infrastructure for the information technology discipline that provides the resources necessary for an organization to meet its current and future business information demand.

Definition of an information technology infrastructure begins with the two basic resources that provide the foundation for information technology, as shown in Figure 4.1. The *platform resource* represents the hardware and system software at an organization's disposal. The *data resource* represents all the data available to an organization, regardless of whether they are automated or nonautomated.

These two resource components support the business activities, as shown in Figure 4.2. The *business activities* represent all business activities in an organization, regardless of whether they are automated or manual. They utilize the data resource and the platform resource to perform specific processes and tasks.

The *information systems* form the fourth component of the infor-

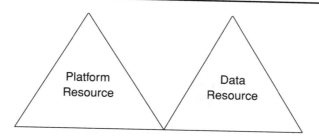

Figure 4.1   Resource components of the information technology infrastructure.

mation technology infrastructure, as shown in Figure 4.3. The information systems represent the implementation of business activities; they use the data resource and reside on the platform resource.

Another way to view the information technology infrastructure is to picture a three-sided pyramid with the base of the pyramid representing information systems and the three sides of the pyramid representing business activity, the data resource, and the platform resource. Then fold the three sides down to form a triangle representing the infrastructure, shown in Figure 4.3.

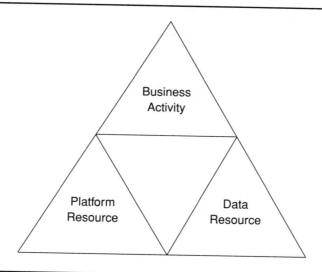

Figure 4.2   Business activity component of the information technology infrastructure.

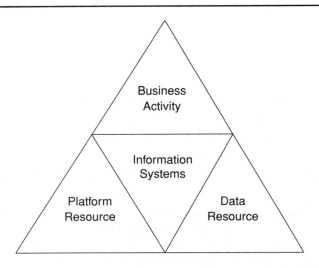

Figure 4.3   Information system component of the information technology infrastructure.

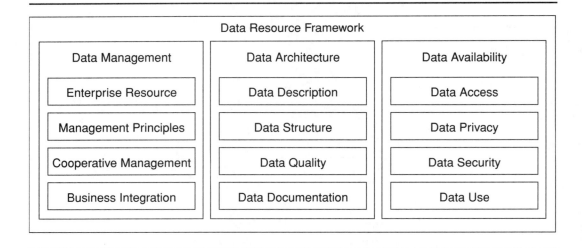

Figure 4.4   The data resource framework.

Data Resource Framework

The information technology infrastructure consists of four *information technology frameworks* for business activities, the data resource, the platform resource, and information systems. The four frameworks have similar constructs, although the details are different. All four frameworks are important for managing information technology, but only the data resource framework is relevant to the current topic of developing an integrated data resource.[1]

The *data resource framework* represents a discipline for the complete development and maintenance of an integrated data resource. Its three components are data management, data architecture, and data availability, as shown in Figure 4.4.

The data management component contains all activities related to management of the data resource. The data architecture component contains all activities related to describing the data, structuring the data, maintaining the data quality, and documenting the data. The data availability component contains all activities related to making data available while properly protecting and securing these data.[2]

All three components of the data resource framework are important for developing and managing an integrated data as a resource. However, the data management and the data availability components are useless without the data architecture component. Without a data architecture, managing the data and making those data readily available to meet the business information demand is very difficult. This chapter's emphasis, therefore, is on the data architecture component.

Data Architecture

The term *data architecture* has been defined as narrowly as being synonymous with a data structure and as broadly as anything associated with managing the data resource, including strategic planning, tactical planning, and personnel. It has been defined so many times and used in so many ways without definition that the term is quite confusing.

An initial definition of a data architecture, based on the data architecture component of the data resource framework, is:

---

[1]The information system framework is adequately represented by the *Framework for Information Systems* promoted by John Zachman.

[2]The activities for each of these components are explained in more detail in Brackett, 1994.

> The component of the data resource framework that contains all activities, and the products of those activities, related to the identification, naming, definition, structuring, quality, and documentation of the data resource for an organization.

This definition, however, is not good enough for developing a formal data architecture. A more formal definition is needed.

The term *architecture* has several definitions. First, it is the art, science, or profession of designing and building structures. Second, it is the structure or structures as a whole, such as the frame, heating, plumbing, and wiring in a building. Third, it is the style of structures and method of design and construction, such as Roman or Colonial architecture. Fourth, it is the design or system perceived by people, such as the architecture of the Solar System.

These basic definitions can be adjusted to provide a more formal definition for a data architecture. First, a data architecture is the art, science, or profession of designing and building a data resource. Second, it is the structure of the data resource as a whole. Third, it is the style or type of design and construction of the data resource. Fourth, it is a system that represents the real world as certain people perceive it. Based on these definitions, the formal definition of a data architecture is:

> The science and method of designing and constructing an integrated data resource that is business driven, based on real-world objects and events as perceived by the organization, and implemented into appropriate operating environments. The overall structure of a data resource that provides a consistent foundation across organizational boundaries to provide easily identifiable, readily available, high-quality data to support the business information demand.

A data architecture is similar to a building architecture. A building architecture has a description that consists of the names and definitions of all the elements, such as pipes, wood, paint, windows, and roofing. It has a structure that shows the relationship of the elements and how they fit together, such as heating, wiring, plumbing, and phone through the walls, floors, and ceilings. It has integrity that ensures the quality of the building, such as size and type of lumber, use of steel reinforced concrete, type of paint, and required maintenance. Finally, it has documentation in the form of plans, blueprints, and specifications about the other three components.

Like the building architecture, a data architecture includes all the components, not just one or two of them. A common perception of a data architecture is the traditional entity relationship diagram prominent in data modeling. The entity relationship diagram is only one technique for defining the structure of an integrated data resource. It does not represent the total data architecture.

The data architecture component of the data resource framework contains four activities. Each of these activities is briefly explained below and is described in more detail in the following chapters:

- Data description is the formal naming and comprehensive definition of all data in an integrated data resource.
- Data structure is the proper logical and physical structuring of data in an integrated data resource.
- Data quality is the maintenance of high-quality data in an integrated data resource.
- Data documentation is the current, complete, ongoing, readily available documentation of the entire data resource.

Common Data Architecture

The traditional perception of a data architecture is usually at the database or the information system level and usually pertains only to newly defined data. It is often difficult to broaden the perception of a data architecture to an organization-wide or inter-organization level and to include both existing disparate data and newly defined data. The concept of a common data architecture resolves this traditional perception.

> The common data architecture is the common context for identifying and understanding all data.

A *common data architecture* is a formal, comprehensive data architecture that provides a common context within which an integrated data resource is developed so that it adequately supports the business information demand.[3] The common data architecture includes all data within an organization, across organizational boundaries, and across disciplines. It includes primitive and derived data; tabular and nontabular data; elemental and combined data; automated and nonautomated data; and historical, current, and projection data.

A common data architecture includes data in purchased software, home-built applications, databases, programs, screens, reports, and documents. It includes data used by traditional information systems,

---

[3]The common data architecture is explained in detail in Brackett, 1994.

expert systems, executive information systems, geographic information systems, data warehouse systems, and object-oriented systems. It includes centralized and decentralized data. A common architecture crosses all business activities, all projects, and all information systems regardless of where they reside, who uses them, or how they are used.

The common data architecture transcends all data.

A common data architecture includes different perspectives of the real world from different organizations and disciplines, which is referred to as the expanded perspective. It also includes perspectives of the real world that change over time, which is referred to as the extended perspective. Including these perspectives within a common data architecture helps people understand how other organizations view the real world. This, in turn, helps organizations cooperate in collecting and sharing data to meet their individual business needs.

The common data architecture is not a generic data architecture. A *generic data architecture* is a standard architecture for a specific purpose, such as purchase orders or student registration. A generic data architecture is an attempt to get organizations to do similar business functions in a similar manner. There are a few generic data architectures because each organization does things slightly differently based on its perspective of the real world and its mission or mandates.

The common data architecture is not a data standard; it encompasses all data standards and provides a way to evaluate standards and identify where they overlap and conflict. It also provides a way to determine which data standards should be used for a specific purpose through the designation of official data. These official data may or may not match specific data standards, but they provide an official set of data for a specific use.[4]

The common data architecture is not a standard data model; it encompasses all data models like *Webster's Dictionary* encompasses all words. Individual projects use subsets of the common data architecture and draw data from the common data architecture to meet the needs of the information system the same way a student draws words from *Webster's Dictionary* and assembles them for a term paper. Projects do not use all data in the common data architecture any more than a term paper uses all the words in *Webster's Dictionary*. If data do not exist in the common architecture, the project defines data according to precise criteria and places them in the common data architecture for subse-

---

[4]Data standards are explained further in Chapter 15.

quent projects, the same as new words are defined and placed in each new release of *Webster's Dictionary*.

> The common data architecture is not a generic or standard data model.

A common data architecture is structurally stable. The data do not change for individual events. Projects come and go, schedules come and go, business activities come and go, information systems come and go, people come and go, the data use changes, and data values go through their life cycle, but the data architecture remains structurally stable.

A common data architecture provides many benefits. One of the most important benefits is discovering the hidden data resource. *Data discovery* is the process of identifying all the data that exist in an organization's data resource and learning the content and meaning of those data. It is the realization that considerable quantities of very useful data are often available. The use of those data to meet the business information demand is limited only by people's imagination once they discover the vast resource of data available to them.

The common data architecture provides a way to integrate data within an organization and across organizations. It enables a shift from reactive data resource management to proactive data resource management by allowing people to determine whether the data exist before they create redundant data. It also enables data refining, data integration, and data deployment.

> The common data architecture enables the shift from reactive to proactive management of the data resource.

The common data architecture supports the data sharing concept explained in the last chapter. Data sharing is often perceived as occurring only between projects or within a specific business scope. This view is better than just sharing data across bridges between systems, but it is not the ideal for sharing data across business functions or across organizations. Data must be shared across business activities and organizational boundaries to realize the full potential of the data resource. The common data architecture provides the foundation for intra-organization and inter-organization data sharing.

Building and implementing a common data architecture does not require restructuring all existing databases or converting existing data files. Data names in programs or data dictionaries do not need to be changed and all documentation referencing data does not need to be changed. The common data architecture represents all data through cross-references that provide the content and meaning without altering databases or information systems.[5]

FORMAL APPROACH

A formal approach to developing an integrated data resource includes new perspectives about how the common data architecture is used to develop and maintain an integrated data resource.

Data Architecture Perspective

A formal approach for bringing disparate data under a common data architecture and developing an integrated data resource is shown in Figure 4.5. The organization's total data resource includes all data within the organization or available to the organization, including disparate data, formal data, and integrated data. The common data architecture includes all formal data and integrated data, as well as the data in information systems and messages to recipients.

---

[5]The process of cross-referencing data to the common data architecture is explained in Chapter 9.

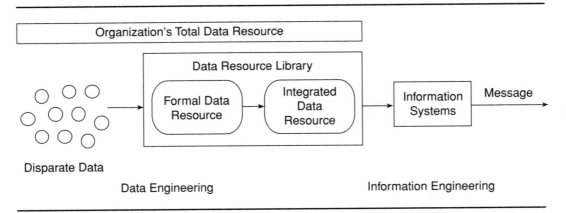

Figure 4.5   The formal data resource management approach.

Real World	Common Data Model	Logical Data Model	Physical Data Model
Object / Event	Data Subject	Data Entity	Data File
Feature	Data Characteristic		
	Data Characteristic Variation	Data Attribute	Data Item
Object Existence / Event Occurrence	Data Occurrence	Data Occurrence	Data Record

Figure 4.6   Relationships between terms.

Disparate data are outside of the common data architecture until they are identified and understood within the context of the common data architecture. Then they become part of the formal data resource. When the data variability and data redundancy of disparate data are reduced, they become part of the fully integrated data resource. Both the formal and integrated data resource are contained in a data resource library that provides data to information systems to use in delivering messages to recipients.

Data Model Perspective

Development of an integrated data resource within a common data architecture requires a new perspective about how the data resource represents the real world and how that data resource is modeled and implemented. Development of an integrated data resource is based on objects and events in the real world that are of interest to the organization, as shown in Figure 4.6. An object is a person, place, thing, or concept in the real world. An event is a happening in the real world. Objects are represented by specific existences in the real world and events are represented by specific occurrences in the real world.

A *common data model* represents all the data available to an organization that have been identified and defined within the common data architecture. It represents the objects and events in the real world that are of interest to the organization, is subject-oriented, and includes all perspectives of the real world. The common data model is the formal representation of the organization's data resource that forms a bridge between the real world and information systems.

A *logical data model* represents the normalized design of data needed to support an information system. Ideally, data are drawn from the common data model and normalized to support the design of a specific information system. If, however, the data are not defined within the common data model, they need to be defined during design of the information system based on the real world and placed in the common data model. They are then available for the next logical data model. This approach speeds the development of logical data models, avoids the situation of paralysis-by-analysis and the continued development of disparate data, and allows many different logical data models to be developed within a common context.

A *physical data model* represents the denormalized physical implementation of data that support an information system. Ideally, the logical data model is denormalized to a physical data model according to specific criteria that do not compromise the logical data model but allow the database to operate efficiently in a specific operating environment. This is the point where a subject data resource becomes relational if the implementation is in a relational database management system and the terms table, row, and column are commonly used.

Data Unit Perspective

Developing common data models, logical data models, and physical data models requires a definition of the specific data units that occur within each data model and an explanation of how those data units are developed. Each of the data units are defined and explained in the following sections.[6] They are used throughout the book to explain the development and use of an integrated data resource.

Objects and Events

A *data subject* represents a person, place, thing, event, or concept about which an organization captures, maintains, and uses data. It is developed from an organization's perspective of an object or event in the real world.

Example: Employee, city, vehicle, and customer account are objects in the real world. Traffic accident, flood, and account deposit are events in the real world. Both objects and events become data subjects based on an organization's perspective of the real world.

---

[6]Additional explanations and examples can be found in Brackett, 1994.

A *data entity* represents a data subject from the common data model that is used in the logical data model. A *data file* represents a data entity from the logical data model that is implemented with a physical data model.

The distinction between terms used in the common data model and a logical data model is made for two reasons. First, when presenting the concept of a subject-oriented data resource to executives and managers, there is often resistance to the terms *entity* and *attribute* and confusion about how a subject data resource is built with *entities*. Using the approach that a subject data resource is built with data subjects based on objects and events in the real world makes more sense and gains better support.

Second, traditional logical data models are built with data entities and their developers perceive that if the model contains data entities, those entities must be the same data entities as those in the common data model. This is not always true. There is not an automatic alignment between the data entities in a logical data model and data subjects in the common data model. Therefore, a distinction is made between data subjects in the common data model and data entities in a logical data model.

Features

A *data characteristic* represents an individual characteristic that describes a data subject. It is developed, directly through measurement or indirectly through derivation, from a feature of an object or event. Each data subject is described by a set of data characteristics.

Example: Birth date, height, weight, and social security number are characteristics about an employee. Make, model, and color are characteristics about vehicles.

A *data characteristic variation* is a variation in the content or meaning of a data characteristic. Each data characteristic in the common data model has one or more variations in content and/or meaning. Data characteristic variations are used to manage the wide variability in the content and meaning of disparate data.

Example: A person's name is a characteristic about a person, but that person's name may be complete or abbreviated and it may be in a normal or an inverted sequence. These different forms are variations of the same characteristic of a person.

A *data attribute* represents a data characteristic variation that is used in a logical data model. A *data item* represents a data attribute from the logical data model that is implemented with a physical data model. It is an individual field in a data record.

A *data characteristic group* is a set of related data characteristics that are commonly grouped together.

Example: Century, calendar year, month, and day are grouped together to form a date.

A *data attribute group* represents the use of a data characteristic group in a logical data model. A *data item group* represents a data attribute group from a logical data model that is implemented with a physical data model. It is a set of related data items that are stored, processed, and displayed together.

Existences and Occurrences

A *data occurrence* is a logical record that represents one existence of an object or one occurrence of an event in the real world. It is used in both the common data model and the logical data model.[7]

Example: Employee *John J. Smith* is represented by a data occurrence in the Employee data subject. A deposit to a checking account is represented by a data occurrence in the Customer Account Transaction data subject.

A *data record* represents a data occurrence from the logical data model that is implemented with a physical data model. It is a physical grouping of data items that are stored or retrieved from a data file.

A *data occurrence group* is a set of related data occurrences in a logical data model that meet a specific set of criteria.

Example: All employees that are certified as pilots form a Pilot Certified Employee data occurrence group. All vehicles that are motorized form a Motorized Vehicle data occurrence group.

---

[7]A data occurrence is sometimes referred to as a *data instance*. Data instance, however, refers to the point in time or the period of time for which a data value accurately represents the real world, not to the existence of an object or occurrence of an event.

A *data record group* represents a data occurrence group from the logical data model that is implemented with a physical data model. It is a set of related data records in a data file.

Coded Data Values

A *data value* represents the individual facts and figures contained in data characteristics, data characteristic variations, data attributes, and data items. An *actual data value* is a measurement, value, or description of a trait or feature of a data subject.

Example: *12/24/87* is an employee's birth date, *blue* is the color of a vehicle, and *127.36* is the balance in a customer's account.

A *data code* is an actual data value that has been encoded in some way.

Example: Codes 1, 2, and 3 represent Probationary Employees, Temporary Employees, and Permanent Employees, respectively.

A *data code* set is a set of data codes that are closely related.

Example: All the data codes pertaining to the type of a vehicle belong together as a set of Vehicle Type Codes, and all the data codes pertaining to land use belong together as a set of Land Use Codes.

Data Megatype Perspective

Developing an integrated data resource within a common data architecture also requires a new perspective of how major types of data are related. A data megatype is a broad grouping of data forms within the common data architecture, as shown in Figure 4.7.[8] The depth dimension represents the transformation from disparate data to integrated data, as described previously. The vertical dimension represents *data megagroups* and the horizontal dimension represents *data megaclasses*.

The *data megaclasses* are broad groupings of data forms that are

---

[8]A *data type* is the form of a data value, such as date, number, string, floating point, packed, and double precision.

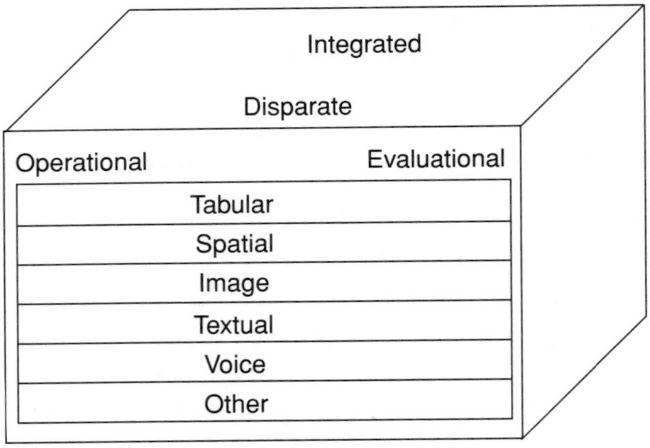

Figure 4.7   Data megatypes.

developed and maintained differently. *Tabular data* are the traditional data that are maintained in traditional databases and are displayed in tabular form. *Nontabular data* are data that are not generally maintained in traditional databases or typically displayed in tabular form, such as spatial, textual, voice, image (photo, digitized image, remote sensed image, or digital ortho-photography), and video.

Textual data are the data processed by textual information management systems, including keyword searches, searches for phrases, and searches for concepts, meanings, and conclusions. Spatial data are the data used in geographic information systems to accurately locate objects on the surface of the Earth or in structures.[9] Image data are the images processed in image management systems. Voice data are the sounds of voices used for analysis or conversion to text.

Nontabular data will play an increasing role in an organization's business activities. They will be routinely captured, stored, manipulated, and displayed to support business activities the same as tabular data. Nontabular data must be included in the integrated data resource to support the business information demand.

The *data megagroups* are broad groupings of data representing both the granularity of data and the time frame that data represent. *Operational data* are the data used in the operational processing of business transactions that support day-to-day business operations. They are detailed, largely primitive data that are kept current to keep the orga-

_____

[9]Spatial data are explained in more detail in Chapter 12.

nization operating. *Evaluational data* are the data used in decision support processing to evaluate trends, projections, and alternatives. They are usually historical, are derived from the operational data, and contain many levels of summarization above the operational data.[10]

SUMMARY

An integrated data resource is developed through a formal data architecture using a formal approach. Development of a formal data architecture begins with an overall perspective of information technology. The information technology infrastructure describes the relationships between the data resource, platform resource, business activities, and information systems. Each of these components has framework describing the contents of that component. The data resource framework consists of a data management component, a data architecture component, and a data availability component. The data architecture component contains activities for data description, data structure, data quality, and data documentation.

A common data architecture is defined based on the components of the data architecture. The common data architecture provides a common context within which all data are identified and defined. It supports extended and expanded perspectives of the real world, and it supports an enhanced, expanded, and extended data resource. It supports the formal data sharing concept and allows an organization to find and use its hidden data resource.

An integrated data resource is developed within a common data architecture using a formal approach. The formal approach begins with a common data architecture that encompasses the data resource library, information systems, and messages to recipients. Disparate data are identified and defined within the common data architecture to form the formal data resource. The data remaining after the redundancy and variability are removed become part of the integrated data resource. Data engineering builds the data resource library and information engineering uses data from the data resource library to prepare messages.

Three different data models are used to develop and maintain the data resource library and the data used by information systems. The common data model represents all data available to an organization from a real-world perspective, the logical data model represents the data used by an information system, and a physical data model represents the implementation of a database. The common data model is

---

[10]Operational and evaluational data are explained in more detail in Chapter 10.

usually developed and maintained by data engineering, and the logical and physical data models are usually developed and maintained by information engineering.

An integrated data resource will not be achieved overnight. The current disparate data situation will get worse before it gets better. How bad it gets depends on how quick an organization takes the initiative and begins developing an integrated data resource. The quicker an organization begins, the quicker it will understand its data and begin integrating, sharing, and utilizing those data to full potential.

QUESTIONS

The following questions are provided as a review of the chapter and to stimulate thought about an architectural approach to developing an integrated data resource.

1. What is the information technology infrastructure?
2. What is the purpose of a data resource framework?
3. What does the data architecture component of the data resource framework represent?
4. What is a common data architecture?
5. What is the formal approach to developing an integrated data resource?
6. What is the architectural perspective for developing an integrated data resource?
7. What does the common data model represent?
8. How is the common data model developed?
9. What does the logical data model represent?
10. How is the logical data model developed?
11. What does the physical data model represent?
12. How is the physical data model developed?
13. What are the data units?
14. What are data megatypes?
15. Why is it necessary to build an integrated data resource?

CHAPTER 5

Data Description

Formal data names and comprehensive data definitions provide the base for understanding the real content and meaning of data.

Data description is the first activity in the data architecture component of the data resource framework. This activity includes the formal naming and comprehensive definition of data. All data, regardless of their location or use, whether they are automated or not, and whether they are primitive or derived, must be formally named and comprehensively defined. A formal name and comprehensive definition provide the context for understanding the true content and meaning of data and understanding what those data represent in the real world. They illuminate the hidden meaning in disparate data that is often lost when knowledgeable people leave an organization.

Understanding the content and meaning of all data is the first step to developing an integrated data resource. If an integrated data resource is to foster understanding about the business, be readily shared across organizational boundaries, and meet the business information demand, the content and meaning of all data in that resource must be known. Simply put, an organization must understand its data in order to properly manage and use those data to support the business information demand.

This chapter explains the techniques for formally naming and comprehensively defining data.[1] It begins with a brief explanation of traditional data naming convention weaknesses, the formal data naming taxonomy with the latest enhancements, and the supporting data naming vocabulary. Examples of formal data names are provided for each component of the enhanced data naming taxonomy. This chapter describes data name abbreviation schemes used to meet physical limitations and the use of shorthand notations for data names. The chapter concludes with guidelines and examples for developing comprehensive data definitions.

DATA NAMES

A data name is the first thing people usually see when they begin dealing with the data resource. These people may include clients, programmers, or database analysts, and they may see a report, a screen, a document, a program, a file listing, or a data dictionary. Regardless of who the people are or what they see, they use the data name to identify, understand, and use data.

A *data name* is a label for a unit of data, whether that unit is a data site, data subject, or data file. A *formal data name* is a label for data that is developed from a formal data naming taxonomy and uniquely identifies that unit of data within the common data architecture. It is fully spelled out, is not codified or abbreviated, does not contain any special symbols, and is not subject to any length restrictions.[2] A few exceptions, which are explained later, allow special symbols and abbreviations in the formal data name.

Each unit of data must be uniquely identified to be properly managed.

All other data names are aliases of the formal data name. Any existing physical data names, any data names that have been shortened to meet physical length restrictions, and any data names that do

---

[1]The development of the data naming taxonomy and supporting vocabulary is thoroughly explained in Brackett, 1994. Only a brief overview is given here with an explanation of the enhancements.

[2]The specific criteria for developing a formal data name are explained in more detail in Brackett, 1994.

not comply with the formal data naming taxonomy and its supporting vocabulary are treated as aliases of the formal data name.

Developing formal data names is a relatively easy, though often ignored, process. Failure to formally name all units of data perpetuates the disparate data cycle. Disparate data can be avoided, redundancy and variability can be reduced, and existing disparate data can be uniquely identified without affecting the applications they support if a few simple techniques are followed for formally naming data.

Data Naming Conventions

Traditional data names usually do not have any structure and often have little or no meaning, resulting in many data name homonyms and synonyms. *Data name homonyms* occur when two or more different data characteristics have the same data name. *Data name synonyms* occur when the same data characteristic has two or more different data names. Traditional data names are usually abbreviations due to physical limitations and are seldom consistent across programs or data files.

Example: CUST_NM and EMP_BD are traditional data names meaning Customer Name and Employee Birth Date.

Current data naming conventions are not robust enough for uniquely identifying all data.

A variety of *data naming conventions* have evolved in an attempt to resolve problems with traditional data names, such as the *Of Language, entity-attribute-class, role-type-class, prime-descriptor-class, entity-adjective-class, entity-attribute-class word, entity-description-class, entity keyword-minor keyword-type keyword,* and *entity keyword-descriptor-domain.*[3] Although these data naming conventions do provide data names that have more structure and meaning than traditional data names, they are not robust enough for uniquely naming all data within a common data architecture.

---

[3]Data naming conventions, and the problems with those conventions, are explained in more detail in Brackett, 1994.

Data Naming Taxonomy

The approach for uniquely naming data within the common data architecture is a formal data naming taxonomy and supporting data naming vocabulary. The *data naming taxonomy* provides a rigorous system for uniquely naming all data units consistently within the common data architecture. It is similar to other formal naming systems, such as the system for naming plants and animals developed in the 1730s by Carolus Linnaeus, the Dewey decimal system, postal zip codes, and chemical names.

> The data naming taxonomy provides a common language for naming data.

The data naming taxonomy establishes formal data names that anyone can use. This common language identifies and names data across applications, across projects, across organizations, and across disciplines.

Analogy: Air-traffic controllers worldwide use English regardless of the country where the air-traffic controller is located or the native language of the pilots. All spoken communication from the pilot to the air traffic controller is in English. Translation to the language of the country is done on the ground and translation to the language of the cockpit is done in the plane. English is the common communication between the cockpit and the air-traffic controller.

The same situation is true with formal data names. As existing disparate data are identified and documented, their local names are cross-referenced (translated) to the formal data name. This approach allows people familiar with their local data to work with those data using their local data name. It also allows people using different local data names to work with each other through a common data name. As new data are identified, they receive a formal data name according to the data naming taxonomy.

A Structural Taxonomy

The data naming taxonomy is a structural taxonomy that is based on data structure rather than on data use. Because data use can vary widely from one application to the next, and data use can change over time, any data naming taxonomy based on use is unstable and eventually leads to data synonyms and homonyms. The structural approach helps people understand the structure of an integrated data resource as well as the meaning of the data in the data resource. The structural approach, however, can lead to three conflicts.

Type conflicts can occur with dissimilar structures. An object or concept may be a data subject to one organization and a data characteristic to another organization.

Example: Post Office Box may be a data subject to the U.S. Postal Service because it manages post office boxes, but it may be a data characteristic in an employee's address.

Dependency conflicts can occur when one organization tracks many occurrences of a data subject, and another organization tracks only one occurrence of a data subject.

Example: One organization may track only one predominant Race or Ethnicity for its employees while another organization may track multiple Races or Ethnicities for its employees.

Key conflicts can occur when different sets of data characteristics form the primary key.

Example: One organization uses Employee Social Security Number to uniquely identify employees and another organization uses the Employee Birth Date and Employee Name Family to uniquely identify employees.

> The data naming taxonomy is based on data structure rather than data use.

Even though the structural approach can lead to conflicts, it is still more useful and more stable than an approach based on use. By understanding the conflicts that can occur and properly using the formal data naming taxonomy, the conflicts can usually be avoided.

Original Taxonomy Components

The original data naming taxonomy consisted of four components for the data site, the data subject, the data characteristic, and the data characteristic variation, as shown below.[4]

Data Site: Data Subject. Data Characteristic, Data Characteristic Variation

A colon follows the data site name, a period follows the data subject name, and a comma follows the data characteristic name.

Example: An employee's name in a logical data model that does not have a physical site might be as follows:

Employee. Name, Complete Normal
Employee. Name, Abbreviated Inverted

Those same names in a physical data model that has a physical site might be as follows:

Seattle Employee: Employee. Name, Complete Normal
Boston Training: Employee. Name, Abbreviated Inverted

A space usually follows the punctuation, but the space may be eliminated for convenience.

Example: The data names without spaces would be as follows:

Employee.Name,Complete Normal
Employee.Name,Abbreviated Inverted
Seattle Employee:Employee.Name,Complete Normal
Boston Training:Employee.Name,Abbreviated Inverted

The punctuation may also be eliminated for convenience as follows:

Example: The data names without punctuation would be as follows:

Employee Name Complete Normal
Employee Name Abbreviated Inverted

---

[4]The first component of the data naming taxonomy was named *data repository*. That name has been changed to *data site* to more adequately reflect its purpose and to avoid any reference to data repository products.

Seattle Employee Employee Name Complete Normal
Boston Training Employee Name Abbreviated Inverted

If determining which words in the data name belong to a specific component is at all difficult, the punctuation should be used.

Enhanced Taxonomy Components

Several enhancements have been added to the original data naming taxonomy to support more intensive management of the data resource within a common data architecture. The components of the enhanced data naming taxonomy are as follows:

Data Site:
[Data Occurrence Selection]
Data Subject.
Data Code Set;
Data Characteristic,
Data Characteristic Variation
(Data Characteristic Substitution)
'Data Code Value'
<Data Version>

A data occurrence selection represents the selection of data occurrences, known as a data occurrence group, from a data subject based on a set of criteria. It precedes the data subject and is enclosed in brackets.

Example: [Pilot Certified] Employee is used for employees that are certified as pilots.

[Diesel Powered] Vehicle is used for vehicles that have diesel engines.

A data code set represents a unique set of data codes within a data subject. It follows the data subject name and is followed by a semicolon.

Example: Disability. Personnel; indicates disability codes used by Personnel.

Disability. Manufacturing; indicates disability codes used by Manufacturing.

A data characteristic substitution represents the substitution of a specific data characteristic variation for a data characteristic. The data characteristic receiving the substitution is enclosed in parenthesis.

Example: Employee. Birth (Date) could have any date variation, such as the following:

Employee. Birth Date, CYMD
Employee. Birth Date, MDY

A data code value represents a specific coded data value. It follows the data characteristic name and is enclosed in quotes. Note that the comma is not needed if there is no data characteristic variation name.

Example: Disability. Personnel; Code 'P' is used for a physical disability

Vehicle. Type Code 'M' is used for a motorized vehicle.

A data version represents a specific version of data. It occurs at the end of the data name and is enclosed in carets.

Example: Boston Training: Employee <1 Quarter 1995> is used for employee data at the Boston Training data site representing data as of the first quarter of 1995.

The components of the data naming taxonomy can be combined in a variety of ways to meet specific needs. The preceding examples give a general idea of how to use the data naming taxonomy. Additional examples are provided later in this chapter and throughout the book.

Data Naming Vocabulary

Class words in the data naming conventions provide a standard structure and format for data values by using standard words to represent classes of data, such as integer, string, date, and name. They increase the meaning of a data name compared to traditional data names. Class words were an early attempt to define data domains and develop data integrity rules. Many of the problems with traditional data names were resolved by using class words in data naming conventions.

> The class word concept has expanded to a data naming vocabulary to support all components of the data naming taxonomy.

The class word convention, however, is not robust enough to support the data naming taxonomy.[5] The convention has been expanded to a full data naming vocabulary to support all components of the data naming taxonomy. The *data naming vocabulary* is a set of common words that are used consistently for forming data names in each component of the data naming taxonomy. A *common word* is a word in the data naming vocabulary that has a consistent meaning wherever it is used.

Example: History is a common word meaning any data that are not current but are saved for historical purposes. Student History, Employee History, and Vehicle History represent historical data for Student, Employee, and Vehicle.

Example: Number is a common word meaning an identifying number, Count means a quantity, and Amount means a monetary value. They provide common meanings for Equipment Identification Number, Room Seating Count, and Sales Transaction Amount.

> The data naming vocabulary provides common words with consistent meanings for all data names.

Five sets of common words are usually defined for data sites, data subjects, data characteristics, data characteristic variations, and data versions. Data occurrence selections and data code sets use the common words for data subjects. Data characteristic variation substitutions use the common words for data characteristics. Data codes values do not have common words.

An initial set of common words is shown in Appendix A. Each organization should enhance this initial set and develop a data naming

---

[5]The reasons for enhancing the class word concept are explained in Brackett, 1994.

vocabulary that supports their particular common data architecture. As additional common words are identified during development of a common data architecture, they should be added to the vocabulary.

Aligning Naming Conventions

Organizations can align the components in existing data naming conventions with components in the data naming taxonomy to take full advantage of the data naming taxonomy. The components in the data naming taxonomy that are not represented in the data naming conventions can be used to enhance the data naming conventions. Aligning data naming conventions and the data naming taxonomy also helps organizations move from more restricted data naming convention to the full data naming taxonomy with a minimum of effort.

Example: An organization uses a data naming convention consisting of a prime word, descriptors, and a class word. The prime word is equivalent to the data subject name; the descriptors and class word are equivalent to the data characteristic name; with the class word representing common data characteristic words. The other components in the data naming taxonomy can be used to further enhance the data naming convention.

Example: An organization uses a data naming convention consisting of a prime word modifier, a prime word, a property modifier, a class word modifier, and a class word. The prime word modifier and prime word are equivalent to the data subject name, the property modifier, class word modifier, and class word are equivalent to the data characteristic name, with the class word representing common data characteristic words. The other components in the data naming taxonomy can be used to further enhance the data naming convention.

Forming Data Names

Formally naming data is a major step in building a common data architecture. Formal data names are part of a cycle of discovery that includes comprehensive definitions and proper structure.[6] The best place to start this discovery cycle is to develop formal data names.

---

[6]Data structuring is explained in Chapter 6.

Data Site Names

A *data site name* is the unique name of a specific data site within a common data architecture. One to four words are usually sufficient to uniquely name a data site. A data site name uniquely identifies the physical location of existing disparate data and the physical location of data deployed throughout an organization or on a network.

Example: Payroll, Seattle Payroll, Dallas IBM 3090 Payroll, and New York Personnel identify specific data sites.

> A unique data site name is necessary to properly document the physical location of data.

Common data site words add consistency and meaning to data site names. Cities, buildings, computers, files, reports, screens, and documents provide common words for data site names.

Example: If data were located in three cities, such as Chicago, Los Angeles, and Dallas, those city names would become common data site words.

The data site name prefixes the data characteristic name to uniquely identify each data characteristic at each data site. The data characteristic name does not change to include the data site name.

Example: A data characteristic name is Employee. Birth Date, CYMD. When that data characteristic is placed at a specific data site it is uniquely identified with the data site name, such as Chicago: Employee. Birth Date, CYMD. The data characteristic at that data site, such as the name in the database, is still Employee. Birth Date, CYMD. It does not become Chicago Employee. Birth Date, CYMD.

Common data site words usually vary from one organization to another. A set of common data site words should be defined and maintained for naming data sites included in the common data architecture. If the common data architecture covers more than one organization, the common data site words must uniquely identify each data site within those organizations.

Data Occurrence Selection Names

A *data occurrence selection name* is the unique name of a selection of data occurrences from a data subject. It must be long enough to be meaningful and uniquely identify the selection of data occurrences, but not so long as to become a definition. One to four words are usually sufficient to uniquely identify a data occurrence group.

Example: [Pilot Certified] Employee, [Retirement Eligible] Employee, and [Temporary] Employee indicate unique data occurrence selections from the Employee data subject.

In some situations, the selection criteria are too detailed to include in the data occurrence selection name, and a more generic data occurrence selection name is used.

Example: [Selection 6] Employee indicates that detailed selection criteria were used. A comprehensive definition of the selection fully explains what the selection represents.

> Data occurrence selection names uniquely identify the selection of data occurrences from a data subject.

Data occurrence selection names can be used with the data site name to represent a specific data occurrence selection from a specific data site.

Example: San Francisco: [Pilot Certified] Employee and Thurston County: [Mature Maple] Timber Stand indicate both the data site and the data occurrence selection.

Common data subject words, described in the next section, are used in data occurrence selection names.

Data Subject Names

A *data subject name* is the unique name of a data subject within the common data architecture and should indicate both the meaning and structure of the data subject. The name must be long enough to be meaningful and unique, but not so long as to become a definition. One to four words are usually sufficient to uniquely identify a data subject and to indicate its meaning and structure. More than four words usually becomes excessive and adds little to the meaning.

Example: Appointment is not unique because there could be a variety of appointments, such as medical appointments, meeting appointments, and employee appointments to positions or committees. Unique data subject names would be Doctor Appointment, Meeting Appointment, Employee Appointment, or Committee Appointment.

> Each data subject name must be unique within the common data architecture.

Common data subject words add consistency and meaning across data subjects and indicate the structure of data within the common data architecture. Words like Activity, History, Suspense, Validation, and Authorization could be common data subject words.

Example: Student, Employee, and Customer data subjects each might have Activity, Suspense, and History data. The combination of the data subjects and the common words produces nine data subject names, Student History, for example, that provide consistency and meaning and indicate the structure of data.

Common data subject words may vary from one organization to another. Each organization should develop and maintain a set of common data subject words. If the common data architecture includes more than one organization, the common data subject words must include all those organizations.

Data Code Set Names

A *data code set name* is the unique name of a data code set within a data subject in the common data architecture. The name must be long enough to be meaningful and unique, but not so long as to become a definition. One to four words are usually sufficient to uniquely identify a data code set. More than four words usually becomes excessive and adds little to the meaning.

Example: Equipment type codes may vary from one organization unit to another or from one organization to another. Equipment Type is the data subject, and each different set of coded data values forms a data code set within that data subject. The data code sets might be named Equipment Type. Sales or Equipment Type. Marketing.

> The data code set name uniquely identifies a specific set of coded data values within a data subject.

Note that the semicolon is left off the data name when there is no data characteristic name following the data code set name. When there is a data characteristic name following the data code set name, the semi-colon is used.

Example: Equipment Type. Sales; Code and Equipment Type. Sales; Name include data characteristic names, as do Equipment Type. Marketing; Code and Equipment Type. Marketing; Name.

Common data subject words are used in data code set names.

Data Characteristic Names

A *data characteristic name* is the unique name of a data characteristic within a data subject in the common data architecture. Every data characteristic represents a specific feature of a data subject. The data characteristic name consists of the data subject name followed by the *feature name*. The data subject name provides uniqueness within the common data architecture, and the data feature name provides uniqueness within the data subject. Together they provide uniqueness for each data characteristic within the common data architecture.

Example: Birth Date is a feature name that identifies the date a person was born. Birth Date prefixed with Customer uniquely identifies the customer's birth date, and Birth Date prefixed with Employee uniquely identifies the employee's birth date.

> The data feature name prefixed with the data subject name provides a unique data characteristic name.

The feature name must be long enough to be unique within a data subject, but not so long as to become a definition. One to five words are usually sufficient to uniquely identify a data feature. More than five words is usually excessive and becomes a definition.

Example: Equipment. Date is not unique or meaningful because there could be many different dates for a piece of equipment. Better data characteristic names might be Equipment. Manufacture Date, Equipment. Purchase Date, and Equipment. Install Date.

Example: A data characteristic name like Date Salesman Said Equipment Would Be Shipped is too long. It could be shortened to Equipment. Salesman Ship Date and provide the same meaning and uniqueness.

The words in a data characteristic name should progress from general to specific.

Example: A person's name could be complete or abbreviated. The words Complete and Abbreviated are placed after the word Name because they are more specific qualifications of a person's name, producing Person. Name Complete and Person. Name Abbreviated.

Another way to understand the sequence of words in a data characteristic name is with implied words.

Example: Day. Number Calendar Year is the number of the Day within a Calendar Year. Putting Number at the end of the name would form Day Calendar Year Number, but the number is not the Calendar Year Number, it is the Day Number. Number belongs with Day, not with Calendar Year. The name would certainly not be Calendar Year Day Number because the data subject is not Calendar Year. In this situation, the implied words might be Day Number within a Calendar Year, or Day Number in Calendar Year sequence.

Data characteristic names must be fully qualified to avoid any uncertainty.

Example: Equipment. Ship Date appears to be fully qualified. However, there could be a planned ship date as stated by the salesman, a planned ship date as confirmed by the factory, and the actual ship date. To be fully qualified, the data characteristic names could be Equipment. Salesman Ship Date, Equipment. Factory Ship Date, and Equipment. Actual Ship Date.

Some adjustment of the general-to-specific rule is acceptable for normal English usage.

Example: In the preceding example, the data characteristic names would have been Equipment. Ship Salesman Date, Equipment. Ship Factory Date, and Equipment. Ship Actual Date if they followed the general-to-specific rule. These data names do not sound right to many people and are adjusted for maximum understanding.

> All data characteristic names must be fully qualified.

The data naming taxonomy allows enough words to fully qualify a data characteristic name.

Example: Person. Weight is not sufficiently qualified because it could be a verbal statement from the person or an actual weight. Even Person. Weight Verbal and Person. Weight Scale still may not be sufficient because the clothes a person wears may make a significant difference in the weight. Data characteristic names like Person. Weight Verbal, Person. Weight Scale Clothed, and Person. Weight Scale Unclothed would be more qualified.

Common data characteristic words add consistency and meaning across data characteristic names. Common words like Date, Number, Quantity, Identification, Value, Amount, and Description provide common meaning.

Example: Equipment. Purchase Date, Class. Description, and Part Order. Quantity uses the common words Date, Description, and Quantity to provide consistent meaning.

The common word Combined means the data characteristic is a concatenation of several other data characteristics.

Example: A person's name and birth date may be combined. The formal name might be Employee. Name Birth Date Combined. The data definition explains the combination.

Combined is not used for an expected combination of data characteristics.

Example: A date consisting of century, calendar year, month, and day would be Date, CYMD without the word Combined.

Combined also is not used when another word, such as Complete, indicates a combination.

Example: Latitude. Degrees, Latitude. Minutes, and Latitude. Seconds may be combined into a single data characteristic named Latitude. Complete.

The common word Value means there are no measurement units for the contents of the data characteristic and a companion data characteristic identifies the measurement units. The term Measurement Units is considered a common data characteristic word even though it is a phrase.

Example: Well. Depth Value contains the value of the well depth measurement and a companion data characteristic Well. Depth Measurement Units contains the measurement units.

An absolute, rigid implementation of common data characteristic words can cause problems. Some generally accepted usages that violate the common words are difficult to change. When a generally accepted usage violates the definition of a common word and it is difficult to alter common usage, the violation is accepted.

Example: License plates on vehicles contain a License. Number that is often not a number, such as XYZ 123. The value of the license number violates the definition of the common word Number, but it is difficult to change the data characteristic name to License. Identifier because of generally accepted usage.

Each organization should develop a set of common data characteristic words and use them consistently for naming data characteristics within the common data architecture. If a common data architecture includes more than one organization, the common data characteristic words must include all those organizations.

Data Characteristic Variation Names

A *data characteristic variation name* is the unique name of a data characteristic variation. The data characteristic variation component of the data naming taxonomy uniquely identifies each content and meaning variation of a data characteristic by adding a variation name after the data characteristic name.

The data characteristic variation name must be long enough to be meaningful and uniquely identify the variation, but not so long as to become a definition. One or two words are usually sufficient to uniquely identify a data characteristic variation.

Example: An employee's complete name may be in several different forms, such as the normal sequence, John William Smith, and the inverted sequence, Smith, John William. The data characteristic is Employee. Name Complete, and the data characteristic variations are Employee. Name Complete, Normal and Employee. Name Complete, Inverted.

Example: An employee's birth date could be in the form of month, day, year or in the form of century, year, month, day. These data characteristic variation names would be Employee. Birth Date, MDY and Employee. Birth Date, CYMD, respectively.

Each variation of a data characteristic must be uniquely identified in the common data architecture.

The same data characteristic often exists in many different lengths that can be identified by the data characteristic variation.

Example: City. Name is a data characteristic, but it can exist as 20 characters and as 35 characters. The data characteristic variation names are City. Name, 20 and City. Name, 35.

More than one data characteristic variation can be used in a data name. The data naming taxonomy allows enough words to completely specify the data characteristic variation.

Example: An employee's name may be complete or abbreviated, and it may be in the normal or inverted sequence, resulting in Employee. Name, Complete Normal; Employee. Name, Complete Inverted; Employee. Name, Abbreviated Normal; and Employee. Name, Abbreviated Inverted.

Example: If Employee. Name, Complete Normal exists in two different lengths of 42 characters and 56 characters, the data characteristic variation names would be Employee. Name, Complete Normal 42 and Employee. Name, Complete Normal 56.

A data characteristic variation can indicate accuracy, resolution, units of measurement, source of data, meaning, content, and a variety of other criteria, as shown in the following examples:

Vehicle. Speed, Estimated and Vehicle. Speed, Measured
Employee. Height, Inches and Employee. Height, Centimeters
County. Code, Numeric and County. Code, Alpha
Person. Birth Date, CYMD Certificate and Person. Birth Date, CYMD
    Verbal

Abbreviations and numbers are acceptable in the data characteristic variation name as these examples demonstrate. Although the data naming taxonomy usually requires fully spelled out names, the use of numbers and abbreviations in selected cases provides the same meaning and keeps the data name from being unreasonably long.

Example: Person. Birth Date, Century Year Month Day or Person. Name Complete, Normal Fifty Six are much longer and cannot be understood as quickly as Person. Birth Date, CYMD or Person. Name, Complete Normal 56.

Special characters are acceptable in the data characteristic variation name even though the data naming taxonomy usually prohibits the use of special characters. However, the use of special characters should be limited only to those that are absolutely necessary. The symbols for pound, at, dollars, and so on, should not be used in a data name.

Example: A combined date and time supplied by the operating system might be System Date/Time. A hyphen might separate words, such as Sub-Surface.

A data characteristic variation name should not be used to indicate a standard. The words standard and official should not be used in a data characteristic name to indicate that its form and content are officially recognized.

Example: State. Code Standard or State. Code Official should not be used to indicate the accepted set of state codes. All sets of state codes should be identified and documented, and then one of those sets should be designated as the official variation.

The word Common can be used as a data characteristic variation common word.

Example: There are several data code sets for Education Level, but none of the sets contains all the data codes. A new data code set is created that contains all the data codes. The data characteristic variations are Education Level. Common; Code and Education Level. Common; Name.

A *common data characteristic variation word* is a common word for data characteristic variations. Common words like Feet, Meters, and Yards provide consistency and meaning to data characteristic variations.

Example: Well. Depth, Feet, Well. Depth, Meters, and Well. Depth, Yards indicate variations in the data characteristic for Well. Depth.

The common data characteristic variation word Irregular means that the data characteristic format or meaning is likely to change from one data characteristic to the next and is unpredictable. This word indicates that some type of analysis is necessary to bring this data characteristic into conformance.

Example: Employee. Name, Irregular indicates that the content of the name is inconsistent; it could be a mixture of complete and abbreviated, and normal and inverted.

More than one common data characteristic variation word can be used in the same data characteristic name.

Example: Variable means the values in a data characteristic have different formats or meanings, and Multiple means multiple values exist in the data characteristic, such as J. Smith and S. Jones.

Person. Name, Variable means the format of the person's name is variable, but there is only one person's name.

Person. Name, Multiple means there are multiple names in one data characteristic, but the format is the same.

Person. Name, Variable Multiple means the format of the person's name varies from one data characteristic to the next and there are multiple names in each data characteristic.

Many data characteristic variations are encountered when disparate data are identified and cross-referenced to the common data architecture. As these variations are encountered, an organization needs to maintain a set of the common data characteristic variation words and use them consistently to identify specific data variations.

Data Characteristic Substitution Names

A *data characteristic substitution name* is the name of a data characteristic that represents the substitution of a specific data characteristic variation. This name is useful for defining a data characteristic when the specific data characteristic variation is unknown or may vary from one location to another.

Example: Employee. (Name Complete) is a data characteristic representing an employee's complete name. Specific variations of the complete name could be normal or inverted sequence, which would result in Employee. Name Complete, Normal and Employee. Name Complete, Inverted after the substitution.

___

Data Code Names

A *data code name* is the formal name of the data code value and uniquely identifies a data code within the common data architecture, not just within the data subject. The data code names must be long enough to be unique, but not so long as to become a definition.

___

Example: Student. Admission Code of 1, 2, and 3 mean New Student, Returning Student, and Continuing Student, respectively, and are acceptable data code names. A data code name like A Student Returning To School After A Lapse of One or More Terms is too long for a data code name. Short data code names, such as New, Returning, and Continuing, are not unique within the common data architecture.

___

> Each data code value must be uniquely named in the common data architecture.

Two to five words are usually sufficient for a unique data code name. More than five words may be necessary in some situations. The data subject name, or an indication of the data subject, should be added as a suffix to make the data code name unique.

___

Example: The data code names of disability codes for speech, hearing, and sight might be Speech Disability, Hearing Disability, and Sight Disability rather than just Speech, Hearing, and Sight.

___

The data code value can be placed in the formal name by putting the value in quotes after the name of the data characteristic or data characteristic variation representing the coded data value.

___

Example: The Student. Admission Code mentioned previously could be added to the formal data name, such as Student. Admission Code '1', Student. Admission Code '2', and Student. Admission Code '3'.

___

Similarly, the data code name can be placed in quotes after the name of the data characteristic or data characteristic variation.

Example: The coded data values names for Student Admission would be Student. Admission Name 'Continuing Student' and Student. Admission Name 'Returning Student'.

Data Version Name

A *data version name* is the unique name of a data version within the common data architecture. The data version name is placed in carets at the end of the data name. It must be long enough to be meaningful and uniquely the specific data version, but not so long as to become a definition. One to four words are usually sufficient to uniquely identify a data version. A comprehensive definition of the data version name fully explains what the data version represents.

Example: <1900>, <16:32:00>, <January 2, 1992>, <3rd Quarter 1994>, <Through 1988>, and <1989 Following> are valid data version names.

Data version names uniquely identify the version of data.

The data version name can be appended to any set of components in the data name.

Example: It can be appended to the data site name to indicate the version of all data at that site, such as Boston Employee:<January 1, 1995>.

Example: It can be appended to the data subject name to indicate the version of data in that data subject, such as Employee.<3rd Quarter 1994>.

Example: It can be appended to the data characteristic name to indicate the version of data for a specific data characteristic, such as Employee.Yearly Income<1993 Year End>.

Each organization should develop a set of common data version words and use them consistently for naming data versions within the common data architecture. If a common data architecture includes more than one organization, the common data version words must include all those organizations.

Data Name Abbreviations

The formal data name is used during logical design of the data resource because no length restrictions exist. When the physical design is developed, the data names often need to be shortened to meet the length restrictions of different products. A *data name abbreviation* is the shortening of the formal data name to meet a product length restriction. A *formal data name abbreviation* is a data name abbreviation that has been consistently abbreviated by a formal algorithm using an established set of word abbreviations. An *informal data name abbreviation* is a data name abbreviation that has not been consistently abbreviated by a formal algorithm or an established set of word abbreviations.

> Data names should be abbreviated according to a formal algorithm and an established set of word abbreviations.

A *word abbreviation set* is a formal set of established word or word phrase abbreviations that is used to shorten a data name. Abbreviations for word phrases should be limited to word phrases that are in common use.

Example: The single word Manage might be abbreviated to Mng or mng, and the word phrase Old Age Survivors Insurance would be abbreviated to OASI or oasi.

A *data name abbreviation algorithm* is a formal algorithm for abbreviating data names using an established word abbreviation set. There are several schemes for developing a word abbreviation set and several algorithms for abbreviating data names.[7]

[7]Word abbreviation schemes and abbreviation algorithms are explained in both Brackett, 1990, and Brackett, 1994.

Ideally, there should be one set of word abbreviations for all data within the common data architecture. Disparate data names, however, may be abbreviated randomly or by a variety of data name abbreviation algorithms. An organization should establish one set of *official word abbreviations* that is applied consistently to all data names according to a formal data name abbreviation algorithm. All other data name abbreviation sets become *unofficial word abbreviations*.

The strategy for establishing one set of official word abbreviations is to identify and document all the existing sets of word abbreviations and then merge those sets into one set of official word abbreviations. Once an official set is developed, formal data name abbreviations can be unabbreviated according to the unofficial word abbreviation set, and then reabbreviated according to the official word abbreviation set.

Example: Empl Brth Dte and Emp Bth Dt were developed by two different abbreviation algorithms. They would be unabbreviated to Employee. Birth Date by their respective algorithms, and then reabbreviated using the official word abbreviations to become Empl Brth Dt.

Informal data name abbreviations, of course, cannot be unabbreviated automatically. They need to be unabbreviated manually to the formal data name. The formal data name can then be reabbreviated according to a formal algorithm and the official word abbreviation set.

Example: Emp_BD and EMPL_BR_DT were not developed by any formal algorithm or set of word abbreviations. They need to be manually unabbreviated to Employee. Birth Date, MDY and then reabbreviated automatically as, for example, empl_bth_dt_mdy.

Data name abbreviations may be all uppercase, upper- and lowercase, or all lowercase depending on the specific operating environment and the organization. They may also be underscored, hyphenated, or separated by blanks depending on the specific operating environment and the organization. The formal punctuation defined in the data naming taxonomy may be retained or it may be dropped. The formal data name abbreviation algorithm should provide the proper format.

Short Data Names

A short data name is a shortened notation for a data name that provides a quick reference to the data, but is not a substitute for the formal data name. Appendix B shows and explains several shorthand notations for data names.

> Shorthand notations for data names provide a quick reference to the data.

DEFINING DATA

All data must have a comprehensive data definition for people to thoroughly understand and fully utilize an integrated data resource. Developing comprehensive data definitions, like developing data names, is a relatively easy, though often ignored, process. Comprehensively defining data helps resolve disparate data and prevent their continued development. It also increases the use of an integrated data resource by improving data sharing and supports more informed business decisions.

> All data must be comprehensively defined.

A *comprehensive data definition* is a formal data definition that provides a complete, meaningful, easily read, readily understood definition explaining the content and meaning of data. Comprehensive data definitions are based on sound principles and a set of guidelines that ensure they provide enough information to clients so that the integrated data resource can be fully utilized to meet the business information demand.

Data Definition Criteria

A comprehensive data definition is developed for each data site, data subject selection, data subject, data characteristic, data characteristic variation, data code, and data version in the integrated data resource. The following guidelines show what is contained in a comprehensive data definition and how it is developed.[8]

---

[8]A complete description of the preparation of data definitions is explained in Brackett, 1994.

> Data definitions must reflect the real-world meaning.

A comprehensive data definition must reflect the real-world business meaning of the data. Because an integrated data resource is a model of the real world, the definitions of those data must reflect the real-world meaning. A data definition must also apply to the entire integrated data resource, whether that data resource represents a single organization or several organizations. It must be consistent across all uses of the data and all business activities. Only one data definition that applies wherever the data are stored or used.

Analogy: The situation is like the definition of Lego blocks. Each Lego block has one definition, and that definition applies whether the block is used to build a boat or a spaceship.

> A comprehensive data definition explains the content and meaning of data, not the use of data.

A comprehensive data definition must not explain the use of data. One problem with traditional data definitions, if they exist at all, is that they explain the use of data. Three problems occur with data definitions based on the use of data.

First, explaining the existing use or uses of data could limit new uses of the data. If people are searching for data to meet their needs and the definitions that they see explain someone else's use of the data, those people's ability to identify data for their need is limited. If data definitions explain the content and meaning of data independent of current uses, people's ability to identify data they need is enhanced. Some examples of possible uses of data can be included in the data definition to help people perceive new uses for data, but the data definition should not contain a full explanation of all data uses.

Example: The definition for an automobile might be a *a vehicle that is used to transport employees to and from work on a daily basis,* which explains one use of an automobile, not the definition of an automobile. Because an automobile can be used for more than transporting employees to and from work on a daily basis, this definition could limit another person's use of an automobile. A data definition that describes what an automobile is helps a person see all types of uses for an automobile.

Second, defining data based on use usually results in disagreements that may never be resolved. It is extremely difficult to get consensus on a data definition that has a wide range of uses. Defining the content and meaning of data promotes agreement on data definitions.

Example: Employee Name might be defined as data used to print paychecks. This definition could cause immediate disagreement from people that use Employee Name for training schedules, affirmative action, or project assignments. To satisfy these uses, the definition must be expanded. The expanded definition only causes more disagreements, which result in an even more expanded definition.

Third, the use of data changes over time depending on the business activities the data support and the organization's information needs. Because data have different uses in different business activities, and because business activities frequently change, the use of data changes over time. Even a comprehensive data definition including all uses will deteriorate as the use of data changes. Keeping data definitions current with their content and meaning is difficult enough, but keeping data definitions current with actual use is impossible.

Example: Employee Name is used for maintaining training schedules. If an organization decided not to maintain training schedules, the definition for Employee Name would become inaccurate. Similarly, if an organization decided to use Employee Name for tracking trip reduction and telecommuting, the definition would become inaccurate.

The use of data is explained in business process descriptions. Each business process uses data in a particular way, and a comprehensive definition of that process includes an explanation of the data use. Defining the use of data in a business process allows the data definition to focus on the content and meaning and remain stable over time.

> The use of data is documented in business process definitions, not in data definitions.

A comprehensive data definition must be complete and meaningful. It must completely define and explain the data and any similarities or differences with closely related data. It must also include anything that is pertinent to a thorough understanding of the data. An excellent guideline for developing data definitions that are complete and meaningful is to prepare definitions people would like to see when they view the definition for the first time. When the people are newcomers to the data resource, what would they like to see in a comprehensive data definition to help them understand the data? What type of information do they need to make the data explicitly clear?

> Comprehensive data definitions must be complete and meaningful enough to ensure a thorough understanding of the data.

A comprehensive data definition should be developed for each different perception.

Example: There could be different definitions for wetlands based on different perceptions of wetlands. Each of these perceptions should have a formal data name, such as Wetlands Shallow, Wetlands Deep, and Wetlands Growth Management, and a comprehensive data definition that explains the similarities and differences. Whenever a reference is made to wetlands, the formal data name is used and the definition accompanying that name explains the specific perception.

No attempt should be made to force a resolution to one data definition because forcing a resolution forces organizations to change their perceptions. It is better to formally name and comprehensively define each different perception and allow resolution to take a normal course.

Comprehensive data definitions should be explicit enough to eliminate any connotative meaning. The *denotative meaning* is the explicit meaning in a data definition. The *connotative meaning* is the idea or notion suggested by a data definition. The connotative meaning is what a person interprets from the definition in addition to what is explicitly stated.

Example: The data definition for Well Depth Feet is the *depth of the Well in feet*. This minimum definition leaves room for many different connotative meanings. Is the depth the total depth of the drilled well, the depth of the casing, the depth to high water, or the depth to low water?

A better name would be Well Total Depth Feet with this definition: *The total depth of the well in feet from the surface of the surrounding ground to the deepest point dug or drilled regardless of the depth of the well casing.*

A general guideline is to have one to two paragraphs of one to three sentences each. Some data definitions may have many paragraphs to avoid any connotative meaning. Other data definitions may provide an adequate meaning in one or two sentences. The data definitions may reference or inherit other data definitions.[9] Appendix C shows examples of comprehensive data definitions.

Data Definition Common Words

Common words may be used to provide consistent meaning in data definitions just as they provide common meaning in data names.

Example: The common word Subtype may be used in a data definition to show that the data is a subtype of a parent data subject, as in *Organization Unit is a subtype of a Jurisdiction representing.* . . . The common word Combined may be used in a data definition to show a combination of more primitive data characteristics, such as *Latitude Complete is a combined data characteristic consisting of Latitude Degrees, Latitude Minutes, and Latitude Seconds.*

> Common data definition words add consistent meaning to comprehensive data definitions.

Several common data definition words are defined in Appendix C. This initial set can be expanded as comprehensive data definitions are created.

SUMMARY

Understanding the content and meaning of data is mandatory for the effective and efficient development and use of an integrated data resource. This understanding is primarily obtained from formal data names and comprehensive data definitions for all data in an integrated

---

[9]Data definition reference and inheritance is explained in Brackett, 1994.

data resource. The process of developing formal data names and comprehensive data definitions is often ignored, but it is relatively easy if a few simple guidelines are followed.

The original data naming taxonomy consists of four components for the data site, data subject, data characteristic, and data characteristic variation. Enhancements are provided for data occurrence selections, data code sets, data characteristic substitutions, and data versions. The data naming taxonomy is based on the structure of data and uniquely names all data in an integrated data resource. It is more comprehensive than data naming conventions because it is applicable to existing disparate data, logical data, and physical data.

The data naming taxonomy is supported by a formal data naming vocabulary that consists of common words for each component of the data naming taxonomy, formal data name abbreviation algorithms, and formal word abbreviations. Common words provide consistent meaning to formal data names. They are an extension of the traditional class word used in data naming conventions.

A variety of short data name notations are available for referencing data units without using the formal data name. These short data names are useful for planing and designing data, for integrating disparate data into an integrated data resource, and for deploying data to appropriate products and sites. They do not, however, substitute for the formal data name.

Comprehensive data definitions reflect the definition of real-world objects as perceived by the organization. They explain the content and meaning of data, not the use of data. They must be complete and meaningful, and emphasize a strong denotative meaning to limit individual connotative meanings. Common data definition words add consistent meaning to comprehensive data definitions. Comprehensive data definitions provide a way for organizations to thoroughly understand all the data in an integrated data resource.

QUESTIONS

The following questions are provided as a review of the chapter and to stimulate thought about how to formally name and comprehensively define data so they can be readily understood and properly managed.

1. What is a formal data name?
2. Why is a formal data name so important?
3. Why are data naming conventions not good enough for an integrated data resource?

4. What was the original data naming taxonomy?
5. Why is the formal data naming taxonomy based on structure rather than use?
6. What are the three type of conflicts that can occur with a taxonomy based on structure?
7. What are the enhancements to the data naming taxonomy?
8. Why are these enhancements necessary?
9. What is the data naming vocabulary?
10. How is the data naming vocabulary related to the traditional class word?
11. What does a data site name represent?
12. Why are common words important in a formal data name?
13. What makes a unique data characteristic name?
14. Why must data characteristic names be fully qualified?
15. Why is it necessary to have data characteristic variations?
16. Why should coded data values have a formal name?
17. Why should data occurrence groups have a formal name?
18. Why should data versions have a formal name?
19. Why is it important to have a formal data name abbreviation algorithm and a formal set of word abbreviations?
20. What are the different notations for short data names?
21. Why are comprehensive data definitions needed?
22. What are the criteria for a comprehensive data definition?
23. Why are the uses of data not included in a comprehensive data definition?
24. Why is it important to minimize the connotative meaning in a data definition?

Data Structure

A culturally acceptable and technically correct data structure is mandatory for development of an integrated data resource.

The disparate data in most organizations are usually poorly structured because they never benefitted from formal logical data modeling, data normalization, or data denormalization processes. The data structure is usually a physical structure of data files developed to meet specific application needs, based on specific perspectives of the real world, and implemented for a specific operating environment. There are usually no formal primary keys or foreign keys, and any relations between data files are based on similar data items. Many older data files were developed in every imaginable way, creating a disparate data structure that often makes it extremely difficult to integrate data.

The disparate data structure gets worse as the size and complexity of the data resource increases. A common data structure must be developed for data to be properly and completely integrated. A common data structure provides a new way of managing data that represents many different perspectives of the real world. It provides a way to understand the structure of disparate data and it provides a foundation for integrating data. Only through a common data structure can a data resource be fully utilized to meet the business information demand.

Chapter 6 explains the concepts, terms, and notations used to develop and document a common data structure. It explains how a com-

mon data structure resolves problems with traditional structural notations and presents alternative perspectives of the real world. This
chapter explains the concepts of primary keys, multiple primary keys,
intelligent primary keys, and dual primary keys. It also describes how
to use subject relation diagrams and subject structure charts. The
chapter concludes with an explanation of the techniques for defining
data classification schemes.[1]

DATA STRUCTURE CONCEPT

Most organizations have considerable quantities of data that were structured in different ways for different reasons. These data support a variety
of different applications in different operating environments that represent different perspectives of the real world. The result is disparate data
structures that make it difficult to integrate the data to meet the business
information demand. A new approach is needed to understand both disparate data structures and multiple perspectives of the real world, and to
integrate those data into a data resource that readily meets the business
information demand. The new approach includes implementing a common data structure and using data sets for managing data.

Common Data Structure

The term data structure is used in many contexts and has many definitions. Within the common data architecture, a *data structure* is a representation of the arrangement, relationship, and contents of data
subjects, data entities, and data files. A data structure includes both
logical data in design models and physical data in databases.

A *disparate data structure* is one of a variety of different data
structures that are based on different perspectives of the real world,
different application support requirements, and different operating environments. A disparate data structure typically represents one perspective of the business and supports a single information system. It is
usually not robust enough to provide a full understanding of the world
it represents.

A *common data structure* is the structure of data within the common data model that provides a full understanding of all the disparate

---

[1]This chapter does not present the physical structure of data, the criteria for
defining primary keys, data normalization or denormalization techniques, or
other routine data structuring techniques. These topics are adequately covered
in previous books by the author.

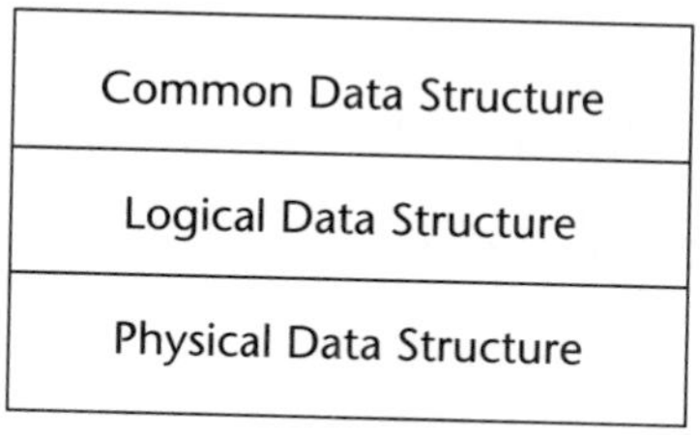

```
┌─────────────────────────────────┐
│      Common Data Structure      │
├─────────────────────────────────┤
│      Logical Data Structure     │
├─────────────────────────────────┤
│      Physical Data Structure    │
└─────────────────────────────────┘
```

Figure 6.1   Three levels of data structures.

data structures and multiple perspectives of the real world those data structures represent. The common data structure encompasses multiple logical data structures, as shown in Figure 6.1. It contains the universe of data subjects and data characteristics for all projects and information systems and represents multiple perspectives of the world.

The *logical data structure* is the structure of data in the logical data model. This structure is a subset of the common data structure that supports a single information system and usually represents a single real world perspective. It contains data entities and data attributes needed in the information system. A logical data structure may represent either disparate data or integrated data.

The *physical data structure* is the structure of data in the physical data model. This structure represents the physical implementation of a logical data structure for an information system in a specific operating environment. It contains data files and data items that support the information system. A physical data structure, like the logical data structure, may represent either disparate data or integrated data.

Data Sets

A *data set* is a unique set of related data characteristics used for a specific purpose, such as a set of data characteristics defining a data subject, a set of data characteristics extracted from a data subject, a set of data characteristics being moved between data sites, or a set of data characteristics in a report or on a screen. A data set is the basic tool for managing data within the common data architecture. All data, whether they are defining a data subject, a form, a screen, a document, a database, or a data flow, are managed as data sets.

A *single data set* is a set of data characteristics belonging to one data subject. A data set can be shown in several forms; however, the outline form is usually the best.

```
Employee
        Employee Name Complete Normal
        Employee Birth Date CYMD
        Employee Educational Level Code
        Employee Hair Color
```

Figure 6.2   Single data set example.

Example: The data characteristics describing the features of an employee are a single data set, as shown in Figure 6.2. The data subject name appears at the top of the data set and the data characteristic names are indented below the data subject name.[2]

A *nested data* set is the situation where two data sets are nested in a one-to-many relationship. The outer, or leftmost, data set represents the parent data subject, and the inner, or nested, data set represents the child data subject.

_____

[2]Note that the punctuation has been left off the data names.

```
Vehicle
    Vehicle License Number
    Vehicle Make Name
    Vehicle Model Name
    Vehicle Manufacturer Name
    Vehicle Color

Vehicle Maintenance
        Vehicle Maintenance Date CYMD
        Vehible Maintenance Total Cost
        Vehicle Maintenance Total Time Hours
```

Figure 6.3   Nested data set example.

```
Empl
    Empl Nm Cmplt Nrml
    Empl Eductn Lvl Cd
    Empl Hair Color
    Empl Eye Color
```

Figure 6.4   A data set with abbreviated data names.

Example: Many maintenance activities are performed on a vehicle, as shown in Figure 6.3. The data characteristics for the Vehicle Maintenance data set are nested within the Vehicle data set because many maintenance activities are performed on a single vehicle.

Data sets can contain either the complete logical data name or the abbreviated physical data name, depending on what the data set represents.

Example: The preceding two data sets above contain the complete logical data names. Figure 6.4 shows a data set containing abbreviated physical data names.

DATA RELATIONS

A *data relation* is an association between data occurrences either in different data subjects or within the same data subject. It provides the connection between data subjects for building the common data structure. A data relation within the common data architecture is an association only; a data relation does not have a name, and does not contain any data characteristics. Anytime a data relation contains data characteristics, a new data subject is defined for those data characteristics.

Common Notation

Data relations are designated with four symbols, as shown in Figure 6.5. A box with bulging sides indicates a data subject; the name of the data subject is inside the symbol. A dashed line connecting two data

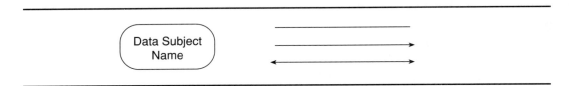

Figure 6.5   Symbols used to represent data relations.

subjects indicates a data relation between those data subjects. The dashed line may have no arrowheads, an arrowhead on one end, or an arrowhead on both ends, and the line may be branched or unbranched.

A dashed line signifies a relationship between data subjects, not a flow of data between data subjects.[3] A solid line, such as a data flow on a data flow diagram, indicates a flow rather than a relationship.

Data Relation Types

A *one-to-one data relation* exists when a data occurrence in one data subject is related to only one data occurrence in a second data subject and that data occurrence in the second data subject is related to only one data occurrence in the first data subject. A one-to-one data relation is designated by a dashed line between two data subjects without any arrowheads.

Example: An employee of a medical clinic may also be a patient in that clinic. Because an employee can be only one patient and that patient can be only one employee, a one-to-one data relation exists between Employee and Patient, as shown in Figure 6.6.

A *one-to-many data relation* exists when a data occurrence in a parent data subject is related to more than one data occurrence in a subordinate data subject, but each of those data occurrences in that subordinate data subject is related to only one data occurrence in the parent data subject. A one-to-many data relation is shown by a dashed line between two data subjects. The end of the dashed line with no arrowhead identifies the parent data subject with one data occurrence,

---

[3]An arrow is used on data relations because it matches the arrows used on directed arcs as defined in traditional graph theory.

Figure 6.6   A one-to-one data relation between data subjects.

and the end of the dashed line with the arrowhead identifies the subordinate data subject with multiple data occurrences.

Example: A vehicle may have many repairs, but each repair applies to only one vehicle, as shown in Figure 6.7. The data relation points from Vehicle to Vehicle Repair indicating that each data occurrence in Vehicle can have many data occurrences in Vehicle Repair.

A *many-to-many data relation* exists when a data occurrence in one data subject is related to more than one data occurrence in a second data subject, and each data occurrence in that second data subject is related to more than one data occurrence in the first data subject. A dashed line with an arrowhead on each end indicates a many-to-many data relation.[4]

Example: A Vehicle can have many Traffic Accidents, and each Traffic Accident can involve many Vehicles, as shown in Figure 6.8. Arrows point to both Vehicle and Traffic Accident, indicating that there are many data occurrences on each end of the data relation.[5]

A *recursive data relation* is a data relation between data occurrences in the same data subject. A recursive data relation may be one-to-one, one-to-many, or many-to-many, the same as data relations between data subjects.

A *one-to-one recursive data relation* exists when a data occurrence within a data subject is related to only one other data occurrence in

---

[4]A many-to-many data relation consists of two one-to-many data relations pointing in opposite directions. By convention, the two data relations are combined into one data relation with an arrow on each end.

[5]The resolution of many-to-many data relations is explained in Brackett, 1994.

Figure 6.7   A one-to-many data relation between data subjects.

that same data subject. A one-to-one recursive data relation is shown as a one-to-one data relation from the data subject to itself. A one-to-one recursive data relation is also known as a *closed recursive data relation* because it forms a closed loop between two data occurrences.

Example: If spouses worked for the same organization, each would have a data occurrence in Employee, as shown in Figure 6.9. Each data occurrence would reference the other data occurrence.

A *one-to-many recursive data relation* exists when a data occurrence within a data subject is related to two or more other data occurrences in that same data subject. A one-to-many recursive data relation is shown as a one-to-many data relation from the data subject to itself. A one-to-many recursive data relation is also known as an *open recursive data relation* because the relationships can be navigated either up or down without coming back to the original data occurrence.

Example: The organizational structure in an organization can be represented in a one-to-many recursive data relation, as shown in Figure 6.10. Each parent Organization Unit can have many subordinate Organizational Units, but each Organizational Unit has only one parent Organization Unit.

Figure 6.8   A many-to-many data relation between data subjects.

Figure 6.9   A one-to-one recursive data relation within a data subject.

A *many-to-many recursive data relation* exists when each data occurrence in a data subject is related to many other data occurrences in that same data subject, and each of those data occurrences is related to many other data occurrences.

Example: Network Component has a many-to-many recursive data relation, as shown in Figure 6.11. Network Component shows how various components on a network are connected to form the network. Each data occurrence in Network Component is related to many other data occurrences in Network Component, and each of those data occurrences is related to many other data occurrences.[6]

DATA RELATION DIAGRAMS

The term *data relation diagram* was previously used to represent data subjects and their relations.[7] That term now refers to a set of three diagrams representing the three types of data models. Each of these data relation diagrams is explained in the following sections.

[6]The resolution of many-to-many recursive data relations is explained in Brackett, 1994.

[7]Brackett, 1994.

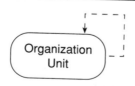

Figure 6.10   A one-to-many recursive data relation.

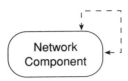

Figure 6.11   A many-to-many recursive data relation.

Entity Relation Diagrams

An *entity relation diagram*, also known as an *E-R diagram*, represents the arrangement and relationship of data entities for the logical data structure. The entity relation diagram is generally acceptable for an information system; however, several problems with the arrangement of entities and the notations make these diagrams unacceptable for the common data architecture.

> An entity relation diagram shows the arrangement and relationship of data entities for the logical data architecture.

First, the arrangement of data entities and data relations is often confusing because no uniform rationale for their placement on the diagram exists. Data entities are not placed in any regular pattern, and data relations often cross or wander around the diagram. Both of these situations cause problems because people spend too much time trying to understand what the diagram represents and not enough time making sure the diagram represents the real world.

Second, names and cardinalities are often placed on the data relations. These conventions add extra detail to the diagram, making it difficult for people to interpret the diagram and verify that it represents the real world. In some conventions, the cardinalities are indicated with symbols rather than numbers, causing additional interpretation difficulty. The data relation names are often a repeat of the cardinality and add nothing to the diagram.

Example: The diagram in Figure 6.12 shows a data relation with notation for zero or one Employee and one or many Paychecks. The data relation also carries two labels, Has Many and Belongs To, meaning an

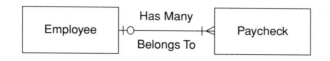

Figure 6.12　　Entity relation diagram with unnecessary detail.

Employee Has Many Paychecks and a Paycheck Belongs to an Employee. There is an unnecessary repetition of detail between the symbols for cardinality and the wording on the data relation.

Third, some entity relation diagram conventions try to show the data attributes on the diagram, either within the data entity or as separate symbols attached to the data entity. These conventions may be acceptable for data entities with a few data attributes, but the diagram becomes confusing when there are several dozen data attributes. In addition, the size of the data entity symbol varies when the data attributes are listed in the data entity symbol. Too much detail and too much variability on the diagram makes it difficult to distinguish relations between data entities and relations between data entities and data attributes.

Example:　The diagram in Figure 6.13 shows relationships between a data entity and the data attributes in that data entity. This diagram becomes confusing when a data entity has many data attributes.

Example:　Figure 6.14 shows the data attributes within the data entity. This diagram also becomes confusing when there are many data attributes for a data entity.

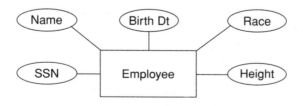

Figure 6.13　　Entity relation diagram with external attributes.

```
┌─────────────────────┐
│                     │
│   EMPLOYEE          │
│ SSN                 │
│ Name                │
│ Birth Dt            │
│ Race                │
│ Height              │
│                     │
└─────────────────────┘
```

Figure 6.14   Entity relation diagram with internal attributes.

Both of these diagrams give people too many things to comprehend at one time. An entity relation diagram should show the data entities and the relations between data entities, not the data attributes. These diagrams also encourage the use of shorter data names, which make the diagrams even more difficult to understand. In many situations, the entity relation diagram is really a diagram representing the physical data files.

> Entity relation diagrams are usually technically correct but are culturally unacceptable.

Fourth, some entity relation diagram conventions try to show the primary and foreign keys on the diagram by placing PK and FK after the data attributes comprising those keys. Again, this convention may be acceptable for data entities with one data attribute in the primary key and foreign keys consisting of different data attributes. When several data attributes are in a primary key and the same data attribute appears in the primary key and/or more than one foreign key, determining which data attributes comprise which key can be difficult.

Example: A country has many universities, universities have many departments, and departments have many courses. A University is uniquely identified by the University Name, a University Department is uniquely identified by the University Name and the University Department Name, and a University Course is uniquely identified by the University Name, the University Department Name, and the University Course Name.

```
┌─────────────────────────────────────────────┐
│              University Course                │
├─────────────────────────────────────────────┤
│  University Name                   PK FK      │
│  University Department Name        PK FK      │
│  University Course Name            PK FK      │
│  University Course Number                     │
│  University Course Description                │
│  University Course Credits                    │
│  University Course Lab Indicator              │
│                                               │
└─────────────────────────────────────────────┘
```

Figure 6.15   Conventional primary and foreign key designations.

There are data relations from University to University Department, from University Department to University Course, and from University to University Course. There are foreign keys from University Department to University, from University Course to University Department, and from University Course to University. The entity relation diagram convention that indicates primary keys and foreign keys with PK and FK does not clearly show the primary and foreign keys, as shown in Figure 6.15. Without the previous description, it would be difficult to determine which data attributes comprise the primary and foreign keys.

Many of these problems are due to the improper development and use of entity relation diagrams. Some people are using entity relation diagrams to develop physical data models for building databases. Others are using them to develop intricate conceptual models that are difficult to understand and implement.

Subject Relation Diagrams

The problems with entity relation diagrams are largely solved with a subject relation diagram. A *subject relation diagram* shows the arrangement and relationship of data subjects in the common data structure. It limits the detail shown on a subject relation diagram so that it is technically correct as well as culturally acceptable. The diagram accurately represents the structure of data subjects in the common data structure and it is acceptable to all people who develop or use it. Details that are not needed for the common data structure are not shown on the subject relation diagram.[8]

---

[8]The criteria for developing a subject relation diagram are explained in Brackett, 1994.

> A subject relation diagram shows the arrangement and relationship of data subjects in a technically correct and culturally acceptable form.

Subject relation diagrams are intended to increase the understanding of a common data structure and the issues surrounding an accurate representation of the real world. They are intended to show all the data subjects and data relations in the common data architecture that are available to individual information systems. The diagrams are not intended to contain the detail necessary for developing a database. The following guidelines highlight the features of a subject relation diagram:

- The data subjects are arranged to increase the understanding of a common data. Data relations generally do not cross.
- The data relations are not named because the names add little additional meaning.
- The cardinality notations are not shown because specific cardinality is part of data integrity, not part of the data structure in the common data architecture. Only the general cardinality is shown with the arrowheads on the data relations.
- Data characteristics are not shown on the subject relation diagram. They are shown on an associated logical data structure.
- Primary and foreign keys are not shown in any form on the subject relation diagram. They, too, are shown on an associated logical data structure.

Examples of subject relation diagrams are shown throughout this chapter and Chapter 14.

File Relation Diagrams

A *file relation diagram* represents the arrangement and relationship of data files for the physical data model. After a logical data model is developed for an information system, that model is denormalized for a specific operating environment. The file relation diagram represents that denormalized model and is used to develop the physical database.[9]

The desired approach is to have a common data model that represents the total data resource. The structure of the common data model is represented on subject relation diagrams. Entity relation diagrams are developed to represent the logical structure of data for each information system by drawing the appropriate data subjects from the common data

---

[9]File relation diagrams are explained in Brackett, 1990 and Brackett, 1994.

model. Additional detail may be added to the entity relation diagrams, such as verb phrases on the data relations, to further clarify the data that supports the information system. File relation diagrams are developed by denormalizing the entity relation diagrams to represent the physical databases in a specific operating environment. All the detail necessary to build the databases is included in the file relation diagram.

Multiple Perspectives

A subject relation diagram may represent multiple perspectives of the real world. It contains the total set of all data subjects and data relations. A subject relation diagram is to common data structures what *Webster's Dictionary* is to books and articles. The common data model contains all possible data subjects and data relations that could be possibly used by any information system.

> The common data structure contains multiple perspectives of the real world.

Example: Race (biological decendency) and Ethnicity (cultural decendency) may be maintained for an Employee. Some organizations may want to capture Race, or Ethnicity, or both for each Employee. Some organizations may want to capture only one Race or Ethnicity, and others may want to capture more than one Race or Ethnicity. Figure 6.16 shows the total set of these possibilities. This subject relation diagram may appear unreasonable at first; however, it represents the total set of possible data subjects and data relations for Race and Ethnicity.

Any specific information system uses only the data subjects and data relations necessary for the business activities it supports. An information system typically will not use all the data subjects and data relations shown in the common data architecture.

> The common data architecture may contain multiple cardinalities.

The common data architecture also contains multiple cardinalities. A specific information system uses only the cardinality relevant to the business activity it supports.

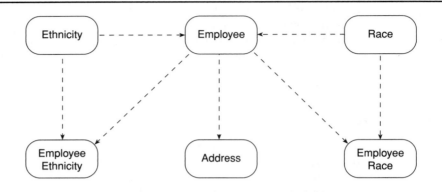

Figure 6.16   The total set of possibilities for Race and Ethnicity.

Example: The subject relation diagram in Figure 6.16 shows an Employee with many Addresses. The first data set in Figure 6.17 shows an Employee data subject with multiple Addresses. However, an Employee may have only one Address for a specific business activity. The second data set in Figure 6.17 shows an Employee data subject with one Address.

Data Subject Hierarchy

A *data subject hierarchy* is a hierarchical structure of data subjects with branched one-to-one data relations. It represents mutually exclusive, or *can-only-be*, situations between data subjects at each level in the hierarchy. A data subject hierarchy is traditionally known as an entity type hierarchy consisting of supertypes and subtypes. In the common data structure, each supertype and subtype is considered a data subject regardless of its level in the hierarchy; therefore, the hierarchical structure is referred to as a data subject hierarchy.

Data subject hierarchies are important for showing multiple perspectives of the real world and for displaying variations in data subjects.

Example: An employee in a university may be a Classified Employee, an Exempt Employee, or Faculty, as shown in Figure 6.18. A Classified Employee may be a Probationary Classified Employee or a Permanent Classified Employee, and a Faculty can be either Tenured Faculty or Nontenured Faculty.[10]

---

[10]Data subject hierarchies are explained in detail in Brackett, 1994.

A data subject can take three forms in a data subject hierarchy. A *virtual data subject* is a data subject that and represents a broad classification of subordinate data subjects. It has no data characteristics of its own. A *true data subject* is a data subject that contains one or more data characteristics that describe the data subject.

Example: A data subject hierarchy is defined for Hazard with subordinate data subjects for Geologic Hazard, Marine Navigation Hazard, and Environmental Hazard. The definitions and data characteristics are substantially different for geologic, marine navigation, and environmental hazards, so each becomes a true data subject with its own data characteristics. Hazard becomes a virtual data subject without any data characteristics.

A *data subject type* is a further breakdown of a true data subject that either has no data characteristics of its own or has data characteristics that inherit their names and definitions directly from a true data subject.

```
Employee
    Employee Name Complete Normal
    Employee Birth Date CYMD

    Employee Address
        Employee Address Line 1
        Employee Address Line 2
        Employee Address City Name
        Employee Address State Name Abbreviation
        Employee Address Zip Complete

Employee
    Employee Name Complete Normal
    Employee Birth Date CYMD
    Employee Address Line 1
    Employee Address Line 2
    Employee Address City Name
    Employee Address State Name Postal Abbreviation
    Employee Address Zip Complete
```

Figure 6.17   Employees with single and multiple addresses.

Example: Using the preceding example, Marine Navigation Hazard may be subdivided into Marine Current Hazard, Shallow Obstacle Hazard, and Narrow Channel Hazard. Each of these subdivisions become data subject types.

The data characteristics in a data subject type carry the parent data subject names to prevent synonymous data names. It is a poor practice to use the data subject type name in the data characteristic names because the synonymous data names make an already difficult situation more difficult.

Example: Many synonymous data characteristic names would be created if the data subject type names in Figure 6.18 were used to prefix the data characteristic names. Names like Employee Birth Date, Classified Employee Birth Date, Exempt Employee Birth Date, and Faculty Birth Date would be created. In reality, all of these data characteristics are Employee Birth Date.

All three data subject forms may exist in the same data subject hierarchy. If a virtual data subject exists, it is the top level. There may be many levels of true data subjects and many levels of data subject types. True data subjects may be subordinate to a virtual data subject or other true data subjects. Data subject types may be subordinate to true data subjects or other data subject types.

A matrix can be used to show which data characteristics are valid

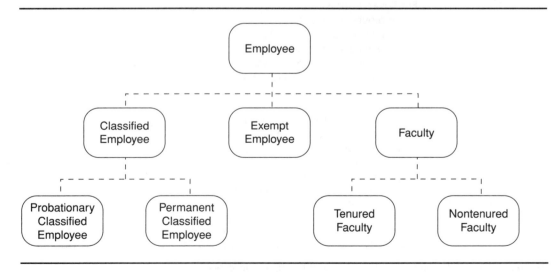

Figure 6.18   Data subject hierarchy example.

for each data subject type. The data subject types are listed across the top of the matrix and the data characteristics are listed down the left side of the matrix. The cells in the matrix are checked to show the data characteristics that are valid for each data subject type.

Example: A data characteristic matrix for Marine Navigation Hazard data subject types is shown in Figure 6.19. The data characteristics all have the Marine Navigation Hazard data subject name. The matrix shows which data characteristics are valid for each type of marine hazard.

Data subject forms are not identified on a subject relation diagram because their identification requires another set of symbols. The intent of a subject relation diagram is to keep it simple so that people can readily understand the structure of data subjects in the common data architecture. Data subject forms are readily identified in their data definition through the use of common data definition words, such as *A virtual data subject representing . . .* or *A subtype of the Employee data subject that . . .*

Presenting Ideas

Subject relation diagrams can present ideas about how an organization views the real world. They can be used to analyze different alternatives for building a data resource that portrays the real world. Subject relation diagrams can document decisions about how the integrated data resource will be structured.

Example: An organization consists of many different departments. Suppose that the initial business rule states that an employee could be temporarily assigned to any department in the organization. Figure

---

	Marine Current Hazard	Shallow Obstacle Hazard	Narrow Channel Hazard
.Hazard Type Code	X	X	X
.Current Speed Knots	X		X
.Minimum Depth Meters		X	
.Minimum Channel Width Meters		X	
.Warning Device Indicator	X	X	X

Figure 6.19   Data characteristic matrix.

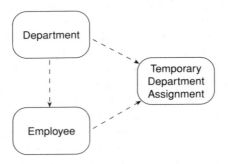

Figure 6.20   Employee temporary assignment to any department.

6.20 shows the data relation diagram for this situation. An Employee belongs to a Department and can be temporarily assigned to any Department through a Temporary Department Assignment.

Further analysis shows a weakness in the business rule. How can an employee be temporarily assigned to a Department where he is permanently assigned? In other words, the subject relation diagram shows that an Employee is permanently assigned to a Department and can be temporarily assigned to Any Department, including the Department where the employee is permanently assigned.

The business rule is changed so that an Employee can be temporarily assigned to any Department other than the employee's Home Department. A data subject hierarchy shows that a Department could be either a Home Department or a Foreign Department with respect to the employee, as shown in Figure 6.21. The comprehensive data definitions make this situation clear.

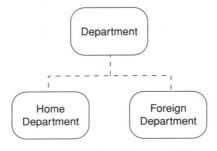

Figure 6.21   Data subject hierarchy for departments.

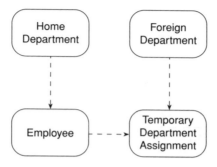

Figure 6.22   Employee temporary assignment to a Foreign Department.

A revised subject relation diagram shows that each Employee belongs to a Home Department and can be temporarily assigned to any Foreign Department through a Temporary Department Assignment, as shown in Figure 6.22. This situation is more reasonable and is what was intended in the first business rule.

A similar situation occurs with projects. The business rules state that Employees belong to Departments, Projects belong to Departments, and an Employee can be assigned to any Project, as shown in Figure 6.23.

If the business rules were changed so that an Employee could only be assigned to a Project that belonged to the employee's Home Department, the subject relation diagram would be changed as shown in Figure 6.24.

If the business rule stated that an Employee could only be assigned

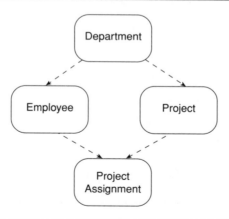

Figure 6.23   Employee assignment to any Project.

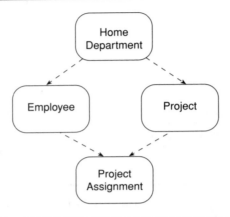

Figure 6.24   Employees assignments to projects in their home departments.

to a Project in a Foreign Department, the subject relation diagram would be adjusted as shown in Figure 6.25.

Even though these examples are simple, they illustrate how subject relation diagrams can show both existing and desired data structures. Subject relation diagrams can be used to compare the structures of the data supporting different systems or the alternative possibilities for

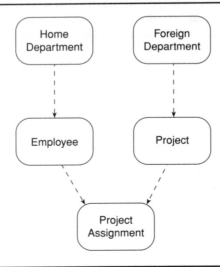

Figure 6.25   Employee assignment to projects in a Foreign Department.

new systems. The notation is simple enough for anyone to understand and use, yet detailed enough to portray the most intricate business rules.

DATA KEYS

A *data key* is a set of one or more data characteristics that have a special meaning and use in addition to describing a feature or trait of a data subject. Data keys are important for uniquely identifying data occurrences in each data subject and for navigating through the data resource. In a common data structure, the most important keys for properly integrating data are primary keys.

Primary Keys

A *primary key* is a set of one or more data characteristics whose value uniquely identifies each data occurrence in a data subject. A primary key is also known as a *unique identifier*. Each data occurrence in a data subject must have a different value in the primary key. If two or more data occurrences in a data subject have the same value in the primary key, no uniqueness exists, and the primary key is not valid.

Several criteria exist for identifying a primary key and assuring its validity across the full range of data occurrences. If a primary key meets these criteria it is a *valid primary key*. If it does not meet these criteria it is an *invalid primary key*.[11]

The *range of uniqueness* for a primary key is the range of data occurrences for which values of the primary key provide uniqueness.

Example: Figure 6.26 shows four primary keys identified for Vehicle. Their ranges of uniqueness are shown on the right. The first primary key is unique for all vehicles. The second is unique for all vehicles in the United States because it contains a license number and a state code. The third is unique for all vehicles in a specific state, because there is no state code. The fourth is also unique for all vehicles in a specific state, but it has a redundant data characteristic.

An *official primary key* is a primary key that is designated as the preferred primary key for a data subject in the integrated data resource. Its value is unique for all data occurrences within the scope of

---

[11]The criteria for designating a primary key are explained in Brackett, 1994.

Vehicle

Primary Key	Unique for all Vehicles.
Vehicle Identification Number	
Primary Key	Unique for Vehicles in the United States.
State Code ANSI	
Vehicle License Number	
Primary Key	Unique for Vehicles in a specific State.
Vehicle License Number	
Primary Key	Unique for Vehicles in a specific State.
Vehicle License Number	
Vehicle Model Name Complete	Redundant

Figure 6.26   Primary key variability for Vehicle.

the common data architecture. An official primary key is usually the one that is used predominantly in an organization. In a common data architecture that spans multiple organizations, however, many primary keys can be in predominant use by different organizations. Ideally, one of these primary keys is selected as the official primary key, the same as within an organization, with the selection based on consensus rather than on predominance of use.

Example: In the previous example, Vehicle Identification Number might be designated as the official primary key because it is unique for all Vehicles within the United States.

A *candidate primary key* is any primary key that has been identified in disparate data, but has not been reviewed for validity or range of uniqueness and has not been designated as any other type of primary key. All primary keys that originate from disparate data are candidate primary keys until their validity and range of uniqueness are determined.

Example: In the vehicle example, all four keys are candidate primary keys until their validity and range of usefulness is determined.

An *alternate primary key* is a primary key whose value is unique for all data occurrences in the scope of the common data architecture, but has not been designated as the official primary key.

Example: In the vehicle example, State Code ANSI and Vehicle License Number might be designated as the alternate primary key because it is unique for all Vehicles in the United States but is secondary compared to Vehicle Identification Number.

A *limited primary key* is a primary key whose uniqueness is limited to a subset of the data occurrences within the scope of the common data architecture. Ideally, a primary key is unique for all data occurrences in a data subject. There are situations with disparate data, however, where a primary key is not unique for all data occurrences. This situation usually occurs when the scope of a data subject is expanded.

Example: If the scope of the common data architecture were a single state, a Vehicle License Number would uniquely identify each vehicle and would be a primary key for Vehicle. Since the scope of the common data architecture is the entire United States, Vehicle License Number would not uniquely identify a vehicle because the same license number exists in many different states. The primary key is limited to a specific state.

An *obsolete primary key* is a primary key that no longer uniquely identifies each data occurrence in a data subject within the common data structure. It is no longer used because it has lost its uniqueness or is not appropriate for some reason. Obsolete primary keys usually result from integrating disparate data and determining that an existing primary key is obsolete. It is documented as obsolete so that it is no longer used.

Example: In the vehicle example, the last primary key is considered obsolete because it has a redundant data characteristic. It is labeled obsolete so that it is no longer used.

Multiple Primary Keys

Disparate data subjects often contain more than one primary key resulting in *multiple primary keys* for a common data subject. All primary keys must be documented and reviewed to determine their validity, range of uniqueness, and whether they contain redundant data characteristics. Primary keys in disparate data frequently have a limited range of uniqueness and often have redundant data characteristics. These situations must be documented so an official primary key can be properly designated.

> All primary keys must be documented so an official primary key can be designated.

One reason for multiple primary keys is different perspectives of the real world. Each perspective could have a different primary key.

Example: In the vehicle example, the Vehicle Identification Number is the most stable primary key because it is permanently affixed to the vehicle by the manufacturer. Manufacturers and law enforcement use this number as a permanent unique identifier of the vehicle even though it is not readily visible. The Vehicle License Number is affixed to the vehicle in a specific state, but it may change within that state or when the vehicle is licensed in another state. It is readily visible and is used to quickly identify a vehicle.

Primary Key Intelligence

Primary key intelligence is an important topic for discussion. Database technicians generally promote nonintelligent, system assigned primary keys because they are stable and easier to maintain. Business clients generally promote intelligent primary keys because they have meaning in the real world, even though they could possibly change.

> The intelligence of primary keys is a frequently debated issue.

An *intelligent primary key* is a primary key whose value has meaning in the real world. It contains a fact that is meaningful with respect to the business. A *nonintelligent primary key* is a primary key whose value does not contain a fact and has no meaning in the real world. It is meaningless with respect to the business.

It is interesting that the terms intelligent and nonintelligent are used with primary keys. Primary keys are composed of one or more data characteristics whose values provide unique identification; however, data characteristics cannot possess intelligence. Primary keys, therefore, cannot be intelligent or nonintelligent. Better terms might be meaningful and meaningless with respect to the business.

A *physical primary key* is an arbitrarily assigned, permanent, nonintelligent primary key that may or may not be visible to the client. Database technicians designate a physical primary key that is useful for managing database stability and performance. It is usually assigned by the database management system, is smaller than an intelligent key, and requires less processing. It is used for physical control of records and operational efficiency in a database management system. If a physical primary key is not visible to the client, it is referred to as a *surrogate primary key*. A *system-assigned primary key* is a physical primary key whose value is assigned by a database management system.

Two problems exist with physical primary keys. First, they create a problem when data from different sources are merged into a single database. Each of the sources could assign primary key values that are unique at that source, but are not unique when the data are merged. The primary key values cannot be changed without rippling the changes to subordinate records, which could be a time-consuming process and would create additional problems if the data were also retained at the source.

A new physical primary key could be created for the merged data, but this action requires additional maintenance to manage two primary physical keys. This process could become unmanageable if there were several levels of merges. The physical primary key could have a different range of values assigned at each source or a source identifier. In either of these situations, the physical primary key has some degree of intelligence even though it is system assigned.

Second, physical primary keys create a problem with normalizing data. People can assign any arbitrary primary key they desire and normalize the data any way they want around that arbitrary primary key.

Example: Vehicles, buildings, and employees could be given the same physical primary key and placed in a data subject for Business Objects. This approach defeats the principle of data normalization and results in a data resource that is not properly structured by data subjects and could lead to disparate data.

Dual Primary Keys

A new perspective about the intelligence of primary keys involves the use of both a meaningful business key and a meaningless physical key. The concept of *dual primary keys* involves the development of both a business primary key and a physical primary key that is system-oriented. The business primary key and physical primary key are variations of the official primary key. Both a *business primary key* and a physical primary key should be defined in the common data structure so that people are aware that both keys exist.

Dual primary keys resolve the primary key intelligence issue.

A business primary key is a meaningful primary key that is usually assigned by business clients and is visible to business clients. It is used to uniquely identify and manage objects and events in the real world and to properly normalize data into data subjects.[12] Business clients select a business primary key that is meaningful to them and helps them determine the validity of a data model. A business primary key supports the business survival, subject-oriented approach to building an integrated data resource. It may be less stable than a physical primary key, but it provides business clients meaningful access to data. It is usually longer than a physical primary key and requires more processing.

Foreign Keys

A *foreign key* is the primary key of a parent data subject that is placed in a subordinate data subject. Its value identifies the data occurrence in the parent data subject that is the parent of the data occurrence in the subordinate data subject. A foreign key must be defined for each data relation to a parent data subject. If there are two data relations to the same parent data subject, such as the resolution of a recursive many-to-many data relation, there will be two foreign keys to the parent data subject. When a one-to-one data relation exists, a foreign key is defined in each data subject.[13]

---

[12]Data normalization is explained in detail in Brackett, 1994.
[13]Foreign keys are explained in detail in Brackett, 1994.

> Foreign keys are important for managing relations between data subjects.

When an official primary key is designated, foreign keys are adjusted to match the official primary key. An *official foreign key* is the foreign key that matches the official primary key in a parent data subject. A *business foreign key* is the foreign key that matches the business primary key. A *physical foreign key* is the foreign key that matches the physical primary key. An *alternate foreign key* is a foreign key that matches an alternate primary key. A *limited foreign key* is a foreign key that matches a limited primary key. An *obsolete foreign key* is a foreign key that matches an obsolete primary key.

SUBJECT STRUCTURE CHART

A subject relation diagram shows the arrangement and relationship of data subjects in the common data model, but it does not show the content of the data subjects. A related subject structure chart shows the content of data subjects. A *subject structure chart* shows the existence and structure of data characteristics within data subjects in the common data structure. It directly supports the subject relation diagram to provide a complete representation of the common data structure. There are corresponding *entity structure charts* and *file structure charts* for the logical data structure and physical data structure, respectively.

> The subject structure chart supports subject relation diagrams.

The subject structure chart shows the primary keys, foreign keys, and data characteristics in a data subject, as shown in Figure 6.27. It contains the data subject name, followed by the primary key or keys, followed by the foreign key or keys, followed by a complete list of the data characteristics.

The official primary key is designated with the label *Official Primary Key* followed by the data characteristics comprising the primary key. Similarly, alternate primary keys are designated with *Alternate Primary Key*, business primary keys are designated with *Business Primary Key*, physical primary keys are designated with *Physical Primary Key*, candidate pri-

```
Employee

    Official Primary Key
        Employee Social Security Number

    Alternate Primary Key
        Employee Name Complete Normal
        Employee Birth Date

    Employee Management Level
        Employee Management Level Code

    Employee Status
        Employee Status Code

    Characteristic List
        Employee Birth Date
        Employee Management Level Code
        Employee Name Complete Normal
        Employee Social Security Number
        Employee Status Code
```

Figure 6.27   Format of the data structure chart.

mary keys are designated with *Candidate Primary Key*, limited primary keys are designated with *Limited Primary Key*, and obsolete primary keys are designated with *Obsolete Primary Key*. Primary keys are placed in the sequence of official primary key, business primary key, physical primary key, alternate primary key, candidate primary key, and obsolete primary key.

Foreign keys are designated with a label showing the name of the parent data subject referenced by the foreign key. The name of the parent data subject helps verify the data relations on the subject relation diagram. The data characteristics comprising the foreign key are listed below the label in the same order they are listed in the parent data subject's primary key. The foreign keys are placed in alphabetical order by the parent data subject name for quick reference.

The complete set of data characteristics is designated with the label *Characteristic List*. The data characteristics contained in the data subject are listed in alphabetical order below the label. This list contains all data characteristics in the data subject, even if they are already listed in primary keys or foreign keys. It provides a complete reference to all data characteristics contained in the data subject.

> The data structure must be separated from the data definitions.

Some data structure conventions attempt to show the data structure in the data definitions. The data characteristics composing the foreign keys are defined in the parent data subject and in each subordinate data subject. These multiple redundant data definitions can easily cause confusion. It is also difficult to visualize the foreign keys when they are imbedded in data definitions. A subject structure chart is the best way to separate the data structure from the data definitions.

The best approach is to develop three pieces of related documentation. A subject relation diagram shows the arrangement and relationship of data subjects in the common data architecture. A subject structure chart lists the contents of each data subject shown on the subject relation diagram. The data definitions provide a comprehensive definition for each data subject, data characteristic, and data characteristic variation. This approach ensures that the common data structure has maximum usefulness and minimum redundancy.

CODED DATA

Coded data are prominent throughout the data resource. Disparate data contain many different sets of data codes that are often undefined and inconsistent. These *disparate data codes* interfere with the proper management and use of an integrated data resource. The concepts of code tables and data code sets help people understand and manage disparate data codes.

Code Tables

A *code table* is a set of coded data values that are closely related. Each set of closely related coded data values, such as education level codes, position type codes, and seniority codes, is defined as a separate code table in the common data structure. A *code table data subject* is a data subject containing a code table.

Example: All the conditions related to disability, such as speech, hearing, sight, and so on, form a disability code table. The disability code table becomes the Disability data subject.

A code table contains a set of closely related coded data values.

Each code table data subject contains at least two data characteristics representing the data code value and the data code name.

Example: Disability contains two data characteristics for Disability Code and Disability Name.

The official primary key for a code table data subject is the data characteristic representing the data code value.

Example: Disability Code is the official primary key for Disability.

If the data code name is unique, which it should be in a properly constructed code table, it will be an alternate primary key.

Example: Disability Name is unique and will be an alternate primary key.

If different levels of detail for data codes exist, a separate data subject is defined for each level.

Example: Land use might have three levels of detail from general land use to specific land use. A separate data subject is established for each level of land use codes, such as Land Use Category, Land Use Group, and Land Use Type. The Land Use Category might be *Agriculture* or *Manufacturing*. The Land Use Group might be *Crops* or *Livestock* within *Agriculture*. The Land Use Type might be *Potatoes* or *Corn* within *Crops*.

A code table is usually defined if a set of names are encountered that could have data codes that already exist in the disparate data or data codes that could be defined later.

Example: If the data values *speech, sight, hearing, mental, physical,* and *developmental* were encountered, a Disability code table would be defined because those data values could be coded. The official primary key would be Disability Name. When data codes are identified, Disability Code becomes the official primary key and Disability Name becomes an alternate primary key.

The use of both official and alternate primary keys allows a subordinate data subject to use either data characteristic for linking to the parent data subject.

If data values that are not likely to be coded are encountered, a code table is not defined. The decision to define or not define a separate code table is not always clear. If there is any uncertainty, it is better to define a separate code table. A code table is also defined if it can be attached to more than one other data subject.

Example: Disability codes could be attached to students, employees, drivers, or schoolchildren. The attachment of one set of disability codes to different data subjects prevents the redundant definition of disability codes for each data subject; therefore, disability codes are defined as a separate code table.

A situation that may be encountered is a formal list of data codes and corresponding names with the option for free text at the end of the list. The option of free text at the end of a formal list is a poor practice because different people may add different data codes and corresponding names in the free text field resulting in a set of coded data values that becomes undocumented and unmanageable. In addition, the code table cannot be used for maintaining data quality. It is better to have a formal list of data codes and corresponding names without any free text capability and add to that list when additional codes are identified.

> The use of free text in a code table is a poor practice.

The only other option is to keep the names as suggested data values that can be entered for a data characteristic and allow free text. In this situation, a code table would not be defined, and coded data values would not be allowed. In other words, a set of suggested data values is presented with the option of free text if the suggested data values are not adequate.

Example: The status of projects might be *not complete, partially complete, complete,* or free text. Free text could be entered if the three suggested data values are not appropriate. The suggested data values are defined similar to the way coded data values are defined.

Data Code Set

Disparate data often have different sets of coded data values or corresponding names for the same code table. These different sets could have the same codes with different names, different codes with the same name, or different codes and different names. A *data code set* is a specific set of data codes within a code table data subject where either the data codes, the corresponding names, or both are different.

Example: There may be different sets of coded data values for education level from different organizations.

Each data code set is uniquely identified by the data subject name and the data code set name.

Example: Different sets of education level codes would be uniquely identified by the data subject name Education Level suffixed with the data code set name representing the source of the data code set. The resulting data code set names might be Education Level University, Education Level National, and Education Level State. The primary keys would be Education Level University Code, Education Level National Code, and Education Level State Code.[14]

Coded Data Trends

In the early days of data processing, there was a trend toward coding data to save space, particularly with the 80-column card constraint and expensive data storage, and to save data entry time. This trend continues today even though there are no 80-column card constraints, data storage is less expensive, database management systems use compression techniques, and considerable data are captured electronically.

[14]The previous convention for naming data code sets, explained in Brackett, 1994, has been changed with the addition of a data code set component to the data naming taxonomy.

> The current trend is toward keeping actual data values.

The new trend is to keep a meaningful data value and not encode the data value. This trend provides data that are readily understandable and provides better support to ad hoc queries and data warehouse systems. Queries are simpler and analyses can be performed faster without the need to decode data for the business client.

Data Group Trends

Traditionally, there was a trend toward grouping data values for convenience and designating a code for each group.

Example: People's ages were grouped into five-year age groups, such as 0–5, 6–10, and 11–15.

The problem with data groupings is that they are defined for a specific purpose. If a data grouping that supports one business need does not support another business need, another data grouping is defined. The result is a wide variety of data groupings and a wide variety of data code sets.

> The current trend is toward not defining formal groups of data values.

The new trend is to retain the actual data value and not define any formal groups of data values. Data groups are created as necessary to meet specific business needs. This new trend supports ad hoc queries by a wide variety of business clients and development of data warehouse systems where data can be grouped by a variety of different schemes to analyze trends and make projections.

DATA CLASSIFICATION

Most classification schemes progress from general to specific, like the animal and plant kingdoms, chemicals, and minerals. The *data classification scheme* is a scheme for classifying data that progresses from general levels to specific levels. The data classification scheme includes working levels and categorical levels of data.

The *working levels of data classification* are the lower three levels of data classification consisting of data subjects, data characteristics, and data characteristic variations. They represent the operational level of data classification. These three levels are used for building the common data architecture and developing an integrated data resource.

The *categorical levels of data classification* are abstract levels of data classification above the working level that provide a broader perspective of data. There are several types of categorical levels, including data classification schemes, data themes, data segments, and data clusters, as shown in Figure 6.28.

Data Classification Scheme

Many people, particularly when dealing with projects involving large quantities of disparate data, have an initial difficulty understanding data at the data subject and data characteristic level. Starting with a higher level data classification scheme helps people understand the data better than if they started at the data subject and data characteristic level.

The levels in a data classification scheme are shown in Figure 6.29. A *data discipline* is the highest level in a data classification scheme representing a broad collection of data, such as water resource, transportation, and education. A *data area*, which is also known as a *data subject area*, is the second level in a data classification scheme representing a subdivision of a data discipline. A *data group* is the third level in a data classification scheme representing a subdivision of a data area. A *data class* is the lowest level in a data classification

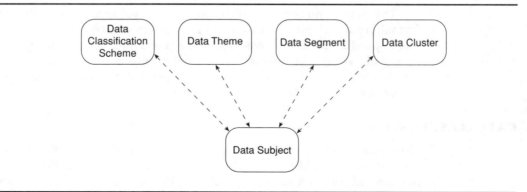

Figure 6.28   Categorical levels of data classification.

```
Data Discipline
   Data Area
       Data Group
           Data Class
               Data Subject
                   Data Characteristic
                       Data Characteristic Variation
```

Figure 6.29   The data classification scheme.

scheme representing a subdivision of a data group. It contains data subjects from the working level.

Each level in the data classification scheme must have a formal name and a comprehensive definition similar to data subjects, except that a suffix defines the level in the classification scheme.

Example: Part of the categorical levels of data classification for the Water Resource Data Discipline is shown in Figure 6.30. The Stream Data Area represents all data about streams and includes data groups for descriptive data, quantity data, and quality data. The Stream Quality Data Group contains data classes for biological data, chemical data, and physical data. The Stream Biological Quality Data Class contains data subjects relating to the biological quality of streams. Similar classifications exist for other water bodies, such as lakes and reservoirs.

```
Water Resource Data Discipline
   Stream Data Area
       Stream Quality Data Group
           Stream Biological Quality Data Class
           Stream Chemical Quality Data Class
           Stream Physical Quality Data Class
           Stream Quantity Data Group
           ....
   Lake Data Area
```

Figure 6.30   Data classification scheme example.

A data classification scheme is usually developed to help people understand disparate data. Developing a data classification scheme should not be a major effort, particularly if it will not help people understand disparate data. If development of a data classification scheme gets in the way of developing a common data structure, it should be abandoned. In other words, developing a data classification scheme is a technique to help people understand data at a higher level. It is not a requirement for developing a common data architecture, nor is it a purely academic exercise.

> Data classification schemes are defined to help people understand data.

Many different data classification schemes may exist, and data subjects may belong to more than one data classification scheme at the same time. There is no single, permanent data classification scheme for all data, and data subjects do not belong to just one data class. Such a system would be too rigid and confining and would not allow different perspectives of the real world. Data classification schemes must be flexible enough to represent different perspectives of the real world. Because many different perspectives of the real world exist, there will be many different data classification schemes.

A data classification scheme cannot be defined ahead of time and presented to people because the understanding that comes from developing the data classification scheme is lost. The involvement of people in the creation of a data classification scheme provides the understanding necessary for them to develop a common data architecture. The discovery process brings people's perspectives together and forms a common vision of the data resource.

> Development of a data classification scheme is a discovery process.

A data classification scheme is usually temporary, although the documentation may be retained to help newcomers understand the data resource. Once disparate data are understood and a common data architecture begins to emerge, there is less need for a data classification scheme. Data classification schemes also can be used to develop topics and keywords for indexing a data clearinghouse, as described in Chapter 8.

Data Themes

Data themes are specific groupings of data subjects for a specific purpose. They are identified within some scope, such as a major project, and are based on the way people view the grouping of data subjects for that project. Data themes are usually temporary and can easily change. They are usually developed for planning or coordination purposes rather than to increase people's understanding of the data.

> Data themes are defined for planning and coordination purposes.

Data themes are different from a data classification scheme and can cross data classification schemes.

Example: The Water Resource Data Discipline has data groups for Lake Quality, Reservoir Quality, and Stream Quality. A Water Quality Data Theme could be defined that crosses the Lake, Reservoir, and Stream data groups to include all water quality data.

A many-to-many relation exists between data themes and data subjects. A data theme can include many different data subjects, and a data subject can be included in many different data themes at the same time.

Data Segments

A *data segment* is a set of data subjects that are closely related by a high frequency of data relations between the data subjects in the set. There is a low frequency of data relations between the data subjects in different data segments.

Example: Vehicle, Vehicle Use, and Vehicle Maintenance are closely related data subjects belonging to a Property Data Segment. Employee, Position, and Job Class are closely related data subjects belonging to the Personnel Data Segment. There are few data relations between data subjects in the Property Data Segment and the Personnel Data Segment.

> Data segments are defined through an affinity of data relations.

Data segments may overlap slightly when a data subject has a relation to data subjects in two different data segments.

Example: In the preceding example, Employees are authorized to operate Vehicles through a Vehicle Authorization data subject. Vehicle Authorization would be included in both the Property and Personnel Data Segments. Employee and Vehicle remain in their respective data segment.

Data segments have relatively rigid boundaries that are defined through an affinity analysis of the data relations. They are more permanent than either data classification schemes or data themes because of the affinity established through data relations. With the exception explained previously, a data subject usually belongs to only one data segment.

Data Clusters

A *data cluster* is a temporary group of data subjects for a specific purpose. It can be any useful combination of data subjects for any specific purpose that cannot be met by any of the other categorical levels.

Example: A particular information system development project involves data subjects that are not uniquely defined by a data classification scheme, a data theme, or a data segment. These data subjects can be defined as a temporary data cluster for the duration of the development project.

> Data clusters are defined for the temporary grouping of data subjects.

A data subject can belong to many data clusters at the same time. If there are many different information system development projects, a data cluster could be defined for each development project. The data subjects involved in each development project would be assigned to that particular data cluster.

Example: Employee could belong to an Affirmative Action Data Cluster, a Payroll Data Cluster, and a Training Data Cluster at the same time.

SUMMARY

The structure of data gets more disparate as the size and complexity of the data resource grows. A common data structure needs to be developed to clarify multiple perspectives of the real world and integrate the disparate data structures. Only through the development of a common data structure will an organization be able to integrate and deploy their data to meet the business information demand.

The common data structure consists of a subject relation diagram and a subject structure chart. The subject relation diagram shows the arrangement and relation of data subjects in the integrated data resource. It resolves many of the problems with traditional entity-relation diagrams and provides a better understanding of multiple perspectives of the real world. A subject relation diagram is also an excellent tool for presenting ideas and alternatives for representing the real world through an integrated data resource. The subject structure chart supports the subject relation diagram by showing the structure of the data characteristics contained in each data subject. It shows all the primary keys, the foreign keys, and a complete list of data characteristics.

The use of a dual primary key resolves the issue of primary key intelligence and supports the development of a common data structure. The dual primary key consists of a business primary key and a physical primary key. The business primary key has a business meaning and is used by business clients to manage objects in the real world. The physical primary key has no business meaning and can be used by database personnel to control the database.

The definition of a code table data subject for each set of related coded data values also supports development of a common data structure. Each distinct set of related coded data values is defined as a separate data subject that contains data characteristics for the data code and a corresponding name. Each set of disparate data codes within a code table data subject is defined as a separate data code set.

Data classification schemes help people understand and manage the common data structure by providing a categorical level of classification above the working level. The working level contains data subjects, data characteristics, and data characteristic variations. The categorical level contains data classification schemes to help people understand data, data themes for planning and coordination, data segments representing the affinity between data subjects, and data clusters for the temporary grouping of data subjects.

The common data structure is a key component of a common data architecture. The development of a technically correct and culturally acceptable common data structure is the only way an organization can increase their understanding of the real world, resolve disparate data structures, and develop an integrated data resource that meets the business information demand.

QUESTIONS

The following questions are provided as a review of the chapter and to stimulate thought about developing and maintaining common data structures.

1. What is a disparate data structure?
2. What is the importance of a common data structure?
3. How is a data set used in managing data?
4. What notations are used to represent data relations?
5. What does a subject relation diagram represent?
6. What are the problems with the use of traditional entity relation diagrams?
7. How do subject relation diagrams resolve these problems?
8. How does a subject relation diagram show multiple perspectives of the real world?
9. What does a data subject hierarchy represent?
10. What is the range of uniqueness for a primary key?
11. What is the difference between an intelligent and a nonintelligent primary key?
12. What are the benefits of having a dual primary key?
13. What is the purpose of a subject structure chart?
14. What is the difference between a code table and a data code set?
15. Why should code tables be defined as separate data subjects?
16. What is the difference between the working levels and the categorical levels of data classification?
17. What is the difference between data classification schemes and data themes?
18. What is the difference between data segments and data clusters?
19. What are the benefits of data classification?
20. How can a common data structure help meet the business information demand?

CHAPTER 7

Data Quality

The need for consistent data quality becomes more important as the size and complexity of a data resource increases.

The quality of a data resource is usually as disparate as the data in the data resource, and that disparity is steadily increasing as new products and techniques become available. Initial work integrating large quantities of disparate data showed that disparate data are far more variable and have much lower quality than first thought. Additional work developing geographic information systems, building data warehouse systems, and distributing data over networks shows that already low data quality can become worse if it is not properly managed.

Traditionally, data quality received limited interest beyond making sure data values were correct. One of the reasons for the limited interest was lack of a formal data architecture within which data quality could be documented and managed. The common data architecture provides the foundation to achieve a consistent quality for a data resource. Organizations must take a much broader and more comprehensive look at data quality to understand the current level of data quality, establish a desired level of data quality to meet the business information demand, and adjust the existing data quality to the desired level.

Chapter 7 begins with an explanation of disparate data quality and the need to develop a consistent data quality. It explains the basic techniques for understanding, documenting, and improving data quality. It describes how proper use of these basic techniques helps resolve disparate data quality and achieve the desired level of data quality. The chapter concludes with an explanation of the prominent data quality issues most organizations face today and an explanation of techniques for managing data quality.

DISPARATE DATA QUALITY

Data quality indicates how well data in the data resource meet the business information demand. Data quality includes data integrity, data accuracy, and data completeness. Data integrity deals with how well data are maintained in the data resource. Data accuracy deals with how well data in the data resource represent the real world. Data completeness deals with ensuring that all data needed to meet the business information demand are available in the data resource.

Disparate data, as explained in Chapter 1, are data that are essentially not alike. *Disparate data quality* is the state of a data resource where the data quality is essentially not alike, or is distinctly different in kind, quality, or character. It is a state where the data quality is not known and does not meet the business information demand. The quality of the existing data in most organizations is as disparate as the data themselves.

Most organizations have disparate data quality.

The data resource in many organizations is continually increasing in both size and complexity. More people are collecting more data and making more changes to those data. The people collecting data have varying levels of qualification and use different techniques and equipment for collecting data. New techniques and equipment for collecting data are constantly emerging. Data quality varies with the level of qualification, the technique, and the equipment.

More data are being aggregated and more analyses are being performed on the data by different methods resulting in more derived data that may be poorly documented. More storage sites are available on personal computers and networks, and data are being moved to and from those sites with increasing frequency and less documentation.

Data quality becomes more important as the size and complexity of the data resource increase. It becomes very important as data are deployed to more products, distributed to more data sites, and used to support a wider range of business activities. Data quality becomes critical as the data resource is used to support changing business activities in a highly dynamic business environment.

Organizations need to understand the quality of their existing data, determine the data quality required to meet the business information demand, and seek to attain the desired data quality. Understanding the quality of existing data is difficult because the data quality is often not known or not documented, and frequently changes over time. If the existing data quality is not understood, it is difficult to establish the desired level of data quality and to adjust the existing data quality to that desired level.

> Disparate data quality must be resolved to have a data resource that meets the business information demand.

The best approach to resolving disparate data quality is to establish a consistent data quality for the data resource. *Consistent data quality* is the state of a data resource where the quality of existing data is thoroughly understood and the desired quality of the data resource is known. It is a state where disparate data quality is known and the existing data quality is being adjusted to the level desired to meet the current and future business information demand. Consistent data quality has one set of comprehensive rules for managing data quality that are uniformly applied to all data in the data resource. The techniques described in the following sections help define the consistent data quality for a data resource.

DATA INTEGRITY

The first component of data quality is data integrity. *Data integrity* is the formal definition of comprehensive rules and the consistent application of those rules to ensure high integrity data. It consists of techniques to determine how well data are maintained in the data resource and to ensure the data resource contains data that have high integrity. Data integrity includes techniques for data value integrity, data structure integrity, data retention integrity, and data derivation integrity.[1]

---

[1]This book presents only the data integrity basics. A previous book (Brackett, 1994) provides detailed examples for data integrity, explains how data integrity is maintained, and describes how data integrity rules are implemented as constraints.

Data Value Integrity

Data value integrity is a subset of data integrity that specifies the allowable values for each data characteristic and each relation between data characteristics within the common data architecture. Data value integrity is specified as data integrity values or data integrity rules. A *data integrity value* is an actual data value or a coded data value that is allowed. A *data integrity rule* is a statement that defines the actual data values or coded data values that are allowed.

Data integrity values can be specified for a single data characteristic.

Example: The set of data code values for Disability specify the allowable values.

Data integrity values can also be specified for a relation between data characteristics.

Example: A relationship exists between Employee Type and Employee Seniority. Certain employee types can only exist with certain employee seniority. The data value integrity for the relation between Employee Type Code and Employee Seniority Code is specified in the first two columns of the table in Figure 7.1. Additional columns can be added for the begin date and end date, or for any other data

---

Employee Type Code	Employee Seniority Code	Begin Date	End Date
1	A	10/1/91	
1	B	10/1/91	
2	B	10/1/91	
2	C	10/1/91	
3	A	10/1/91	
3	B	10/1/91	
3	C	10/1/91	12/31/92
4	A	08/1/92	
4	C	08/1/92	

Figure 7.1   Data value integrity table.

characteristics relating to the relation between Employee Type Code and Employee Seniority Code. The begin and end dates are useful when the data values or relationships between data values change over time.

Data integrity rules can be specified for data characteristics.

Example: *Maximum 3-digit numeric* is a data integrity rule for Employee Age, and *Maximum 34-character alphabetic right justified* is a data integrity rule for Organization Name.

Data integrity rules can be specified as a more formal notation.

Example: The data integrity rule for Employee Birth Date CYMD might be as follows:

1960 <= Employee Birth Date CY <= Current Calendar Year.

Similar data integrity rules could be defined for the month and day portions of the employee's birth date.

Another formal notation for data integrity rules is a set of options.

Example: If the values for a project status were *Completed, Partially Completed, Not Started,* or *Canceled,* the notation would be as follows:

Project Status Name = {Completed | Partially Completed | Not Started | Canceled}

Any of these forms is acceptable for defining and documenting data value integrity. The important points to remember are that data value integrity must be properly defined, and it must be defined in a manner that is understandable and acceptable to business clients.

Conditional Data Value Integrity

Conditional data value integrity specifies whether the values in data characteristics are required, optional, or prevented under certain conditions. The notations *R, O,* and *P* represent *Required, Optional,* and *Prevented* respectively. Mathematical notations, such as *1* for required, *0,1* for optional, and *0* for prevented could be used, but they generally have less meaning for business clients and should be avoided.

```
Student
    Student Name                              Required
    Student Birth Date                        Required

Customer
    Customer Name                             Required
    Customer Monthly Income                   Optional

Vehicle
    Vehicle Horsepower
    Motorized Vehicles                        Required
    NonMotorized Vehicles                     Prevented
```

Figure 7.2   Conditional data value integrity table.

Example: A student's name and birth date are required; a customer's name is required, but monthly income is optional; and a vehicle's horsepower is required for motorized vehicles, but prevented for nonmotorized vehicles. These conditions are specified in a *conditional data value integrity table*, as shown in Figure 7.2.

Conditional data value integrity can also be specified as a *conditional data value integrity rule*.

Example: Vehicle Horsepower in the preceding example can be stated as rules, as shown in Figure 7.3.

Conditional data value integrity can be specified in a *conditional data integrity value matrix*. A conditional data integrity value matrix is developed with the data characteristics down the left side and the data

```
If Vehicle is Motorized          Then Vehicle Horsepower is Required
If Vehicle is Nonmotorized       Then Vehicle Horsepower is Prevented
```

Figure 7.3   Conditional data value integrity rules.

	Temporary Employee	Permanent Employee	Faculty
Employee Name	R	R	R
Employee Birth Date	R	R	R
Employee Anniversary Date	O	R	P
Employee End Date	R	P	P
Employee Faculty Tenure Status	P	P	R

Figure 7.4   Conditional data integrity value matrix.

subject subtypes across the top. The cells in the matrix indicate whether a specific data characteristic is required, optional, or prevented for a specific data subject subtype.

Example: There are three subtypes of employees: temporary employees, permanent employees, and faculty. Not all data characteristics for employees are applicable to all subtypes of employees. The conditional data integrity value matrix is shown in Figure 7.4.

Conditional data integrity rules can be shown in a more formal notation. Optional data characteristics are shown in a set separated by a vertical rule.

Example: If either the employee's age or the employee's birth date were required, the notation would be as follows:

Employee = {Employee Age Years | Employee Birth Date CYMD}

This notation can be expanded to show sets of data that were mutually exclusive.

Example: If either the manufacturer and model of a vehicle, or the vehicle identification number were required, the notation would be as follows:

Vehicle = {Manufacturer Name, Vehicle Model Name | Vehicle Identification Number}

This notation can be used in a wide variety of situations to show the options for data characteristics or the values of data characteristics.

Any of these forms is acceptable for defining conditional data value integrity. Like data value integrity, the important points to remember are to properly define conditional data value integrity and to define conditional data value integrity in a manner that is understandable and acceptable to business clients.

Data Domains

Data value integrity is defined in data subjects like any other data and is part of an integrated data resource. A *data domain* is a data subject or data characteristic that contains data integrity values or data integrity rules. It defines the values that a data characteristic can contain under specific conditions. A *data value domain* is a data domain that contains a set of data integrity values. It can contain a list of values that may be continuous or disjointed or a list of value combinations for several related data characteristics. It can contain begin and end dates defining the time frame for which data values are valid. A *data rule domain* is a data domain that contains data integrity rules. The data integrity rules may also have begin and end dates defining the time frame for which data values are valid.

Every data characteristic must have a corresponding data domain that specifies allowable values.

Example: In the previous examples, data domains are defined for Disability Codes, for the relationship between Employee Type Code and Employee Seniority Code, and for the three data subjects with conditional data values. The data subject names for those data domains are *Disability Integrity, Employee Type Seniority Integrity*, Student Integrity, Customer Integrity, and Vehicle Integrity, respectively. Notice the use of a common data subject word Integrity for those data subjects.

If multiple data characteristic variations exist within a data characteristic, each of those data characteristic variations must have a data domain. One of the easiest ways to determine whether a data characteristic variation exists is to review the data domain. If more than one data domain exists, there is more than one data characteristic variation.

A data attribute in a logical data model, as explained in Chapter 4, represents one data characteristic variation and has one corresponding data domain. One major reason for identifying data characteristic variations and corresponding data domains is to ensure that when a data characteristic variation is selected from the common data architecture to be an attribute in a logical model it has a formal data domain.

> Every data characteristic or data characteristic variation must have a data domain.

Data value domains must have a data domain for each of the data characteristics in that domain. This *data domain integrity* is an important part of the consistent data quality for an integrated data resource.

Example: Disability contains a set of Disability Codes that is the data domain for any data characteristic containing disability codes. Disability has two data characteristics for Disability Code and Disability Name. Each of these data characteristics requires a data domain defining their allowable values. The data rule domain for Disability Code is *A 1-digit number* and the data rule domain for Disability Name is *A maximum 16-character alphanumeric string.*

> Data value integrity must be continued until a data integrity rule is defined.

Data value integrity must be progressively defined until a data integrity rule is defined. The implied data integrity rule for data integrity rules is *An alphanumeric string of unlimited length.* This technique provides a shell of *primary data value integrity rules* around an integrated data resource. These primary data value integrity rules are developed through the definition of business rules to ensure that the data adequately support the business information demand.

Default Data Values
Default data values are often used in data edits. In many situations, this practice is acceptable.

Example: The current date could be entered for a credit application, or an initial credit limit could be entered based on specific data in the credit application.

In other situations, however, default data values may not be acceptable.

Example: If a student's classification is not known when they first enter a university, *Freshman* is entered as the default value. This default is inappropriate because students may enter a university as sophomores, juniors, seniors, or graduates.

Default data values should be audited to ensure data quality is maintained.

The best practice is to not have default data values. If default data values are allowed, their use should be audited to ensure that the default value is valid. If the audit shows the default data value is not valid, the process should be changed to so the default data value is correct. This self-correction process for default values improves data quality.

Data Structure Integrity

Data structure integrity is a subset of data integrity that specifies the integrity for data relations. Data structure integrity may be documented in a diagram, a matrix, or a table.

A *data structure integrity diagram* shows data structure integrity in a diagram.

Example: The existence of an Employee requires the existence of a Person, but existence of a Person does not require the existence of an Employee, as shown in Figure 7.5. Existence of a Student prevents the existence of a Prospective Student, and the existence of a Prospective Student prevents the existence of a Student. The existence of an Employee does not require the existence of a Paycheck, but existence of a Paycheck requires the existence of an Employee.

A *data structure integrity matrix* shows data structure integrity as a matrix.

Example: The same data structure integrity shown in Figure 7.5 is shown as a matrix in Figure 7.6. The data structure integrity matrix is not as graphical as the diagram, but it shows the possibility of other conditions, such as those between Student and Person, and between Perspective Student and Person.

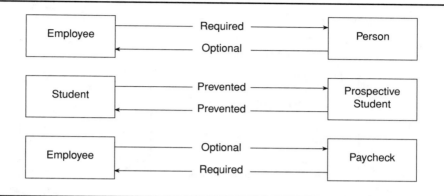

Figure 7.5   Data structure integrity diagram.

A *data structure integrity table* shows data structure integrity as a table.

Example: The same data structure integrity shown in Figure 7.5 is shown as a table in Figure 7.7.

The data structure integrity table is not as graphic as the data structure diagram and does not show other possibilities like the data structure matrix, but it takes less space. A data structure integrity diagram or data structure integrity matrix is generally used to identify structural data integrity, and a data structure integrity table is generally used for documentation.

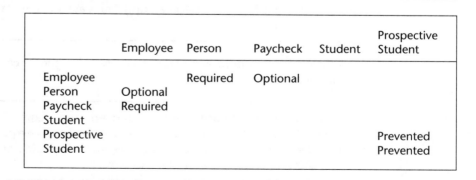

	Employee	Person	Paycheck	Student	Prospective Student
Employee		Required	Optional		
Person	Optional				
Paycheck	Required				
Student					
Prospective Student					Prevented Prevented

Figure 7.6   Data structure integrity matrix.

```
Person
   Employee Optional

Employee
   Person Required
   Paycheck Optional

Paycheck
   Employee Optional

Student
   Prospective Student Prevented

Prospective Student
   Student Prevented
```

Figure 7.7   Data structure integrity table.

Conditional Data Structure Integrity

Conditional data structure integrity specifies the cardinality for data relations. *Cardinality* is the number of data occurrences allowed on either side of a data relation. In the common data architecture, cardinality is documented with data integrity, not with the data structure. Cardinality is documented in a conditional data structure integrity table or as conditional data structure integrity rules.

Example: Students can have zero, one, or many Degrees; Undergraduate Students cannot have any Degrees; and Graduate Students must have one or more Degrees.

A *conditional data structure integrity table* shows cardinality in a table form.

Example: The cardinality between Student and Degree is shown as a table in Figure 7.8. The number of degrees for an Undergraduate Student is *0*, or *Prevented*. The number of degrees for a Graduate Student is one or more, commonly shown as *1,M* or *Required*.

A *conditional data structure integrity rule* shows cardinality as a rule.

Student			
	Undergraduate	0	Degree Prevented
	Graduate	1,M	Degree Required

Figure 7.8 Conditional data structure integrity table.

Example: The cardinality between Student and Degree is shown as a rule in Figure 7.9.

Either the tabular form or rule form is useful for documenting conditional data structure integrity. The cardinality can be shown on an entity relation diagram, if desired, by using the symbols *0; 0,1; 0,M;* or *1,M* meaning *zero, zero or one, zero-to-many,* or *one-to-many,* respectively.

Conditional data structure integrity rules can also be shown in a more formal notation.

Example: The cardinality between Employee and Dependent might be stated as Employee: *0 <= Dependent <= n* or as *Employee: 0,n Dependent.* The data structure integrity between Employee and Position might be stated as *Employee:1,3 Position Appointment.*

Conditional data structure integrity, such as the can-also-be situation, can be shown in a data subject hierarchy.

Example: Wells can be either water wells, geothermal wells, inspection wells, or recharge wells, as shown in Figure 7.10. The Well Type Code in Well Type designates the type of well.

If Student is Undergraduate	Then Degree Prevented
If Student is Graduate	Then Degree Required

Figure 7.9 Conditional data structure integrity rule.

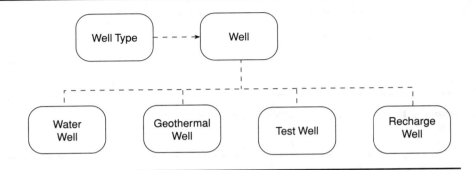

Figure 7.10   Data subject hierarchy showing conditional data structure integrity.

The conditional data structure integrity can be shown with the same formal notation used for data characteristics and data characteristic values:

Example: *Well = {Water Well | Geothermal Well | Inspection Well | Recharge Well}*

Any of these forms are acceptable for defining data structure integrity and conditional data structure integrity. The important points to remember are to properly define data structure integrity and conditional data structure integrity and to define them in a manner that is understandable and acceptable to business clients.

Referential Integrity

Referential integrity is the part of data structure integrity that ensures a parent data occurrence exists for each subordinate data occurrence. A subordinate data occurrence cannot be added if no parent data occurrence exists, and a parent data occurrence cannot be deleted if subordinate data occurrences still exist.

Example: A Customer Order cannot be added without a corresponding Customer, and a Customer cannot be deleted if corresponding Customer Orders exist.

Referential integrity is usually required in the common data architecture and does not need to be explicitly stated for every data relation. Exceptions for data warehouse systems will be explained in Chapter 10.

Data Retention Integrity

Data are often changed or discarded based on current business operations without consideration for the future value of those data. *Data retention integrity* is a subset of data integrity that specifies criteria for preventing the loss of critical data through updates or deletion. It considers the future value of data to determine what data should be retained and how they should be retained. It looks to the future to determine the unknown or hidden usefulness of the data.

Data retention integrity is specified for both data occurrences and data characteristics. A *data occurrence retention rule* specifies exactly how long a data occurrence is retained and what is done before a data occurrence is deleted. It specifies the procedure to preserve the historical significance of the data occurrence and the data characteristic values in that data occurrence. Possible procedures for preserving the historical significance of data include creating an audit trail for all or part of the data characteristics in the data occurrence, moving the data occurrence or selected data characteristics to a history file, rolling up data values to a higher level, and deleting data occurrences with no action.

Example: The data occurrence retention rule for Employee is shown in Figure 7.11.

A *data characteristic retention rule* specifies what is done when a data characteristic value is updated or deleted. It specifies the procedure to preserve the historical significance of data characteristic values. Possible procedures for maintaining the historical significance include an audit trail for the data value changes or rolling up the data values to a higher level.

Example: A few data characteristic retention rules for Employee are shown in Figure 7.12.

Employee

An Employee data occurrence may be deleted after January 31 of the year following the end of his employment. All data characteristic values in that data occurrence are moved to Employee History.

Figure 7.11   Data occurrence retention rule example.

Employee

Employee Birth Date CYMD may be updated without retaining the previous value. It is never deleted.

Employee Age Years may be updated or deleted at any time without any tracking.

Employee Name Complete Normal may be updated after the existing value is placed in Employee Audit Name Complete Normal with a corresponding Employee Audit Date CYMD. It is never deleted.

Figure 7.12   Data characteristic retention rule example.

Data retention rules are maintained in a data subject or data characteristic the same as other data integrity rules. The data occurrence retention rules are maintained with the data subject. The data characteristic retention rules are maintained with the data characteristic. Details for maintaining data retention integrity rules are explained further in Chapter 8. The important point to remember is that data retention rules must be properly defined so that they can be implemented.

Data Derivation Integrity

A data resource often contains considerable derived data. The derivation procedure and the procedure for maintaining derived data need to be properly documented to ensure high-quality data. Redundant data and replicated data are also prominent in an organization's data resource. The existence of redundant and replicated data and the maintenance of those data also need to be properly documented to ensure high-quality data.

Derived Data

Data derivation is the process of creating a data value from one or more contributing data values through a data derivation algorithm. *Derived data* are any data that are derived through a data derivation process. *Active derived data* are any data that are derived from contributing data characteristics that still exist and whose values can change. Active derived data must be rederived when the contributing data values change or when new contributing data values appear. *Static derived data* are any data that are derived from contributing data characteristics that no longer exist or whose values will never change. There is no need to rederive static derived data.

Data derivation integrity is a subset of data integrity that specifies the criteria for data derivation and for derived data maintenance. The specification includes the contributing data characteristics, the data derivation procedure, and the timing for data derivation.

A *data derivation diagram* specifies the data characteristics contributing to the derived data characteristic. A rectangle represents data characteristics and a solid line with an arrow represents the direction of data derivation. The name of the data characteristic is placed in the rectangle. The arrow points from the contributing data characteristics to the derived data characteristic. The data derivation procedure is implied in the solid line.

The four types of data derivations are shown in Figure 7.13. The top diagram represents *data generation* where a data value is derived from a data derivation procedure without a contributing data characteristic.

Example: The generation of random numbers for a statistical analysis is an example of data generation.

The second diagram represents a *single contributor data derivation* where a data value is derived from one contributing data characteristic and a data derivation procedure.

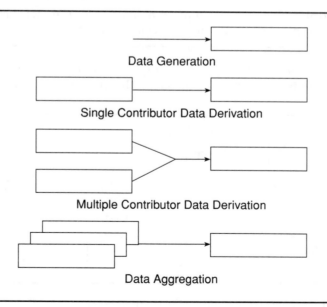

Data Generation

Single Contributor Data Derivation

Multiple Contributor Data Derivation

Data Aggregation

Figure 7.13   Types of data derivations.

Example: The derivation of kilometers from miles is represented as an equation:

Road Segment Length Kilometers = Road Segment Length Miles × 1.60935

Example: The derivation of a person's age from their birth date and the current date is represented as an equation:

Employee Age Years = Current Date CY – Employee Birth Date CY

The third diagram represents a *multiple contributor data derivation* where a data value is derived from two or more contributing data characteristics and a data derivation procedure.

Example: The derivation of Well Type from Well Casing Material and Well Depth is shown in Figure 7.14.

The bottom diagram represents a *data aggregation* where a data value is derived from the aggregation of two or more contributing data characteristics in different data occurrences within the same data subject.

Example: The derivation of Account Balance from Account Transactions is an example of a data aggregation, as shown in Figure 7.15.

A *data derivation procedure* is an algorithm, equation, logical expression, or matrix that specifies the procedure for deriving data.

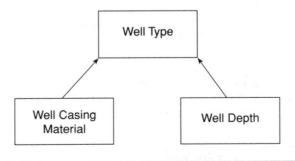

Figure 7.14   Data derivation diagram for multiple contributors.

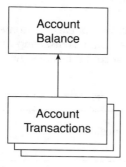

Figure 7.15   Data aggregation diagram.

Example: The data derivation procedure for Well Type is shown in Figure 7.16. The procedure is in the form of a matrix showing the conditions of Well Casing Material and Well Depth for deriving Well Type. A statement about the timing of rederivation appears below the matrix.

Example: The data derivation procedure for Account Balance Amount is shown in Figure 7.17. The procedure includes a statement about the rederivation of Account Balance Amount.

The data aggregation procedure can also be shown in a more formal notation.

Well Casing Material	Well Depth	Well Type
Black Steel	< 10 Feet	1
Black Steel	11 to 100 Feet	2
Black Steel	> 100 Feet	3
Stainless Steel	< 50 Feet	4
Stainless Steel	50 Feet +	5

Well Type is rederived immediately when either Well Casing Material or Well Depth changes.

Figure 7.16   Data derivation algorithm for Well Type.

> The new Account Balance Amount is derived for each Customer at midnight of each working day by applying the Account Transaction Amount for the working day to the previous day's Account Balance Amount for that Customer.

Figure 7.17   Data derivation algorithm for account balance.

Example: The aggregation of the trip miles during a month for a motor pool vehicle might be shown as follows:

$$Vehicle\ Month\ Miles = \sum\nolimits_{January\ 1}^{January\ 31} Vehicle\ Trip\ Miles$$

The problem with most active derived data is that once they are derived they are usually not updated when the values of their contributing data characteristics change or when new contributing data characteristics are added, or they are updated inconsistently. When the values of contributing data characteristics change or new contributing data characteristics are added, the values of the active derived data characteristics must be rederived in order to be valid.

Derived data maintenance is the process for ensuring that active derived data are properly rederived when their contributing data characteristics values change or when new contributing data characteristics appear. *Derived data maintenance criteria* specify the frequency and timing for rederiving active derived data, such as immediately, daily at midnight, and monthly on the first workday of the month.

Example: The derived data maintenance criteria for Well Type and Account Balance are shown in previous examples.

Derived data, particularly active derived data that are routinely rederived, need to carry a version identification. The data version component of the data naming taxonomy provides the version identification. The version identification becomes extremely important when comparing data or analyzing trends and projections.

Example: The Account Balance Amount in the previous example would be suffixed with the version, such as Account Balance Amount <January 8, 1995>.

Redundant Data

The existing data resource often has redundant data even though the objective is to limit redundant data to foreign keys. *Redundant data* is the situation where the same data characteristic value exists at two or more data sites. Redundant data were created, stored, and maintained independently of each other and are often unknown to the organization. Because the existence of redundant data is usually unknown, the data values are inconsistently updated and frequently do not match.

Redundant data must be identified, documented, and properly maintained to ensure high-quality data. *Redundant data integrity* is the process of identifying, documenting, and maintaining redundant data until the redundancy can be eliminated or reduced to a manageable level. *Redundant data maintenance* is the process of maintaining consistent values in each existence of a redundant data characteristic. The timing for redundant data maintenance is documented as part of the redundant data integrity.

Redundant data integrity can be documented in a diagram or a table. A *redundant data diagram* specifies the data characteristics representing the official data source and the redundant data characteristics that should be maintained from that official data source. A rectangle represents a data characteristic and a solid line with an arrow on one end represents the maintenance of redundant data. The arrow points from the official data characteristic to the redundant data characteristics and represents the process to maintain redundant data.

Example: An employee's birth date may exist in the employee file, the payroll file, and the training file. The employee file is designated as the official data source and the other two files are redundant data sources that must be maintained from the official data source, as shown in Figure 7.18. Anytime Employee Birth Date is entered or changed in the Employee file, it is immediately changed in the Payroll file and the Training file.

A *redundant data table* specifies the data characteristics in the official data source and the redundant data characteristics that are maintained from the official data source as a table.

Example: The redundant data table for employee birth dates is shown in Figure 7.19. The timing of the update is shown in a statement at the bottom of the table.

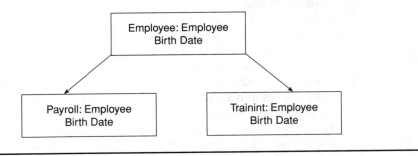

Figure 7.18   Redundant data diagram.

Replicated Data

Data can be replicated to distribute data to various data sites. *Data replication* is a formal process of creating exact copies of a set of data from the data site containing the official data source and placing those data in at other data sites. A *data replicate* is a set of data copied from a data site and placed at another data site during data replication. Data replicates are not the same as redundant data. Each data replicate is planned, known, documented, and properly maintained. Data replication is explained in more detail in Chapter 13.

DATA ACCURACY

The second component of data quality is data accuracy. *Data accuracy* deals with how well data stored in the data resource represent the real world. It includes a definition of the current level of data accuracy and the necessary adjustment in data accuracy to meet the business needs. It ensures that the current level of data accuracy is known and that the appropriate level of data accuracy can be achieved. The level of data

---

Employee: Employee Birth Date CYMD
Payroll: Employee Birth Date CYMD
Training: Employee Birth Date CYMD

Immediate update to Payroll and Training.

Figure 7.19   Redundant data table.

accuracy must be known and must be adjusted to meet the business information demand.[2]

No fundamental level of data accuracy exists. Each organization determines the desired level of data accuracy required for each data characteristic to meet its business needs. When the existing level of data accuracy is determined for each data characteristic, which can be highly variable, adjustments can be made to bring the existing data accuracy to the desired level. The common data architecture supports the determination of the existing and desired data accuracy.

Scope

Data accuracy includes many tangible and intangible items. Tangible items include the method used to identify objects and events in the real world, the method of collecting data about those objects and events, the time when data were collected, and the method that was used to enter data into the data resource. Tangible items include precision, scale, resolution, currentness, the level of detail, the degree of reproducibility, collection frequency, data instance, data volatility, data version, data lineage, and anything else about how well data represent the real world.

> Data accuracy includes many tangible and intangible items.

Intangible items include the person that captured and input the data, the person that declared the data value to be correct, and the confidence people have about the data. Confidence in the person or organization collecting data or the method of collection is reflected in confidence about the data, regardless of the accuracy of the data. Loss of confidence in a few pieces of data might destroy confidence in an integrated data resource.

Data Currentness

Data currentness is a measure of how relevant a data value is compared to the real world or how out-of-date the data value has become. Data currentness depends on the data instance, the data volatility, and the data collection frequency.

---

[2]This book presents only the data accuracy basics. A previous book (Brackett, 1994) provides detailed examples for data accuracy and explains how data accuracy is controlled and changed.

> Data currentness is how relevant data are compared to the real world.

The *data instance* is the point in time or the period of time for which the data value accurately represents the real world. Within the common data architecture, data instance is not the same as a data occurrence. The data instance must be known for all data.

Example: The data instance for the vital signs of a patient during heart surgery is a few seconds, the cost of living index is a specific month, a building's size is several years, and a person's birth date is permanent.

Data volatility is how quickly the data representing the real world become inaccurate, which is dependent on how quickly the real world changes. It is the rate at which data cease to accurately represent the real world. The volatility of all data must be known to define its accuracy.

Example: Data for a patient during heart surgery might change every few seconds, but a person's name often remains unchanged during that person's lifetime.

The *data collection frequency* is the frequency at which data are collected from the real world. The collection frequency must be known for all data.

Example: A patient's vital signs during heart surgery might be collected every second, and the population of a city might be collected every 10 years.

A relationship exists between collection frequency and data volatility. The frequency of data collection must match the volatility of the data. Data that are not kept fresh will deteriorate, and spoiled data result in a less accurate data resource.

Example: If a patient's vital signs were taken every hour during heart surgery, the patient may die before the change was noticed and corrective action taken, but measuring the population of a city every day would not show significant changes.

> The frequency of data collection must match the data volatility.

Data currentness is maintained by adjusting the data collection frequency to the event frequency. The *event frequency* is the frequency at which an event occurs or an object changes in the real world. If changes occur more frequently than the data are captured, events will be missed, and the data will not be current.

Event changes may be continuous or discrete. If the event change is continuous, such as the flow of a stream, an *arbitrary event* is established to capture data at the frequency desired by the organization, such as hourly or daily. If different organizations require different levels of accuracy, the arbitrary event should be the most frequent data collection desired. If an event is discrete, such as an automobile accident, the data collection frequency should be during the event or as soon after the event as necessary to meet the organization's needs. If different organizations have different data collection frequencies, the earliest data collection frequency should be used.

> Data about events are collected to meet the organization's needs.

Data timeliness is how quickly data representing the world are captured, entered into the data resource, distributed to data sites, and made available for use. It is a measure of how quickly the data resource represents changes. Data timelines includes collecting data in the most efficient manner, editing the data as near the source as possible, and correcting data errors with a minimum delay. Data currentness is improved by decreasing the time from data collection to data availability.

Data Lineage and Heritage

A *data origin* is the location where a data value originated, whether it was collected, created, measured, generated, derived, modified, or aggregated. It could be a field measurement, a laboratory analysis, a complaint from a customer, or a survey of opinions. *Data tracking* is the process of tracking data from the origination to their current data site.[3]

---

[3]Data tracking is explained in more detail in Brackett, 1994.

> Data tracking is the process of trading data from their origins to their current data sites.

A *data source* is a specific data site where data are stored and can be obtained. A *primary data source* is the first data site where the original data are stored after their origination. A *secondary data source* is any data site where data acquired from another data site are stored without alteration or modification. The data for a secondary data source may come from a primary data source or another secondary data source. If data are altered or modified in any way at a data site, that data site becomes a primary data source for those new data.

An *official data source* is any data site where the official data, the record of reference, are stored. When redundant data exist, it is the data site that contains the official source of data for extraction to develop an integrated data resource or to replicate to other data sites. A *nonofficial data source* is any data site where data that are not the record of reference are stored. It is a data site where redundant data are located that should not be used for data extraction to develop an integrated data resource or to replicate to other data sites.

An official data source may be different from the primary data source.

Example: Data may originate from field measurements, which is the data origin, and be stored in the collecting organization's database, which is the primary data source. The field measurements from several collecting organizations are transferred to a central location without alteration, which becomes the secondary data source. The central location is the official data source for those field measurements.

Data tracking documents the movement of data from their origin, through primary data sites, to secondary data sites. It documents any alterations or modifications to the data, the addition of new data, and the creation of derived or aggregated data. It is a process to help understand and manage the movement of data within and between organizations.

Data tracking is an important process for determining the data lineage. *Lineage* is the direct descent from an ancestor, to the descendants of a common ancestor that is regarded as the founder of the line. Lineage is commonly used for biological or cultural descendants, but can be applied to data: *Data lineage* is a process to track the descent of data values from their origins to their current data sites. It includes determining where the data values originated, where they were stored, and how they were altered or modified. It is a history of where data values originated and how they were altered or modified to their present form.

Data lineage is the descent of data values from their origins to their current data sites.

Data lineage can be documented for a specific data characteristic or a set of data characteristics, for a data occurrence or a set of data occurrences, or for a data file or a database. Data lineage is documented with a data lineage diagram, data sets documenting each data flow, data definitions for each data characteristic in the data set, and a narrative statement.

A *data lineage diagram* is a diagram that shows the flow of data sets from their origin to their current data sites. It shows where the data originated, the flow of data sets between data sites within organization or across organizations, and the data sites where the data are currently located. The data sites are indicated with an oval, representing the physical storage of data, with the name of the data site inside the oval. The data sets moving between data sites are indicated by a solid line with an arrow pointing in the direction of the data flow.

Example: The data lineage diagram for payroll and training data is shown in Figure 7.20. The Payroll data set moves from the West Region

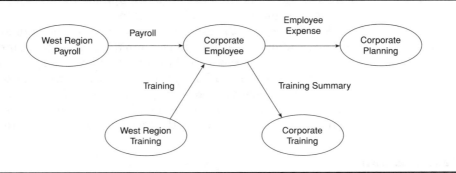

Figure 7.20   A data lineage diagram.

Payroll data site to the Corporate Employee data site, and Training moves from West Region Training to Corporate Employee. Employee Expense moves from Corporate Employee to Corporate Planning, and Training Summary moves from Corporate Employee to Corporate Training.

A data set shows the data in each data flow between data sites and the data stored at each data site. Each of the data characteristics involved in a data flow or stored at a data site have a comprehensive data definition. A supporting statement describes the history of the data from their origin to their current data sites and includes any information that is not contained on the data lineage diagram, in the data sets, or in the data definitions. Data lineage can contain any other documentation, such as the data derivation procedures.

Data lineage is not the same as data derivation or data distribution. Data lineage describes the history, or life cycle, of data values from their origination. Data derivation, as described earlier, describes the contributing data characteristics and procedures for deriving data values. Data distribution, as explained in Chapter 13, describes the replication and distribution of data from the official data source to a nonofficial data source.

Data heritage is the content and meaning of data from their origins to their current data sites.

Heritage is something transmitted by or acquired from a predecessor, or something possessed as a result of one's natural selection or birth. Heritage, like lineage, usually applies to biological or cultural descendants, but can be applied to data.

Data heritage is the content and meaning of the data at the time of their origination and as they move from their origin to their current data sites. It is a statement of how the content and meaning were altered during their life cycle. Data lineage describes the paths that data followed and how they were altered during their life cycles, and data heritage describes the original content and meaning of data and how the content and meaning were changed as they moved from data site to data site.

Temporal Data

Temporal data are becoming more important as the size and complexity of the data resource increases and as the interest in data warehouse systems and on-line analytical processing increases. *Temporal* means related to, concerned with, or limited by time. It is derived from *tempus*, meaning time. *Temporal data* are any data that represent a point in time or a time interval—they have a time component.

Example: Employee Birth Date CYMD is temporal data about an Employee, and Vehicle Accident Date CYMD and Vehicle Accident Time HM are temporal data about a Vehicle Accident.

> Temporal data are an important component of data accuracy.

Several different types of temporal data are documented. The *event time* is the time an event happened in the real world. The *identification time* is the time an organization found out about the event. The *collection time* is the time data were collected about the event. The *entry time* is the time a transaction was entered into the data resource. The *distribution time* is the time data were distributed to a data site.

Temporal data must be collected to the level of detail necessary to meet the business activity needs.

Example: Geologic times, such as Eocene, Miocene, or Pleistocene, are used to date rock formations. Century, year, month, and day are used for birth dates. Hours, minutes, and seconds are used for patients during surgery. Small fractions of seconds are used in nuclear physics experiments.

A single time or a time interval can be collected for data occurrences or for data characteristics. A *time point* is a single time for a data occurrence or data characteristic. A *time interval* is a begin and end time for a data occurrence or data characteristic.

The names for temporal data follow the data naming taxonomy described in Chapter 5. The type of temporal data can be shown with a common word, such as Event, Identification, Collection, Begin, End, Date CYMD, or Time HM.

Example: Temporal data names might be Training Class Begin Date CYMD and Training Class End Date CYMD, Employee Name Change Entry Date CYMD, and Traffic Accident Event Date CYMD.

> Temporal databases manage temporal data better than relational databases.

A relational database is oriented to current values and does not adequately handle temporal data. Temporal data, such as audit trails, history data, and archive data, can be maintained in a relational database, but such a database does not have a built-in capability to regenerate data for a past or future date. *Temporal databases*, also known as *time relational databases*, have the capability to store temporal data and manage data based on those temporal data.[4] They can recreate data values for past or future dates based on the temporal data values.

Data Versions

Data versions are a critical component of data accuracy. A *data version* is a set of data values that represent the real world at a specific point in time. Data versions are identified with a data version name and corresponding definition, as explained in Chapter 5. Temporal data are a key component of the data version name and definition because they show the point in time or time interval the data values represent.

> A data version is critical for determining the time and method of data preparation.

The method of data preparation is also a key component of a data version, such as the query used to develop a set of data values. The method of data preparation must be documented as part of a data version to fully understand how the data values were developed. The comparison of different sets of analyses or summarizations that are based on different data methods of data preparation are meaningless without a data version. The data version must be known so the data can properly support business activities and decisions.

---

[4]Time relational data is described in Brackett, 1990.

Multiple Source Updates

The situation often exists where data from a single data source are made available to many organizations and those organizations begin making adjustments to those data to more accurately reflect the real world. The adjustments are often done independently and are not synchronized in any way, resulting in multiple data sources and conflicting data versions. The data quality can be severely affected if updates from multiple data sources are not properly synchronized.

Example: The 1990 Census is distributed to many different jurisdictions, and those jurisdictions begin making adjustments to the census based on more recent data. Anyone wanting current census data would need to contact many different jurisdictions and would have difficulty determining which set of adjusted data was the most current or most accurate.

There are two techniques to resolve multiple data sources and conflicting data versions. The first technique is to establish a central data source that contains the most recent data versions, regardless of the origin of those data versions. Current data are then available from this central data source. Contributing organizations are the primary data source for enhanced or updated data, but they are not the official data source. The central data source is the official data source for the dissemination of current data, even though it is a secondary data source.

Example: Census data are updated by each jurisdiction and sent to the central data source. Anyone desiring current census data can go to that central data source for the most recent census data.

> Multiple data sources are managed through a central data source and data versions.

The second technique is to establish unique data names for each primary data source and develop data version names using those primary source data names. Data are updated and enhanced at the decentralized data sites, which are both the primary data source and the official data source. A comprehensive definition of each data version explains the details of how the population data were enhanced. A clearinghouse can help people locate the data sources that contain data meeting their business needs.

Example: Census data might be maintained at several locations. Formal data names might be Frost County Population <Jones & Associates Version 2>, Frost County Population <County Planning Version 1>, and Highland County Population <Growth Management July 1993>.

Proactive and Retroactive Updates

Temporal databases allow proactive and retroactive updating. *Proactive updates* are updates made to the data resource today that will not become effective until some future date. Proactive updates require at least an entry date and an effective date.

Example: A river will be closed to navigation for dredging. The begin date and end date for the closure, and the date of data entry, are entered into the data resource.

Proactive updates are beneficial because they set the stage for something to happen at a future date. They are also beneficial because they can show a series of pending updates, such as product price increases, that can be used for trend analysis. Proactive updates are not beneficial, however, if the effective data is not observed and the data are used inappropriately.

Example: A product price may be entered to be effective at a future date and may be quoted as available today.

> Proactive and retroactive updates provide benefits, but need to be properly managed.

Retroactive updates are updates made to the data resource today that were effective at some past date. Retroactive updates require at least an entry date and an effective date.

Example: A customer's account was not properly credited with a deposit, resulting in overdrafts and charges. A correction is made with a retroactive update which rippled forward and eliminated the overdrafts and the charges.

Retroactive updates are beneficial because they make data effective on the date corresponding with the actual event in the real world. Retroactive updates are not beneficial because they change historical data and any analysis or derivation based on those data will be in error. The best way to manage retroactive updates is to document the updated data as a new data version. Any derivation or analysis on the updated data would contain the data version before the retroactive update. When a more recent data version appears, it would indicate that any previous derivation or analysis would be in error.

DATA COMPLETENESS

The third component of data quality is data completeness. *Data completeness* is an indication of whether all the data necessary to meet the current and future business information demand are available in the data resource. It deals with determining what data are needed to meet the business information demand and ensuring that those data are captured and maintained in the data resource so they are available when needed.[5]

> Data completeness ensures that all the data necessary to meet the business information demand are available in the data resource.

Data completeness is managed through data resource surveys and data resource inventories. A *data resource survey* is a high-level determination of an organization's data needs and the data available to the organization based on a higher level data classification scheme. It is usually done first to set priorities for conducting more detailed data resource inventories.

A *data resource inventory* is a detailed determination of the orga-

---

[5]Data completeness is covered in more detail in Brackett, 1994.

nization's data needs and the data available to the organization based on data subjects and data characteristics. It usually follows the data resource survey to identify data needs and existing data in greater detail. These two processes together often uncover a hidden data resource that could be immediately available to the organization.

A data resource survey includes a data needs survey, a data availability survey, and a data survey analysis. A *data needs survey* is a high-level determination of the data an organization needs to meet the business information demand. A *data availability survey* is a high-level determination of data that are currently available to the organization. A *data survey analysis* compares the data needs survey with the data availability survey to identify data that already exist and data that need to be acquired. The priorities of the business strategies, the data needed to support those strategies, and the degree to which those data needs are met are used to identify critical data required to meet the current and future business information demand and plan the acquisition of those data.

A data resource inventory includes a data needs inventory, a data availability inventory, and a data inventory analysis. A *data needs inventory* identifies data subjects and data characteristics needed to support an organization's business activities. A *data availability inventory* identifies the existence of data subjects and data characteristics and obtains detailed information about them. The *data inventory analysis* compares data needs from the data needs inventory with the data available from the data availability inventory to determine what data subject and data characteristics exist and what data subjects and data characteristics need to be acquired.

Data suitability is the part of data completeness that indicates how suitable data are for a specific business activity. The same data may be more suitable for one business activity and less suitable for another business activity.

MANAGING DATA QUALITY

Data quality is a big problem for many organizations. The data quality is not known and most data have never been audited or validated in any manner. An organization usually needs to understand its existing data quality and improve the quality of the data in their data resource if that data resource is to successfully support the business information demand. Improving the data quality is a complex process that begins with the realization that the existing data quality is disparate and ends with achievement of consistent data quality.

Data Quality Improvement

Data quality improvement is the process of changing data quality to the level desired to support the business information demand. Several other terms are used to represent data quality improvement, such as data scrubbing, data purification, data cleansing, data hygiene, and data cleanup. They are all synonymous with data quality improvement.

> Data quality improvement can be either prospective or retrospective.

Two basic types of data quality improvement exist. *Prospective data quality improvement* is the process of improving only the quality of new data coming into the data resource, but generally ignoring improvement of data quality for data already in the data resource. *Retrospective data quality improvement* is the process of improving the quality of data that already exist in the data resource. An organization usually begins its data quality improvement with prospective data quality improvement and then decides if the benefits of retrospective data quality improvement are worth the effort.

Data Quality Criteria

Data quality improvement begins by establishing data quality criteria. The data quality criteria include all of the items described previously pertaining to data integrity, data accuracy, and data completeness. Both existing and desired data quality criteria may be developed. *Existing data quality criteria* are the criteria documenting the data quality that currently exists in the data resource. *Desired data quality criteria* are the desired criteria needed to support the business information demand.

> Data quality criteria can be determined from existing data or applied to new data.

The process of determining the existing data quality criteria cannot be fully automated because it requires knowledgeable people to understand the disparate data quality. Usually the existing data quality is either unknown or known by a few people but not documented, and automated tools are largely useless. Automated tools can support knowledgeable people and document the results of their analysis, but tools cannot replace the thought process involved in discovering the existing data quality criteria. The application of the desired data quality criteria to new data entering the data resource could be largely automated.

Data Quality Techniques

Two basic techniques for determining and improving the quality of data exist. The *inductive data quality* technique is a specific-to-general process where the existing data are analyzed and data quality criteria are developed from those existing data. The existing data quality criteria are then reviewed to determine whether they are acceptable criteria. If the criteria are not acceptable, they are adjusted to the desired level. The inductive data quality technique is useful for understanding the existing data quality and beginning the development of the desired data quality criteria.

The *deductive data quality* technique is a general-to-specific process where the desired data quality criteria are first developed and then applied either to existing data to determine the level of compliance or to new data to ensure that they meet the desired criteria. Existing data that do not meet the desired data quality criteria are analyzed to determine whether they can be adjusted or whether the criteria need to be adjusted. The deductive data quality technique is useful for determining the existing level of data quality and for ensuring that data quality is at the desired level.

Both the inductive and deductive techniques can be combined into a cyclic process to improve the quality of the data in the data resource, as shown in Figure 7.21. Existing data quality criteria are developed through the inductive technique, analyzed to determine whether they are appropriate, and then adjusted to the desired data quality criteria that support the business information demand. The desired data quality criteria are then applied to both existing data and new data through the deductive data quality technique to ensure that the data resource has the desired quality.

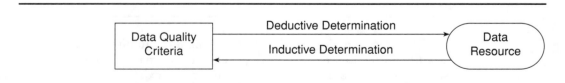

Figure 7.21   Data quality determination.

Data Quality Process

The *data quality process* is a process to document and improve data quality by using both the deductive and inductive techniques. It is a systematic process of examining the data resource to determine its level of data quality and ensuring that the data quality is adjusted to the level necessary to support the business information demand. It is a process to routinely audit the data to determine their integrity and accuracy. The data quality process includes five steps.

Realizing Disparate Data Quality

It is relatively easy for an organization to realize that the quality of data in the data resource is not at the desired level and to make the decision to adjust the data quality. In many situations, an organization already knows that the data quality is disparate and is ready to begin a process of data quality improvement.

Understanding Existing Data Quality

The difficult task is understanding and documenting the existing data quality. The existing data quality is documented through the inductive data quality process described previously. A portion of the data resource, preferably a portion critical to the business operation, is selected for analysis. The data in that portion of the data resource are reviewed and documented using the techniques described previously for defining data integrity and data accuracy. The result is a set of existing data quality criteria representing the data in the selected portion of the data resource.

Determining Desired Data Quality

The desired data quality criteria that support the business information demand are then developed by reviewing the existing data quality criteria and adjusting those criteria as necessary. The adjustment is usually toward increasing the data quality criteria. In some situations, however, the data quality criteria may be decreased. Without knowing the existing data quality criteria, it is often difficult to determine the desired data quality criteria. An organization must have a thorough understanding of the existing data quality criteria to begin adjusting the data quality.

Adjusting Data Quality

The data in the selected portion of the data resource are then adjusted through the deductive data quality process using the desired data quality criteria. The adjustment may be either prospective for new data coming into the data resource, or retrospective for data that already exist. Most organizations apply the desired data quality criteria prospectively, but the decision to apply the desired data quality criteria retrospectively depends on the level of effort involved and the potential benefit.

In many situations, the existing data cannot be improved because the details are not available, and the benefits would not justify the effort. Those data, however, cannot be removed from the data resource because they do have some value. To meet the situation, different *data certification levels* can be established, such as high-quality data, moderate-quality data, and low-quality data. The lower levels of certification are downward adjustments to the desired data quality criteria.

Data quality certification designates the level of data quality.

Data that fail the desired data quality criteria are passed through progressively lower levels of data quality criteria until they pass. When they pass, they are certified at that level of data quality. This process of *data quality certification* is useful for evaluating the quality of disparate data and for identifying the official data sources.

Tracking Data Quality

The adjustments to data quality can be tracked to ensure that the desired data quality criteria are acceptable and are being applied appropriately. If the desired data quality criteria are not acceptable, they are adjusted and reapplied. This cyclic, self-correcting process continues until the desired data quality criteria are acceptable. This process can also be used proactively to identify data that fail the desired data quality criteria and adjust the processes for collecting or creating those data to ensure they pass the desired data quality criteria.

There is no absolute measure of data quality, and no standard scale for determining the quality of the data resource or for tracking the improvement in data quality. Without a good measure of data quality, organizations do not know the level of their data quality or the progress they are making for improving data quality.

Data quality improvement can be measured with the data quality improvement process and data quality criteria.

When the data certification levels are established, data can be run through the data certification criteria at any time. If the data quality has improved and the data are run through the data quality criteria again, they may pass at a higher level. The quantity of existing data passing each data certification level indicates the current state of the data resource. Changes in the quantity of data passing at each level of data quality certification indicate how much data quality is being improved. Even though this approach is subjective, it provides an organization with a way to measure its existing data quality and the improvement in data quality.

SUMMARY

Data quality indicates how well the data resource supports the business information demand of an organization. The data resource in most organizations is characterized by disparate data quality—data quality that is not meeting the business information demand. The primary reason for the disparate data quality is legacy systems. Legacy systems create and store data to meet specific needs with limited data edits or validation and little documentation. As legacy systems are replaced or changed, most understanding of the data quality that does exist is lost.

The bad news is that data quality is getting worse, not better, as the size and complexity of the data resource increases. With more people developing more systems and capturing more data with many different techniques, there is less control over data. The development of data warehouse systems, geographic information systems, and client/server applications without a common data architecture and formal data quality criteria makes the situation even worse.

Organizations need to gain control of their data quality by understanding the existing data quality, establishing data quality criteria that support the business information demand, and improving the quality of their data to the desired level. Improving the quality of data is a very complex issue that is not easily resolved, but it is not impossible if done within the common data architecture.

Data quality consists of data integrity, data accuracy, and data completeness. Data integrity deals with how well data are maintained in the data resource. It consists of criteria for defining and maintaining the correct data values, the proper data structure, the appropriate retention of critical data, and the timely preparation of derived data. Data accuracy deals with how well data represent the real world. It has a very wide scope from the precision of measurements to confidence in the data. Data completeness is the process of ensuring that all data needed to meet the business information demand are readily available in the data resource. It is managed through high-level data resource surveys and detailed data resource inventories that determine the data needs and the data availability.

One important data quality aspect is improving the currentness of data through analysis of the data instance and the volatility of data, and adjustment of the collection frequency to ensure that data adequately represent the real world. Another important aspect is determining the data lineage and data heritage through the data tracking process. Primary and secondary data sources are identified, as well as official and nonofficial data sources, to determine where data originated and where the record of reference is located. Managing the time component of data through data versions and temporal databases is another important aspect of data quality as larger quantities of data are saved for the analysis of trends and projections. Updating multiple data sources to keep them synchronized and using proactive and retroactive updating are also important aspects of data quality.

High-quality data adequately reflect business reality, and managing data quality is often synonymous with managing the business. Disparate data quality must be improved to a level that supports business management. Data quality improvement can be prospective for new data entering the data resource, and it can be retrospective for data already in the data resource. Data quality improvement is achieved by realizing that disparate data quality exists, determining the existing data quality, defining the desired data quality to support the business, changing the data quality from the existing to the desired level, and tracking the changes.

Data quality can be measured subjectively by establishing levels of data criteria. The highest level of data quality criteria is the desired data quality criteria. Intermediate levels of data quality criteria are developed down to the existing data quality criteria. Data are then passed through these data quality criteria to determine the current level of data quality and to track the improvement of data quality over time.

The analysis and improvement of data quality within the common data architecture shifts emphasis from apparent or perceived data quality that people believe the data resource has to the true data quality. The responsibility for analyzing and improving data quality rests with everyone in the organization. Everyone must pull together to develop and implement consistent data quality for the entire data resource so it supports the business information demand.

QUESTIONS

The following questions are provided as a review of the chapter and to stimulate thought about what data quality is and how data quality can be documented, controlled, and changed to the desired level.

1. What is the current state of data quality in most organizations?
2. Why is data quality continuing to get worse in most organizations?
3. What is the purpose of establishing a consistent data quality?
4. What does data quality include?
5. How are data value integrity and conditional data value integrity documented?
6. Why must all data integrity ultimately be defined with a data integrity rule?
7. How are data structure integrity and conditional data structure integrity documented?
8. What does data retention integrity specify?
9. What does data derivation integrity specify?
10. What does redundant data integrity specify?
11. What does data accuracy include?
12. What is data currentness?
13. What is the relationship between data instance, data volatility, and data capture frequency?
14. How are data tracking, data lineage, and data heritage related?
15. What is the difference between primary and secondary data sources, and official and nonofficial data sources?
16. Why is temporal data becoming more important?
17. How are multiple data sources kept synchronized?
18. What are the advantages of proactive and retroactive updating?
19. What is data completeness?
20. What is the difference between prospective and retrospective data quality improvement?
21. What is the difference between existing and desired data quality criteria?
22. What is the difference between the inductive and deductive data quality processes?
23. How is existing data quality determined?
24. How is data quality improved?
25. How is data quality measured?

## CHAPTER 8

Metadata

Quality metadata are critical for thoroughly understanding and fully utilizing an integrated data resource.

The metadata in most organizations are becoming at least as disparate as the data. If metadata exist at all, they are often incomplete, out of date, poorly written, hard to locate, and difficult to understand. Considerable metadata are retained by knowledgeable people who are retiring or moving to other jobs, resulting in a complete loss of those metadata. The problem increases as the size and complexity of the data resource increases, such as with data distribution, data warehouse systems, and geographic information systems. The problem becomes severe as more people collect and store more data.

An organization needs to develop a robust set of metadata that adequately describes the data resource and place those metadata in a formal index to the data resource so it can support the business information demand. Readily available high-quality metadata provide both data resource managers and business clients a more complete awareness and understanding of the data resource. Only through a complete awareness and understanding of the data resource can it be fully utilized to support business activities.

Chapter 8 begins by describing the disparate metadata situation that exists in most organizations, including the metadata dilemma and the disparate metadata cycle that perpetuates this dilemma. This chapter describes the shock that organizations suffer when they realize the lack of metadata prevents full utilization of their data resource. This chapter then presents a new perspective about the types of metadata and the development of common metadata and describes the development and use of a metadata warehouse that can provide readily available high-quality metadata. The chapter concludes by describing how metadata quality and metadata changes can be managed to fully utilize an integrated data resource.

METADATA SITUATION

The current status of metadata in most organizations is bad. The metadata are becoming as disparate as the data. This situation limits the integration and sharing of data within and among organizations which often results in an unmet business information demand. The current status of metadata must be understood so that metadata can be enhanced to support full utilization of an integrated data resource.

Disparate Metadata

Disparate data, as explained in the first chapter, are data that are essentially not alike, or are distinctly different in kind, quality, or character. *Disparate metadata* are metadata that are essentially not alike, or are distinctly different in kind, quality, or character. Metadata often do not exist, or if they do exist, they are incomplete, out of date, poorly written, and difficult to understand. They often exist only in knowledgeable people who create or use the data. Metadata are frequently scattered through many documents and are often difficult to locate. When the metadata are located, they may not completely explain the content, meaning, or quality of data.

> Most existing metadata do not provide a thorough understanding of the data.

Massively disparate metadata is the situation where the metadata are scattered across multiple jurisdictions, such as health care or water resource, or across multiple disciplines, such as growth management or water resources. These metadata are extremely difficult to integrate for a complete awareness and understanding of the data that are available. In many situations, massively disparate metadata are more difficult to integrate than the data.

Knowledgeable people, such as business clients and programmers, retain considerable metadata that were never formally documented. Organizations are on the threshold of losing these knowledgeable people as they retire or move on to other job opportunities and the metadata they retain. This is a permanent loss of information about the data resource!

Disparate Metadata Cycle

The bad news is that many organizations are not making any attempt to improve their metadata. Organizations that are making an attempt to improve their metadata often make little progress. At the same time, different people using different methods continue to capture or create new data. These new data are often not documented any better than previous data, in spite of better tools and techniques for documentation. Worse yet, they are documented differently in a variety of different tools resulting in the creation of additional disparate data.

> The metadata disparity is increasing faster than ever.

The current emphasis on capturing and maintaining good metadata is a long-awaited trend. Many products, such as data warehouse systems and geographic information systems, are capturing and storing metadata about the data stored within those products. These data can be easily distributed with the data so that people can understand the data. This approach to capturing and maintaining metadata has two problems, however. The first problem is that these independent sets of metadata are often not consistent across products; different metadata are captured and stored in many different forms. The second problem is that these separate sets of metadata cannot be readily integrated for one comprehensive view of all data available to an organization.

The rapid increase in metadata disparity is the result of a disparate metadata cycle similar to the disparate data cycle. The *disparate metadata cycle* is a self-perpetuating cycle where disparate metadata are being produced faster than ever before. Organizations are caught in a trap of needing more and more data to support their business activities, yet having fewer resources to manage those data properly. The result is limited development of metadata, which results in a lack of awareness and understanding about data that already exist. This lack, in turn, encourages the collection or creation of new data rather than the use of existing data.

> Disparate metadata lead to additional disparate data.

The collection and creation of new data without the benefit of readily available high-quality metadata perpetuates the creation of disparate data. In other words, the lack of good metadata not only limits full utilization of the data resource, but it leads to the collection and creation of additional disparate data, which are not properly documented, leading to increased metadata disparity. The cycle continues unchecked in most organizations.

Metadata Dilemma

The disparate metadata cycle creates a metadata dilemma similar to the data dilemma. A *metadata dilemma* exists when an organization has a critical need for readily available high-quality metadata to fully utilize the data resource, yet the organization is actively creating and collecting new data without maintaining adequate metadata. This situation seems to require a choice between maintaining good metadata to fully utilize an integrated data resource and continuing to develop data to meet the current business information demand.

> The metadata dilemma is a severe blow to most organizations.

The metadata dilemma creates a double blow for most organizations. First, the data dilemma allows the creation of disparate data which are difficult to integrate and share across application and organization boundaries. Second, the metadata cycle not only makes it difficult to integrate and share metadata, but it limits the awareness and understanding of existing data, which perpetuates the collection and creation of additional data that are not properly documented. The disparate data blow is severe enough, but the disparate metadata blow can be disastrous for many organizations.

Metadata Shock

Realizing the existence of disparate metadata is a shock for most organizations similar to the disparate data shock. *Metadata shock* is the realization that existing metadata do not, will not, and cannot, provide readily available high-quality information about the data resource. Metadata shock is the sudden realization that the metadata dilemma really exists and is severely limiting use of the data resource. Metadata shock is the panic an organization feels when it realizes the disparate metadata situation is getting worse rather than better.

> The data resource is virtually useless without readily available high-quality metadata.

The metadata shock usually becomes a profound need for readily available high-quality metadata to increase the awareness and understanding of the data resource. An organization needs to know where the data originated, how they were captured or created, where they are located, how they are maintained, and who maintains them. It needs to know the official data source, the data quality, and how data quality changes over time.

The need to improve data quality, as described in the last chapter, emerges as the need for readily available high-quality metadata is met. Resolving the metadata dilemma is the first step to resolving the data dilemma and improving data quality. A firm commitment to the development of readily available high-quality metadata must be made to develop and fully utilize an integrated data resource.

A NEW PERSPECTIVE

A new perspective about developing and maintaining metadata breaks the disparate metadata cycle, resolves the metadata dilemma, and promotes full utilization of an integrated data resource. The new perspective includes an understanding of the different types of metadata and the concept of common metadata.

Metadata Types

Metadata have traditionally been defined as data about the data. This traditional definition was useful until the need for increased data awareness and understanding, the resolution of data disparity, and an integrated data resource became important. As organizations began looking at what data were available, how those data present a view of the world, the quality of those data, and the metadata defining those data, it became clear that the traditional definition of metadata was no longer sufficient.

> A new perspective of metadata helps resolve the metadata dilemma.

The terms currently used in the common data architecture pertaining to metadata are shown in Figure 8.1. These objects and events that occur in the real world are shown on the right side of the diagram.[1]

Foredata are the upfront data that describe those objects and events. Foredata are the data that people use to track or manage objects and events in the real world. Foredata include both data representing the objects and events and data about the quality of the data representing the objects and events.

Example: *John Smith, Swift River, 12/23/1992,* and *$125.83* are foredata about objects and events in the world.

Example: *Only people employed by the state, rivers in the northern region,* and *to the nearest 10 feet* are foredata about the quality of data representing objects and events in the real world.

Metadata are the data describing the foredata. They are the afterdata that provide definitions about the foredata, including the foredata that describe objects and events and data about the quality of data describing the objects and events.

Example: The definitions of Stream Name Complete, Person Birth Date CYMD, and Well Depth Feet are metadata describing data about objects and events.

Example: The definitions of Well Depth Measurement Accuracy and Timber Layer Coverage are metadata describing the quality of the data about objects and events.

Meta-metadata are the data describing the metadata. They are the data that provide the framework for developing high-quality metadata.

---

[1]Appendix D contains a more academic presentation of the derivation of these terms.

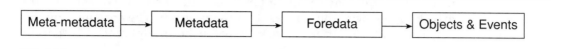

Figure 8.1   Diagram of data and metadata types.

Example: The definitions of data entity, data characteristic, data characteristic variation, and data code set are meta-metadata.

Common Metadata

Disparate data exist largely because there are no well-defined, consistent, commonly accepted metadata. Many organizations are developing standard metadata, commonly known as data standards, in an attempt to resolve the data disparity. These standards often mandate how data should be designed, captured, named, structured, and documented.

The problem with standard metadata is that they are quite variable. They are often physically oriented, contain data names that are not fully qualified, are inconsistently abbreviated, and have minimal definitions. They often describe the methods of capture, the storage format, and the use of data. Some standard metadata provide only conceptual definitions with no additional detail and others are presented in a mathematical notation that is difficult to understand.

Disparate data exist because there are no commonly accepted metadata.

Standard metadata are often not consistent between organizations. Metadata range from a conceptual overview of the real world to detailed physical specifications for a particular database management system. They have varying formats with different levels of detail. They often have gaps, overlaps, and conflicts causing considerable confusion for the people trying to resolve data disparity.

The current approach to standard metadata is not working. This approach is an attempt to mandate the way out of a problem without fully understanding the problem. Organizations developing standard metadata often have good intentions, but these organizations are attacking the symptom rather than the problem. They are making the disparate data situation worse rather than better by creating disparate metadata.

The bad news is that disparate metadata are being actively produced and there is little hope of encouraging organizations to develop standard metadata in a consistent manner. The result is that there really are no data standards because standards, by definition, do not conflict. The development of more data standards only clarifies that no data standard exists.

The existence of conflicting data standards means there is no data standard.

The reason for the development of disparate metadata is that there are no well-defined, consistent, commonly accepted meta-metadata standards. Few organizations attempt to develop standard meta-metadata to resolve the disparate metadata situation. The disparate metadata situation can be prevented with the development of standard meta-metadata.

The common data architecture provides the standard for meta-metadata. *Common meta-metadata* are the architecture component of the common data architecture consisting of formal data names, comprehensive data definitions, common data structure, and consistent data quality. The common meta-metadata provide the framework for the development of common metadata.

The common data architecture is the construct for common meta-metadata.

Common metadata are metadata developed within the common data architecture to provide all the detail necessary to thoroughly understand the data resource and how it can be improved to meet the business information demand. Common metadata resolve the metadata disparity. The resolution of metadata disparity leads to the resolution of data disparity and promotes the development of data that are consistent across all organizations and all disciplines.

> The common data architecture provides common meta-metadata for the development of common metadata.

Knowledgeable people must develop common metadata if they are to be useful. The best way to develop good common metadata is to include business experts, domain experts, and data experts in the development effort. The business experts know the specific business rules and processes unique to the organization or organizations within the scope of the common metadata. The domain experts know the discipline involved in the common metadata, such as water resources, health care, surveying, and land use. The data experts know how data are managed from the real world through logical design to physical implementation.

> Development of common metadata must include business experts, domain experts, and data experts.

Many attempts at developing common metadata do not include all of these experts. Most attempts include business and/or domain experts, but do not include data experts. One reason for the proliferation of disparate metadata is the failure to include data experts, particularly a qualified data architect, in the development effort. Only when qualified data architects who are familiar with the common data architecture are included in the development of common metadata will those metadata be robust enough to stop the development of disparate metadata.

METADATA WAREHOUSE

The best way to implement and maintain common metadata is through a metadata warehouse. A metadata warehouse goes beyond traditional data dictionaries, data catalogues, and data repositories to provide a personal help desk for increasing the awareness and understanding of the data resource. It provides a usable, understandable index to the data resource supported by client-friendly search routines. Without a good index to the data resource, people are not aware of data that are available, cannot fully understand those data, and cannot use those data to meet the business information demand.

Metadata Warehouse Concept

A *metadata warehouse* contains the common metadata and client-friendly search routines to help people fully understand and utilize the data resource. It contains common metadata about the data resource in a single organization or an integrated data resource that crosses multiple disciplines and multiple jurisdictions. It contains a history of the data resource, what the data initially represented, and what they represent now. The metadata warehouse is a repository for common metadata about tabular and nontabular data, centralized and distributed data, and automated and nonautomated data. The search routines are used to determine what data are available, what they represent, where they are located, and how they can be accessed.[2]

> The metadata warehouse contains the common metadata.

The primary objective of the metadata warehouse is to provide a comprehensive guide to the data resource. Supporting objectives for the metadata warehouse are to provide the following:

- A lexicon of the common words used in formal data names and prominent data name abbreviation schemes
- The data description, data structure, and data integrity for the common data architecture
- The definitions of various classification schemes for data in the common data architecture
- A thesaurus for identifying data that exist within the common data architecture
- A glossary of business words, terms, and abbreviations that support use of the data resource
- An inventory of data maintained by various organizations and cross-references between those data and the common data architecture
- A directory of organizations maintaining data and contacts in those organizations for obtaining additional information about existing data
- Data translation schemes between data variations to support data sharing within and between organizations

---

[2]The concept of a metadata warehouse, like its forerunner the data resource guide, was conceived and developed by the author.

- A clearinghouse for data sources, unpublished documents, and projects pertaining to the data resource
- Rapid, client-friendly access to the metadata warehouse so clients can readily identify, understand, and use the data resource

A metadata warehouse can be active or passive. A *passive metadata warehouse* depends on people to update it when new data enter the data resource. An *active metadata warehouse* is automatically updated when new data enter the data resource. The passive approach is best while disparate data are being identified and understood. The active approach is best when an integrated data resource is developed and all data are completely understood and documented within the common data architecture.

Metadata Warehouse Architecture

Figure 8.2 shows a strategic model of a metadata warehouse. The common data architecture consists of Data Subjects that contain one or more Data Characteristics and one or more Data Code Sets. Each Data Characteristic contains one or more Data Characteristic Variations. Each Data Code Set contains many Data Codes and at least two Data Characteristic Variations for the code value and the code name.

The logical data architecture consists of Data Entities that represent Data Subjects. Each Data Entity contains one or more Data Attributes that represent Data Characteristic Variations. Each Data Attribute can contain Data Codes that correspond to the data codes in a Data Code Set. The physical data architecture consists of Data Files that represent Data Entities. Each Data File contains one or more Data Items that represent Data Attributes.[3]

A *common metadata model* documents the architecture of the metadata warehouse. Common metadata are part of the common data architecture and are modeled the same as any other data, such as personnel, finance, or equipment.[4]

Metadata Warehouse Components

The metadata warehouse consists of 10 major components containing the common metadata. The components are briefly described below. A complete description of each component, including a detailed common metadata model for each component, appears in the following sections.

---

[3]In a relational database management system, data files are referred to as tables, and data items are referred to as columns.

[4]Chapter 14 provides more information on this topic.

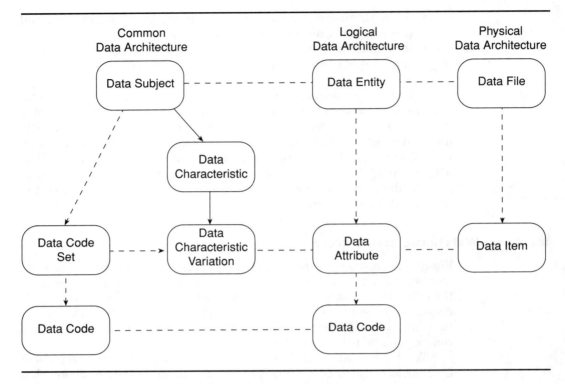

Figure 8.2   Strategic metadata warehouse model.

The data naming lexicon contains common words and word abbreviations for the data naming taxonomy in the common data architecture.

The data dictionary includes formal names and comprehensive definitions for all data in the common data architecture.

The data structure is the structure for all data in the common data architecture.

The data integrity contains rules for all data in the common data architecture.

The data thesaurus contains synonyms for data subjects and data characteristics in the common data architecture.

The data glossary contains definitions of words, terms, and abbreviations related to the common data architecture.

The data product reference is inventory of existing data, including definitions, structure, integrity, and cross references to the common data architecture.

The data directory contains descriptions of organizations maintaining data sources, unpublished documents, and data projects and contacts in those organizations.

The data translation schemes are translation algorithms and explanations for data variations in the common data architecture.

The data clearinghouse contains descriptions of data sources, unpublished documents, and projects related to the data resource.

Data Naming Lexicon

The *data naming lexicon* contains the vocabulary that supports the data naming taxonomy. It contains the common words used to form data names, and it contains prominent sets of word abbreviations used to shorten data names.

> The data naming lexicon contains common words and sets of word abbreviations.

The metadata model for the data naming lexicon component is shown in Figure 8.3. Data Name Common Word Type indicates the type of data name, such as *Data Site, Data Selection, Data Subject, Data Characteristic, Data Characteristic Variation*, and *Data Version*. Data Name Common Word contains the common words and their definitions. Data Name Word Set contains the names and definitions of specific sets of word abbreviations. Data Name Word Abbreviation contains the words or phrases that appear in data names and their abbreviations.

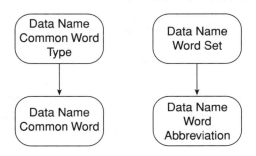

Figure 8.3   Data naming lexicon metadata model.

Data Characteristic Lexicon

Count   The quantity of objects that exist or have occurred. Not the same as Amount or Number.

Number   A number that identifies an object. Not an Amount, Capacity, Code, or Quantity.

Quantity The capacity or count of something. Not a Value, Amount, or Number.

Figure 8.4   Common words for data characteristic names.

Example: Several common words used in data characteristic names are shown in Figure 8.4. A more complete list of common words appears in Appendix A.

The data naming lexicon also contains sets of word abbreviations for words or phrases that appear in a data name. Ideally, only one set of word abbreviations exists. However, organizations often have multiple sets of word abbreviations to meet different length restrictions. There are often different sets of word abbreviations in different organizations. The data naming lexicon can contain many sets of word abbreviations.

Example: Several word abbreviations are shown in Figure 8.5. Anytime a word is used in a data name, such as *management*, the root word is identified (*manage*), all manifestations of that word are identified, and all those words are abbreviated. This procedure ensures that all words are abbreviated in a consistent manner.[5]

The Data Name Word Set contains a description of the algorithms used to abbreviate data names and the conditions under which each algorithm is used. If the abbreviation algorithm uses different sets of word abbreviations for data subject and data characteristic names,

[5]More detailed descriptions of word abbreviations are contained in Brackett, 1990, and Brackett, 1994.

Manage	Mng
Managed	Mngd
Management	Mngt
Manager	Mngr
Manages	Mngs
Managing	Mngg

Figure 8.5   Data name word abbreviation example.

they are explained in the description of the algorithm. The data naming lexicon assists automatic abbreviation and unabbreviation of data names by passing the full data name through the algorithm to obtain the abbreviated data name or passing the abbreviated name through the algorithm to obtain the full data name. The data naming lexicon is maintained by adding new common words, new word abbreviation sets, and new word abbreviations whenever they are identified.

Data Dictionary

The *data dictionary* is an alphabetical list of the formal data names and comprehensive data definitions for data sites, data subjects, data characteristics, data characteristic variations, data codes, and data versions within the common data architecture. The data dictionary does not include data product definitions, which are contained in the data product reference.

The metadata model for the working levels of data classification is shown in Figure 8.6. Data Subjects contain many Data Characteristics that

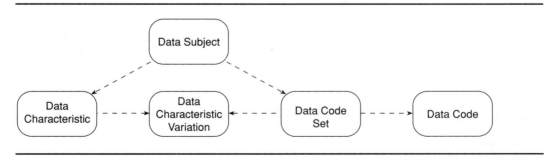

Figure 8.6   Data dictionary metadata model for the working levels.

contain many Data Characteristic Variations. Data Subjects also contain many Data Code Sets that contain many Data Codes. Each Data Code Set has at least two Data Characteristic Variations for the data code value and the data code name.

The metadata model for the categorical levels of data classification is shown in Figure 8.7. Data Subjects have a many-to-many relation to Data Disciplines, Data Segments, Data Themes, and Data Clusters. These many-to-many relations are resolved with Data Discipline Subject, Data Segment Subject, Data Theme Subject, and Data Cluster Subject respectively. Data Subject, Data Discipline, Data Segment, Data Theme, and Data Cluster carry the specific data definitions. The four data subjects resolving the many-to-many relations simply show the data subjects that belong to each categorical level.

Data accuracy is documented in the data dictionary through the data name, the data definition, companion data characteristics, or data values. Using the data name is good for separating data with different levels of accuracy, but it is poor when there are several different levels of accuracy.

Example: The data name, such as Well Depth Estimated or Well Depth Surveyed, can show the accuracy of the data.

Using the data definition is good for explaining the accuracy in detail, particularly when the accuracy is more subjective.

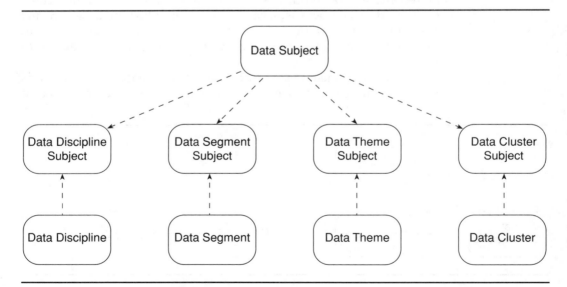

Figure 8.7   Data dictionary metadata model for the categorical levels.

Example: The definition *Well depth is estimated by dropping a rock, counting the seconds till a splash is heard, and calculating the depth* explains the data accuracy.

Companion data characteristics can be established for the data value and the accuracy of that data value. This technique is good when there are many levels of accuracy, but it can be abused when people combine values with different levels of accuracy for an analysis.

Example: Well Depth Meters Value and Well Depth Accuracy Codes are companion data characteristics. Well Depth Meters Value contains the measurement, and the common word *Value* indicates that there is a companion data characteristic. The companion data characteristic, Well Depth Accuracy Code, indicates the accuracy.

There can be more than one companion data characteristic.

Example: Well Depth Value may have many different measurement units and many different accuracy codes. The common word *Value* indicates one or more companion data characteristics. The two companion data characteristics are Well Depth Measurement Units and Well Depth Accuracy Code.

The format of the data value can indicate the accuracy.

Example: Well Depth Meters contains values such as *23*, *47.6*, and *114.77*. The number of decimal places indicates the accuracy.

This technique is good if people use the notation appropriately; however, it is not appropriate if a fixed format is used.

Example: A fixed format of two decimal places shows the first value in the preceding example as *23.00*, indicating that the measurement was to 0.01 meter, which is not true.

The data dictionary is maintained by constantly adding and adjusting data definitions. Anytime new data are defined within the common data architecture, data are cross-referenced to the common data architecture, or existing data definitions are enhanced, those changes must be entered in the data dictionary.

Data Structure

The *data structure* contains the structure of data within the common data architecture. It does not include the structure of any data products. The structure of data products is contained in the data product reference.

The data structure metadata model is shown in Figure 8.8. Data Subjects have many Data Characteristics and many Primary Keys. Primary Keys have a Primary Key Type, such as *Official*, *Alternate*, *Candidate*, and *Obsolete*. The many-to-many relation between Primary Keys and Data Characteristic Variations is resolved with Primary Key Characteristic. The same situation is true with Foreign Keys, with the exception that Foreign Keys have both a local and a parent Data Subject. Data Subjects also have a many-to-many relation with Subject Relation Diagrams, which is resolved with Data Subject Location. Subject Relation Diagrams can be *Strategic*, *Tactical*, or *Detailed*, as shown by the Subject Relation Diagram Type.

The data structure component is maintained through constant addition and enhancement. Anytime new data structures are defined or existing data structures are changed, the data structure documentation is adjusted accordingly.

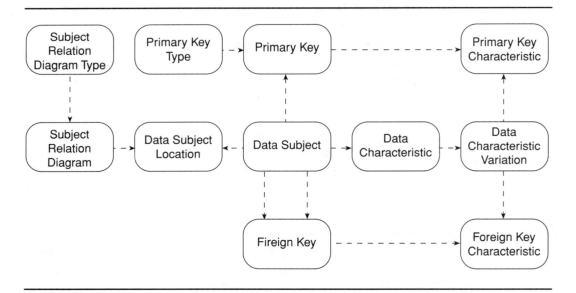

Figure 8.8   Data structure metadata model.

Data Integrity

Data integrity rules are important for maintaining integrity of the data resource, but they are often difficult to define and document. Chapter 7 defined data integrity. *Data integrity* contains the data integrity documentation for data subjects and data characteristics in the common data architecture. It does not include data accuracy, which is documented in the data dictionary. It does not include data integrity for data products, which is contained in the data product reference.

The data integrity metadata model is shown in Figure 8.9. Data Subjects contain many Data Characteristics. Data Characteristics can have a Data Derivation Procedure and a Data Derivation Type. Each Data Subject can have many Foreign Keys that represent data relations. The data relations may belong to a Data Relation Set. The Data Relation Set Type indicates whether the Data Relation Set is a *Data Subject Hierarchy*, *Mutually Exclusive Parents*, or *Data Categories*.

Data value integrity is defined as either a rule or a set of allowable values. If the data value integrity is defined as a rule, it is documented as a data characteristic in the metadata Data Characteristic. If the data value integrity is defined as a set of values, it is documented as a separate data subject with a data characteristic referencing that data subject in the metadata Data Characteristic.

Conditional data value integrity is defined as a separate data subject showing the allowable combination of data values, with a data characteristic referencing that data subject in the metadata Data Characteristic. The options for data characteristics within a data subject, such as *Optional* or *Required*, are shown as a matrix in a data characteristic in the metadata Data Subject.

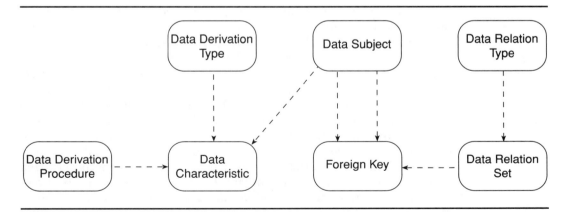

Figure 8.9   Data integrity metadata model.

A data domain does not manifest itself as a data subject in the common metadata model. A data domain is either documented as a data characteristic in the metadata Data Characteristic or as a data subject referenced by a data characteristic in the metadata Data Characteristic.

A foreign key represents a data relation between two data subjects or a recursive data relation to the same data subject. Data structure integrity is documented as data characteristics in the metadata Foreign Key. Cardinality of the data relation is documented as a data characteristic in the metadata Foreign Key. A data relation may belong to a data relation set, such as a data subject hierarchy, mutually exclusive parents, or data categories. In this situation, the foreign keys involved in the set belong to a Data Relation Set. Data Relation Type indicates whether the data relation set is a *Data Subject Hierarchy*, *Mutually Exclusive Parents*, or *Data Categories*.

A matrix of data characteristic options for data subject types in a data subject hierarchy, such as *Required*, *Optional*, or *Prevented*, is documented as a matrix in a data characteristic in the metadata Data Subject.

Data retention can be defined for data occurrences or data characteristics. The data retention for a data occurrence is documented as a data characteristic in the metadata Data Subject, such as what is done with subordinate data occurrences when the data occurrence is deleted and how referential integrity violations are resolved. The data retention for an individual data characteristic is documented as two data characteristics in the metadata Data Characteristic. One data characteristic documents retention when the individual data value changes, and the other data characteristic documents retention when the data occurrence is deleted. In some situations, the data retention for both data characteristics may be the same and in other situations the data retention may be different.

Data derivation is defined as a specific procedure for an individual data characteristic or as a general procedure that can be used by several data characteristics. If the data derivation procedure is for an individual data characteristic, it is documented as a data characteristic in the metadata Data Characteristic. If the data derivation procedure is a general procedure, it is documented in the metadata Data Derivation Procedure, which is referenced by a data characteristic in the metadata Data Characteristic. The Data Derivation Type indicates whether the data derivation procedure has no contributor data characteristics (generation), is a procedure with one contributing data characteristic, is a procedure with many different contributing data characteristics, or is a procedure with one contributing data characteristic from many different data occurrences (aggregation).

Data integrity rules are maintained through constant enhancement. Anytime there is a new data integrity rule or a change in existing data integrity, the data integrity documentation is adjusted accordingly.

Data Thesaurus

The *data thesaurus* contains a set of data name synonyms to help people locate the particular data they need. It provides a reference between similar names or business terms and the common data names.

An integrated data resource can become quite large. The quantity of references to data subjects and data characteristics in the data resource can grow at an exponential rate and become larger than any one person can comprehend. The data thesaurus provides a place to document references to common data names.

The data thesaurus metadata model is shown in Figure 8.10. Data subjects can be referenced by many different business phrases and each business phrase can reference many different data subjects, putting Data Subjects and Data Subject Business Phrases in a many-to-many relation. The many-to-many relationship is resolved with a Data Subject Thesaurus Phrase that contains specific references from business terms to data subject names. The same situation is true for data characteristics.

A data thesaurus is maintained by constantly adding new references each time new data subjects or data characteristics are defined or each time new references are identified for existing data subjects or data characteristics. Most of the new references are identified when new data are defined. Three techniques for identifying data thesaurus entries exist.

First, a data name is broken down into phrases that could be placed in the thesaurus. Typically, a data name may be referenced by two to ten phrases.

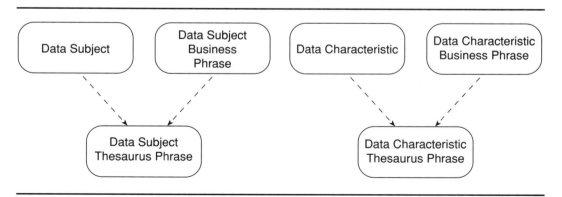

Figure 8.10   Data thesaurus metadata model.

Example: Employee Appointment is broken down into Employee and Appointment, and Employee Performance Evaluation is broken down into Employee, Performance, Evaluation, Performance Evaluation, and Employee Evaluation. Each of these phrases is entered into the thesaurus, as shown in Figure 8.11.

Each organization must decide the extent of phrases used in the data thesaurus.

Example: Words like Type, Class, and Status, which are common in many data names, should not be placed in the thesaurus. They are too common and not useful to locating specific data.

Second, related data names are identified and documented. It is helpful to review each data definition to determine these additional references.

Example: Employee Appointment places Employees in Positions. References should be entered from Employee Appointment to Position and from Position to Employee Appointment.

Third, references from words or phrases used by clients are added to the thesaurus. Clients frequently use business terms that are different from the formal data names. These business terms need to be added to the thesaurus. Reviewing the data glossary provides additional phrases to added to the thesaurus.

Appointment	Employee Appointment
Employee	Employee Appointment
Employee	Employee Performance Evaluation
Evaluation	Employee Performance Evaluation
Performance	Employee Performance Evaluation
Performance Evaluation	Employee Performance Evaluation
Employee Evaluation	Employee Performance Evaluation

Figure 8.11   Data subject thesaurus examples.

Duties	Position
Job	Position
Personnel	Employee
Responsibility	Position
Staff	Employee
Worker	Employee

Figure 8.12   Additions to the data subject thesaurus.

Example: Staff, Worker, and Personnel are phrases clients use when referring to Employees, and Job, Responsibility, and Duties refer to Position. These phrases are added to the thesaurus, as shown in Figure 8.12.

The same procedure is followed for data characteristics. The data characteristic name, excluding the data subject prefix, is broken down into phrases that could be entered into the thesaurus.

Example: Employee Anniversary Date CYMD, Employee Birth Date CYMD, and Customer Birth Date CYMD might be entered, as shown in Figure 8.13. The word Date would probably not be entered as a phrase. Data characteristic variations, such as CYMD, may or may not be entered at the discretion of the organization.

Anniversary	Employee Anniversary Date CYMD
Anniversary Date	Employee Anniversary Date CYMD
Birth	Customer Birth Date CYMD
Birth	Employee Birth Date CYMD
Birth Date	Customer Birth Date CYMD
Birth Date	Employee Birth Date CYMD

Figure 8.13   Additions to the data characteristic thesaurus.

The data thesaurus needs constant maintenance when data names are changed. All references must be changed from the old data name to the new data name. This process requires careful searching of the thesaurus for all references to old data names and changing those references to new data names. It also requires searching for old data names used as references to other data names and changing them to the new data names. If this maintenance is not done, the thesaurus rapidly deteriorates.

Data Glossary

The *data glossary* contains an alphabetical listing of words, terms, and abbreviations and their definitions. The data glossary does not contain abbreviations for the words used in data names. Those are contained in the data naming lexicon. It does not contain data definitions. Those are contained in the data dictionary.

The data glossary metadata model is shown in Figure 8.14. Glossary Item is a word, term, or abbreviation that either contains a definition or a reference to another item that contains a definition. A Glossary defines the source for a set of data definitions, similar to a bibliographic reference. A Glossary may belong to a specific Data Discipline, such as health care or education.

Example: A glossary definition is shown at the top of Figure 8.15. The word or term is followed by a definition. The definition may contain a reference to the source of the definition.

Example: An abbreviation is shown at the bottom of Figure 8.15. Typically, the abbreviation is listed with a reference to the fully spelled out term, but no definition is listed. A separate entry is made for the fully spelled out term and the definition.

Figure 8.14   Data glossary metadata model.

> Water Diversion   The removal of water from a stream, lake, reservoir, or any other surface water body into a canal, pipe, or other conduit.
> OASI   Old Age Survivors Insurance

Figure 8.15   Data glossary example.

Multiple definitions for the same word or term are usually shown with a number in parenthesis after the word or term.

Example: Multiple definitions for wetlands would be shown as *Wetland (1)*, *Wetland (2)*, and so on, and the source of the each definition would be indicated.

The data glossary is maintained by continually adding new definitions and enhancing existing definitions. Anytime a new word, term, or abbreviation is found that may not be clear to clients, or may require further explanation, it is added to the glossary. Anytime an existing definition is unclear or confusing, it is enhanced so that clients thoroughly understand all words, terms, and abbreviations.

Data Product Reference

Existing data are referred to as data products because they are a product of some development process. The *data product reference* contains documentation about data products, including data names and definitions, data structure, data accuracy and integrity, and cross-references to the common data architecture. It documents the results of data resource inventories, but it does not contain the results of data resource surveys. Data resource surveys are documented in the data clearinghouse.

The data product metadata model is shown in Figure 8.16. Data Product, Data Product Group, Data Product Unit, and Data Product Code form the data product structure.[6] Data Subject, Data Characteristic, Data Characteristic Variation, Data Code Set, and Data Code form the common data architecture. The primary cross-reference between data products and the common data architecture is between Data Product Item and Data Characteristic Variation. Cross references may be made between Data Product Entity and Data Subject, and between Data Product Code and Data Code.

---

[6]Data products are described in more detail in Chapter 9.

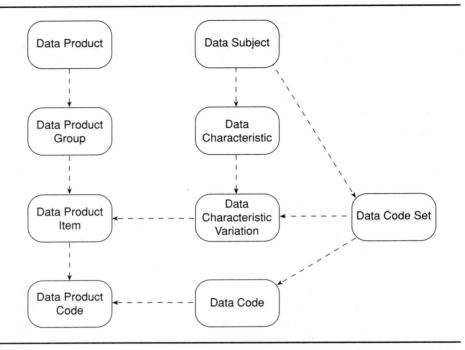

Figure 8.16   Data product reference metadata model.

Data product names and definitions are documented in the Data Product, Data Product Group, Data Product Item, and Data Product Code data subjects. A physical database is usually documented as a Data Product, a data file is usually documented as a Data Product Group, and a data item is usually documented as a Data Product Item. The physical parameters for data files are documented in Data Product or Data Product Group. The format, physical parameters, and accuracy of data attributes are documented as a narrative statement in Data Product Item.

A logical data model that does not correspond to the common data architecture is documented as a Data Product, a data entity is documented as a Data Product Group, and a data attribute is documented as a Data Product Unit. Geospatial data layers are usually documented as a Data Product Group.

The data product structure is documented as either entity relation diagrams or file relation diagrams in Data Product. The diagrams may be in either their original form or a modified form. The modified form retains the same structure but uses the notations used in the common data architecture for data entities, data files, and the relations between them. The modified form may include additional data entities not shown on the original diagrams, such as code tables, to help people understand the structure of existing data. The original form is readily recognized by people familiar with the data product. The modified form provides a common notation across all data products.

An entity structure chart or a file structure chart is documented with Data Product. If neither of these charts is available, one may be created and documented in Data Product.

Data product integrity, if it exists, is documented in Data Product Group and Data Product Unit as appropriate. A general statement about data integrity for a data product is documented in Data Product. Data product integrity may be documented in a narrative form or with any other notation, such as those shown in the last chapter, to help people understand the existing data integrity.

Cross-references are made between data products and the common data architecture so that existing data can be readily understood in a common context. The primary cross-reference occurs between Data Product Unit and Data Characteristic Variation. Additional cross-references may occur between Data Product Group and Data Subject and between Data Product Code and Data Code. The cross references allow people to identify what existing Data Product Units represent in the common data architecture and all manifestations of Data Product Units for each Data Characteristic Variation. Chapter 9 explains cross-references in more detail.

Data product documentation and cross-references are maintained through constant modification. Whenever new data are identified, they are entered into the metadata warehouse and cross-referenced to the common data architecture. Any additional information or adjustments to the cross-references are added to the metadata warehouse. If existing data cease to exist because of conversion to an integrated data resource, the documentation may be retained for historical reference, or it may be deleted from the metadata warehouse.

Data Directory

The *data directory* contains information about organizations that maintain data, such as contacts in those organizations, how data can be acquired from the organization, other general information about data access and availability, and the terms and conditions for accessing data. It does not include information specific to any data product. That information is contained in the data product reference.

The data directory metadata model is shown in Figure 8.17. Organizations have one or more Organization Contacts. Both Organizations and Organization Contacts can be connected to Data Products and to Clearinghouse Items to identify the data owners and contact points for those data owners.

The data directory requires constant maintenance. New organizations are constantly being added as data are identified and cross-

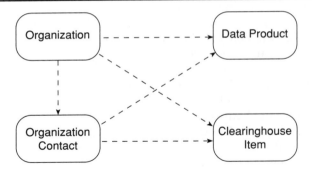

Figure 8.17   Data directory metadata model.

referenced to the common data architecture. In addition, contact people within organizations are constantly changing. Information about the availability of data and terms and conditions for accessing or acquiring data frequently change. All of these changes need to be made to the data directory so that it provides current information to clients.

Data Translation Schemes

The *data translation scheme* contains the data translation schemes between common data characteristic variations when those data characteristic variations represent measurements or format variations. They are not used to translate data between data characteristic variations that represent differences in content or meaning.[7] Data translation schemes usually translate data between official data characteristic variations and nonofficial data characteristic variations. They may translate data between official data variations if more than one official data variation has been designated or between nonofficial data variations if the need exists.

The data translation scheme metadata model is shown in Figure 8.18. A Data Translation Scheme converts the values from a source Data Characteristic Variation to a target Data Characteristic Variation. A Data Translation Scheme can also reference another Data Translation Scheme so that specific data translations can use a general translation scheme, such as date translations.

Data translation schemes are maintained by constantly adding new translation schemes. Whenever official data variations are designated and translation schemes are developed and accepted, they are added to

---

[7]Chapter 9 describes data translation schemes in more detail.

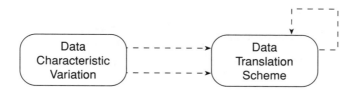

Figure 8.18   Data translation scheme metadata model.

the data translation scheme component. Data translation schemes may be removed when the data characteristics being translated no longer exist.

Data Clearinghouse
Data sharing within large organizations and among many different organizations involves both the sharing and exchange of existing data and cooperation on the collection of new data. Considerable emphasis is placed on identifying and sharing data, but limited emphasis is placed on cooperation to collect new data. The result is that many organizations collect critical data redundantly and ignore less critical data. If organizations cooperate on data collection and data sharing, they could prevent redundant data collection and collect additional less critical data for the same resources. The *data clearinghouse* provides a mechanism for collecting, classifying, and distributing information about data sources, unpublished documents, and projects related to the data resource.

The data clearinghouse metadata model is shown in Figure 8.19. A Clearinghouse Item can be either a *Data Source*, a *Document*, or a *Project*, as shown by Clearinghouse Item Type. A document can have one or more Document Authors as shown by Clearinghouse Item Author. A Clearinghouse Item can be represented in one or more Geographic Areas, as shown by Clearinghouse Item Geographic Area. A Geographic Area can be a *City*, *County*, *Township*, *Quadrangle*, *Hydrologic Unit*, or *Water Resource Inventory Area*, as shown by Geographic Area Type. A Clearinghouse Item can be referenced by one or more Clearinghouse Topics, as shown by Clearinghouse Item Topic. Each Clearinghouse Topic can be referenced by one or more Clearinghouse Keywords, as shown by Clearinghouse Topic Keyword.

A *data source* is any source of data from a specific organization, such as a database or data file. A data source may include nonautomated data, but it does not include unpublished documents containing data. Data sources are identified and documented through data resource surveys. Only general information to raise the awareness of the data source is collected during data resource surveys and documented in the data clearinghouse. Detailed data are collected during data

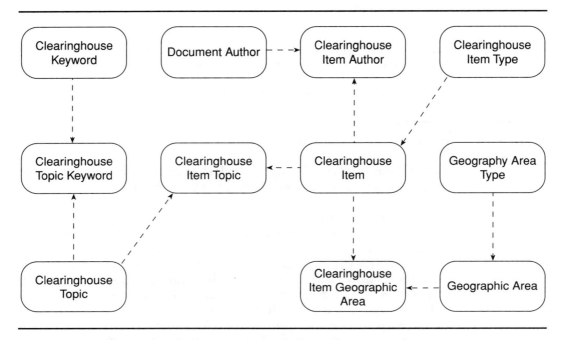

Figure 8.19   Data clearinghouse metadata model.

resource inventories and placed in the data product reference, not in the data clearinghouse.

Only primary data sources are usually documented in the data clearinghouse. Data are disseminated from these primary data sources to organizations that need those data to support their business information demand. In many cases, organizations receiving data modify those data in some way or add additional data and become primary sources. These new or modified data are then disseminated to other organizations. This value-added process forms a network of data flowing between organizations.[8]

Published documents appear in formal bibliographic references and do not need to be included in the data clearinghouse. Unpublished documents, however, are constantly being produced, but do not appear in formal bibliographic references even though they may contain useful data. An unpublished document is any document containing useful data that should be part of the data resource, but is not listed in a formal bibliographic reference, such as consultant studies, field surveys

---

[8]Data resource surveys are described in more detail in Brackett, 1994.

and project reports. References to unpublished documents, and the authors of those documents, are maintained in the data clearinghouse.

Data projects are constantly being planned, implemented, and completed. A *data project* is any formal project pertaining to the collection, generation, organization, management, or documentation of data that is, or should be, part of the data resource. Generally, only current, planned, and desired data projects are entered into the data clearinghouse. Completed data projects are usually not of interest because their results appear in either a formal bibliographic reference or an unpublished document in the data clearinghouse. Current and planned data projects are of general interest to many organizations. Desired projects are projects of interest to an organization, but the organization does not have the resources to plan or implement the project. If interest can be generated across several organizations, the resources may be available to plan the project.

A single-level index to data clearinghouse items through keywords may not be appropriate. Defining keywords for all possible business terms can result in many cross references to clearinghouse items and extensive cross-reference maintenance. A two-level reference scheme of business keywords and core topics reduces the number of references to clearinghouse items and still provides access through a wide range of business terms. *Clearinghouse topics* are core topics used to reference clearinghouse items. *Clearinghouse keywords* are any business words or terms that reference clearinghouse topics.

Example: Figure 8.20 shows clearinghouse keywords and topics. Clearinghouse Keywords, such as *Forest* and *Trees*, are shown on the left. The Clearinghouse Keywords reference Clearinghouse Topics, such as *Timber*, which are shown on the right. The Clearinghouse Topics are used to reference Clearinghouse Items.

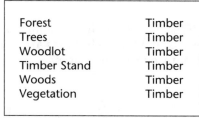

Forest	Timber
Trees	Timber
Woodlot	Timber
Timber Stand	Timber
Woods	Timber
Vegetation	Timber

Figure 8.20   Clearinghouse keyword and topic reference example.

Clearinghouse keywords and topics are developed by a team of business experts and domain experts. The business experts provide input about possible business terms that could become clearinghouse keywords, and the domain experts provide input about possible core topics that could become clearinghouse topics. In some situations, it is difficult to get started developing keywords and topics. Data themes, data areas, data groups, and data classes often provide initial topics to start the process.

Clearinghouse keywords and topics are not the same as the entries in a data thesaurus. Clearinghouse keywords and topics provide an index to data sources, unpublished documents, and data projects that may contain useful data. They are developed by business experts and domain experts. The data subject thesaurus and data characteristic thesaurus provide an index to formal data names in the common data architecture and are developed largely by data experts, although business experts often provide related terms. They are based on words and word strings from the common data names and on words and word strings closely related to the common data names.

Clearinghouse items can be accessed by several different techniques. The primary access is through clearinghouse keywords and topics and through geographic areas. The clearinghouse keywords and topics provide access by subject, and the geographic areas provide access by location. Additional access to clearinghouse items is through document names, document author names, project names, and organizations.

The data clearinghouse must be constantly enhanced to be complete and current. Organizations are constantly changing their data sources, producing more unpublished documents, and completing, starting, or establishing new data projects. If the data clearinghouse is not kept current with these changes, it will not help organizations cooperate on data collection and data sharing. Periodic surveys should be conducted to ensure the data clearinghouse is complete and current.

MANAGING METADATA

Managing metadata is at least as difficult as managing data. However, managing metadata is easier if a few techniques are followed for developing high-quality metadata and for managing versions of metadata.

Metadata Quality

Ideally, metadata must accurately represent the data, the same as the data must accurately represent objects and events in the real world. Metadata often do not have the quality desired to represent data, the same as the data often do not have the quality desired to represent objects and events. The quality of the metadata relies heavily on the integrity of the people creating the metadata. An implied truth in labeling principle for metadata says people are doing the best job possible to collect and document metadata. A counterpart to this principle says client beware because the metadata quality may not be at the level desired, even though people had good intentions when developing those metadata.

The biggest problem with metadata is the unknown. Metadata often do not exist, are not readily available, or are not comprehensive. The best approach to developing metadata is to document the original data products and provide additions to that documentation as more information is discovered.

Creating data product metadata is a discovery process.

Metadata documented for data products can be rolled forward to their counterparts in the common data architecture through the data cross-references. These metadata are used to develop common metadata and to verify that data cross-references are appropriate. Through additions to the metadata, adjustments of data cross-references, and enhancements to common metadata, the existing data quality can be thoroughly understood and the desired level of data quality can be determined.

Business experts, domain experts, and data experts should form a cooperative partnership to develop data product metadata. Each of these experts has knowledge and skills that contribute substantially to developing data product metadata during the discovery process. Common metadata are ensured by strongly emphasizing that these experts develop complete, accurate metadata for any new development effort. Development of common metadata should be a high priority item for any development project and for any production project that develops new data.

Common metadata must have a strong connotative meaning.

Common metadata must provide a complete understanding of the content and meaning of data. They must fully explain what the data represent in the real world. Common metadata must be presented in a syntax that is both correct and acceptable to anyone reviewing the metadata.

They must provide a connotative meaning that is complete enough to prevent any substantial denotative meaning from the reviewer.

Metadata Versions

Objects and events are constantly changing, and the data resource is constantly being adjusted to accurately reflect those changes. One major problem with common metadata is properly managing changes in both data and metadata. Both the semantics and syntax of data may change over time depending on how people use data and how applications and edits adjust data. The semantics and syntax of metadata may also change over time, depending on how they represent the data. How can changes in data and metadata be documented and presented to people so they understand what the data represented at a specific point in time?

Data changes are indicated through data names and data definitions. Minor changes in data definitions that enhance the understanding but do not alter the content or meaning are made with a revision date in the data definition. Significant changes in data definitions that alter the content or meaning are made with a data version attached to the data name.

The data version name for significant data subject changes may be a letter, a number, a date, a date range, or any other meaningful name identifying the data version.

Example: If the definition of Employee changed from *all people on site paid directly by the organization* to *all people on site paid directly by the organization or indirectly through contractors*, the data version names could be Employee <A> and Employee <B>, Employee <1> and Employee <2>, or Employee <Pre 1980> and Employee <Post 1980>. Data version names like <Old> and <New> should be avoided because they do not easily accommodate additional changes. Comprehensive data subject definitions explain the differences.

Data structure changes, such as new data relations, obsolete data relations, different cardinalities, and different primary keys, are best documented with a new subject relation diagram and subject structure chart. The diagram and chart carry a date that indicates when the changes were effective. Effective begin and end dates may also be added to the data integrity documentation.

Significant data characteristic changes are documented with a data version name attached to the data characteristic name or with companion data characteristics.

Example: Road Segment Length Miles <1960-1975>, Road Segment Length Miles <1976-1990>, and Road Segment Length Miles <Post 1991> indicate a different accuracy for measuring the length. Better data version names might be <0.1 Miles>, <0.01 Miles>, and <0.005 Miles>.

Example: Companion data characteristics could also be used to indicate the differences in accuracy using Road Segment Length Miles and Road Segment Length Accuracy. The accuracy could also be indicated by using the precise number of decimal places in the data value as explained earlier. Comprehensive data characteristic definitions explain the differences and details.

Data version names could be used to indicate effective begin and end dates for data characteristics, but is not required.

Example: Employee Hair Color Name <Pre 1985> indicates that an employee's hair color information was collected prior to 1985. Similarly, Employee Eye Color Name <Post 1993> indicates that an employee's eye color has been collected since 1993.

Data characteristic variations represent different forms of the same data characteristic, not different data characteristics. Comprehensive data characteristic definitions explain the differences in the two data characteristics.

Example: A change from Patient Age Years to Patient Age Months is represented by two data characteristic variations for Patient Age. The data values may be collected differently, but they can be readily converted through data translation schemes.

Significant data characteristic changes are documented with data versions, not with data characteristic variations. A comprehensive data definition explains the difference.

Example: If Patient Age Years were collected differently, the data version name is used to show the difference. Patient Age Years <Pre 1990> and Patient Age Years <Post 1990> indicate a change in Patient Age.

Significant data code changes are documented with begin and end dates. When new data codes are added to a data code set, the effective begin date is entered. When a data code becomes obsolete, the effective end date is entered. If a data code is split into two or more new data codes, the original data code has an effective end date and each of the new data codes have an effective begin date. If two or more data codes are combined, each of the original data codes has an effective end date and the new data code has an effective begin date.

If a new set of data codes is established, the data characteristic or the data code set containing those data codes has an effective begin date. If an entire set of data codes becomes obsolete, the data characteristic or the data code set containing those data codes has an effective end date.

Metadata changes are documented the same way as data changes because they are part of the common data architecture. Changes to metadata follow the same notations described above for data. The metadata model is managed the same as the data model to reflect changes over time.

SUMMARY

The state of metadata in most organizations is at least as bad as the state of data. Metadata are disparate within organizations and massively disparate across organizations. Disparate metadata are developed by a disparate metadata cycle, similar to the disparate data cycle, which is creating a metadata dilemma that could be disaster for the data resource. An organization must go through the shock of realizing its metadata are not promoting a fully utilized data resource to meet the business information demand.

High-quality metadata are needed to understand existing data quality, determine the desired data quality, adjust the existing data quality, and fully utilize the data resource. Because the size and complexity of an organization's data resource increases rapidly, the faster an organization can develop common metadata, the more quickly it can stabilize and fully utilize the data resource. Development of common metadata is not a small task but it can be achieved with a new perspective of metadata.

The new perspective of metadata includes foredata describing objects and events in the real world, common metadata describing the foredata, and common meta-metadata describing the metadata. The common data architecture provides common meta-metadata within which common metadata are developed. The common meta-metadata provide a mechanism to move from the current situation of disparate metadata to common metadata that cross multiple jurisdictions and multiple disciplines.

A metadata warehouse contains the common metadata that provides a formal guide to an integrated data resource, helps manage the data resource, and ensures maximum utilization of the data resource. The metadata warehouse includes components for the data naming lexicon, data dictionary, data structure, data integrity, data thesaurus, data glossary, data product, data directory, data translation schemes, and data clearinghouse. These components are documented in a common metadata model.

The metadata warehouse can be a stepping stone from no formal metadata management to the use of robust repositories that include documentation for the entire information technology infrastructure. It provides a quick, less expensive approach to maintaining high-quality data about the existing data and the integrated data resource. It is method-independent and requires fewer resources to maintain than a full repository. In some cases, the metadata warehouse is more robust for documenting the data resource than most repositories.

Common metadata are best developed through the cooperative efforts of business experts, domain experts, and data experts who work in a discovery mode to understand the existing data resource and develop common metadata. Development of common metadata that have a strong semantic meaning and an understandable syntax will break the disparate data cycle, resolve the dilemma, and provide an integrated data resource that is fully utilized.

QUESTIONS

The following questions are provided as a review of the chapter and to stimulate thought about the existing status of metadata and how common metadata can be developed.

1. What are disparate metadata?
2. Why is the disparate metadata situation getting worse rather than better?
3. What is the disparate metadata cycle?
4. Why could the metadata dilemma be disaster for many organizations?
5. What is metadata shock?
6. How is the new metadata perspective different from traditional metadata?
7. How do common metadata differ from standard metadata?
8. What are the common meta-metadata?

9. What is a metadata warehouse?
10. What is the common metadata model?
11. What does the data naming lexicon contain?
12. What does the data dictionary contain?
13. How do the data structure and data integrity relate to the data dictionary?
14. How do the data thesaurus and the clearinghouse keywords and topics differ?
15. What does the data product reference contain?
16. What does the data clearinghouse provide?
17. How is high-quality metadata achieved?
18. How are data subject changes documented?
19. How are data characteristic and data code changes documented?
20. Why are high-quality metadata really needed?

## CHAPTER 9

Data Refining

> Data refining is the first step to developing an integrated data resource within the common data architecture.

Considerable disparate data exist within an organization and across many organizations. These disparate data need to be integrated into a single data resource so they the data can be fully utilized to meet the business information demand. The integration of disparate data, called data refining, is one phase of the overall process of integrating all data within the common data architecture.

Data refining is a semantic refining process for understanding the content and meaning of disparate data without altering those data or affecting the operation of information systems. It is accomplished by identifying disparate data, uniquely naming and defining them, cross-referencing them to the common data architecture, designating official variations and primary data sources, and developing an integrated data resource. It increases the awareness and understanding of data that already exist and reduces the variability and redundancy inherent in disparate data.

Chapter 9 begins with an explanation of the data refining concept and how disparate data are represented as data products. It explains how data products are uniquely named, defined, and structured and how disparate data quality is evaluated. It presents techniques for developing cross-references between data products and the common data architecture, identifying the variability in disparate data, designating official data variations, and developing data translation schemes. The chapter concludes by explaining how data are prepared for physical integration.[1]

DATA REFINING CONCEPT

Refining removes impurities from crude or impure material to form useful products, such as refining crude oil. *Data refining* refines disparate data within a common context to increase the awareness and understanding of the data, remove data variability and redundancy, and develop an integrated data resource. Disparate data are the raw material and an integrated data resource is the final product.[2]

Analogy: The data refining process is similar to the oil refining process that takes crude oil, refines it into usable products, stores those products for future use, and discards waste products.

> Data refining integrates disparate data within the common data architecture to support the business information demand.

The term *data refining* is used rather than *data re-engineering* because most disparate data were never engineered in the first place; therefore, they cannot be re-engineered. Data refining is one aspect of the total data engineering discipline.

Data Refining Approach

Data refining is a semantic process for understanding disparate data. *Semantic data refining* is the process of cross-referencing disparate data to the common data architecture to understand their content and meaning without changing the data or impacting the day-to-day operation information systems. It is a nondestructive, no-impact process that increases data awareness and understanding and reduces data variability and redundancy through cross-references.

---

[1]A few techniques have been changed slightly since Brackett, 1994. These changes will be explained as they are encountered.

[2]Data refining is not the same as data mining. The latter term represents the statistical analysis of the data resource to discover patterns and trends.

> Semantic data refining is a nondestructive, no-impact process to under-
> stand and resolve disparate data.

Data refining is accomplished by inventorying and uniquely identifying existing data. Data characteristic variations that correspond to
data product units are identified or created, and cross-references are
made between the data product units and the corresponding data characteristic variations. When the cross-references are completed, the data
variability is analyzed and official data variations are designated. Data
translations are prepared between the data characteristic variations to
support data sharing and physical data integration.

Data refining should not be limited to just data in databases and
their supporting documentation. It should include the data defined and
maintained in programs. The data defined and maintained in programs
may not be written to or read from data files; however, they need to be
understood the same as data that exist in databases. Identifying and
documenting data contained in programs is one step to resolving the
millennium date problem.[3]

Data refining is a complex process that requires looking at each
piece of disparate data to determine its content and meaning. It is a
discovery process that starts with an initial common data architecture
and enhances it to represent all disparate data. The process involves
knowledgeable people who analyze disparate data and cross-reference
them to the common data architecture. Data refining is an evolutionary
process that uses the knowledge hidden in people and products to
develop robust metadata for existing data.

Once an organization realizes its disparate data situation and com-
mits the resources to developing an integrated data resource, the biggest
difficulty is getting started. The concepts and techniques described in the
following sections help people get started with the data refining process.
Once the process begins, the success builds enthusiasm, and it is easy to
gain additional commitment for refining data and building an integrated
data resource. The results are well worth the effort.

Data Product Concept

Data refining begins with establishing an overall structure for uniquely
identifying and defining all disparate data. The overall structure for

---

[3]The millennium data problem is described in more detail in the last chapter.

disparate data is a hierarchy of data products. The term *data products* is used because all disparate data are the product of some development effort.[4]

> A *data product* is a major, independent piece of documentation of any type that contains the names and/or definitions of disparate data, such as a dictionary, a database, a major project, or a major information system.
>
> A *data product group* is a major grouping of data within a data product, such as a data entity, data file, a data record, a data record type, a screen, a report, a document, or a program.
>
> A *data product unit* is an individual element of data in a data product group, such as a data attribute, a field in a record, or an element on a screen, or data in a program.
>
> A *data product code* is a coded data value that exists in a data product unit.

Disparate data are defined as a hierarchy of data products for data refining.

Disparate data may be unstructured or semi-structured. *Unstructured disparate data* are disparate data that do not conform to any type of naming, definition, structure, or quality criteria and have no similarity to the common data architecture. Databases are defined as data products, data files are defined as data product groups, and data items are defined as data product units.

Example: Older databases and data files are typical examples of unstructured disparate data.

Semi-structured disparate data are disparate data that are at least partially structured by some method, but are not equivalent to the common data architecture. They conform to some type of naming, definition, structure, and quality criteria, but not those of the common data architecture. An information system, development project, or data model is usually defined as a data product, data entities are defined as data product groups, and data attributes are defined as data product units.

---

[4]Two terms were changed since Brackett, 1994. Data product subject was changed to data product group, and data product characteristic was changed to data product units to prevent any confusion between data products and the common data architecture.

DATA PRODUCT NAMES

Unstructured disparate data names are usually short, inconsistent, and often meaningless. There are many synonyms and homonyms that do not uniquely identify each data file, data item, or data code value. Semi-structured data names are usually better than unstructured disparate data names, but they still may not uniquely identify each data entity, data attribute, and data code value. All disparate data must be uniquely named using the data naming taxonomy prior to being cross-referenced to the common data architecture.

Data Naming Taxonomy

The data naming taxonomy provides unique identification for all disparate data, as shown in Figure 9.1. The data site, data subject, and data characteristic components of the data naming taxonomy uniquely identify data products, data product groups, and data product units for unstructured and semi-structured disparate data. The data characteristic variation component is meaningless for uniquely identifying disparate data.

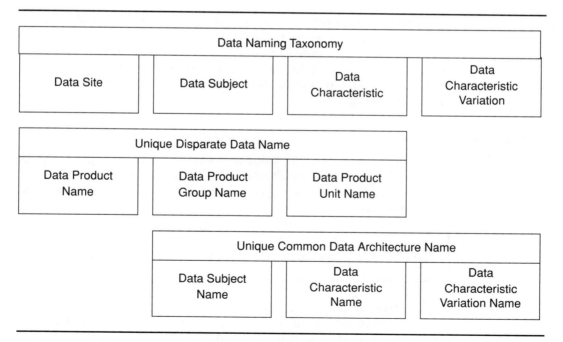

Figure 9.1   Unique data names from the data naming taxonomy.

The data subject, data characteristic, and data characteristic variation components provide unique common data names within the common data architecture. Data site is meaningless for understanding disparate data.

Data Products

Each data product is uniquely named within the scope of the data refining effort using the data naming taxonomy. A unique data product name starts the sequence of unique names for all disparate data.

Example: Health Department Data Dictionary, County Water Sampling Project, Financial Information System, and Traffic Investigation Unit are unique data product names.

> A unique data product name starts the unique identification of disparate data.

A unique data product name usually does not exist and is developed when the data product is first identified. If the data product name is not unique, the identification of disparate data will not be unique, and the data refining effort will not be successful. Organizations must plan ahead to ensure unique data product names from the beginning of the data refining effort.

Data Product Groups

Each data product group is uniquely named within a data product. The data product name provides uniqueness within the scope of the data refining effort, and the data product group name provides uniqueness within the data product.

> Data product group names are unique within a data product.

Unstructured disparate data may have a single record type or they may have multiple record types that become data product group names. Any major grouping of unstructured disparate data could become a data product group name.

Example: Vehicle is a single record type that becomes a data product group. Control Record, Summary Record, and Transaction Record are multiple record types, and each becomes a data product group.

Semi-structured disparate data usually have a data entity name that may be close to a data subject name.

Example: Personnel, Employee, and Customer become data product group names.

Data product group names are relatively easy to identify.

Example: PERS.DATA.NEW, BUDGET.DATA, or IBM 3090 PERS.DATA.NEW are typical data file names. Daily Financial Transaction Report, Monthly Vehicle Accident Summary, and Water Sample Analysis Results are typical report or screen names. Water Sample, Accident, and Account are typical data entity names.

When these data product group names are added to their data product names, a unique data product group name is created.

Example: IBM 3090: PERS.DATA.NEW, Financial Information System: Daily Financial Transaction Report, and Woodland County: Water Sample are unique data product group names.

Data Product Units

Each data product unit is uniquely named within the data product group. A data product unit is uniquely identified by the data product name, the data product group name, and the data product unit name.

> The data product unit name must be unique within a data product group.

Data product unit names are easy to identify because they already exist in the documentation. Unstructured disparate data names are usually short and abbreviated.

Example: EMP_BD and SHIP_DT are unstructured disparate data names.

Semi-structured disparate data names are usually more meaningful.

Example: Employee Birth Date and Shipping Date are semi-structured disparate data names.

Data product unit names are shown exactly as they appear in the data product, such as fully capitalized, underscored, or abbreviated. There is no alteration in their format or spelling.

Example: Data item names in a data file like TYPE, CODE, STATUS, and DATE become data product unit names.

When combined with the data product and data product group names, each data product unit is uniquely named.

Example: Financial Information System: Daily Financial Transaction Report. Status is a unique data product unit name.

Data Product Codes

Each data product code value is uniquely identified within the data product unit. A data product code is uniquely identified by the data product name, the data product group name, the data product unit name, and the data product code value.

Data product codes are uniquely identified by the value, not the name.

Data product codes always have a value and may have definitions without names, names without definitions, or neither name or definition. Many times it is difficult to tell whether a phrase is the name or a definition; therefore, a data product code is identified by the data product code value rather than the data product code name.

Example: Financial status codes N and A are uniquely identified by the data product name, the data product group name, the data product unit name, and the data code value, as in the following:

Financial Information System: Daily Financial Transaction Report. Status 'N'
Financial Information System: Daily Financial Transaction Report. Status 'A'

DATA PRODUCT DEFINITIONS

The task of finding a definition for disparate data can be frustrating and confusing for most people, particularly for unstructured disparate data. Most unstructured disparate data do not have good definitions, if they have any definitions at all. Semi-structured disparate data usually have some data definitions, but they may not be comprehensive. Developing comprehensive data definitions for disparate data is necessary for a thorough understanding of the content and meaning of those data.

Data product definitions seldom exist and are usually developed during data refining. They must comprehensively define a data product and the scope of data included in that data product.

Data product group definitions usually do not exist for unstructured disparate data and may exist for semi-structured disparate data. A good definition of each data product group should be prepared to help people understand what the data product group represents.

Data product item definitions are usually short phrases or single sentences and may be oriented to the entry or purpose of the data.

Data product code definitions are usually names or short phrases, if they exist at all. If a definition exists, it should be retained as stated in the original documentation.

> Data product unit and data product code definitions can be extended as additional information is gained.

Disparate data definitions can be extended based on information gained during data refining. An *extended data product definition* includes the definition as it appears in the original documentation, followed by any additional information gained during data refining. The additional information should contain a date, the name of the person extending the definition, and the source of the extended definition. Because disparate data generally represent specific uses of data, a definition of the use can help identify and define the content and meaning of those data. The extended data definitions may include the use of data to gain more understanding about what the data represent. However, the use of data cannot be included in a comprehensive data definition.

Do not assume that disparate data definitions are complete and accurate. Most disparate data definitions were either developed early in a project and forgotten or developed after the project was completed. Definitions developed early in a project were probably altered during the project, but the documentation was probably not changed. Definitions developed after the project were based on memory, which is poor at best.

DATA PRODUCT STRUCTURE

Ideally, all data go through a formal data modeling process, including data normalization and data denormalization. Most unstructured disparate data, however, never went through a formal data modeling process, and the data keys, data files, and data items are seldom consistent with a common data architecture. Semi-structured disparate data usually went through some type of data modeling process and may be more consistent with a common data architecture.

The physical structure of disparate data is documented with a file relation diagram and a file structure chart. The logical structure of disparate data is documented with an entity relation diagram and an entity structure chart.[5]

File Relation Diagram

A *file relation diagram* is a diagram that shows data files and the data relations between those data files. Two symbols are used to prepare a file relation diagram. An oval represents a data file with the name of the data file inside the oval. A dashed line represents a data relation between data files. The data relation has an arrow on one end representing a one-to-many data relation, the most prominent data relation between data files; a line with no arrows represents a one-to-one data relation. In most cases, there are no many-to-many data relations between data files.

Example: A file relation diagram containing three data files for Employee, Position, and Employee Appointment is shown in Figure 9.2.

---

[5]Disparate data structure is described in more detail in Brackett, 1994.

A file relation diagram shows data files and the relations between those files.

A file relation diagram may or may not exist for disparate data. If a diagram does exist, it may contain any symbols or notations the developer decided to use at that time. There are usually no consistent symbols or notations between file relation diagrams, and often no consistent symbols or notations within a file relation diagram.

File relation diagrams for disparate data can be documented in either their original form using the original symbols and notations, or they can be documented in a modified form using the common data architecture notation and symbols, as described in Chapter 6. If a file relation diagram does not exist, one is prepared using the common data architecture notation and symbols.

File Structure Chart

A *file structure chart* is a listing of the data keys and data items in each data file. It looks similar to a subject structure chart, but it shows data keys rather than primary keys and foreign keys. A *data key* is one or more data items used as access into a data file to store or retrieve data. The data keys are usually named or numbered to match the naming convention required by the database management system where the data files are maintained.

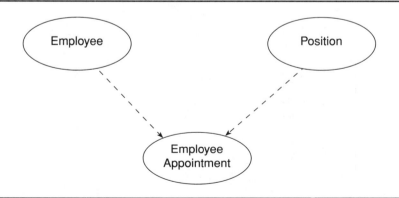

Figure 9.2   File relation diagram for employee data.

Usually no file structure chart exists for unstructured disparate data. The closest documentation is a listing of the data items. There may be some indication of primary keys or foreign keys on the list, but those indications may not truly represent the data file. A file structure chart may exist for semi-structured disparate data. The best approach is to prepare a file structure chart for every data product containing data files. If a data product does not contain data files, a list of the data items is usually sufficient for preparing cross-references to the common data architecture.

Example: The file structure chart for an Employee data file using abbreviated names is shown in Figure 9.3. A file structure chart for an Employee data file using full names is shown in Figure 9.4.

Entity Relation Diagram

An *entity relation diagram* is a diagram that shows data entities and the data relations between those data entities. Two symbols are used to prepare an entity relation diagram. A box with bulging sides, the same symbol that represents a data subject, represents a data entity. A

```
Employee_File

Data Key
    Empl_SSN
    Emp_BD

Data Key
    Dept_File
    Dept_ID

Data Item List
    Empl_SSN
    Emp_BD
    Dept_ID
    Emp_Nam
    Empl_Ht
    Empl_Wt
```

Figure 9.3   File structure chart with abbreviated data names.

```
Employee

      Data Key 1
          Employee Social Security Number

      Data Key 2
          Employee Name Complete Normal
          Employee Birth Date CYMD

      Data Item List
          Employee Birth Date CYMD
          Employee Height Feet
          Employee Name Complete Normal
          Employee Social Security Number
          Employee Weight Pounds
```

Figure 9.4   File structure chart with full data names.

dashed line represents a data relation between data entities. The data relation has an arrow on one end to represent a one-to-many data relation, an arrow on both ends to represent a many-to-many data relation, and no arrows to represent a one-to-one data relation.

An entity relation diagram is prepared for semi-structured disparate data.

An entity relation diagram usually exists for semi-structured disparate data. If a diagram does exist, it may be documented in its original form with the original symbols and notations, or it may be documented in a modified form using the same symbols and notations used for the common data architecture. If a diagram does not exist, one is created using the symbols and notations described above.

Entity Structure Chart

An *entity structure chart* is a listing of the primary keys, foreign keys, secondary keys, and data attributes in each data entity. It looks the same as a subject structure chart, except that it may have secondary keys. An entity structure chart usually exists for semi-structured data.

If one does not exist, it should be prepared to document the logical structure for disparate data.

DATA PRODUCT QUALITY

Most disparate data have incomplete, inconsistent, and highly variable data integrity and data accuracy that are not formally documented. The data integrity and data accuracy for disparate data must be identified and documented to fully understand those data.[6]

Data Product Integrity

Disparate data seldom have formal data value integrity rules. Disparate data frequently have several, often incomplete and conflicting, data domains because data products were developed by different people for different uses. Often a mixture of data rule domains and data value domains exist within a data product. A data rule or data value domain must be identified and documented for each data product unit during data refining.

> The data integrity must be identified and documented to fully understand disparate data.

Disparate data seldom have formal data structure integrity rules, and they often have different and conflicting data structure integrity rules. The data structure integrity rules for disparate data are determined by identifying data relations that exist in disparate data. This process is often difficult because data relations are not readily visible and are usually not documented. Many developers of disparate data did not even attempt to maintain any structural integrity, let alone document it. Data structure integrity must be identified and documented for all disparate data during data refining.

Disparate data often have different data derivation rules. Each data product unit is analyzed to determine whether it is derived. Identifying derived data is relatively easy, but identifying the data derivation algorithm is often difficult. The algorithms may be buried in program code, or they may even be done outside the information system. If a data product unit is derived, a data derivation algorithm must

---

[6]Disparate data integrity is described in more detail in Brackett, 1994.

be identified and documented, including the data characteristics contributing to the derivation.

Disparate data frequently have no data retention rules or may have conflicting data retention rules. Generally, updating and deleting is done without regard for the data needs of other applications or the future need for historical data. Data may be retained by manual procedures or by programs that are unknown or undocumented. Formally documenting data retention rules often leads to a better understanding of how existing data might be retained to support future business activities. Data retention rules must be identified and documented for each data product characteristic during data refining.

Data redundancy is seldom known, let alone consistently maintained, for disparate data. If data redundancy is known and maintained in disparate data, the rules are documented and aggregated the same as derived data algorithms. Most identification of redundant data is done within the common data architecture by reviewing all the data product units contributing to a data characteristic. When redundant data are identified, the primary data source is designated and rules are established for maintaining the redundant versions.

Data Product Accuracy

Data accuracy includes precision, resolution, scale, granularity, significant digits, reliability, source, method of collection, type of equipment used, method of analysis, method of calculation or estimation, adjustments made, person or organization involved, confidence, data instance, and data volatility. Disparate data have widely different degrees of accuracy, although the accuracy is frequently unknown or not readily apparent. The accuracy cannot be changed or improved during data refining. It can only be identified and documented to increase the understanding of the data.

Data accuracy must be identified and documented for all disparate data.

Data accuracy can be documented as a single data characteristic with the accuracy shown in the variation name.

Example: Lake Size Acres Estimated 1:24000 Photo means the size of a lake was estimated from 1:24,000 scale aerial photographs, and Lake Size Acres Surveyed means the size of the lake was surveyed.

A single data characteristic is best when only a few possibilities for different data accuracy exist and all are frequently used.

Example: If there were only three levels of accuracy for the size of a lake and there were usually values for one or two of those data characteristics, three single data characteristics would be used.

Data accuracy can also be documented with companion data characteristics where one data characteristic contains the value and the other data characteristic contains the accuracy.

Example: Lake Size Acres could have companion data characteristics such as Lake Size Accuracy Code or Lake Size Determination Code.

Example: Water Samples have many Water Sample Analyses. Each Water Sample Analysis represents one result, such as nitrogen or chloride, that is designated by a parameter code. The companion data characteristics are Water Sample Analysis Result Value and Water Sample Analysis Measurement Units because the measurement units vary from one type of analysis to another.

Companion data characteristics are acceptable as long as the measurement units for each specific type of analysis are consistent. Alternatively, the measurement units could belong to the parameter; however, this is a data normalization issue, not a data naming issue. Companion data characteristics are best when many possibilities for accuracy exist, but only one exists in any data occurrence.

Example: If 20 different methods of determining the size of a lake existed and only one of those was used, companion data characteristics would be used.

DATA CROSS-REFERENCE

The content, meaning, and format of disparate data are highly variable. The more disparate data that an organization maintains, the greater the variability. Also, the more disperse an organization is, the greater the variability of the data. The greater the variability of disparate data, the more difficult it is to gain control of those data.

The key to gaining control of disparate data is cross-referencing them to the common data architecture. Cross-referencing is the most important task in the entire data refining process. This simple task requires considerable thought and analysis to determine the content and meaning of data before making the cross-reference. Once the cross-reference is made, the other tasks of determining the variability, designating official data variations, and developing translation schemes is relatively easy.[7]

Data Cross-Reference Approach

Cross-referencing disparate data begins by identifying and defining data products, data product entities, data product units, and data product codes. A *data cross-reference* is a link between disparate data names and common data names. The primary cross-reference is between data product units and data characteristic variations. A cross-reference may also be made between data product groups and data subjects and between data product codes and data codes.

> Data cross-references link disparate data to the common data architecture.

Some data cross-references are determined easily and others require considerable searching and analysis to determine their correct counterpart in the common data architecture. The best approach is to make data cross-references as soon as enough information is available to make the cross-reference with reasonable certainty. Generally, 70 to 80 percent of the cross-references are easy to make once the content and meaning of data are determined. Usually, 15 to 20 percent are more difficult to make and require some additional analysis. Five to 10 percent are extremely difficult to make and require considerable investigation to determine their content and meaning. Data cross-referencing is a critical process that requires a thorough understanding of both data products and the common data architecture. It also requires tremendous patience and diligence to make sure appropriate data cross-references are made.

---

[7]Data cross-referencing is described in more detail in Brackett, 1994.

Data Product Group

A *data subject cross-reference* is a data cross-reference between a data product group and a data subject when a one-to-one relationship between the data product group and the data subject exists and all data product units belong to that data subject. Data product groups are usually not cross-referenced to data subjects because they seldom represent single data subjects. This is particularly true with unstructured disparate data. Some semi-structured data product groups represent single data subjects, and a cross-reference can be made. Making a data cross-reference between a data product group and a data subject implies that all data attributes in that data product group belong to the same data subject

---

A data subject cross-reference is made only when a data product group matches a single data subject.

When geographic information systems are cross-referenced to the common data architecture, each database is defined as a data product and each data layer is defined as a data product group.

Example: A geographic information system contains data layers for timber, soil, and roads. These data layers are defined as data product groups and are cross-referenced to Timber Type, Soil Unit, and Road Segment in the common data architecture.

Data product groups may be cross-referenced to true data subjects or data subject types in a data subject hierarchy.

Example: An Employee data file may represent only permanent employees and would be cross-referenced to an Employee subtype for Permanent Employee. Similarly, a data file for Permanent Employees might have been expanded to include all employees. It would be cross-referenced to the Employee data subject.

Data Product Unit

A *data characteristic cross-reference* is a data cross-reference between a data product unit and a data characteristic variation. All data product units are cross-referenced to data characteristic variations during data refining, even if a cross-reference exists between the data product group and corresponding data subject. These data characteristic cross-references show the data characteristic variation that represents each data product unit.

> Every data product unit is cross-referenced to a data characteristic variation during data refining.

Determining a data characteristic cross-reference is based on reasoning, definitions, and knowledge about the data product's attributes. A data product unit definition is reviewed and the common data architecture is searched for an appropriate data characteristic variation. If a match is not found, a new data characteristic variation is defined, and the data cross-reference is made. Data characteristic cross-referencing may take many iterations and many reviews with knowledgeable people to determine the appropriate cross-reference.

A *data characteristic cross-reference list* shows data characteristic cross-references. Data product units are listed on the left exactly as they appear in the data product, including sequence, spelling, capitalization, and punctuation. Headings show data products and subheadings show data product groups. The corresponding data characteristic variations are shown on the right.

Example: A typical data characteristic cross-reference list is shown in Figure 9.5.

Data characteristic cross-references are made to data characteristic variations, not to data characteristics. Because considerable variability exists in disparate data, the cross-references must be made to data characteristic variations to identify that variability. Therefore, each data characteristic in the common data architecture has at least one variation to support cross-references.

> Each data characteristic has at least one variation for cross-references.

Every data product unit has a corresponding data characteristic variation. A data product unit that represents more than one elemental data characteristic is not split during data cross-referencing. A corresponding data characteristic variation is defined and a cross-

Water Right File

    Control Number
        TYPE WATER   Water Resource Category Code
        OLD NEW   Water Right Number Status Code
        ASSIGNED NUMBER   Water Right Number
        STAGE   Water Right Stage Code
        RECORD MODIFIER   Water Right Record Modifier

    AA Transaction
        TRANS CODE   Water Right Transaction Code
        STATUS   Water Right Status Code
        NAME   Water Right Processor Name Variable
        NUMBER OF POD/W   Water Right Removal Site Count
        REPEAT POD/W   Water Right Removal Repeat Count
        LOCATION OF POD/W   Water Right Removal Location Detail
        WRIA   Water Resource Inventory Area Number
        SECTION   Water Right Section Number
        TOWNSHIP   Water Right Tier Number
        RANGE   Water Right Range Number

Figure 9.5   Data characteristic cross-reference list.

reference is made to that data characteristic variation. The data characteristic variation should be labeled *Obsolete* or *Limited*, and the definition should explain the situation and the valid data characteristics variations that should be used. This technique ensures that there is a corresponding data characteristic variation for every data product unit and people understand exactly what every data product unit represents.[8]

A *combined data product unit* contains two or more data characteristics that should not be combined. A corresponding combined data characteristic variation is created and a cross-reference is made to that data characteristic variation. The data characteristic variation is labeled *Obsolete*, and the definition contains references to all the elemental data characteristics.

---

[8]This technique is a change from Brackett, 1994, where data product units representing more than one data characteristic were split during cross-referencing. Splitting data product units during cross-referencing is no longer a valid technique.

Example: An employee's name and birth date are combined into one data product unit. A corresponding data characteristic variation is created for Employee Name Birth Date Combined, and a cross-reference is made to that data characteristic variation. The data characteristic definition explains that the appropriate data characteristics are Employee Name Variable and Employee Birth Date MDY.

An *irregular data product unit* does not have a consistent content or format. Irregular data product units are cross-referenced to an irregular data characteristic variations that have a status of *Obsolete*.

Example: Emp-Nam contains an employee's name in an irregular format and is cross-referenced to Employee Name Irregular, which is labeled *Obsolete*. A data characteristic variation is designated to replace the obsolete data characteristic variation, such as Employee Name Complete Normal, and data are ultimately converted to that data characteristic.

A *variable data product unit* contains different data attributes under different situations. Generally, a record type indicates which specific data product unit exists in a particular field. Data cross-references are usually made using the record type.

Example: A file contains data about computer hardware. Each hardware component does not contain the same data characteristics. Different data product units are placed in same physical fields depending on the record types, and record types are created for computers, controllers, and modems. Record type 1 is a *Computer* record, and Field_1 contains Hardware Computer Channel Count. Similarly, record type 2 is a *Controller* record, and Field_1 contains Hardware Controller Port Count, as shown in Figure 9.6.

A *multiple data product unit* contains several values in the same data product unit. A corresponding data characteristic variation is created, and a cross-reference is made to it. The resolution of multiple values becomes a normalization issue within the common data architecture.

Example: The names of team members involved in taking water samples are listed in Team Member Names. A corresponding data characteristic variation is created for Water Sample Team Member Name Multiple, and the cross-reference is made to that data characteristic variation.

```
┌────────────────────────────────────────────────────────────┐
│                                                              │
│     1      Computer                                          │
│            Field_1          Hardware Computer Channel Count  │
│                                                              │
│     2      Controller                                        │
│            Field_1          Hardware Controller Port Count   │
│                                                              │
│     3      Modem                                             │
│            Field_1          Hardware Modem Baud Rate         │
│                                                              │
└────────────────────────────────────────────────────────────┘
```

Figure 9.6   Variable data characteristic cross-reference.

The data naming taxonomy allows as much detail as necessary to adequately name a data characteristic variation.

Example: An employee's name could be Employee Name Complete Normal for the complete name in the normal sequence, Employee Name Complete Normal 30 for a 30-character length, or Employee Name Complete Normal 30 Left for left justification. Common words, such as *Multiple*, *Variable*, *Combined*, and *Irregular*, can be added for additional detail.

Data cross-references can become very elaborate, particularly when the original documentation is intricate and confusing. Appendix E shows a data cross-reference example involving many layers of nested definitions.

Data Product Code

A *data code cross-reference* is a data cross-reference between a data product code and a data code. Data product codes do not need to be cross-referenced to data codes if the data code values are the same in the data product and the common data architecture. Only the data product unit containing the data codes needs to be cross-referenced to the data characteristic variation representing the data codes. Data product codes must be cross-referenced to data codes if the data code values are different from the data codes.[9]

---

[9]Routine data code cross-referencing is described here. Data code cross-referencing for more complex situations, such as splitting and combining data code sets and data codes, is described in detail in Brackett, 1994.

> Data product codes are cross-referenced to common data codes only if they are different.

A *data code cross-reference list* shows the data code values that correspond to the data product code values. The data product code is listed on the left, followed by the data code value and the data code name.

Example: Vehicle Type Codes represent *Trucks*, *Cars*, *Busses*, and *Motorcycles* as shown in Figure 9.7. The data product unit containing the data codes is cross-referenced to the corresponding data characteristic variation as explained previously.

Usually there is only a data product unit representing the data code value; there is not a data product unit for the data code name. If a data product unit exists for the data code name, it is cross-referenced to a corresponding data characteristic variation.

If a data product unit contains data code names, those names are placed in the data code cross-reference list. This format is used when the data code values are the same and the data code names are different, when the data code names are the same and the data code values are different, or when both data code names and data code values are different.

Example: A cross-reference list for data code values and names is shown in Figure 9.8.

Data Product Code Value	Data Code Value	Data Code Name
1	T	Truck
2	C	Car
3	B	Bus
4	M	Motorcycle

Figure 9.7   Data code cross-reference.

Data Product Code Value	Data Product Code Name	Data Code Value	Data Code Name
1	Truck	A	Truck
2	Auto	B	Car
3	Bus	C	Bus
4	M/C	D	Motorcycle

Figure 9.8   Data code cross-reference with names.

Data Product Inventory

Many organizations do not want to start an active data cross-referencing initiative until they have identified all their existing disparate data. When they know the scope of disparate data, they can identify the critical data and start a cross-referencing initiative. An inventory approach helps an organization determine the scope of its disparate data and helps set priorities for data cross-referencing that will provide an immediate benefit.

> An inventory approach helps set priorities for data cross-referencing.

The data cross-reference techniques described previously support an inventory approach. First, databases are identified and documented as data products, usually through a data resource survey. Then the files are identified and documented as data product groups, beginning with the critical databases, usually through a data resource inventory. Next, the data elements in each data file are identified and documented as data product units, including the data product codes. Finally, the data product units are cross-referenced to the common data architecture based on priorities that will provide the most benefit.

An inventory approach to understanding disparate data is often enlightening and builds enthusiasm for continuing the data refining process. Priorities can be adjusted as the project progresses based on a better understanding of the scope and importance of disparate data. The early results can be used to develop a common data architecture that supports new development projects.

DATA VARIABILITY

When data cross-referencing is completed, data subjects, primary keys, data characteristic variations, and data codes are analyzed to determine the extent of data variability. An understanding of existing data variability helps establish official data variations.[10]

Primary Key Variability

After data cross-referencing, there are often as many as 12 to 15 primary keys. Each of these primary keys is considered a candidate primary key. Each candidate primary key is reviewed to determine its validity as a primary key and its range of uniqueness. The primary keys are then designated as official, alternate, limited, or obsolete as necessary.

Data Subject Variability

Data subject variability usually results from different perspectives of the real world that occurred when data were developed. These different perspectives cannot be discarded or radically changed. They must be incorporated into a common view of the real world so that everyone understands the complete real world and where their business fits into that real world. Data subject variability is best documented on a data subject hierarchy.

> Data subject hierarchies are useful for documenting data subject variability.

Example: A partial data subject hierarchy for Person is shown in Figure 9.9. A Person can be a Health Care Person, an Employment Person, or an Education Person. An Employment Person can be a Retiree, an Employee, or an Employment Candidate. An Employee can be Faculty, a Classified Employee, or an Exempt Employee.

Data Characteristic Variability

Data product units usually have many format and content variations that are represented by the corresponding data characteristic varia-

---

[10]Data variability is described in more detail in Brackett, 1994.

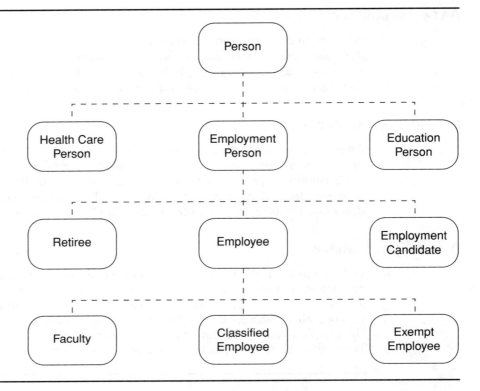

Figure 9.9   Data subject hierarchy for data subject variability.

tions. Data characteristic variations are documented in a *data characteristic variation list* that shows data characteristic variations under their parent data characteristic.

Example: The data characteristic variations for the Person Name data characteristic are Person Name Complete Normal, Person Name Complete Inverted, Person Name Abbreviated Normal, and Person Name Abbreviated Inverted, as shown in Figure 9.10.

Data characteristic length variations are be documented in a *data characteristic length variation list*. The data characteristic variations are listed under their respective data characteristics, and the length variations are listed under the data characteristic variations. The data characteristic variation name is formed by adding the length variation to the end of the data characteristic variation name.

```
Person Name
    Person Name Complete Normal
    Person Name Complete Inverted
    Person Name Abbreviated Normal
    Person Name Abbreviated Inverted
```

Figure 9.10   Data characteristic variation list.

Example: Person Name Complete Normal can be 48, 56, or 60 characters long, as shown in Figure 9.11.

Data Code Value Variability

Disparate data codes also have many data code value and data code name variations. A *data code variation* is the same data property that is represented by more than one data code value.

Example: Sight Disability can have a code of 2 in one database and a code of S in another database.

Each different set of properties is defined as a separate data subject. Each different set of data codes for the same set of properties is defined as a separate data code set represented by a specific data characteristic variation for the data code value.

Example: Disability and Vehicle Type are separate sets of properties and are defined as separate data subjects. Disability School Code and Disability Employment Code or Vehicle Type Motor Pool Code and Vehicle License Type Code are separate data code sets within Disability and Vehicle Type.

```
Data code variations are managed as data code sets.
```

Data code value and name lengths may both vary. These length variations are identified and managed as data characteristic variations.

```
Person Name
    Person Name Complete Normal
        Person Name Complete Normal 48
        Person Name Complete Normal 55
        Person Name Complete Normal 60
    Person Name Complete Inverted
        Person Name Complete Inverted 48
        Person Name Complete Inverted 55
    Person Name Abbreviated Normal
        Person Name Abbreviated Normal 30
        Person Name Abbreviated Normal 20
    Person Name Abbreviated Inverted
        Person Name Abbreviated Inverted 26
```

Figure 9.11   Data characteristic length variation list.

Example: The Vehicle Type Code License data subject is found in two different information systems. One system uses two-digit codes, and one system uses one-digit codes. The data characteristic variations names are Vehicle Type License Code 1 and Vehicle Type License Code 2. Similarly, the code names are different lengths and are defined as Vehicle Type License Name 20 and Vehicle Type License Name 16.

A *data code matrix* contains all the data code sets for one set of data properties. It identifies the variability between the data code values and data code names for a data code set. The names of the data code sets are listed across the top of the matrix, and the individual data code values and names are listed under their respective data code sets.

Example: Different data code sets for disability are shown in Figure 9.12. The data subject is Disability, and the data code sets are Disability School, Disability Employment, and Disability Health.

A data code matrix is built by aggregating all the data product codes according to their corresponding data characteristic variations.

Example: In the preceding example, six data characteristic variations represent three different sets of data product codes: Disability School

Disability School		Disability Employment		Disability Health	
10	Sight	A	Seeing	V	Vision
20	Hearing	H	Hear	S	Sound
30	Physical	P	Physical	A	Accidental
40	Developmental	D	Developed	G	Genetic

Figure 9.12　　Data code matrix for disability.

Code and Disability School Name, Disability Employment Code and Disability Employment Name, and Disability Health Code and Disability Health Name.

A data code matrix can also have one set of data code names and several sets of data code values. The property name is listed on the left and the data code values for each data code set are listed on the right.

Example: Disability codes with only one property name and several sets of data codes are shown in Figure 9.13.

OFFICIAL DATA VARIATIONS

When the extent of data variability is determined, official data variations are designated to support short-term data sharing and long-term development of an integrated data resource. An *official data variation* is a data variation that has been accepted by the consensus of knowledgeable people for short-term data sharing and long-term development of an integrated data resource. A *nonofficial data variation* is a data variation that was not designated as an official data variation.

> Identifying official data variations resolves the data variability in disparate data.

Official data variations are designated by the consensus of a team of knowledgeable people. The frequency of existence, frequency of use, data definitions, formats, and desires of the organization for an integrated data resource are all considered, and an appropriate data vari-

Property	School	Employment	Health
Sight	10	A	V
Hearing	20	H	S
Physical	30	P	A
Developmental	40	D	G

Figure 9.13   Data code matrix with one set of data code names.

ation is designated as the official data variation. The official data variations hold their status and the nonofficial data variations become *Limited* or *Obsolete* so they are no longer perpetuated.[11]

Official Primary Key

Each primary key identified in the disparate data becomes a candidate primary key in the common data architecture. Each candidate primary key is reviewed to determine its validity and range of uniqueness. Official primary keys are designated based on their validity and uniqueness within the scope of the common data architecture. An *official primary key* is a primary key that has been designated as official by the consensus of knowledgeable people.

> An official primary key is designated for each data subject.

Both business and physical primary keys are designated from the official primary keys. Limited primary keys are designated if they are valid for a limited range of uniqueness. Obsolete primary keys are designated if they are no longer valid or useful. All other candidate primary keys become alternate primary keys.

Official Data Characteristic Variations

When the range of data characteristic variability is determined, official data characteristic variations are designated. An *official data characteristic variation* is a data characteristic variation that has been designated by a consensus of knowledgeable people. All data characteristic

---

[11]Designation of official data variations is explained in detail in Brackett, 1994.

variations are reviewed for each data characteristic, and an official data characteristic is designated. If an existing variation is not acceptable as the official data characteristic variation, a new data characteristic variation is defined and designated as the official data variation. An official data characteristic variation is indicated with an asterisk (*) in front of the data characteristic variation name.

Example: Four employee birth dates were identified during data cross-referencing, as shown in Figure 9.14. After reviewing the variations and considering the approach of a new century, Employee Birth Date CYMD was designated the official data characteristic variation. It is identified with an asterisk and is placed at the top of the data characteristic variation list. The other data characteristic variations become nonofficial variations.

An *official data derivation algorithm* is a data derivation algorithm documenting the derivation of a data characteristic that has been designated as official by a consensus of knowledgeable people. After data cross-referencing is completed, the disparate data derivation algorithms are aggregated to their respective data characteristic variations. When an official data characteristic variation is designated, the data derivation algorithms for all the data characteristic variations within the parent data characteristic are reviewed, discrepancies are resolved, and an official data derivation algorithm is designated.

An *official data retention rule* is a data retention rule that has been designated as official by a consensus of knowledgeable people. After data cross-referencing is completed, the data retention rules are aggregated to the data characteristic variations. When official data characteristic variations are designated, the data retention rules for all the data characteristic variations within the parent data characteristic

---

```
Employee Birth Date
   *Employee Birth Date CYMD
   Employee Birth Date YMD
   Employee Birth Date MDY
   Employee Birth Date DMY
```

Figure 9.14   Official data characteristic variation designation.

are reviewed, and an official data retention rule is designated or developed.

After data cross-referencing is completed, the data accuracy is reviewed for each data characteristic to determine the existing level of data accuracy. The desired level of data accuracy is established based on the organization's desires and the existing level of data accuracy. It may be desirable to aggregate several data characteristic variations from different data product units into companion data characteristics. This approach puts several different levels of data accuracy into two data characteristics. The original data characteristics are abandoned, and the data product units are cross-referenced to the paired common data characteristics, as shown previously.

Official Data Domains

An *official data domain* is a data domain in the common data architecture that has been designated as official by a consensus of knowledgeable people for maintaining data quality. After the official data characteristic variations are designated, the data domains for each nonofficial data characteristic variation are reviewed and compared. The discrepancies are resolved by consensus to provide an official data domain. Enhancements identified in the official data domain may be applied to existing data product characteristics to improve their integrity.

Official Data Codes

After the data code variations are identified and documented, one data code set in each data subject is designated as official. An *official data code set* is a set of data codes that has been designated as official by a consensus of knowledgeable people. If an existing data code set is not acceptable, a new data code set is defined and designated as the official set. All other data code sets become nonofficial.

> One official set of data codes must be designated for the integrated data resource.

Example: The data code sets listed previously for disability are reviewed. The Disability School Name is designated official, and Disability Employment Code is designated official, as shown in Figure 9.15. The data characteristic variations representing the official data code values and data code names are identified with an asterisk.

DATA TRANSLATION SCHEMES

When official data variations are designated, data translation schemes are developed. A *data translation scheme* is a translation between data characteristic variations when those data characteristic variations represent measurements or format variations. Data translation schemes are not the same as data derivation algorithms that create data characteristic values from contributing data characteristics.

Data translation schemes are usually developed between official and nonofficial data characteristic variations; however, they may be developed between nonofficial data characteristic variations if the need arises. Data translation schemes are developed by a consensus of people knowledgeable about the different data characteristics and data codes.

Data Characteristic Translation

A *data characteristic translation scheme* translates data values between variations of the same data characteristics. Data characteristic translation schemes are developed only for format and value variations, not for meaning, content, or accuracy variations.

Example: A data translation scheme is developed between Well Depth Estimated Feet and Well Depth Estimated Yards. A data translation scheme cannot be developed between Well Depth Estimated Meters and Well Depth Measured Feet because a different accuracy is involved.

Disability School Name	Disability Employment Code
Sight	A
Hearing	H
Physical	P
Developmental	D

Figure 9.15 Official data code set designation.

> Data characteristic translation schemes are developed only for format and value variations, not for accuracy or meaning variations.

   Two translation schemes are created between data characteristics because translation usually occurs both directions.

Example: Four birth dates for employees are listed in Figure 9.14. Employee Birth Date CYMD is designated as the official data characteristic variation. Data translation schemes are developed both directions between Employee Birth Date CYMD and Employee Birth Date YMD, between Employee Birth Date CYMD and Employee Birth Date MDY, and between Employee Birth Date CYMD and Employee Birth Date DMY, resulting in six data translation schemes.

> Translation schemes are developed both ways between data characteristic variations.

   Data characteristic translation schemes can be simple, such as the translation between units of measurement.

Example: The translation between feet and yards.

   Data characteristic translation schemes can also be more complex.

Example: Translation of a person's name from Person Name Complete Normal to Person Name Complete Inverted involves a set of instructions to parse and rearrange the name components.

   Data translation schemes between data characteristic length variations are relatively simple. If a shorter data characteristic variation is translated to a longer data characteristic variation, the data values are moved and aligned right or left as necessary. If a longer data characteristic variation is translated to a shorter data characteristic variation, the values may be too long. Additional criteria must be supplied, such as truncation right or left, to handle data values too long for the receiving data characteristic variation. Justification translations, such as right- and left-justified, are easy to define.

Data translation schemes can also be complex for variable and irregular data characteristics. Additional information is usually required to make these data translations, and knowledgeable people are usually required to review the data values and make the determinations. Expert systems may be able to provide some assistance with variable or irregular data translations.

Example: The translation between Person Name Irregular and Person Name Complete Normal is complex.

Data translation schemes between a combined data characteristic and elemental data characteristics are relatively easy.

Example: Translation between the Person Name Complete Normal, and Person Name First, Person Name Middle, and Person Name Family requires parsing and movement. Translation from the elements to the combined is a simple concatenation.

Data Code Translation

A *data code translation scheme* translates data between data code sets. Data code translation schemes, like data characteristic translation schemes, can be simple where a one-to-one relation between data values exists.

Example: The data translation scheme for disability codes is the table shown in Figure 9.13. No additional translation schemes are necessary.

Data code translations may combine many disparate codes into one official code. These many-to-one data code translation schemes are also easy to define; however, a reverse translation is impossible without additional information.

Example: There are many detailed data product codes for the termination of an employee's employment. These data codes are combined into fewer data codes, as shown in Figure 9.16. Translation from the left to the right is easy, but translation from the right to the left is impossible without additional information.

Employee Termination Code A	Employee Termination Code B
10 through 13	1
14	3
21 through 23	3
40 through 44	2
45	3
46 through 47	2

Figure 9.16   Data code value translation scheme.

DISPARATE DATA INTEGRATION

The final phase of data refining is to physically integrate disparate data into an integrated data resource. Physical integration reduces the redundancy and variability inherent in disparate data. The resulting data resource is more usable because the data are more accurate, more easily maintained, and quicker to identify and access.

> Disparate data integration reduces data redundancy and data variability.

The approach is to establish a scope for data integration, identify existing data redundancy and data variability with that scope, designate official data sources, and physically integrate the data according to those official designations. Designating official data sources reduces data redundancy, and designating official data characteristic variations reduces data variability. The steps are explained in the following sections.[12]

Integration Scope

The first step for integrating disparate data is to identify the data subjects involved in physical integration. An organization usually starts with data that are critical to the operation of the business and progress

---

[12]The physical integration of data is explained in detail in both Brackett, 1990 and Brackett, 1994.

to data that are less critical. Some disparate data will never be cross-referenced and integrated because they are essentially unusable and have no historical value. There is no reason to expend any effort cross-referencing and integrating these data.

Example: If the scope of physical integration is employee data, the data subjects related to employees are identified, such as Employee Position and Employee Appointment. The data products containing data related to those data subjects are identified, such as payroll files, affirmative action files, and training files.

Official Data Source

The next step is to designate the official data sources for the values of each data characteristic. An *official data source* is the data product unit designated as the source for extracting data values to populate the integrated database. An *official data source table* is prepared showing all the data product units corresponding to each data characteristic within the data integration scope. It is a table of redundant data product units used for designating the official data value source. The official data value source is indicated with a pound sign (#) in front of the data product unit name.

Example: A partial official data source table for the employee data integration is shown in Figure 9.17. The data product units for the data products within the data integration scope are listed for each data subject and data characteristic within the data integration scope. The official data value sources are PYRL.EMPL_NM for the Employee Name and AA.EMP_BIRTH for the Employee Birth Date.

Note that there may not be one data site that is the official data source for all data characteristics. The official data sources may come from many different data sites, as shown in Figure 9.17.

Official Data Variation

The third step identifies official data characteristic variations. An *official data characteristic* variation table is prepared showing official data characteristic variations. Data characteristics are listed within their parent data subjects, and the data characteristic variations are listed

```
Employee
    Employee Name
        # PYRL.EMPL_NM
          AA.EMP_NAME
          TRAIN.EMPLYE_NAME
    Employee Birth Date
          PYRL.EMPL_BD
        # AA.EMP_BIRTH
          TRAIN.EMPLYE_BDATE
```

Figure 9.17   Official data source table.

within their parent data characteristics. The official data characteristic variation is indicated with an asterisk (*) in front of the data characteristic variation name.

Example: A partial official data characteristic variation table for the employee data integration is shown in Figure 9.18. The official data characteristic variations are Employee Name Complete Normal and Employee Birth Date CYMD.

Integration Table

The fourth step prepares an *official data integration table* from the official data value source table and the official data characteristic variation table. The nonofficial data product units are removed from the data characteristic source table, and two columns are added for the source data characteristic variation representing the source data product units and the target official data characteristic variation. If these two data characteristic variations are different, a data translation is required.

Example: The two tables shown in Figures 9.17 and 9.18 are combined, as shown in Figure 9.19. Both the employee's name and birth date need to be translated to the proper data characteristic variation during data integration.

```
Employee
    Employee Name
        *Employee Name Complete Normal
        Employee Name Complete Inverted
    Employee Birth Date
        *Employee Birth Date CYMD
        Employee Birth Date YMD
        Employee Birth Date MDY
```

Figure 9.18   Official data characteristic variation table.

Physical Integration

The fifth and last step for integrating disparate data is to perform the physical data integration based on the official data integration table. Data values are extracted from the official data value source, translated if necessary, and placed in the integrated data resource. The primary keys for each data file are used to access the existing database, and the official primary key is used in the integrated data resource.

One difficulty is identifying data records in different disparate databases that represent the same data occurrence. Listing the primary key attributes in the official data value source table, official data characteristic variation table, and official data integration table usually resolves the difficulty.

Data Product Unit	Source Data Characteristic Variation	Target Data Characteristic Variation
Employee		
Employee Name		
# PYRL.EMPL_NM	Employee Name Complete Variable	* Employee Name Complete Normal
Employee Birth Date		
# AA.EMP_BIRTH	Employee Birth Date YMD	* Employee Birth Date CYMD

Figure 9.19   Official data integration table.

SUMMARY

The only way to thoroughly understand and properly manage disparate data is to cross-reference them to the common data architecture. Data refining is the process for cross-referencing disparate data to the common data architecture to increase the awareness and understanding and to remove variability and redundancy. Data refining is a semantic, nondestructive, no-impact process that does not change the data or affect the day-to-day operation of information systems.

Disparate data are defined as a hierarchy of data products, data product groups, data product units, and data product codes in preparation for data refining. Traditional databases and data files are usually considered unstructured disparate data, and project or information system data models are usually considered semi-structured disparate data. The data site, data subject, and data characteristic components of the data naming taxonomy are used to uniquely name the data products. Both original and extended data definitions are maintained for data products.

The physical structure of unstructured disparate data is documented with file relation diagrams that show data files and the relations between them and with file structure charts that show data keys and data items for each data file. The logical structure of semi-structured disparate data is documented with entity relation diagrams that show data entities and the relations between them, and with entity structure charts that show primary keys, foreign keys, secondary keys, and data attributes for each data entity. Data integrity, data accuracy, and data redundancy are also documented for all data products.

Data cross-referencing is the connection between disparate data and the common data architecture. The primary cross-reference is between data product units and data characteristic variations. Cross-references can be made between data product groups and data subjects if the data product group represents one data subject. Cross-references can also be made between data product codes and data codes if the data code values are not identical. Every data product unit is cross-referenced to a corresponding data characteristic variation. All multiple, irregular, variable, and combined data product units are resolved within the common data architecture.

When data cross-referencing is completed, the variability for primary keys, data subjects, data characteristics, and data codes is evaluated. Official primary keys, data characteristic variations, and data code sets are designated. Official data integrity and data accuracy are established. Data translation schemes are developed between data characteristic variations and data code sets. Finally, official data sources are designated in preparation for the physical integration of disparate data.

Data refining is one phase of the overall process of integrating all data within the common data architecture. It is a major phase of data integration that resolves the redundancy and variability of existing data and starts development of an integrated data resource that can be fully utilized to meet the business information demand.

QUESTIONS

The following questions are provided as a review of the chapter and to stimulate thought about integrating disparate data into an integrated data resource with the data refining process.

1. What is the data refining process?
2. Why is the data refining process a semantic process?
3. Why is a hierarchy of data products important for cross-referencing disparate data?
4. What is the difference between unstructured and semi-structured disparate data?
5. How is the data naming taxonomy used to uniquely identify all disparate data?
6. How are disparate data definitions extended?
7. How is the structure of unstructured disparate data documented?
8. How is the structure of semi-structured disparate data documented?
9. How are data product integrity and data product accuracy documented?
10. What is the purpose of a data cross-reference?
11. What is the primary type of data cross-reference?
12. When are data product entities cross-referenced to data subjects?
13. When are data product codes cross-referenced to data codes?
14. How is data subject variability documented?
15. How is data characteristic variability documented?
16. How is data code variability documented?
17. What are official data variations?
18. How are official primary keys designated?
19. How are official data characteristic variations designated?
20. How are official data codes designated?
21. What are data characteristic translation schemes?
22. What are data code translation schemes?
23. What are official data sources?
24. How does data refining support the integration of data within the common data architecture?

Evaluational Data

The data in data warehouse systems cannot be allowed to become as disparate as the existing tabular data are today.

Data warehouse systems are becoming prominent in many organizations for storing historical data to analyze trends and make projections regarding business alternatives. Considerable information is available for evaluating the need for a data warehouse system, prioritizing development of a data warehouse system, managing data warehouse system projects, and so forth. Not much information is available on developing a data warehouse system within a common data architecture, transforming disparate data into a data warehouse system, or managing the levels of summarized data within the data warehouse system.

An otherwise successful data warehouse system project can fail from improper transformation of the data going into a data warehouse system or the improper summarization of data within a data warehouse system. Organizations must learn how to develop a data warehouse system within a common data architecture through a formal data transformation process and to properly summarize the data in the data warehouse system to ensure that those data accurately represent the business.

Chapter 10 explains the management of data within a data warehouse system.[1] It begins with the concept of how a data warehouse system supports comprehensive business analysis. A new perspective for

---

[1]Chapter 11 explains the transformation of data into the data warehouse system.

managing the evaluational data in a data warehouse system within a common data architecture is explained, including the description, structure, and integrity of evaluational data. The chapter concludes with an explanation of evaluational data management.

DATA WAREHOUSE SYSTEM CONCEPT

Many organizations have been in existence for some time and have accumulated considerable quantities of data that could be useful for business planning. Historical trends and future projections could be used to analyze business alternatives and make more informed decisions that could gain or maintain a competitive advantage. The sad news is that the wealth of information that exists in disparate databases is not being tapped and used to the benefit of the organization. Organizations are missing a golden opportunity to analyze and understand their business.

Decision Support

Business executives and managers need a broader understanding of their business and the dynamic business environment. They need to anticipate change and respond quickly to changes in the business environment to remain competitive. Business executives and managers must analyze business patterns and trends, evaluate alternative courses of action, ask what-if questions, and use the results to seize opportunities. It is extremely important for business executives and mangers to have the decision support they need to keep their organization on the leading edge.

Good support for more informed decisions is the key to remaining competitive.

Decision support includes any tools or products that support more informed decision making, such as executive information systems (EIS), decision support systems (DSS), and on-line analytical processing capability (OLAP). These tools provide a higher level of business intelligence through analyzing historical data, evaluating future trends, setting goals, and measuring performance, identifying variances, allocating resources, and adapting to unanticipated events. They provide a capability to discover and harvest additional information and insights from the masses of detailed operational data that are available or are discarded prematurely.

Good decision support requires an integrated, stable, well-managed data resource. It requires determining what data are needed, extracting and refining those data from disparate databases, loading them into a data warehouse system, and properly managing them within the data warehouse system. It requires the ability to rapidly access and analyze large quantities of historical data without compromising the performance, integrity, or security of operational systems. It also requires the ability to properly integrate and manage both detailed data that support daily business transactions and summary data that support extensive business analysis.

Data Resource Support

The major problem with developing a data warehouse system and providing good decision support to an organization is disparate data. The data are often so disparate that even if they were thoroughly understood, it would be difficult to integrate them into a data warehouse system. The effort involved in thoroughly understanding and integrating disparate data is so overwhelming that many organizations do not even attempt to implement a data warehouse system or implement one improperly.

Good decision support cannot be based on disparate operational data. Disparate operational data cannot be loaded directly into a data warehouse system with any hope of providing adequate decision support. Successful decision support requires a stable, complete, accurate data resource. An organization must gain control of its disparate operational data before any type of successful decision support can be considered.

> Good decision support cannot be based on disparate data.

A second major problem providing good decision support is the inability of most organizations to properly develop and manage level upon level of summary data. They rely on products to summarize data and to drill down to more detailed data without understanding the basic concepts of data summarization. In addition, many data modelers propose managing only the primitive data because they believe derived data will take care themselves if the primitive data are properly managed. This is not true! Failure to properly design and manage summary data is the primary cause of the high failure rate of decision support systems.

> Summary data must be properly managed to provide good decision support.

A third problem providing good decision support is that data are often discarded after their operational usefulness is over. Their historical value is not recognized and there is little concern over any potential use for evaluating the business. Decision makers are often unaware that valuable operational data exist and could be used for business analysis. Organizations must develop and maintain good metadata to be aware of the historical value of operational data so they can be saved for decision support.

> Organizations must stop the development of disparate data by properly managing decision support data.

A fourth problem organizations face is providing enhanced decision support capability. Traditional decision support data are tabular; however, the amount of nontabular data, such as the data in geographic information systems, imaging and remote sensing systems, and text information management systems, is increasing. These nontabular data could be valuable for the analysis of trends, projections, and alternatives that may far exceed the decision support benefits of tabular data. Both tabular data and nontabular data that have significance for decision support must be properly integrated into a data warehouse system to provide the next level of decision support.

Data Warehouse System Definition

Data warehouse systems are a prominent industry trend that provides organizations the capability to analyze business patterns, trends, and alternatives. The term, however, has become a catchall phrase and is beginning to lose its meaning. It is rapidly becoming the latest silver bullet for solving all the disparate data problems. A *data warehouse system*, as defined by W. H. Inmon is a subject-oriented, integrated, time-variant, nonvolatile collection of data in support of management's decision making process.[2]

A data warehouse system is a repository of consistent historical

---

[2]W. H. Inmon, 1994.

data that can be easily accessed and manipulated for decision support. It will support the next generation of executive information systems, decision support systems, and on-line analytical processing that help organizations become more competitive. It can also support the refining of disparate operational data and business process redesign initiatives. The application and potential payback of a data warehouse system is limited only by people's imagination if the data are properly managed.

> Data warehouse systems support enhanced data visualization and decision support.

A data warehouse system provides enhanced capabilities for data visualization. *Data visualization* is the process of creating and presenting a chart from a set of data based on a set of attributes. It deals with understanding patterns, trends, and relationships in historical data and providing visual information to the decision maker. Data visualization provides a way to sift through huge volumes of data to find meaning, conclusions, and results. It exploits the human capability to analyze and understand historical data and evaluate alternatives for an organization to remain competitive.

A good data warehouse system has both hard data and soft data. *Hard data* are the historical facts and figures about operating the business. *Soft data* are the opinions, comments, explanations, observations, and evaluations about the business. Soft data enhance the value of the hard data and support more informed decisions.

The real danger with a data warehouse system is brute-force physical development and extensive uncoordinated summarization and analysis of historical data. The availability of powerful, client-friendly data warehouse system products encourages the bulk loading of disparate operational data and random, undocumented data analysis. A data warehouse system provides the capability to analyze large quantities of data, but it does not address the issue of the difficulty of integrating disparate operational data. The result is another level of disparate data for organizations to manage and possible disastrous business decisions.

Dual Database Concept

Operational processing, also known as *on-line transaction processing* (OLTP), is appropriate for supporting the daily business operations, but is inappropriate for decision support. Decision support processing, also known as *on-line analytical processing* (OLAP), is appropriate for supporting the analysis of business trends and projections, but is inappropriate for daily business transactions. It requires a formality that conflicts with on-line transaction processing. A single copy of data will not work for both formalities.

> A dual database resolves the formality conflicts between operational and decision support processing.

The diagram in Figure 10.1 summarizes the different formalities between operational processing and decision support processing. W. H. Inmon's latest books adequately explain the differences between operational and decision support processing.[3]

A *dual database concept* consisting of an operational database and an decision support database resolves the conflict between the two formalities. An *operational database* contains current, detailed data to support on-line transaction processing, and a *decision support database* contains historical and summary data to support on-line analytical processing. The dual database concept eliminates the storage of large quantities of summary data in operational databases, which double in size about every two years. It also eliminates the chance of analytical processing affecting the integrity of operational data. The dual database concept eliminates the performance degradation of operational databases resulting from extensive data analysis.

A NEW PERSPECTIVE

Proper management of the two data formalities requires an enhanced perspective of data management. It requires a perspective that separates the operational data from the decision support data and properly manages both types of data to support their respective business needs. It also requires a perspective that ensures both data formalities are managed within the common data architecture.

Evaluational Data

The new perspective for managing the two data formalities begins by looking at the two basic things an organization does with their data. Organizations use data to operate the business and they use data to

---

[3]W. H. Inmon, 1990 and 1994.

	Operational	Decision Support
Volatility	Dynamic	Static
Currentness	Current	Historical
Instance	Single time	Time variant
Granularity	Primitive and detailed	Derived and summary
Updates	Continuous, random	Scheduled, periodic
Structure	Static	Dynamic
Normalization	Highly normalized	Moderately normalized
Indexes	Minimum indexes	Maximum indexes
Flexibility	Low, repetitive	High, heuristic
Performance	High, quick response	Low, long response

Figure 10.1   Differences between operational and decision support processing.

evaluate the business. The data that support these two basic functions are termed operational data and evaluational data.

> Organizations use data to operate the business and evaluate the business.

Operational data are data used in the operational processing of business transactions that support day-to-day business operations. They are detailed, largely primitive data necessary to keep the organization operating. An *operational database* contains operational data.

Evaluational data are data used in decision support processing to evaluate trends, projections, and alternatives. They include any data necessary to evaluate the current status, trends, and patterns about an organization's business and make projections to analyze future alternatives. They may include both tabular and nontabular data. Evaluational data are usually derived from the operational data and contain many levels of summarization above the operational data. An *evaluational database* contains evaluational data.

Several other terms could be used instead of evaluational, such as corporate, strategic, organizational, institutional, analytical, transformational, directional, planning, enterprise, archival, historical, investigational, warehouse, and informational. None of these terms, however, is as meaningful as evaluational. The term *informational* is particularly inappropriate because the evaluational data are still data until they form a message that is relevant to a person at a point in time, the same as operational data. The term *information warehouse* is equally inappropriate because information is not stored; only data are stored. The term *evaluational* represents how the data are used similar to the way *operational* represents how those data are used.

Data Architecture

The common data architecture is independent of the product where the data are stored, as shown in Figure 10.2. Generally, operational data exist in database management systems and support on-line transaction processing, and evaluational data exist in data warehouse systems and support on-line analytical processing. Some evaluational data, however, may exist in database management systems and some operational data may exist in data warehouse systems. Therefore, the type of data being stored is independent of the product storing the data.

Buy a data warehouse system; build an evaluational database.

The separation of the common data architecture from the products where data are stored and maintained leads to a basic principle regarding data warehouse systems. An organization builds an evaluational database, which may reside on any platform. The organization may buy a data warehouse system product for storing and maintaining a evaluational data and performing on-line analytical processing. An organization does not build a data warehouse system.

	Database Management System	Data Warehouse System
Operational Data	Predominant	Minimal
Evaluational Data	Minimal	Predominant

Figure 10.2   Data architecture and data storage independence.

> Evaluational data are managed within the common data architecture.

Evaluational data must be designed, developed, and managed within a common data architecture so that disparate operational data can be understood and properly integrated into the evaluational database. There may be separate evaluational databases, and an evaluational database may be distributed over a network, but evaluational data are still built within the common data architecture. Evaluational data do not belong to a different data architecture. An enhanced notation is necessary to model and manage the complexity of evaluational data, but that notation is part of the common data architecture. It is not a separate architecture!

Data Dimensions

A *data dimension* is a representation of a single set of objects or events in the real world, such as Employee, Customer, Vehicle, Product, and Building. A *single dimension data subject* is a data subject that represents one data dimension.

Example: Employee, Position, and Employee Appointment are single dimension data subjects.

On-line transaction processing is *single dimension processing* that uses single dimension data subjects in an operational database. It is also referred to as *dynamic data analysis* because the data values are constantly changing to reflect changes in the real world.

A *multiple dimension data subject* is a data subject that represents two or more dimensions.

Example: Product Order, which represents Product Items, Customers, Sales Personnel, Sales Regions, and Dates, is a multiple dimension data subject.

> Multiple dimension processing requires multiple dimension data subjects.

On-line analytical processing for decision support is *multiple dimension processing*, also known as *multiple dimension analysis*, that uses a combination of single dimension and multiple dimension data subjects. It is also referred to as *static data analysis* because the data values do not change. Multiple dimension processing allows simultaneous analysis of multiple data dimensions through a slice-and-dice process that could support a business analyst's wildest dreams.

Evaluational Data Perspective

Evaluational data contain a combination of single dimension and multiple dimension data subjects that support multiple dimension processing. A *data perspective* is a set of related data subjects in the evaluational database consisting of a central multiple dimension data subject surrounded by several single dimension data subjects that qualify the central data subject. The central multiple dimension data subject is the *data focus*, also known as the *fact table*. The surrounding single dimension data subjects are known as *qualifying data subjects*. At least one of those qualifying data subjects must represent time.[4]

Example: A data perspective for motor pool vehicles contains a multiple dimension data focus for Vehicle Trip and qualifying single dimension data subjects for Department, Employee, Vehicle, Destination, and Day, as shown in Figure 10.3.

An evaluational database usually has only one data focus for a data perspective, but several may exist depending on the complexity of the data. There are usually eight or ten qualifying data subjects in each data perspective, but there may be more depending on the number of dimensions being analyzed. An evaluational database can also have more than one data perspective depending on the extent of the business analysis. A massive multiple dimension database may have dozens of perspectives and hundreds of dimensions that may require massively parallel computers for extensive analysis.

EVALUATIONAL DATA DESCRIPTION

Formal data names and comprehensive data definitions are absolutely essential for the proper management of evaluational data. They pro-

---

[4]Appendix F shows an example of an evaluational data model.

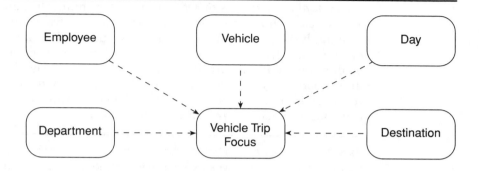

Figure 10.3 Data perspective for vehicle trips.

vide unique identification and complete information about the existence, meaning, and location of evaluational data. They also describe the transformation of disparate operational data to evaluational data and the summarization of evaluational data.

Data Subjects

Evaluational data are defined and managed as data subjects, the same as operational data. The qualifying data subjects are the same single dimension data subjects that appear in an operational database.

> Evaluational data are managed as data subjects like operational data.

A *focus data subject* is the central multiple dimension data subject that is developed during the transformation of operational data to evaluational data.[5] It contains the most detailed nonvolatile data in the evaluational database and forms the *primitive evaluational data* from which other evaluational data are derived. It is the lowest level for *drilling down*.

Example: Vehicle Trip Focus, shown in Figure 10.3, is a focus data subject containing primitive evaluational data.

---

[5]Chapter 11 describes data transformation.

A *summary data subject* is the central multiple dimension data subject containing the summary data resulting from multiple dimension analysis. It contains the derived evaluational data that are developed from either the primitive evaluational data or other derived evaluational data during multiple dimension analysis. When multiple dimension analysis is performed on the focus data subject, the results in stored in a summary data subject. The data values are volatile and can change whenever the data are rederived.

Example: The data in Vehicle Trip Focus, shown in Figure 10.3, could be summarized for Employee by Vehicle by Employee by Destination by Day or for Vehicle by Department by Day. Each of these summarizations forms a different summary data subject.

Data Subject Names

Focus data subjects are named the same as their corresponding data subjects in the operational database, suffixed with the common word *Focus*. The data in the focus data subject are basically the same as those in the corresponding operational data subject, but they may be lightly summarized or may be normalized differently.[6]

Example: The Vehicle Trip Focus, shown in Figure 10.3, is developed from its counterpart, Vehicle Trip, in the operational database.

> Evaluational data subjects are uniquely named with the data naming taxonomy.

Summary data subjects are named the same as the focus data subjects from which the data were derived, except the suffix is changed from the common word *Focus* to the common word *Summary*.

Example: Data resulting from the multiple dimension analysis of Vehicle Trip Focus would be stored in Vehicle Trip Summary.

[6]Chapter 11 explains the different normalization for focus data subjects.

Because many different analyses can be performed on the same focus data subject, resulting in many different summary data subjects, the summary data subject becomes a *summary data subject set*. The specific summary data subjects developed within that set are further qualified with a number. The numbers are usually assigned sequentially from one as new data are developed.

Example: Vehicle Trip Summary becomes a summary data subject set. Data summarized from Vehicle Trip Focus for Employee by Vehicle by Employee by Destination by Day would be named Vehicle Trip Summary 1, and data summarized for Vehicle by Department by Day would be named Vehicle Trip Summary 2.

Summary data subject names must be specific enough to provide full understanding.

Example: Vehicle Trip Summary 1 should be used rather than just Trip Summary because there could be a variety of different types of trips within an organization.

Summary data subject names, however, should not try to include all the qualifying data subjects involved in the analysis. The summary data subject set name with numerical qualifiers is better. A comprehensive definition explains the analysis process.

Example: Vehicle Trip Destination Employee Department Day is too long and makes it difficult to identify the summary data subject set. Vehicle Trip Summary 1 and Vehicle Trip Summary 2 are better names.

Data Characteristic Names

The data characteristics in summary data subjects are prefixed with the data subject set name. This technique provides maximum meaning and minimizes the effort to prepare and maintain comprehensive data characteristic definitions. The same data characteristic can appear in many specific summary data subjects within the same summary data subject shell.

Example: All data characteristics the Vehicle Trip Summary data subject set are prefixed with Vehicle Trip Summary, not with Vehicle Trip Summary 1, Vehicle Trip Summary 2, and so on.

The specific data characteristic name uniquely identifies the content and meaning of that data characteristic.

Example: The summary data characteristics in Vehicle Trip Summary might be Vehicle Trip Summary Total Miles, Vehicle Trip Summary Net Miles, Vehicle Trip Summary Total Passengers, and Vehicle Trip Summary Average Passengers.

Not all summary data characteristics exist in every summary data subject within a summary data subject set. A *data characteristic matrix* is prepared for each summary data subject set to identify which data characteristics are valid for each summary data subject. The summary data subjects are listed in alphabetical sequence on the left side of the matrix and the data characteristics are listed alphabetically across the top of the matrix. The cells are checked if the data characteristic is valid for a summary data subject.[7]

Data Selection

The data occurrence component of the data naming taxonomy identifies the data occurrences selected for an analysis.

Example: A summary data subject resulting from the analysis of vehicle trips over 500 miles would be named [Over 500 Miles] Vehicle Trip Summary 4.

If the selection is very detailed, the common word *Selection* followed by a specific selection number is used to identify the selection criteria. A comprehensive definition explains the selection criteria.

Example: [Selection 5] Vehicle Trip Summary 4 could be the name of a very detailed selection.

---

[7]Chapter 6 explains data characteristic matrixes.

Data Versions

Data version identification is very critical for evaluational data. The data version component of the data naming taxonomy identifies the data version used for the analysis.

Example: The analysis of vehicle trips over 500 miles based on evaluational data last updated with first quarter 1994 data would be named as follows:

[Over 500 Miles] Vehicle Trip Summary 4 <1st Quarter 1994>

The data version notations help people readily distinguish between the results of different analyses.

Example: [Over 500 Miles] Vehicle Trip Summary 4 <1st Quarter 1994> and [Under 500 Miles] Vehicle Trip Summary 6 <2nd Quarter 1994> are two different data versions.

Data Definitions

Each data perspective should have a perspective comprehensive data definition that provides an understanding about what the summary data subjects in that perspective represent. The definition explains the multiple dimension data focus and the single dimension qualifying data subjects. That definition applies to all summary data subjects in the set. A more detailed definition is prepared for each summary data subject explaining exactly what it represents and the specific qualifying data subjects.

> A comprehensive data definition is prepared for each data perspective, summary data subject, and summary data characteristic.

Each data characteristic also has a comprehensive data definition that explains what the characteristic represents and how it was derived. The complete query may be documented for summary data characteristics. A comprehensive data definition is also prepared for data characteristics that are calculated each time they are requested. It does not make any difference whether a data characteristic is stored in a database or calculated when it is requested, it still has a comprehensive data definition.

EVALUATIONAL DATA STRUCTURE

The structure of evaluational data is defined and documented within the common data architecture similar to operational data. The primary differences with evaluational data are their multiple dimensions and the levels of summarization. Enhancements to the data structure notations used for operational data help people understand what the evaluational data represent and how they are managed.

Primary Keys

The primary keys in evaluational data must be meaningful to the business. Arbitrary and system-assigned keys may be easy to use, but they are useless for proper management of evaluational data. These keys cause considerable confusion and misunderstanding about the qualifying data subjects and the summarization of data within multiple dimension data subjects.

The primary keys in evaluational data must have a business meaning.

The primary key of a focus data subject should consist of the business keys from all the qualifying data subjects, including one or more data characteristics representing time. The time data characteristics provide the time-variant aspect to evaluational data. They add the time dimension that makes evaluational data temporal, or time relational.[8]

Example: The primary key characteristics in Vehicle Trip Summary are Vehicle License Number, Department Name, Employee Social Security Number, Destination Name, and Vehicle Trip Date CYMD.

The data characteristics in a primary key are not sequence-dependent. Their sequence can be changed without affecting their unique identification of each data occurrence. Generally, the data characteristics in the primary key of a summary data subject are kept in alphabetical sequence for easy identification and comparison of summary data subjects.

---

[8]Time relational data are explained in Brackett, 1990.

Example: Changing the sequence of the primary key data characteristics in Vehicle Trip Focus does not change the unique identification of each Vehicle Trip.

A different set of data characteristics in a primary key identifies a different summary data subject. The number of possible summary data subjects in a summary data subject set is two to the power of the number of data characteristics in the primary key minus one ($2^n - 1$). The number of meaningful summary data subjects is usually considerably less than the number possible.

Example: If three data characteristics exist in the primary key of a summary data subject set, seven summary data subjects are possible. If five data characteristics exist in the primary key, 31 summary data subjects are possible.

> A different set of primary key data characteristics indicates a different data subject.

All data characteristics in the primary key must have a qualifying data subject.

Example: Vehicle Trip Date CYMD in Vehicle Trip Focus requires a qualifying data subject for Day, which has a primary key of Date CYMD. Similarly, if Vehicle Trip Date CYMD were replaced with Vehicle Trip Quarter Number to summarize data by quarter, a Quarter qualifying data subject would be defined.

Subject Relation Diagram

A data perspective is shown on a subject relation diagram with the data focus at the center and the qualifying data subjects surrounding the data focus, as shown in Figure 10.3. This subject relation diagram, minus the data relations, becomes a shell for documenting summary data subjects. A separate subject relation diagram is developed for each summary data subject showing only the data relations from the qualifying data subjects that are valid for the summary data subject.

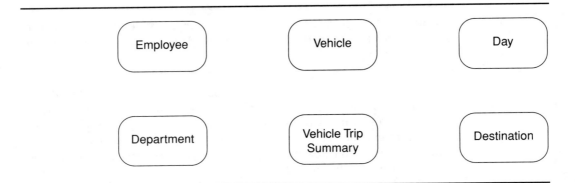

Figure 10.4   Subject relation diagram shell for Vehicle Trip Summary.

A subject relation diagram shell is created for each data perspective.

Example: The data perspective for Vehicle Trip Focus is shown in Figure 10.3. A subject relation diagram shell is developed from this data perspective by changing Vehicle Trip Focus to Vehicle Trip Summary and removing all the data relations, as shown in Figure 10.4.

A subject relation diagram is developed from the shell for each summary data subject that is created.

Example: When Vehicle Trip Summary 1 was created by removing Employee Social Security Number, a subject relation diagram would be created as shown in Figure 10.5. Data relations are shown from Department, Vehicle, and Destination because they are the qualifying data subjects for Vehicle Trip Summary 1. A data relation is not shown from Employee because it is not a qualifying data subject.

The subject relation diagram shell could include several different dates, such as day, month, quarter, and year, as shown in Figure 10.6. One-to-many data relations are shown between Day, Month, Quarter, and Year to show the summarization of temporal data. The time dimension used for a specific summary data subject is indicated by the data relation.

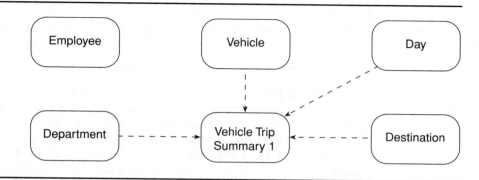

Figure 10.5   Subject relation diagram for Vehicle Trip Summary 1.

Summary Data Subject Matrices

Creation and maintenance of all these subject relation diagrams is valid, but is time consuming. It is also difficult to sort through a large quantity of subject relation diagrams to find the desired diagram; therefore, subject relation diagrams are seldom maintained for summary data subjects.

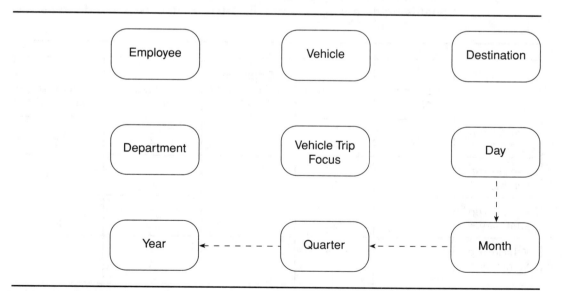

Figure 10.6   Subject relation diagram with many date dimensions.

A summary data subject matrix provides the notation for managing summary data.

A more effective and efficient notation for defining and managing summary data subjects is a matrix. A *simple primary key matrix* is prepared for each data perspective that identifies the primary key data characteristics for all summary data subjects in that perspective. The primary key data characteristics are listed alphabetically across the top of the matrix and the summary data subjects are listed alphabetically on the left of the matrix. Cells in the body of the matrix are checked to show which data characteristics comprise the primary key of each summary data subject.

Example: The simple primary key matrix for Vehicle Trip Summary is shown in Figure 10.7.

If the qualifying data subjects have more than one data characteristic in the primary key and the same data characteristic exists in more than one primary key, a *detailed primary key matrix* may be developed showing the primary key characteristics by qualifying data subject. The qualifying data subjects are still listed in alphabetical order, and the

	Department Name	Destination Name	Employee Social Security Number	Vehicle License Number	Vehicle Trip Date CYMD
Vehicle Trip Summary 1	X	X		X	X
Vehicle Trip Summary 2		X	X	X	X
Vehicle Trip Summary 3		X		X	X
Vehicle Trip Summary 4				X	X

Figure 10.7 Simple primary key matrix for Vehicle Trip Summary.

data characteristics within the primary key are listed in alphabetical order within the qualifying data subject. This matrix is larger, but it provides more detail about the primary key characteristics for each qualifying data subject.

The best approach is to prepare a subject relation diagram for the data perspective showing the data focus and all the qualifying data subjects and one primary key matrix to support that diagram. Either form of the matrix is useful for visualizing and understanding the summary data subjects in a data perspective. If both matrixes are maintained, they must be kept synchronized to prevent confusion.

EVALUATIONAL DATA INTEGRITY

The data integrity for evaluational data is different than the data integrity for operational data. The static nature of data values, the dynamic nature of data relations, and the multiple levels of data summarization require a slightly different approach to data integrity.

Data Relations

The data relations are usually different for evaluational data than for operational data.

Example: Operational data may require that a Product be purchased from only one Supplier at a particular time. Because evaluational data are historical and time variant, a Product could be purchased from many Suppliers. Operational data would have a one-to-many data relation from Supplier to Product, and evaluational data would have a many-to-many data relation between Supplier and Product, as shown in Figure 10.8.

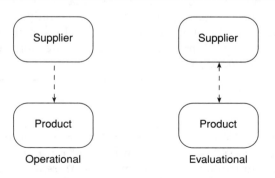

Figure 10.8   Different data relations between operational and evaluational data.

Operational data relations are relatively static, but evaluational data relations may change. The reason for this difference is that operational data must comply with specific business rules, but evaluational data are independent of business rules.

Example: The data relations between Product, Product Purchase, and Supplier in an operational database are static. The data relations between summary data subjects, such as Product Purchase, and their qualifying data subjects, such as Product, Supplier, and Customer, frequently change depending on the type of analysis desired.

> Evaluational data have less referential integrity than operational data.

Evaluational data generally have less referential integrity because data are not updated and the data relations are dynamic.

Example: Product Purchase data may be maintained as evaluational data without any corresponding Supplier data. If the operational referential integrity required between Product Purchase and Supplier data were implemented for an evaluational database, it would prevent storage of only Product Purchase data.

Also, some evaluational data may be retained for a longer period of time than other evaluational data.

Example: Product Purchase data may be retained for analysis for five years, and Supplier data may be retained for analysis only one year. Implementation of the operational referential integrity in the evaluational database would prevent removal of the Supplier data while Product Purchase data remained.

Data Normalization

Generally, evaluational data are not fully normalized like operational data. This difference reduces the number of data subjects to provide more efficient multiple dimension analysis. More analysis can be done in the multiple dimension data subject without navigating many data relations to get data from other data subjects. The data are more redundant, but the processing is faster.

> Evaluational data are not fully normalized like operational data.

Generally, data not needed for multiple dimension analysis are retained in the qualifying data subjects. Data that are needed for multiple dimension analysis are placed in the data focus.

Repeating groups (first normal form) can be left unnormalized so that parent data characteristics appear in each subordinate data occurrence in the data focus.

Example: Product Purchase is the data focus and Product, Vendor, and Customer are the qualifying data subjects. Data characteristics in Product, Vendor, or Customer that are needed for multiple dimension analysis are placed redundantly in each Product Purchase data occurrence.

Interattribute dependencies (third normal form) are also frequently left unnormalized to replace data code values with data code names.

Example: Product Type is a code table qualifying Product Purchase. The Product Type Code is contained in Product Purchase, but the Product Type Name must be obtained from Product Type. To prevent extra navigation to obtain the name of the product type, Product Type Name is placed in Product Purchase.

If coded data values are retained in the data focus, such as Product Type Code, a corresponding code table data subject must be maintained to supply the names for those coded data values. The qualifying data subject contains all the coded data values that are valid during the time period represented by the data focus, not those currently valid for operational data. Effective begin and end dates may be maintained in the qualifying data subject to show the valid time period for each coded data value.

Example: People generally do not want to know that 155 units of product 4857 were shipped to store 98306 in city 993 on January 3, 1995. They would rather know that 155 units of tomato soup were shipped to Ben's Supermarket in Chicago on January 3, 1995.

Not fully normalizing repeating groups and interattribute dependencies is known as vertical data replication. *Vertical data replication* is the replication of data values from a parent data subject to subordinate data subjects for more efficient processing. It usually occurs in evaluational data, but may occur in operational data under special circumstances.

Data Summarization

Evaluational data can be summarized to get a more generalized view about patterns and trends. *Data summarization* is the process of summarizing primitive evaluational data or derived evaluational data to create more generalized derived evaluational data. *Data generalization* is the process of creating successive layers of summary data. It is a process of zooming out to get a broader view of a problem, trend, or situation.

Data summaries are developed by removing primary key data characteristics.

Data generalization is done by removing data characteristics from the primary key. The removal of one or more data characteristics from the primary key results in the summarization of that data dimension. The removal of primary key data characteristics creates a new summary data subject. The remaining primary key data characteristics form the primary key for the new summary data subject.

Example: The removal of Employee Social Security Number in the previous example means that the resulting data are summarized for all Employees. The resulting primary key contains Vehicle License Number, Department Name, Destination Name, and Vehicle Trip Date CYMD. The results are stored in Vehicle Trip Summary 1.

Example: The removal of Department Name means the resulting data are summarized for all Departments. The resulting primary key contains Vehicle License Number, Employee Social Security Number, Destination Name, and Vehicle Trip Date CYMD. The results are stored in Vehicle Trip Summary 2.

Example: The removal of both Employee Social Security Number and Department Name results in summarizing data for all Employees and Departments. The resulting primary key contains Vehicle License Number, Destination Name, and Vehicle Trip Date CYMD. The results are stored in Vehicle Trip Summary 3.

Example: Affirmative Action Summary 5 represents Race by Month by Job Classification with a primary key of Race Code, Month Number, and Job Classification Code. Removing Job Classification Code from the primary key results in the elimination of Job Classification leaving Affirmative Action Summary 6 with a primary key of Race Code and Month Number.

Data specialization is the process of viewing data in more detail, often known as drilling down. It is a process of zooming in to get a more detailed view of a pattern or trend. The process of drilling down to more detailed data is the opposite of data generalization. Adding one or more data characteristics results in more detailed data.

Example: The addition of Employee Social Security Number to Vehicle Summary 3 means the data are summarized by Employee; Vehicle Trip Summary 2 contains the data.

Example: Personnel Summary 6 represents Position by Month with a primary key of Position Number and Month Number. Drilling down to more detail for Job Classification is done by adding Job Classification Code to the primary key. The resulting Personnel Summary 5 represents Position by Month by Job Classification.

> Data generalization and specialization is the management of primary keys.

The previous examples clearly demonstrate that the primary keys must contain meaningful, business-oriented data characteristics. The use of system-assigned, meaningless primary keys makes it difficult to properly manage data generalization and data specialization and usually leads to disparate evaluational data.

Data Summarization Levels

Evaluational data contain a range of summary data from lightly summarized to highly summarized. Primitive evaluational data are *lightly summarized* by removing one, or a few, data characteristic from the primary key of the data focus, leaving the majority of data characteristics in the primary key. Lightly summarized data are known as having *fine granularity*.

Example: Vehicle Trip Focus can be lightly summarized by removing one or two data characteristics from the primary key, such as Employee Social Security Number, as described previously.

The data can be *highly summarized* by removing additional data characteristics from the primary key of the data focus until, ultimately, only one remains. Highly summarized data are known as having *coarse granularity*.

Example: Vehicle Trip Focus can have most of the data characteristics from the primary key removed leaving only two, such as Vehicle Trip Date CYMD and Employee Social Security Number.

The number of summary data subjects possible for a data perspective is $2^n - 1$, where n is the number of primary keys in the data focus, as explained previously. The number of possible pathways to those summary data subjects is much larger. A data derivation diagram could be created to show how the more detailed summary data subjects contribute to the more general summary data subjects.

Example: A subject relation diagram could be created showing how Vehicle Trip Summary 1 (removal of Employee Social Security Number) contributed to Vehicle Trip Summary 3 (removal of Employee Social Security Number and Department Name).

A data derivation diagram could be created for all possibilities in a data perspective, as shown in Figure 10.9. The data focus is shown at the bottom of the diagram with all the data characteristics in the primary key, represented by the letters a, b, c, d, and e. Some of the possible pathways through lightly summarized data to highly summarized data are shown in the diagram with their primary key data characteristics.

A complete derived data diagram shows a network of possible routes to all summary data subjects in a data perspective. A more useful derived data diagram should be developed that shows the possible routes to all valid summary data subjects in a data perspective. The permanent data subjects can be designated on that diagram along with the preferred route for developing and maintaining those permanent data subjects. A corresponding primary key matrix for the data perspective shows the primary key data characteristics for each summary data subject.

MAINTAINING EVALUATIONAL DATA

Evaluational data must be maintained even though their data values are nonvolatile. There are constant additions and possible deletions from an evaluational database, as well as constant rederivations as new data are added.

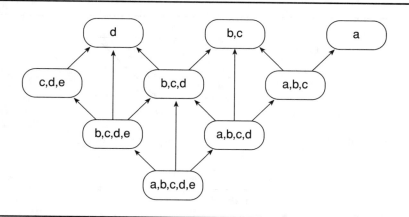

Figure 10.9   Derived data diagram for a data perspective.

Data Addition

An evaluational database grows by enhancing it with new sets of data, by expanding it with more detail within the existing scope, and by extending the scope into new business areas, as shown in Figure 10.10. *Evaluational data addition* is the process of adding new data to an evaluational database.

Evaluational data enhancement is the addition of a new set of primitive data occurrences to the evaluational database within its existing scope.

Example: The evaluational database for Vehicle Trip data is enhanced on the tenth of every month with vehicle trip data from the previous month.

An evaluational database is enlarged by expanding the detail or extending the scope.

Evaluational data expansion is the addition of more data subjects, data occurrences, and data characteristics within the existing scope of the evaluational database.

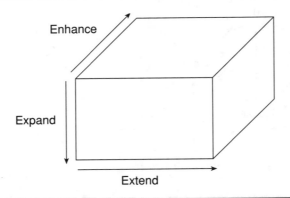

Figure 10.10   Evaluational data addition.

Data subject expansion is the creation and maintenance of more derived summary data subjects in the evaluational database within its existing scope.

Example: The analysis of Vehicle Trip Focus makes frequent use of Vehicle Trip by Department by Quarter. A new permanent summary data subject is created and maintained for this use.

Data occurrence expansion is the addition of more data occurrences to an evaluational database.

Example: Expanding the time period for analyzing vehicle trips from five years to 10 years results in the addition of five years of new data occurrences.

Data characteristic expansion is the addition of more derived data characteristics to an evaluational database within the existing scope of the evaluational database.

Example: Data characteristics for Vehicle Trip Summary Total Cargo Pounds, Vehicle Trip Summary Average Cargo Pounds, and Vehicle Trip Summary Maintenance Cost are added.

Evaluational data extension is an increase in the scope of an evaluational database into new business areas. Extending the scope requires development of a new set of data transformations to transform and load the data necessary to support the new scope.

Example: An organization may diversify; for example, a grocery store may go into the sporting goods business. Several organizations may merge. An organization may develop an evaluational database incrementally.

Data Removal

Normally, new evaluational data are continually added to the evaluational database on a regular schedule. However, evaluational data can be removed from an evaluational database in some situations. *Evaluational data removal* is the process of removing unnecessary or unused data from an evaluational database. It is an approach to keeping evaluational data clean and organized.

An evaluational database may shrink by removing detail or decreasing the scope.

Evaluational data reduction is the removal of a set of primitive data occurrences from the evaluational database. It is the opposite of data enhancement.

Example: The evaluational database for Vehicle Trip data is reduced by removing two years of the oldest data.

Evaluational data contraction is the removal of data subjects, data occurrences, or data characteristics from the data warehouse system. It is the opposite of evaluational data expansion.

Data subject contraction is the removal of one or more summary data subjects from an evaluational database because they no longer need to be maintained for analysis. It is the opposite of data subject extension.

Example: Vehicle Trip by Department by Quarter is no longer needed for analysis and is removed from the evaluational database.

Data occurrence contraction is the removal of a set of data occurrences from an evaluational database. It is the opposite of data occurrence extension.

Example: The time period was shortened from 10 years to seven years for Vehicle Trip data, and the oldest three years of data are removed from the evaluational database. Vehicle Trip data are maintained for only five years and the addition of each new quarter's data results in removal of the oldest quarter's data.

Data characteristic contraction is the removal of one or more data characteristics from an evaluational database. It is the opposite of data characteristic extension.

Example: Summary data characteristics that were maintained are no longer used and are removed to conserve space. Summary data characteristics are used infrequently, and it is easier to create them when needed than to maintain them.

Evaluational data retraction is the removal of primitive and derived evaluational data subjects resulting from a reduction in the scope of the evaluational database. It is the opposite of evaluational data extension.

Example: An organization dropped a line of business and no longer needs the data for analysis, an organization decides further analysis in no longer needed for a particular business area, or there was a wrong guess about developing a segment of the evaluational database. The corresponding data are removed from the evaluational database.

Data Rederivation

When a new version or modification of evaluational data exists, any permanent derived evaluational data must be rederived to reflect the new version or modification. *Evaluational data rederivation* is the process of automatically rederiving summary data when a version or modification change to any of their contributors occurs. As explained previously, the rederived data have a new version or modification number and a corresponding definition.

> Summary data can be automatically rederived if the data derivation scheme is known.

When new data are routinely added to the evaluational database, the frequency and timing of those additions, and any data rederivations resulting from those additions, should be made available to any client using the evaluational database.

Example: New Vehicle Trip data occurrences are added monthly on the 10th of the month, and all summary data based on those new data occurrences are rederived on the 15th of the month.

Example: Vehicle maintenance summary data could be maintained for only 24 months. The addition of a new month of vehicle maintenance data results in the deletion of the oldest month's data.

An organization needs to determine which summary data are to be routinely rederived, which summary data are to be custom rederived, and which summary data are to remain static.

Data Version

Keeping track of data versions is extremely important for properly managing evaluational data. Every multiple dimension analysis is based on a specific version of data, and that version must be readily identified. The results of any multiple dimension analysis is version dependent. If different versions of data are summarized, the version of each qualifying data subject as well as the version of the resulting data subject must be known.

High-quality multiple dimension analysis is version dependent.

Evaluational data versions are identified with the data version component of the data naming taxonomy. The specific format of the version component for evaluational data is a *version identifier* followed by a *modification identifier* with a period separating the two identifiers:

<version identifier.modification identifier>

The version identifier may be any combination of words, letters, or numbers as explained in Chapter 5. In most cases, a date is included in the identifier to represent the time variant nature of evaluational data. The modification identifier could be any combination of words, letters, or numbers, but it is usually a sequential number or letter.

The version identifier uniquely identifies a new set of evaluational data resulting from the addition of data to an evaluational database or the removal of data from an evaluational database.

Example: New insurance claim data are added to the evaluational database every quarter. The data version could be the latest quarter included in the database, such as <1st Quarter 1994>, <2nd Quarter 1994>, or <3rd Quarter 1994>.

The *modification identifier* uniquely identifies a change to one or more data values within an existing set of data, not the addition of a new set of data. Although primitive evaluational data are nonvolatile, there are rare situations where the primitive evaluational data values are wrong and need to be changed to accurately reflect history. When the data values are changed, the version identifier remains the same, and the modification identifier is changed.

Example: If data values in Vehicle Trip Focus <Version 6> changed, the new data version would be Vehicle Trip Focus <Version 6.1>.

Any summary data derived from a new version or modification also receives a new version or modification with a corresponding definition of the reason for the new version or modification.

A data version modification identifier shows a change in primitive evaluational data values.

The data version definition explains the reason for the new version or modification. The reason could be a regular addition of data occurrences, a random addition of data occurrences, an expansion of the time period, a change in the duration that data are retained for analysis, deletion of data occurrences, or any other reason.

Data Perspectives

A major aspect of managing evaluational data is identifying the data subjects included in a data perspective. One approach to identifying data subjects is the *business question approach* where the basic business questions to be answered are identified and used to define the data perspectives to answer those questions.

Example: Basic questions for vehicle trips might be related to which employees in which departments take trips to which destinations at what time of the month and year or which departments use which type of vehicles during the year. The qualifying data subjects are Employee, Vehicle, Department, Destination, and Day, and the central data subject is Vehicle Trip. Therefore, Vehicle Trip Focus is the data focus, and the qualifying data subjects are Employee, Vehicle, Department, Destination, and Day.

> Data perspectives are defined through an analysis of business questions and primary keys.

The problem with the business question approach is that all questions listed by business clients are not well grouped. The questions may be mixed between vehicles, financial, purchasing, and employee. The real work comes in segmenting the business questions into sets with a central data focus. A good approach to segmenting the business questions is to group the questions by major data subject areas and then determine the data focus and qualifying data subjects for those data subject areas.

The data perspectives in an evaluational database are not totally separated. A data perspective may share qualifying data subjects with other data perspectives, forming a network of data perspectives and qualifying data subjects. It could be helpful to develop a complete data model for evaluational data showing all the data perspectives and how they are related through common qualifying data subjects.[9]

Another approach to identifying data subjects is the *primary key approach* where a matrix of primary key data characteristics for all data subjects identified by the business questions is reviewed to determine the data perspectives. A dense matrix, meaning most of the cells are checked, usually represents a single data perspective. A sparse matrix, meaning the checked cells form disjointed groups, usually indicates several different data perspectives. Each group of checked cells identifies a potential data perspective, and the overlapping cells identify common qualifying data subjects. Each potential data perspective is reviewed to identify a data focus and determine whether that data focus will answer the business questions.

These two approaches are generally used together to develop the basic structure of an evaluational database. When the data perspectives are identified, including a data focus and qualifying data subjects for each data perspective, the specific summary data subjects can be identified as explained previously. The appropriate diagrams and matrixes are then developed to document the evaluational database.

Metadata

Metadata are critically important for the proper management of evaluational data for two reasons. First, *operational metadata* are important to identify the existing disparate operational data so an organization knows

---

[9]Chapter 14 explains how to develop a common data model.

what data are available and understands those operational data, and to properly identify the official data source and official data variation. Second, *evaluational metadata* are important to track the evaluational data that are available and to understand what they represent. An active data refining initiative helps prepare the operational metadata, and an active tracking initiative helps maintain the evaluational metadata.

The question is always asked: how far should an organization go in maintaining evaluational metadata? The answer is far enough so that business analysts can thoroughly understand the evaluational data and how they can be accessed. Generally, the same level of detail is maintained for evaluational metadata as is maintained for operational data using the different notations described previously.

Metadata about the available evaluational data, the origins of primitive evaluational data, how the operational data were transformed, the available summary data, how summary data are created and maintained, subject relation diagrams of data perspectives, supporting primary key matrixes, and the enhancement and rederivation time and frequency are most useful. The metadata should also include an explanation of the adjustments to data integrity and the levels of data accuracy. They should explain any discrepancies inherent in the disparate operational data that could not be corrected during data transformation.

Developing evaluational data within a common data architecture prevents evaluational data refining.

Development of comprehensive evaluational metadata and access to those metadata are mandatory for effective and efficient use of an evaluational database. The lack of comprehensive, readily available evaluational metadata prevents an organization from fully utilizing those data to analyze its business. If business analysts do not know the evaluational data that are available or what they represent, they are unable to use those data. Comprehensive evaluational metadata must be prepared, maintained, and readily available. Evaluational metadata must be maintained for primitive evaluational data, but do not need to be maintained for all derived evaluational data.

A *permanent data subject* is a data subject that remains in the evaluational database permanently. A primitive evaluational data subject is considered permanent, as well as any derived evaluational data subjects that are used frequently, whether they are continuously maintained or generated when needed. Evaluational metadata must be maintained for all permanent data subjects.

A *temporary data subject* is a summary data subject that remains in the database for a shorter period of time. It may be created and maintained for the duration of an analysis project and then discarded. It is not maintained for long periods because it is easier to recreate than to maintain. Evaluational metadata may be maintained for a temporary data subject. If metadata are not maintained, a comprehensive definition of the data must accompany those data so they are completely understood and properly used.

A *transient data subject* is a summary data subject that is created for a particular analysis and deleted. It is not maintained beyond a specific analysis. Evaluational metadata are usually not maintained for transient data subjects, although a comprehensive definition of the data must accompany those data.

Active documentation can routinely provide evaluational metadata.

Active documentation is the process of automatically capturing and storing the algorithm for creating a summary data subject. This self-documenting process for evaluational data automatically provides useful metadata without business analyst or data analyst involvement. Active documentation can provide suggested summary data subject names based on the existing data focus names and summary data subject names. It can enhance the primary key matrix and maintain other metadata that are easily determined during multiple dimension analysis. Business analysts or data analysts would need to develop initial evaluational metadata and provide evaluational metadata that are not easily determined during multiple dimension analysis.

An *intuitive data warehouse system* tracks the analysis performed on evaluational data, adds or suggests the addition of permanent summary data subjects or queries based on frequency of use, and deletes or suggests the deletion of summary data subjects and queries based on a lack of use. It is a powerful feature that makes a data warehouse system useful to an organization and helps maintain evaluational data. It also eliminates unnecessary data rederivation.

Searching evaluational data for trends and suggesting structural improvement requires a thorough understanding of the data.

If both evaluational data and evaluational metadata are properly developed and maintained within a common data architecture, evaluational data can be fully utilized. In addition, disparate evaluational data will not be developed, and there will be no need for evaluational data refining. Evaluational data must be designed and developed within the common data architecture to support comprehensive business analysis. Those that claim derived data do not need to be modeled or documented are perpetuating the disparate data problem and severely limiting an organization's ability to analyze its business.

Data Exploration and Mining

Data exploration is the process of routinely searching evaluational data for patterns, trends, and exceptions. Data exploration usually starts with an incomplete definition of the search criteria and an unknown volume of data. As patterns, trends, and exceptions are discovered, the search criteria are refined and the volume of data may be changed. It is a learning process that continues until relatively sound patterns are discovered.

An *active data warehouse system* routinely searches for trends and patterns in evaluational data. It is an active process that searches an evaluational database for trends, patterns, and exceptions. When possible trends or patterns are found, business analysts are notified so they can perform additional analyses or take any action they deem necessary.

Data mining, also known as *data harvesting*, is the process of utilizing the results of data exploration to adjust or enhance business strategies. It builds on the patterns, trends, and exceptions found through data exploration to support the business. It applies the knowledge gained to improve business processes or transform the business.

> Data exploration and data mining maximize the investment in the data resource to support the business.

Data exploration and data mining are not the same as data discovery. Data discovery, as described earlier, is the process of finding the hidden data resource that exists in disparate operational data. Data exploration and data mining find and utilize the patterns, trends, and exceptions through the analysis of evaluational data.

SUMMARY

Most organizations want to stay competitive in a dynamic business environment. Staying competitive requires a continuous, comprehensive analysis of the business to make more informed decisions about business alternatives. A comprehensive analysis of the business requires large quantities of consistent historical data that can be analyzed many different ways. The problem most organizations face is large quantities of disparate operational data that are redundant, highly variable, and largely unknown. These disparate data cannot support comprehensive business analysis.

Implementation of a dual database concept in which detailed operational data support business operations and summarized evaluational data support business analysis provides the base for meeting both operational and analytical needs. The dual database concept provides a foundation for integrating operational and evaluational data within a common data architecture.

Evaluational data are developed within the common data architecture. Data perspectives are defined with a multiple dimension data focus and single dimension qualifying data subjects. A subject relation diagram and a primary key matrix for each data perspective provide the detail for managing evaluational data. Data generalization (summarization) and data specialization (drilling down) is done through the management of primary keys. The analysis of high-use summary data subjects and the pathways to maintain those summary data subjects provide a balance between maintaining data and recreating data.

Evaluational data are managed through the addition of new data, the removal of unnecessary data, and the rederivation of summary data. Version control is critical in an evaluational database and is managed through the data version component of the data naming taxonomy. A version identifier shows the addition or removal of data, and a modification identifier shows a change in data values. Comprehensive, readily available metadata help business analysts locate and use evaluational data to analyze the business.

Developing an evaluational database is a real area of discovery. Business questions identify data perspectives that are used for business analysis. Results of the business analysis lead to more questions, possible addition of more evaluational data, and more analysis. This decision support cycle continues, and the evaluational database constantly evolves to support the cycle. The evaluational database grows, often geometrically, as it evolves. The only way to properly design and manage the growth and evolution of an evaluational database is to develop it within a common data architecture.

QUESTIONS

The following questions are provided as a review of the chapter and to stimulate thought about the managing and documenting evaluational data within a common data architecture.

1. Why is decision support important to an organization?
2. Why does the current data resource not adequately support decision support?
3. What is a data warehouse system?
4. What problem does the dual database concept solve?
5. What are evaluational data?
6. How do evaluational data differ from operational data?
7. What is a data perspective?
8. What is a data focus?
9. What is a summary data subject set?
10. How are summary data subjects and characteristics named and defined?
11. Why are primary keys important for designing and managing evaluational data?
12. What is a summary data subject shell?
13. How do primary key matrixes resolve the problems with summary data subject shells?
14. Why are evaluational data relations more dynamic than operational data relations?
15. Why are evaluational data more unnormalized than operational data?
16. What does data summarization accomplish?
17. Why is it important to properly manage summary data subjects?
18. How can an evaluational database grow and shrink?
19. How are evaluational data versions identified?
20. How are data perspectives identified?
21. Why are metadata important for managing evaluational data?
22. What is data exploration?
23. What is data mining?
24. Why do evaluational data need to be managed within a common data architecture?

## CHAPTER 11

Data Transformation

Disparate data need to be formally transformed before they can become part of an integrated data resource.

The development of high-quality evaluational data, whether or not they are stored in a data warehouse system, requires a formal transformation of the operational data, particularly if they are disparate. One major problem developing an evaluational database to support business analysis is the transformation of disparate operational data to consistent evaluational data. Disparate operational data that are just dumped into an evaluational database will not provide any support to the organization and could provide disastrous results.

Transforming disparate operational data to consistent evaluational data, however, is not the only purpose for data transformation. Data may be also be transformed between operational data and evaluational data within the integrated data resource, between disparate operational data and operational data in the integrated data resource, and between historical data and evaluational data. Data transformation is a process that can be used anywhere in an organization's data resource.

Chapter 11 begins with an explanation of the data transformation concept and how data transformation is performed within the common data architecture. This chapter presents a data transformation perspective and explains the possible data transformation routes. A matrix showing which of the data transformation steps is used in the different data transformation routes is presented. Each of the 10 data transformation steps is described with examples.

DATA TRANSFORMATION CONCEPT

The theme throughout this book has been to survive on disparate data until they can be transformed into an integrated data resource. *Data transformation* is the formal process of transforming data in the data resource within a common data architecture. It includes transforming disparate data to an integrated data resource, transforming data within the integrated data resource, and transforming disparate data. It includes transforming operational, historical, and evaluational data within a common data architecture.[1]

Data should not be moved from one database to another without formal data transformation. Some people think that all that needs to be done is to move disparate data into a data warehouse system or through a data scrubber or convert data values, and the disparity will be solved. This is not true! These perceptions make the solution to a very big problem look all too easy. Data scrubbers and data converters will not transform disparate operational data to consistent evaluational data. They may perform some minor data conversions and data value adjustments, but they will not handle the critical issues of data transformation.

Transforming data is not a trivial task.

Disparate data need to be formally transformed to resolve any existing data disparity and to prevent and new data disparity. Data transformation is not a trivial task. It is a formal process that requires careful planning to ensure an organization can survive on its disparate data while developing an integrated data resource.

Data Transformation Perspective

The data transformation perspective is shown in Figure 11.1. Disparate data are shown on the left side of the diagram and integrated data are shown on the right side of the diagram. Historical data are shown at the top of the diagram, operational data are shown in the middle of the diagram, and evaluational data are shown at the bottom of the diagram. The data transformation paths are shown by lines with arrowheads pointing in the direction of the transformation.

Disparate operational data are the current-value operational data

---

[1]Data transformation was first described by the author in Brackett, 1990.

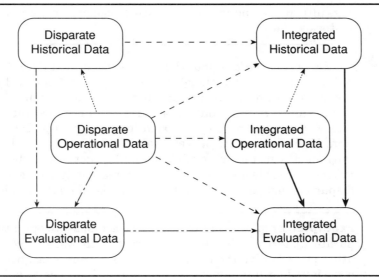

Figure 11.1   Data transformation perspective.

that support daily business transactions. They are the disparate data, including both tabular and nontabular data, that most organizations currently use to support their daily business operations. They are not desirable data, but they do exist and must be managed.

Example: Employee data are stored in a variety of different data files that support payroll, training, affirmative action, position assignment, and a variety of other employee functions. They are disparate data, but they support daily business operations.

Disparate historical data are the disparate operational data that have been archived either as individual data values or as full records. They have been saved or archived in their disparate form, but they are time-variant because they represent the operational values at different points in time. Like the disparate operational data, they are not desirable, but they do exist and must be managed.

Example: Individual employee data values are saved for historical purposes whenever a data value changes. The data value, date, and any other relative data are moved to a historical file for payroll, training, affirmative action, and position assignment, creating disparate historical data.

Disparate evaluational data are evaluational data developed from either disparate operational data or disparate historical data without any data refining or any attempt to resolve the data disparity. They are disparate operational data that have been dumped into a data warehouse system with no transformation or only superficial transformation. Unlike disparate operational data and disparate historical data, they usually do not currently exist and do not need to be created. They are not desirable data because they immediately create another level of disparity that further magnifies the disparate data problem.

Example: Employee data from both the disparate operational and disparate historical files are moved to a data warehouse system in an attempt to resolve the data disparity. A system-assigned primary key is assigned for uniqueness. The disparity, however, is not resolved and multiple dimension analysis is performed on the disparate data yielding uncertain results.

Integrated operational data are a subject-oriented, integrated, time-current, volatile collection of data that support an organization's daily business activities. Time-current and volatile means the data values change to reflect the real world as often as necessary to support business operations. They represent a single data instance and can be used for making operational decisions. Integrated operational data are also known as *operational data stores*.

Integrated operational data are the current-value operational data that are part of the integrated data resource. They are either disparate operational data that have been transformed to the integrated data resource, or they are operational data that comply with the common data architecture and are entered directly into the integrated data resource. Integrated operational data are the desirable operational data for supporting an organization's daily operations.

Example: Employee data from the disparate payroll, training, affirmative action, and position assignment data files are transformed to an integrated employee file in the integrated data resource. The data disparity is resolved and all employee data are integrated into one data file.

Integrated historical data are integrated operational data that have either been archived as individual data values or as full records from integrated operational data, or they are disparate operational or disparate historical data that have been transformed to the integrated data resource. They are time-variant because they represent operational values at different points in time. Integrated historical data, like integrated operational data, are desirable data.

Example: Employee data from the existing disparate payroll, training, affirmative action, and position assignment history files are transformed to an integrated employee history file in the integrated data resource. The data disparity is resolved and all historical data for employees are integrated into one data file.

Integrated evaluational data are a subject-oriented, integrated, time-variant, nonvolatile collection of data to support management's decision-making process, as explained in Chapter 10. They contain multiple data instances that provide a historical trend for making strategic decisions. Integrated evaluational data are also known as data warehouse systems.

Integrated evaluational data that are part of the integrated data resource. They are developed from integrated historical or integrated operational data or from disparate operational data that have been transformed to the integrated data resource. Like integrated operational and integrated historical data, they are desirable data.

Example: Employee data are routinely transformed from the integrated operational and historical data files to the integrated evaluational database on a monthly basis. Those integrated evaluational data are used for multiple dimension analysis about employees.

The integrated evaluational data could be offloaded to a historical evaluational database if necessary. Each organization needs to determine whether its evaluational data are valid but are not frequently used and can be moved to off-line storage or bulk storage devices.

Example: The vehicle trip evaluational database continues to grow as new trip data are added every month. Most of the multiple dimension processing is done on the last three to five years' worth of data, but older data may have some value. Vehicle trip data older than five years are moved to off-line storage, but can be reloaded if necessary.

Data Transformation Routes

The diagram in Figure 11.1 shows many different routes between the major segments of the data resource. Some of these routes are desirable, some are acceptable, and others are unacceptable.

The bold solid lines in the diagram represent the desirable data transformation routes. They transform integrated historical and integrated operational data to integrated evaluational data. The short dashed lines simply represent the storage of historical operational data and are not part of data transformation.

Example: Integrated operational vehicle trip data are routinely saved as historical data whenever the operational data values change. Integrated vehicle trip data, including both operational and historical data, are routinely transformed to integrated evaluational data on a monthly basis.

The broad dashed lines represent acceptable data transformation routes. They transform disparate historical or disparate operational data to the integrated data resource. They are not desirable because extensive data transformation is required, but they are acceptable because disparate data do exist and do need to be transformed to an integrated data resource.

Example: Disparate operational vehicle trip data have been routinely saved as disparate historical data. They are currently transformed and saved as integrated historical data to begin resolving the data disparity. They are no longer saved as disparate historical data. Existing disparate historical vehicle trip data are transformed to integrated historical data to eliminate those disparate data.

Example: Disparate operational vehicle trip data are transformed to integrated operational data to resolve the operational data disparity. Both sets of data may need to be maintained until all applications can be converted to use the integrated operational data. Disparate operational trip data can also be transformed to integrated evaluational data to support multiple dimension analysis.

The dotted and dashed lines represent unacceptable data transformation routes. They show the movement or partial transformation of disparate historical or disparate operational data to disparate evaluational data or the transformation of disparate evaluational data to integrated evaluational data. The first two transformations should not be performed because they create additional disparate data. The latter transformation should be performed only if disparate evaluational data have already been created and the operational and historical data no longer exist. If the operational and historical data still exist, they should be formally transformed to integrated data.

Example: Disparate vehicle trip data, both operational and historical, could be moved to an evaluational database with minimal data transformation in an attempt to resolve the data disparity. This approach, however, makes the disparate vehicle trip data even more disparate and should be avoided in favor of formal transformation to the integrated data resource.

Example: Disparate evaluational vehicle trip data that already exist could be transformed to integrated evaluational data if the operational and historical data no longer exist. If the operational and historical vehicle trip data still exist, they are transformed to the integrated data resource using the more acceptable data transformation routes.

Data Transformation Matrix

The formal data transformation process includes 10 distinct steps, as explained in the next section. All of these data transformation steps, however, do not need to be performed for each of the data transformation routes described previously. The matrix in Figure 11.2 shows which data transformation steps are necessary for each of the data transformation routes. The symbols at the top of the columns represent the 10 data transformation steps.

DATA TRANSFORMATION STEPS

Data transformation must be done carefully and methodically. The target data must be identified and modeled, and the source data needed to develop those target data must be identified. The source data, either current or historical, are then extracted from the official data sources. Any historical data are reconstructed into full records. The data are then translated to official data variations and recast for historical continuity. The source data are restructured according to the target data model and summarized to the desired level. The source data are then

	IE	IO	EX	TR	RC	RS	RC	SU	LO	RE
Disparate Operational to Disparate Evaluational	X	X	X						X	
Disparate Operational to Common Operational		X	X	X		X			X	X
Disparate Operational to Common Historical			X						X	
Disparate Operational to Common Evaluational	X	X	X	X	X	X	X	X	X	X
Disparate Historical to Common Historical	X	X	X						X	
Disparate Historical to Disparate Evaluational										
Disparate Evaluational to Common Evaluational	X	X	X	X	X	X	X	X	X	X
Common Operational to Common Evaluational										
Common Historical to Common Evaluational										

Figure 11.2   Matrix showing use of data transformation steps.

loaded into the target database and reviewed to determine whether the data transformation process was successful. Each of these 10 steps is described in the following sections.

> Data transformation supports the integration of data within a common data architecture.

Identify Target Data

The first data transformation step is to identify and model the target data. The scope of the process is defined, including a description of the data that are to be transformed and the purpose for the data transformation. A logical data model of the target data is developed within the common data architecture to identify the desired target data and the official data variations for those data.

Example: Disparate operational employee data are to be transformed to integrated operational employee data within the integrated data resource. A logical model is developed for the integrated employee data showing the official data variations for all employee data.

> A logical data model must be developed for the target data.

If the target data are in the integrated data resource and the official data variations have not been determined, data transformation cannot continue. The official data variations for the integrated data resource must be determined, preferably through the data refining process, before data transformation can continue.

If the target is an evaluational database, the historical time period is defined as part of the scope.

Example: The time period may be 30 years or more for pharmaceuticals, 10 to 20 years for personnel data, and one to three years for cellular phone data.

The logical data model shows the data focus and qualifying data subjects for each data perspective, and it shows the degree to which the data are not fully normalized.

Example: Integrated evaluational vehicle trip data are needed for multiple dimension analysis. A logical data model is developed for the integrated evaluational data showing the data focus and qualifying data subjects. The degree to which the data are not fully normalized is shown by the placement of redundant data in subordinate data subjects.

Identify Source Data

The second data transformation step is to identify the official data sources for data needed to produce the target data identified in the first data transformation step. If the source data are part of the integrated data resource, a logical data model of the integrated data resource is used to identify the official data sources.

Example: Integrated operational employee data are to be transformed to integrated evaluational data for multiple dimension analysis. The logical data model of the integrated operational employee data, which was developed for the transformation of disparate employee data to integrated employee data, identifies the official data sources.

> An active data refining initiative is mandatory for a successful data warehouse.

If the source data are disparate data, those data need to be refined by the data refining process described in Chapter 9. One of the biggest delays in transforming disparate data, and a step often ignored, is identifying the official data sources. An active data refining initiative that formally identifies official data sources is required to support the formal data transformation of disparate data. Data transformation should not continue unless the disparate data have been through the data refining process.

Example: The disparate operational Vehicle Trip data are put through the data refining process to identify the official data sources. These official data sources will be used for preparing the target evaluational data.

Extract Source Data

The third data transformation step is to extract the source data from the official data sources and place them in an interim database for further data transformation. If the source data are already in the integrated data resource, there is usually only one data source, which is the official data source.

Example: Integrated employee data have only one source for each data characteristic, which is shown in the logical data model for integrated employee data.

If the source data are disparate data, the official data sources may not be in the same data file. Data may need to be extracted from several different data files.

Example: The official data sources for disparate employee data are located in different data files. The employee's name and social security number comes from the payroll file. The employee's birth date and education level come from the training file. The employee's ethnicity, race, and management level come from the affirmative action file. The employee's seniority comes from the position assignment file.

If the source data are disparate and the official data sources have not been designated, data transformation cannot continue. The disparate data must go through the data refining process to designate the official data sources before data transformation can continue.

Two different data extraction processes for evaluational data exist. *Initial data extraction* is the process that first extracts the operational data to build the evaluational database. This is a one-time process that starts the evaluational database.

Example: Five years' worth of operational vehicle trip data are desired to load the evaluational database.

Enhanced data extraction is the ongoing process that extracts snapshots of the operational data on a regular basis for enhancing the evaluational database.

Example: Vehicle trip data are extracted from the operational database monthly on the tenth of the following month to enhance the evaluational database.

> Data extraction takes official data from disparate operational databases.

A detailed explanation of the mechanisms for data extraction, including data conversion, is beyond the scope of this book. *Data conversion* is the process of changing data from one physical environment to another. This process makes any changes necessary to move data from one electronic medium or database product to another. The best approach, particularly with disparate data, is to develop an interim database where the data can be transformed before they are loaded into the target database.

Reconstruct Historical Data

The fourth data transformation step is to reconstruct any historical data that exist as less than complete data records. Operational data are frequently saved, either as individual data values or as full data records, whenever current data values change. These historical data could be valuable, particularly for multiple dimension data analysis.

> Historical data need to be reconstructed into full data records for an evaluational database.

Historical data that are saved as full records do not need to be reconstructed. Historical data that are saved as individual data values, however, need to be reconstructed into full data records during data transformation to provide time relevance. This reconstruction is usually done by taking the current operational data record back through time to create historical data records. Whenever a changed data value is found in the historical data file, a historical data record is created and stored with that data value. That new data record is stepped back chronologically until another changed data value is found in the historical data file. The process continues until no more data values exist in the history data file.

Example: Employee data values were saved, with corresponding dates, whenever a critical data value changed. These historical data are very useful for multiple dimension analysis and need to be reconstructed to full data records for the evaluational database. Each employee data record is taken back through time and a historical employee data record is created anytime a changed data value is found in the employee history file.

Translate Data

The fifth data transformation step is to translate the extracted source data to the official data variations if they are not already in the official data variation. This step is particularly important when disparate data are transformed to the integrated data resource because it reduces the data variability inherent in disparate data and ensures data consistency in the integrated data resource. The content of the data, such as data codes, measurement units, formats, sequences, and lengths are translated to a consistent form.[2]

Example: All of the employee dates, such as birth dates, are converted to Date CYMD. All of the codes, such as Ethnicity Code and Race Code, are

---

[2]Data translation is described in Chapter 10 and is described in more detail in Brackett, 1994

translated to an official set of codes. All names are translated to the individual components, such as Employee Name Family and Employee Name Individual.

Data translation is not as important for data transformation within the integrated data resource because all data should be in the official data variation.

> Data translation reduces the data variability.

Translating disparate data requires that those disparate data go through the data refining process to determine their data variation. It also requires that that the official data variations be designated for those data. If both of these tasks have not been completed, data transformation cannot continue.

Recast Data

The sixth data transformation step is to recast the extracted source data for historical continuity. This process alters the structure of operational data so that they have a consistent structure for the entire time period represented in the evaluational database. The process takes different operational data structures that exist over time and recasts them into a consistent structure for multiple dimension analysis. Data recasting is not a translation of data values. It is an alteration of the structure of historical operational data to provide historical continuity.

> Data recasting provides a common historical perspective for evaluational data.

Many problems need to be overcome during data recasting. Primary keys often change over time, the content and meaning of data change over time, and there are missing periods of data, differences in data structures, and differences in accuracy and integrity. These differences come from different perspectives of the real world, inconsistent business rules, and different physical implementations.

Data recasting aligns these differences to a common historical perspective. It rewrites history to a common base; however, the detail must be available to make the alignment. In some situations the detail is not available and all data cannot be recast to a common historical perspective. When operational data are highly disparate, different data recasting schemes may be tried to find the scheme that provides the best common historical perspective. Thoroughly understanding disparate operational data through data refining helps to select an appropriate data recasting scheme with minimum difficulty.

Data refining is mandatory to determine the data recasting scheme.

Historical data are generally recast to the current operational structure. This approach, however, may not be best for multiple dimension analysis. Data may need to be recast to a previous structure rather than the current structure. Because any point in time is acceptable for data recasting, different time points may be tried to determine any changes in the patterns and trends from different historical points. Also, the data structure may be changed again, and the determination needs to be made whether the new data will be recast backwards or if all previous data will be recast to the latest change. Each organization must determine what type of multiple dimension analyses is needed, what point in time the recast data should represent, and what data recasting scheme works best.

Data recasting may involve combining data into fewer data subjects, or splitting data into more data subjects.

Example: Salaries and sales figures may be combined from weeks or months into quarters or years, or they may be broken down from quarter to weeks and months.

Example: Boundaries could change, such as political boundaries or sales regions, resulting in different sets of data.

Example: Data may be realigned between calendar years, state fiscal years, and federal fiscal years, or they may be realigned to different monthly boundaries, such as the first and last day of the month or months split between the ninth and tenth of the month.

Example: Product identifiers or names may be changed for the same product.

Example: Different aging categories may be used for delinquent accounts.

Restructure Data

The seventh data transformation step is to restructure the source data according to the target data model. Data restructuring is not the same as data translation or data recasting. Two types of restructuring can occur during data transformation.

> Data restructuring alters the structure of the data.

Evaluational data restructuring ensures that all the data necessary for multiple dimension analysis are in multiple dimension data subjects. It unnormalizes repeating groups and interattribute dependencies for efficient processing as described in the data normalization section in Chapter 10. The data needed for multiple dimension analysis are copied from single dimension qualifying data subjects and placed in the multiple dimension data focus. An organization must decide which data characteristics will be used for multiple dimension analysis and make sure those data characteristics are in the data focus.

Logical data restructuring involves the restructuring from the logical data model of the source data to the logical data model of the target data. It includes any changes in the logical structure from disparate data to integrated data and any changes in the logical structure from operational to evaluational data.

Example: The logical structure of the source disparate employee data shows that employee data exist in several different places, such as payroll, training, affirmative action, and position assignment. The logical structure of the target integrated employee data shows those data in one employee data subject. Restructuring the employee data involves moving the data from the disparate data sources into one integrated Employee data record.

Example: The logical structure for the operational Vehicle Trip data is fully normalized, and the logical structure for the evaluational Vehicle Trip Focus is largely unnormalized. Restructuring the Vehicle Trip Focus data involves replicating data from the qualifying data subjects to the data focus.

Physical data restructuring involves the denormalization of the data from the logical data model to the physical operating environment represented by the physical data model. A discussion of all the physical operating environments and the possible data denormalizations that could occur for those operating environments is beyond the scope of this book.

Example: The employee data will be placed in an ADABAS database management system and will be denormalized to be operationally efficient in that system.

Example: The Vehicle Trip data will be placed in a Prism data warehouse system on Sybase and will be denormalized to be operationally efficient in that environment.

Summarize Data

The eighth data transformation step is to summarize the source data to the level desired for the target data. Data summarization can occur either in operational data or when operational data are transformed to evaluational data. Summarizing operational data is relatively easy.

Example: Vehicle Trip data are summarized to a month, creating Vehicle Trip Month with the data characteristics Vehicle Trip Month Miles, Vehicle Trip Month Trip Count, and so on.

Operational data are summarized to the most detailed level that can be obtained when drilling down in the evaluational database. They could be the operational data supporting business transactions, or a level of summarization above the operational data. An organization must determine the lowest level of detail needed in the evaluational database by balancing the volume of data that will be in the evaluational database, the type of multiple dimension analysis desired, and the time to perform the analysis.

Example: Vehicle Trip data are placed in an evaluational database at a quarter level of detail. The Vehicle Trip data are summarized from a daily basis to a quarterly basis. A quarter identifier in Vehicle Trip Focus identifies the quarter, and a Quarter qualifying data subject is created.

Load Data

The ninth data transformation step is to load the transformed data into the target database. It includes any data conversion necessary for the physical operating environment and any data editing that was not done in the previous steps.

The only major task during data loading is final data editing and taking action when data fail the edits. All transformed data should be edited to ensure their quality is at the level desired for the target database. A final editing as the data are loaded is a check to make sure that data quality was maintained or improved during data transformation. Not having a final data edit could allow low-quality data to enter the target database.

Edit failures are not likely if the previous steps in data transformation were done properly. The extraction, reconstruction, translation, recasting, and restructuring steps should have prepared the data so they pass any edit criteria placed on the target database. If the transformed data do fail the edits, the previous data transformation steps should be reviewed and adjusted.

After the transformed data are successfully loaded, the interim database could be retained in case additional or adjusted transformations are necessary. Those transformations can be made to the interim database and the target database can be reloaded. When the transformed data are acceptable, the interim database may be eliminated. The original data, however, should be retained in case the data needs to be recast or otherwise retransformed. Those data may be placed in archival storage, but they should be retained for future use.

Review Data

The tenth data transformation step is to review the target data to determine whether they were transformed correctly. A check is made to ensure that the transformation process was appropriate and all transformed data are correct according to the logical data model and expectations. If the check reveals that the data are not as expected, the data transformation process needs to be adjusted and the data reloaded. This process continues until the data are correct.

SUMMARY

Data transformation is a formal process for transforming data in the data resource within a common data architecture. It is an important process for helping an organization manage and survive on their disparate data while developing an integrated data resource. Data transformation is not a trivial process, however, in spite of claims by a variety of products promoted for cleansing data. It requires careful thought and planning to be successful.

Data transformation is based on a perspective of the data resource that includes historical, operational, and evaluational data that can exist either in a disparate data environment or in an integrated data resource. The perspective includes nine formal data transformation routes, of which two are desirable, four are not desirable but are acceptable, and three are undesirable. The data transformation process includes 10 specific steps which support, in whole or in part, the nine data transformation routes.

The data transformation process begins by identifying and modeling the target database. Next the source data necessary to develop the target data are identified. This step requires the data refining process if the source data are disparate data. The required data are then extracted from the official data variations and placed in an interim database.

Any historical data that were stored as individual data values are reconstructed into full data records. Next the interim data are translated to the official data variations, which also requires the data refining process. The interim data are then recast for historical continuity and restructured to meet the requirement of the target data resource. If the data are being transformed to an evaluational database, they are summarized to the lowest level of detail desired.

Finally, the transformed data are loaded into the target database and reviewed to ensure they are complete and correct as expected. If the data are not complete and correct, the data transformation steps are adjusted and the data are re-transformed. This process continues until the transformed data are complete and correct.

The data transformation process helps an organization resolve its disparate data when it is used carefully and methodically. Disparate operational data can be transformed to integrated operational data, and applications can be converted to the integrated operational data on a scheduled basis without impact. Evaluational databases can be developed for multiple dimension analysis without affecting operational processing. Historical data can be saved when operational data values change and used for multiple dimension analysis.

Data transformation helps an organization survive on its disparate data without affecting business operations while an integrated data resource is designed and developed.

QUESTIONS

The following questions are provided as a review of the chapter and to stimulate thought about transforming data.

1. What is data transformation?
2. Why is data transformation necessary?
3. Why do products like data warehouse systems, data scrubbers, and data converters not support data transformation?
4. What is the data transformation perspective?
5. Where do operational data stores fit into the data transformation perspective?
6. Where do data warehouse systems fit into the data transformation perspective?
7. What are the possible data transformation routes?
8. What are the desirable data transformation routes?
9. What are the acceptable data transformation routes?
10. Why are some data transformation routes unacceptable?
11. What does the data transformation matrix show?
12. What are the 10 data transformation steps?
13. How do data reconstruction, data recasting, and data restructuring differ?
14. Why is it necessary to put disparate data through the data refining process before data transformation?
15. How does data transformation help an organization survive on disparate data?

## CHAPTER 12

Spatial Data

Organizations must gain control of spatial data before they become as disparate as tabular data.

Geographic information systems are a powerful tool for supporting the business activities of an organization. Their ability to store, manipulate, and display mapping information electronically, and often on short notice, allows managers to make more informed decisions. The ready availability and increasing capability of geographic information systems takes decision making to new heights of efficiency and effectiveness.

The problem with geographic information systems, however, is that data are usually collected and stored independently by different organizations for their specific use. These data are often redundant and inconsistent between organizations, and often within organizations, making it difficult to combine the data and produce meaningful results. If this situation continues, the data in geographic information systems will become as disparate as the data in traditional information systems and will be at least as difficult to correct.

Chapter 12 begins with an explanation of geographic information systems, how they support an organization, and the current spatial data situation. It presents a new perspective for managing spatial data within the common data architecture. This chapter explains the method of describing and structuring spatial data and maintaining their integrity and accuracy. The chapter concludes with a explanation about how spatial data are aggregated and integrated with tabular data.

A DATA PERSPECTIVE

The capabilities of geographic information systems is rapidly increasing which provides increased support for more informed decision making. The ready availability of client-friendly geographic information systems, however, is adding to an already monumental quantity of disparate data. The effectiveness of geographic information systems for decision support could be severely compromised if the data are not properly managed.

Decision Support

Spatial data are a type of nontabular data with a spatial component that allows them to be precisely located on some base, such as the Earth. Spatial data in their raw form within a geographic information system might be considered tabular because they could be displayed in tabular form. This is not, however, the normal method for displaying spatial data because they have little meaning in tabular form.

A *geographic information system* is an organized collection of computer hardware, software, geographic data, and personnel designed to efficiently capture, store, update, manipulate, analyze, and display all forms of geographically referenced information.[1] This kind of system provides a repository for spatial data and a tool for manipulating spatial data to produce maps electronically, the same as data warehouses are a product for storing and manipulating evaluational data. The use of a geographic information system directly supports more informed decision making.

Geographic information systems originally contained geographic and environmental data, which was the origin of the name geographic information systems. They stored, manipulated, and displayed data related to the geography of the Earth. Geographic information systems have gone far beyond their original capability and can now provide much broader decision making support.

> Geographic information systems have rapidly expanded their capability and use for decision support.

---

[1]*Understanding GIS: The ARC/INFO Method*, Environmental Systems Research Institute, Inc., 1990.

Geographic information systems are expanding into demographics, such as population density, crime patterns, health and disease, job market, customer marketing, and socio-economic status. They are being used to establish trends, make projections, and predict the future outcome of various alternative plans, such as the spreading or recession of pollution with various abatement efforts. Geographic information systems are being used to perform what-if analyses to reduce the errors of guessing, such as the environmental impacts of population growth, strip mining, clear cutting, and hazardous waste disposal. They are being used to store aerial photo images and satellite imagery to support traditional map information.

Geographic information systems are becoming more powerful for integrating tabular and nontabular data through various referencing schemes and are expanding into areas not related to the Earth's geography. They are beginning to be used for mapping structures, such as buildings, because they can readily reference tabular data related to spatial objects; something computer-aided design (CAD) systems cannot do. Increased capabilities for storing and manipulating three-dimensional data, such as underground aquifers or the wiring in buildings, will continue to be added to geographic information systems. They also have potential in the biological and physical sciences. Increasing capabilities for time-variant data, such as the movement of populations or building remodeling, will also be added.

Even though the name still persists, geographic information systems are really *spatial information systems*. They can capture, store, manipulate, and display all types of two-dimensional, three-dimensional, and time-variant spatial data. Data about the geography of the Earth, populations on the Earth, and structures not related to the Earth can be processed by spatial information systems. Historical data can be analyzed and used to establish patterns and trends and make projections and predictions. Geographic information systems can provide tremendous support for the really tough decisions that need to be made today.

Data Situation

The disparate data situation in most organizations exists largely with tabular data developed over the last several decades, but it is just beginning to happen with spatial data. The high interest in spatial data, the increased capability of geographic information systems, and the reduced cost of geographic information systems and hardware dramatically increases the rate of spatial data capture and storage. The extension of spatial data from environmental and Earth-related interests into demographics, structures, biology, physical sciences, and other areas further increases the rate of spatial data capture and storage.

Spatial data are rapidly becoming as disparate as tabular data.

The impending problem with spatial data is rapidly increasing quantities of disparate spatial data that cannot be easily integrated, which is the same situation organizations already face with their tabular data. In addition, geographic information systems have the capability to store tabular data to describe spatial features independent of tabular database management systems. These tabular data create another level of disparity if they are not kept synchronized with the tabular data in tabular database management systems.

Spatial data need to be shared at least as much as any other type of data, and they need to be integrated with tabular data. The independent development of spatial data within and among organizations prevents those data from being readily shared. Organizations need to gain control of their spatial data to prevent further disparity. If spatial data are not controlled, they will become as disparate as tabular data within a few years and will be extremely difficult to integrate.

Common Data Architecture

Spatial data are managed within a common data architecture the same as any other data in the data resource. Some people claim that spatial data are a different type of data and must be managed within a different architecture. This claim is no more true with spatial data than it is with evaluational data. A few enhanced notations and techniques are needed to properly manage spatial data within a common data architecture, but spatial data can be managed and integrated with other spatial data and with tabular data to meet the business information demand.

Spatial data are developed and managed within the common data architecture the same as any other data in the data resource.

Many organizations currently developing and maintaining spatial data are thinking locally and producing global junk. They need to think in terms of a global data architecture for all tabular and nontabular data and develop local data to meet specific needs within a common architecture. Thinking globally and acting locally provides the best data possible, allows those data to be readily shared across diverse organizations and disciplines, and maximizes the utilization of limited resources.

Thinking globally and acting locally leverages each organization's investment in their data resource. This forward thinking avoids redundant data collection and unnecessary gaps in the data needed to support business activities. Thinking globally and acting locally resolves the dilemma of a high demand for current, accurate data, often on short notice, and not having the data resource available to support that demand. It supports an organization in its effort to be successful in an increasingly dynamic business environment.

Organizations need to gain control and increase the awareness and understanding of spatial data before they become as disparate as tabular data. They need to integrate spatial data with tabular data to meet the business information demand and provide better decision support. Organizations must take a data view, not a product or platform view, because data cross product and platform boundaries. Spatial data must be managed from a data perspective within a common data architecture.

Spatial Data Definitions

A new perspective for managing spatial data within a common data architecture begins with a definition of terms. Many of these terms already exist today, but a few are new to explain different types of spatial data. The major difference with the new perspective is the separation of spatial data relating to the Earth and spatial data relating to structures not associated with the Earth. Just because spatial data are, or could be, maintained and manipulated in a geographic information system does not mean they are geographic data.

Geographic is derived from *geo* meaning Earth and *graphein* meaning to write to describe. Literally it means describing the Earth. *Geographic data* are any data that locate, identify, or describe objects on the Earth. Data about roads, streams, topography, vegetation, and political boundaries are geographic data.

Demographic is derived from *demos* meaning population and *graphein* meaning to write or describe. Literally it means describing populations. *Demographic data* are any data that locate, identify, or describe populations. Demographic data can be related to the Earth the same as geographic data.

Example: Data about school children, population growth, transportation patterns, and customer needs are demographic data.

A geospatial object is any natural feature, constructed feature, or boundary on, above, or below the Earth's surface. The object may be a point, a line, an area, or a three-dimensional object.

Example: A stream, a school, a county, and an aquifer are geospatial objects.

Geospatial data are any data that represent the geographic location and identifying characteristics of a geospatial object. They place objects on, above, or below the surface of the Earth and uniquely identify those objects. A *geospatial database* is any database containing geospatial data.

Example: The begin and end locations of a stream segment and the stream segment identification, the location and name of a school, and the boundaries and name of a county are geospatial data.

A *structure* is an object with elements arranged in a definite pattern or organization that bear a relationship to each other.

Example: A building, a plane, a boat, a circuit board, and a living organism are structures.

Structographic is a new term derived from *structus* meaning structure and graphein meaning to write or describe. Literally, it means describing a structure. *Structographic data* are any data that locate, identify, or describe objects on, in, or around a structure.

Example: Data about rooms, entrances, wiring, and plumbing in buildings, planes, and boats are structographic data.

Structospatial is derived form *structus* meaning structure and *spatium* meaning of, relating to, involving, or having the nature of space. Literally it means spatial locations on, in, or around a structure. A *structospatial object* is any feature or boundary on, in, or around a structure. The object may be a point, a line, an area, or a three-dimensional object.

Example: An electrical outlet, plumbing, floor plans, and rooms are structospatial objects.

Structospatial data are any data that represent the location and identifying characteristics of a structospatial objects. They place structospatial objects on, in, or around a structure and uniquely identify those objects. A *structospatial database* is any database containing structospatial data.

Example: Data about plumbing, wiring, and structural support in a building are structospatial data.

Spatial is a general term including both geospatial and structospatial. *Spatial data* include both geospatial data and structospatial data. A *spatial database* is any database that contains geospatial or structospatial data. These general terms will be used in the following discussions unless reference is made specifically to *geospatial* or *structospatial*.

SPATIAL DATA DESCRIPTION

For the most part spatial data are described within the common data architecture the same as operational data and evaluational data. A few new definitions are needed to support description of spatial data within the common data architecture, however.

Data Layers

A *data layer* is a separate and distinct set of related spatial data that are stored and maintained in a spatial database. It represents a particular theme or topic of interest in the real world and is equivalent to a data subject over a given area. A *geospatial data layer* contains geospatial data, and a *structospatial data layer* contains structospatial data.

Example: A data layer might be defined for the county roads in a county or for the wiring in a building. A data layer is represented as a rhomboid, as shown in Figure 12.1.

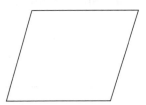

Figure 12.1   The symbol for a data layer.

A *data layer extent* is the outer boundary, or the limits, of a data layer.

Example: The data layer extent for the county roads in a county would be that county's boundary.

The *data layer coverage* is the portion of a data layer extent for which data are captured and stored in a spatial database. The data layer coverage is always within the data layer extent.

Example: The data layer coverage for county roads may be only the rural areas of a county, and the data layer coverage for wiring may be only the new addition to a building.

There could be several different data layer coverages within a data layer extent.

Example: There may be three separate urban areas in a county resulting in three separate data layer coverages for urban areas, or there could be three different areas of damage in a building resulting in three separate data layer coverages.

A *data layer exclusion* is the portion of a data layer extent for which data are not captured and stored. It is the reverse of a data layer coverage. In some situations, it is easier to describe the exclusions than to describe the coverage.

The *extent of interest* is the outer boundary of an area that is of interest to an organization for a specific business purpose. It may be part of a data layer extent, a complete data layer extent, or multiple data layer extents.

Example: The extent of interest for all county roads in Western Washington is all counties in Western Washington, and the extent of interest for wiring on all floors of a building would be the entire building.

A *primitive data layer* is a data layer that represents one set of objects or events in the real world.

Example: County roads, streams, schools, cable raceways, and plumbing are primitive data layers.

A *derived data layer* is a data layer built by combining two or more primitive or derived data layers to meet a specific business need. A derived data layer represents two or more sets of objects or events in the real world.

Example: The county road data layer and the stream data layer could be combined to show bridge and culvert locations.

Example: Plumbing, wiring, and cable raceways may be combined to show the wiring infrastructure of a building.

Spatial data need some form of control, or base, for properly registering and aligning spatial objects. The control is usually provided through a *spatial reference system* that provides the horizontal (x and y), and sometimes vertical (z), control necessary for accurately positioning spatial objects and events. A spatial reference system also provides control for combining the data between two or more data layers.

A *geospatial reference system* provides the control for accurately placing spatial objects and events on, above, or below the surface of the Earth.

Example: The Public Land Survey and State Plane Coordinates are geospatial reference systems.

A *structospatial reference system* provides the control for accurately placing spatial objects and events on, in, or around a structure.

Example: The architectural drawing could be the control for a building.

Georeferencing is the process of accurately placing geospatial objects on, above, or below the surface of the Earth according to a spatial reference system. The term is developed from *geo* meaning Earth and *referre* meaning to carry back. *Structoreferencing* is the process of accurately placing structospatial objects in, on, or about a structure according to a spatial reference system. The term is developed from *structus* meaning structure and *referre* meaning to carry back.

A spatial reference system provides the foundation for developing and maintaining data layers, as shown in Figure 12.2.

A *framework data layer* is a primitive data layer that is basic to many map and business data layers. It is based on a spatial reference system and provides the base for developing specific data layers and business data layers.

Example: Digital elevations, transportation routes, land parcels, and surface water bodies could be geospatial framework data layers.

Example: Wiring, plumbing, stairwells, and elevators could be structospatial framework data layers.

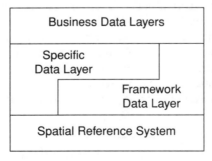

Figure 12.2   Data layer relationships.

A *specific data layer* is any primitive data layer, other than a framework data layer, that is of interest to an organization. It has a more specific, limited interest than a framework data layer. A specific data layer can be based on either a spatial reference system or a framework data layer.

Example: Population, crime, disease, geologic hazard areas, and vegetation type are geospatial specific data layers.

Example: Office layout, exit routes, and room usage are structospatial specific data layers.

A *business data layer* is any derived data layer resulting from an aggregation of framework or specific data layers to meet specific business needs.

Example: Population density, crime statistics, and family socio-economic status could be combined to form a geospatial business data layer for analyzing crime patterns.

Example: Office layout, electrical outlets, and cable raceway openings could be combined to form a structospatial business data layer for office planning.

Spatial Data Layer Names

Spatial data are named with the data naming taxonomy the same as any other data. A data layer is equivalent to a data subject and is named with the data subject component of the data naming taxonomy. The common data subject word Spatial is appended to the name.

Example: Timber Stand Spatial, Vegetation Spatial, Soil Unit Spatial, and Transportation Spatial are typical geospatial data layer names.

Example: Wiring Spatial, Plumbing Spatial, and Electrical Spatial are typical structospatial data layer names.

> Each data layer is uniquely named using the data subject naming component.

The location or source of a data layer is indicated by the data site component of the data naming taxonomy.

Example: Thurston: Timber Stand Spatial and Pierce: Timber Stand Spatial identify the geospatial data layers representing timber stands in Thurston and Pierce Counties.

Example: Architect: Wiring Spatial and Contractor: Wiring Spatial identify the structospatial data layers representing the planned and the actual wiring for a building.

The selection of specific objects or events from a data layer is indicated by the data occurrence selection component of the data naming taxonomy.

Example: Thurston: [Mature Hemlock] Timber Stand Spatial and Pierce: [Young Alder] Timber Stand Spatial identify the selection of mature hemlock timber stands in Thurston County and the selection of young alder timber stands in Pierce County.

Example: Architect: [High Voltage] Wiring Spatial and Architect [Low Voltage] Wiring Spatial identify the selection of high- and low-voltage wiring in a building.

The version of a data layer is identified with the data version component of the data naming taxonomy. Some spatial data change on a regular basis. The more frequently spatial data change, the greater the need for specific data version identification.

Example: Thurston [Mature Hemlock] Timber Stand Spatial <1991> and Thurston [Mature Hemlock] Timber Stand Spatial <1994> show two different versions of mature Hemlock timber stands in Thurston County.

Example: Contractor [High Voltage] Wiring Spatial <Planned> and Contractor [High Voltage] Wiring Spatial <As Built> show two different versions of the wiring for a building.

The data version component can include both a version identifier and a modification identifier, the same as evaluational data. The version identifier shows a new set of data, and the modification identifier shows a change in existing data values.

Example: A new set of more recent data for the timber layer would be indicated by a change in the version identifier, such as Thurston [Mature Hemlock] Timber Stand Spatial <1993>. A change in data values for an existing version of data would be shown with the modification identifier, such as Thurston [Mature Hemlock] Timber Stand Spatial <1991.1>.

Data version identification is critical for spatial data.

The scale at which data were collected and the method of data collection can be placed in the data layer name to provide uniqueness as long as the data layer name is not too long.

Example: Frost County Wetland Spatial 1:12,000 Photo <County Planning Version 1> indicates that the data layer contains the first version of data concerning the wetlands in Frost County that was collected at a scale of 1:12,000 by the county's planning division using aerial photo interpretation.

Example: Frost County Wetland Spatial 1:4,000 Survey <County Engineer Version 4> indicates that the data layer contains the fourth version of data concerning the wetlands in Frost County collected at a scale of 1:4,000 by the county engineer using a field survey.

Example: Structure Weakness Spatial 1:400 <Contractor A> and Structure Weakness Spatial 1:200 <Contractor B> show two different versions of structural weaknesses in a building.

When data layers are combined, a data layer name that indicates the combination is developed using the common data subject word Combined before Spatial.

Example: The aggregation of the timber data layer and the soil data layer is Timber Soil Combined Spatial.

The data layer definition explains how the data layers were combined. If several different aggregations of the timber and soil data layers were made, a sequential number is added.

Example: Timber Soil Combined Spatial 1 and Timber Soil Combined Spatial 2 are different aggregations of the same data layer combination.

Data layers that are developed and printed to meet a specific request, but are not saved electronically, should be uniquely named for identification and documentation. The unique name should include the source of the data, the data layer name, and the data version. The version and modification identifiers and the sequence numbers for combined data layers are both useful for identifying maps printed from a spatial information system. Organizations may consider printing the unique name on the map if the map is released outside the organization.

Printed maps must be uniquely defined the same as data layers.

The data characteristics in a data layer are named the same as any other data characteristic. Data characteristics carry the name of the tabular data subject corresponding to the data layer. They do not have the common word Spatial in their name.

Example: The Soil Unit data subject corresponds to the Soil Unit Spatial data layer. The data characteristics are prefixed with Soil Unit, not with Soil Unit Spatial.

Spatial Data Definition

Spatial data are comprehensively defined the same as any other data. Each primitive and derived data layer is comprehensively defined so people thoroughly understand what the data layer represents and how it was developed. The business data layer definitions need to explain exactly what data were selected and how they were aggregated.

> Comprehensive spatial data definitions are a key component of good metadata.

Data versions also need to be comprehensively defined so people thoroughly understand what each data version represents and why it was created. The data version definition could be included in the data layer definition if it applies only to that data layer, or it could be kept separately if it applies to more than one data layer. If both the version identifier and modification identifier are used, each must be comprehensively defined.

Each map that is printed from a spatial information system should have a comprehensive definition. All too often a map is found and the data used to create the map are unknown. A good comprehensive definition of the data used to produce the map and the method used to create the map prevent misinterpretation and inappropriate conclusions and decisions.

SPATIAL DATA STRUCTURE

Spatial data are structured and documented within the common data architecture using the same notations and diagrams used for tabular data. The difference is the one-to-one relation between data layers and their corresponding data subjects and the use of foreign keys as a reference between spatial data and tabular data.

Data Relations

Data layers are shown with the data subject symbol and data relations are shown with dashed lines and arrows. A one-to-one data relation exists between a data layer and its corresponding data subject. Use of the common word Spatial in the data subject name indicates a one-to-one data relation between a single occurrence in the tabular data subject and the corresponding single object or event in the spatial data layer.

Example: Soil Unit Spatial and Soil Unit and Road Segment Spatial and Road Segment readily identify the data layers and their corresponding data subjects, as shown in Figure 12.3.

Figure 12.3   Data relations between spatial data and data subjects.

A data layer could have data relations to two or more data subjects when data layers are aggregated.

Example: The aggregation of the Soil Unit Spatial and Timber Stand Spatial to a Soil Timber Combined Spatial results in data relations to two data subjects, as shown in Figure 12.4.

A data subject could also have data relations to two or more data layers when data are aggregated in many different ways.

Example: The Soil Unit Spatial could be aggregated with both the Timber Stand Spatial and the Stream Spatial to form the Soil Timber Combined Spatial and the Soil Stream Combined Spatial, as shown in Figure 12.5.

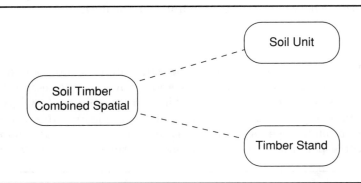

Figure 12.4   Data relations to multiple data subjects.

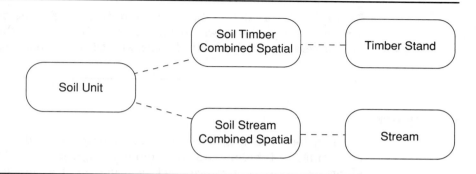

Figure 12.5   Data relations to multiple data layers.

There are usually few data relations between data layers, except when data layers are aggregated. In many situations, a data layer is not actually developed, or is developed only temporarily, for data layer to data layer analysis.

Example: The aggregations for the Soil Unit Spatial, Timber Stand Spatial, and Stream Segment Spatial are shown on a subject relation diagram, as shown in Figure 12.6. Notice the one-to-many data relations between the primitive data layers and the combined data layers. Each Soil Unit and each Timber Stand could appear many times in the combined layer. The one-to-many data relations are really a resolution of the many-to-many data relations between the primitive data layers.

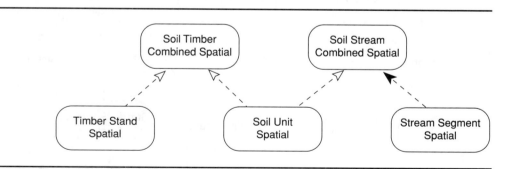

Figure 12.6   Data relations between spatial data layers.

Example: A complete subject relation diagram for the timber, soil, stream example is shown in Figure 12.7. It contains the primitive data layers, the derived data layers, and the corresponding data subjects.

Primary Keys

Primary keys are as important for managing spatial data as they are for managing tabular data. In tabular data, a primary key uniquely identifies a data occurrence, such as a person or a vehicle. In spatial data, a primary key uniquely identifies an object or event, such as stream segment, a school building, or a traffic accident location. The objects and events in a data layer are equivalent to the data occurrences in the corresponding data subject.

Ideally, the primary key for a data subject and the primary key for its corresponding data layer are identical.

Example: The primary key for each school building in a School Building data subject is School Building Name. That same primary key should be used in School Building Spatial so the spatial and tabular data can be integrated.

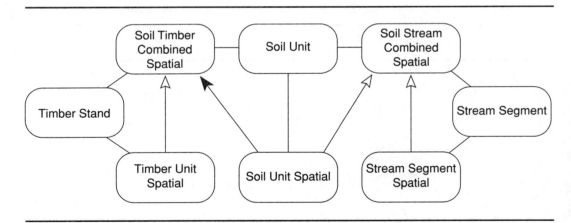

Figure 12.7   Complete subject relation diagram for spatial data layers and data subjects.

System-assigned keys should be avoided because the same primary key will not be assigned in a geographic information system and a database management system. If a system assigned key is used, a meaningful business key should also be maintained for a better understanding of the data layer, and it should be identical in both the spatial and tabular databases.

> Data layer primary keys should be meaningful business data characteristics.

Many primitive objects are created when data layers are aggregated to meet a specific business need.

Example: The Timber Stand Spatial with a primary key of Timber Stand Identifier, Soil Unit Spatial with a primary key of Soil Unit Number, and Slope Class Spatial with a primary key of Slope Class Code are aggregated. The resulting Timber Combined Spatial has many small primitive units resulting for the overlap between timber stands, soil units, and slope classes. These primitive units are uniquely identified with a primary key of Timber Stand Identifier, Soil Unit Number, Slope Class Code, and a Timber Combined Sequence Number. The sequence number is necessary in case a duplicate primitive unit exists.

Geocoding is the process of designating primary keys for geospatial objects and maintaining those unique identifiers in both the geospatial data layers and related tabular data subjects so that the tabular and spatial data can be related. *Structocoding* is the process of designating primary keys for structospatial objects and maintaining those unique identifiers in both the structospatial data layers and related tabular data subjects so that the tabular and spatial data can be related.

A foreign key is, or should be, maintained in both the data layer and the data subject when data layers and data subjects are in a one-to-one data relation. These foreign keys are necessary to support the integration between spatial data and tabular data. Ideally, the primary keys in a data layer and its corresponding data subject are identical, and the foreign keys are identical as well. If the primary keys are different between the data layer and its corresponding data subject, the foreign keys will also be different.

SPATIAL DATA QUALITY

The quality of spatial data, particularly data accuracy, is critical for the proper management and use of spatial data to support business needs. Location is a key component of spatial data, and the accuracy of the location is vital to the proper placement of objects on the Earth or in structures. The accuracy of spatial data is often unknown and might not be at the desired level. The major accuracy problems are documenting the current accuracy of existing data and adjusting that accuracy to the desired level.

Datums

A *datum* is something used as a base for calculating or measuring. Sea level is a traditional datum for measuring elevations, and latitude/longitude is a traditional datum for locating objects on the Earth's surface. A *geodatum* is a datum for aligning objects on, above, or below the Earth's surface. A *structodatum* is a datum for aligning objects in, on, or around a structure.

The designation and use of consistent horizontal and vertical geodatums is mandatory for the accurate placement of geospatial objects. If different geodatums are used, geospatial objects are inconsistently placed on the Earth, and it is difficult to combine data with meaningful results. The establishment of consistent horizontal and vertical geodatums ensures that geospatial data are accurately placed on the Earth.

Consistent horizontal and vertical geodatums must be established.

Organizations must use an established horizontal geodatum, such as the North American Datum 83(91), known as NAD 83(91). If another horizontal geodatum is used, it should be precisely documented and related to an established horizontal geodatum. Organizations must also use an established vertical geodatum, such as the North American Vertical Datum of 1988, known as NAVD 88. If another vertical geodatum is used, such as a local vertical geodatum, it should be documented and related to an established vertical geodatum.

The designation and use of a consistent structodatum, such as a point, a line, or a plane, is mandatory for the accurate placement of structospatial objects in, on, or around a structure. If different structodatums are used, structospatial objects cannot be accurately placed in a structure and it is difficult to combine different layers of data. The establishment of a consistent structodatum for each structure ensures that structospatial data can be accurately placed and integrated.

Linear Referencing Systems

Linear referencing systems are a technique for measuring the length along a linear object. Linear referencing systems apply to both geospatial linear objects, such as roads, streams, and bus routes, and structospatial linear objects, such as wires or pipes. A linear referencing system for geospatial linear objects is a *geolinear referencing system*, and a linear referencing system for structospatial linear objects is a *structolinear referencing system*.

An initial starting point, known as the *anchor point*, is established and the accumulated distance is measured along the linear object from that anchor point. The accumulated distance may be measured in miles, kilometers, or any other convenient unit of measurement. Objects such as bridges and events such as stream flow measurements are located by a unique identifier for the linear object and the accumulated distance from the anchor point.

Example: A bus route is established in a specific area of a city. The bus route has a unique identification and an anchor point. The accumulated distance is measured along the bus route from that anchor point, and each bus stop is located by the accumulated miles from the anchor point. Each bus stop is uniquely identified by the bus route number and the accumulated miles. The times of arrival at each bus stop are calculated from the distance and the average speed of the bus.

Linear referencing is an excellent technique for locating points along linear objects. There is, however, a problem when the linear object changes.

Example: A stream cuts a new channel during spring floods or a highway is relocated causing the linear object to be longer or shorter. The accumulated distance beyond the change is not the same as it was before the change occurred. Any object or event that is located by the new accumulated distance will not have a proper relationship with objects or events before the change occurred.

This situation, known as *linear referencing disparity*, makes it extremely difficult to analyze data over a period of time. The analysis of traffic accidents or stream flow volumes is difficult when the locations are based on different accumulated distances. Previous locations could be adjusted to the latest accumulated distance, but the results of analyses already performed would be inaccurate. Locations could be converted to a common coordinate base, such as latitude/longitude. The common coordinate base may be the only method acceptable for managing data over an extended period of time.

An alternative method is to label each object or event with a linear referencing system version. A different linear referencing system version is defined when a change occurs to a linear object. A common coordinate base is determined when an analysis is performed and the objects or events are converted to that common coordinate base based on the linear referencing system version. The original object or event data are not altered.

Another problem is the existence of multiple linear referencing systems for the same linear object.

Example: Linear referencing systems for a stream could have different anchor points, such as low tide, mean tide, and high tide. The accumulated distances for any particular object or event along that stream are different depending on the anchor point. Different linear referencing systems may also use different measurement units.

A third problem with linear referencing systems is the unique identifiers for linear objects. Unique identifiers are primary keys and must conform to the criteria for designating primary keys. One of those criteria is that the values of the primary key must not change. Many unique identifiers designated for linear objects contain values that can change.

Example: A railroad line might be designated by the owner of the railroad and a line number. A portion of that railroad line might be sold to another railroad company causing a change in the value of the primary key. A similar situation might occur when highways are changed between a state and a county causing the route numbers to change.

A fourth problem with linear referencing systems is whether distances were measured horizontally or topographically. It is relatively easy to get horizontal distances in a geographic information system and more difficult to get topographical distances. It is relatively easy to get topographical distances in the real world and more difficult to get horizontal distances. Any linear referencing system should state explicitly whether the distance is measured horizontally or topographically.

These situations could severely affect data quality and must be resolved. Each linear referencing system must be uniquely named, a stable primary key must be designated, a single anchor point must be established, and the measurement units and method must be consistent. If there are three different anchor points, there are three different linear referencing systems that must be uniquely named.

Example: The linear referencing system for Big Bully creek based on mean tide using miles is Big Bully Creek Mean Tide Miles. A linear referencing system based on high tide using kilometers might be Big Bully Creek High Tide Kilometers.

If the length or course of a linear object changes, there would be a new version for the linear referencing system for that linear object.

Example: If Big Bully creek cut a new course, the new linear referencing system after the course was cut is Big Bully Creek Mean Tide Miles <Version 2>.

When objects show continuous change, the frequency at which those changes are captured and stored in a spatial information system should be documented. The frequency depends on the specific business needs. Data versions become more important as the frequency of data capture increases and should be used to indicate the time when data were collected.

Linear Addressing Systems

A *linear addressing system* is a technique for establishing addresses along linear objects that do not change over time. It is a fixed addressing system that does not change if the linear object changes.

Example: The mileposts commonly seen along highways and freeways are a linear addressing system for roads. These mileposts are placed when the road is established and are not changed if the length of the road changes. The address points remain the same even though the linear distance between the address points may increase or decrease.

> Linear addressing systems have fixed points that do not change over time.

The location of objects or events are determined by a relative offset from the linear address system. Those fixed offsets can be converted to a common coordinate system for analysis, if necessary.

Example: A location of *500 meters north of Milepost 36 on Interstate 74* does not change because the measurement is relative to a fixed point.

The only problem with a linear addressing system is an offset on an old segment of a linear object that no longer exists. This situation is documented with a version identifier the same as with linear referencing systems.

Example: An event occurred *0.6 mile south of Milepost 144 on State Route 16*. Subsequent to the event, the road location was changed so the event is on a portion of the roadway that no longer exists. Each road segment has a linear address version identifier that goes with the event.

Geographic Areas

Many different geographic areas are designated for different business uses. All of these sets of geographic areas are important for at least one business purpose.

Example: A state may have as many as 300 different sets of geographic areas established, such as state legislative districts, state congressional districts, fire districts, school districts, county road districts, library districts, cemetery districts, sewer districts, transportation analysis zones, counties, and cities.

The problem with many sets of geographic areas is that they overlap and the data collected for one set of geographic areas are difficult to apply to another set of geographic areas.

Example: The data collected for fire districts is difficult to integrate with the data collected for law enforcement districts, and the data collected for library districts is difficult to integrate with data for school districts.

> Data quality is an issue when data are integrated between geographic areas.

Any adjustments to data from one set of geographic areas to another open up a data quality issue.

Example: If an even distribution of objects or events in one set of geographic areas is assumed, such as population distribution or school districts, and the data are integrated with an assumed even distribution of objects or events in another set of geographic areas, such as election results by legislative district, the quality of the results may be in question.

Data quality issues need to be considered when data are integrated between different sets of geographic areas.

Linear Object Segmentation

Linear object segmentation is a technique where an object or event can be located on segments of a linear object or across segment boundaries of adjacent linear objects. Multiple objects or events with different boundaries can be co-located on one or more connecting linear objects.

Example: Road segments are defined between intersections. One road segment has three different types of surfacing material, four different projects for widening the shoulders, and two scenic areas. The surfacing, shoulder widening, and scenic areas all have different beginning and ending points and all overlap. They also extend into other road segments.

> Linear object segmentation is important for events and objects that cross linear object boundaries.

Points are designated within a linear object that represent the beginning and ending of the segments for these objects or events.

Example: A shoulder widening project may begin at mile 62.4 in road segment 74 and extend to mile 64.3 in road segment 76. A resurfacing project may begin at mile 63.2 in road segment 74 and end at mile 64.4 in road segment 76. A scenic area begins at mile 61.9 in road segment 74 and ends at mile 62.5 in segment 74.

Linear object segmentation allows a linear object to be segmented multiple ways so objects and events can be accurately located.

Metadata

Metadata are data that help people understand the data. They are needed to easily identify, readily obtain, and effectively use data to meet the business information demand. As the data resource becomes larger and more complex, the need for complete, current, accurate, and readily available metadata is mandatory. Without proper metadata, the data resource cannot be effectively or efficiently used.

> Spatial data need good metadata about location accuracy and data heritage.

Spatial data are part of the data resource and need good metadata the same as any other data. They particularly need good metadata about the accuracy of locations, either on, above, or below the Earth's surface or in, on, or about a structure, and the heritage of data values. Many different methods of location determination are available. Precise data need to be maintained about the method of location determination and the accuracy of the location. Also, spatial data can be easily changed, which directly affects any tabular data integrated with the spatial data. Accurate determination of the source and reason for any

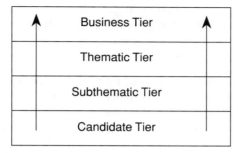

Figure 12.8   The four-tier concept for spatial data.

changes is important for maintaining the quality of spatial data and the tabular data related to spatial data.

MANAGING SPATIAL DATA

The management of spatial data within a common data architecture centers around several basic concepts and techniques. The combination of these concepts and techniques ensures that spatial data are properly developed, can be readily integrated with other spatial data, and can be readily integrated with tabular data. The concepts provide a way to share spatial data to meet business needs and leverage limited resources.

Spatial Data Tiers

Data layers can be grouped into tiers representing levels of data aggregation. A *spatial data tier* is a set of data layers representing a particular level of spatial data aggregation. The *four-tier concept* for spatial data contains four spatial data tiers, as shown in Figure 12.8.

The *candidate tier* consists of data layers that are temporary data layers that are used for entering and adjusting data, determining what data to combine into a subthematic data layer, or determining how to combine data to form a subthematic data layer. It is a candidate for building subthematic data layers.

Example: Candidate geospatial data layers are defined for pumping stations, treatment plants, interceptor sewers, settling ponds, manholes, outfalls, storm water drains, and storm water outfalls for a waste water infrastructure.

Example: Candidate structospatial data layers might be defined for different sets of wiring, plumbing, or other building infrastructure components.

The *subthematic tier* consists of primitive data layers that collectively contribute to a major data theme in a fully enhanced thematic data layer. There are usually one or more permanent data layers in a sub-thematic tier, but there may be none if there is a single layer in the thematic tier.

Example: Subthematic geospatial data layers might be developed for waste water facilities, interceptor sewers, storm water drains, gravity sewers, and storm water outfalls that contribute to the waste water infrastructure data theme.

Example: Subthematic structospatial data layers might be developed for wiring, plumbing, and cable raceways that contribute to a building infrastructure data theme.

The *thematic tier* consists of primitive or derived data layers that represent a major data theme, such as transportation, land use, surface water, or waste water infrastructure. The data layers in the thematic tier may be framework data layers, or map data layers. Data layers in the thematic tier are usually permanent, but they may be temporary or nonexistent, depending on the use and importance of data layers in the subthematic tier.

Example: Geospatial data themes may be designated for transportation, surface water bodies, and vegetation.

Example: Structospatial data themes may be designated for infrastructure, occupancy and usage, and major structural components.

The *business tier* consists of data layers that are a combination of data layers from the thematic and/or subthematic tiers to meet business needs. There are relatively few thematic and subthematic data layers, but there can be many extractions and combinations of those data layers that meet business needs. The data layers in the business tier may be permanent or temporary depending on the continued business needs.

Example: Geospatial data layers for roads, rivers, and bridges may be combined to meet a specific business need.

Example: Structospatial data layers for electrical, phone, and computer network outlets might be combined.

The business tier represents the business data layers shown in Figure 12.2. The thematic and subthematic tiers represent the framework data layers and specific data layers shown in Figure 12.2. They provide a way to classify or group data layers according to major and minor themes.

Spatial Data Themes

The development of spatial data themes and spatial data subthemes helps to organize spatial data within the common data architecture. Major spatial data themes are defined, and spatial data subthemes are defined within these spatial data themes.

Example: Transportation, education, surface hydrology, and vegetation could be spatial data themes. Freeways, state highways, county roads, city streets, and private roads could be subthemes within the transportation theme.

The spatial data subthemes are defined based on corresponding data subjects, such as Soil Unit Spatial and Soil Unit, so that spatial and tabular data can be easily integrated. Data subjects are defined based on how an organization perceives the real world, and data layers are based on corresponding data subjects; therefore, data layers support how an organization perceives the world.

Spatial data themes are defined based on how organizations view the world.

The best approach to defining spatial data themes and subthemes is to develop a *spatial data hierarchy* that includes both current and future spatial data needs. Separate spatial data theme hierarchies may be developed for geospatial data and structospatial data resulting in a *geospatial data hierarchy* and a *structospatial data hierarchy*. Existing spatial data are aligned with these hierarchies and new spatial data are developed within the hierarchies. The framework data layers are defined within the spatial data thematic hierarchy. *Critical data layers* for emergency preparedness and response are designated within the spatial data thematic hierarchy and usually become a high priority for development.

> A spatial data hierarchy provides templates for developing consistent data layers.

The data layers in the spatial data hierarchy provide *data layer templates* for developing data layers. Initial emphasis should be placed on developing data layer templates for the framework data layers and the critical data layers. The remaining data layer templates can be defined on a priority basis based on the collective needs of all organizations involved.

Seen Areas

Data layers can be developed for *seen areas*. A seen area is an area of the landscape that is visible and can be seen from another area of the landscape. A *point seen area* is the portion of the landscape that be seen from a specific point on the landscape.

Example: The landscape that can be seen from a roadside viewpoint is the point seen area of that roadside viewpoint.

A *line seen area* is the portion of the landscape that can be seen from a linear feature on the landscape.

Example: The total landscape that can be seen from a road through a natural area is the line seen area of that road.

An *area seen area* is the portion of the landscape that can be seen from another area on the landscape.

Example: The total landscape that can be seen from a park is the area seen area of that park.

Duplicate Data Layers

Duplicate data layers exist when the same spatial data layer extent is maintained redundantly by different organizations.

Example: Several organizations maintain a data layer for the county roads in Wilderness County.

Each organization enhances their data layer differently based on changes they identify in the real world. These independent enhancements, though good for the organization making the enhancement, often provide conflicting or inconsistent data. The result could be different analytical results and inappropriate or conflicting business decisions.

Enhancements to duplicate data layers need to be synchronized.

Duplicate data layers should be synchronized by developing a procedure for coordinating the enhancements and disseminating those enhancements. If appropriate, a central geospatial database that contains all current enhancements should be designated for each duplicate data layer. Organizations can enhance that central database and draw current versions from that central database.

Alternatively, one organization can be designated as the primary organization responsible for enhancements to a data layer extent. The enhancements are disseminated from that primary organization. Primary organizations may be designated for different data layer extents as long as the data layer extents are maintained from a common data layer template.

Data Layer Extents

Multiple data layer extents exists when different organizations maintain multiple extents of the same spatial data theme. If different organizations design and maintain their data layer extents differently, it is very difficult to edge-match those data layers without some type of conversion or adjustment.

Example: Frost County maintains a county road data layer for its county, and the adjoining Wilderness County maintains a county road data layer for its county.

> Multiple data layer extents are synchronized through data layer templates.

Multiple data layer extents are best managed by using the data layer templates described previously. If each organization involved in maintaining a data layer extent for the same spatial data theme uses the same data layer template, the data layer extents easily edge-match. The result is easy integration of spatial data between different organizations.

Time-Variant Spatial Data

Spatial data represent the objects and events at a point in time. *Time-variant spatial data* is the situation where multiple versions of a spatial data extent are maintained over a period of time.

Example: Yearly snapshots of population density would show the changes in population over time.

The concept of time-variant spatial data becomes more important as the capability and price performance of spatial information systems improve. Ultimately, *spatial evaluational databases* could be used for the analysis of trends and projections using spatial data. The integration of traditional *tabular evaluational databases* and spatial evaluational databases will provide the next level of decision support.

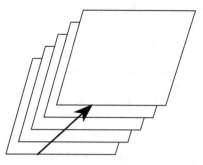

Figure 12.9   Vertical data layer aggregation.

> Data versions are mandatory for managing time-variant spatial data.

The problem with time-variant spatial data is tracking changes in locations. At any point in time (a data instance), a spatial object is in a certain location. At another point in time (another data instance), that object is in another location. Analysis of the change in location over time shows the progression of that object. When the progression is compared with supporting tabular data, appropriate management decisions can be made, or management alternatives can be proposed. The proper use of data version identification is mandatory for managing time-variant spatial data.

Data Layer Aggregation

Data layer aggregation is the process of combining data layers to get a more enhanced data layer. Data layers can be aggregated vertically within or between spatial data tiers to form a more enhanced data layer, as shown in Figure 12.9. *Vertical data layer aggregation* is the combination of two or more data layers to form a more enhanced data layer. Aggregation may occur with either geospatial data layers or structospatial data layers.[2]

---

[2]*Tiling* is a term used in spatial information systems to represent the management of portions of a data layer. It refers to the physical management of a data layer, not to the logical design or management of spatial data.

Example: The waste water facilities, interceptor sewers, storm water drains, gravity sewers, and storm water outfall data layers could be combined to form the waste water infrastructure data layer.

Example: Building wiring, plumbing, network cables, and phone line data layers could be combined to form a building infrastructure data layer.

The vertical aggregation of data layers can be shown in a *vertical data layer aggregation diagram* that looks similar to a subject relation diagram and a data derivation diagram. The symbol for data subjects is used for data layers, but the lines showing the aggregation are solid lines rather than dashed lines, with the arrow pointing in the direction of the aggregation. The diagram is used for documenting the derivation of data layers through aggregation.

Example: The aggregation of mature fir timber stands and soil units is shown in Figure 12.10. The first step is the extraction of mature fir timber stands from the Timber Stand Spatial, and the second step is to

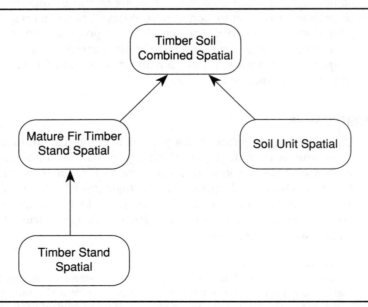

Figure 12.10   Vertical data layer aggregation diagram.

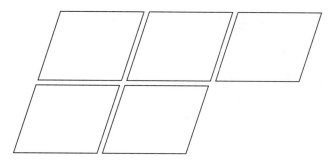

Figure 12.11   Horizontal data aggregation.

aggregate the mature Fir timber stands with the soil units from the Soil Unit Spatial to form the Timber Soil Combined Spatial 1.

Data layers can be aggregated horizontally to form a larger data layer extent. *Horizontal data layer aggregation* is the edge connection of two or more data layer extents, usually from different organizations, so that the same data layer can provide an expanded data layer for a specific extent of interest, as shown in Figure 12.11.[3]

Example: The county road data layers from several counties could be combined to show the county roads for Western Washington.

Data layers can be aggregated chronologically to provide a history of changes. *Chronological data layer aggregation* is the aggregation of successive time periods for a specific data layer extent, as shown in Figure 12.12.

Example: The spread and recession of surface water pollution could be tracked over time and compared to pollution abatement efforts. The changing pattern of building occupancy and use could be tracked over time and evaluated for the structural impact of constant remodeling.

[3]Horizontal data layer aggregation is often referred to as tiling. Tiling, however, represents the physical management of portions of a data layer within a spatial information system.

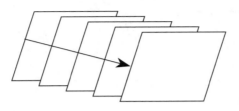

Figure 12.12 Time-variant data layer aggregation.

Three-Dimensional Aggregation

Vertical, horizontal, and chronological data aggregation are combined into a *three-dimensional data layer aggregation* concept, as shown in Figure 12.13. Vertical data layer aggregation combines data layers to form a more enhanced data layer. It occurs between any tiers, as shown by the vertical arrows. Horizontal data layer aggregation connects data layer extents for the same data layer to provide a larger extent. It occurs in any of the top three tiers, as shown by the horizontal arrows. Chronological data layer aggregation combines time periods for a data layer to provide a history of changes. It occurs in any of the top three tiers.

The three-dimensional data layer aggregation forms a network of aggregations. The difficulty with a network of aggregations is a loss of control over spatial data. Different organizations perform different aggregations on different versions of data using different algorithms to

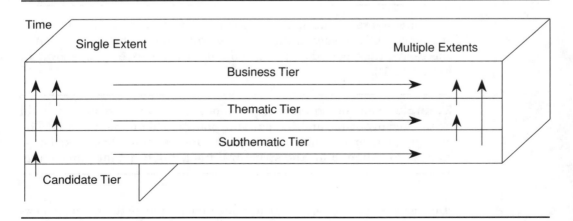

Figure 12.13 Three-dimensional concept for spatial data management.

meet different business needs. The pathway of data layer aggregation and the algorithms used for data layer aggregation vary widely and are often undocumented, resulting in uncertainty about what a combined data layer represents. Data layer aggregation criteria must be developed using the most efficient aggregation pathway and consistent aggregation algorithms. The data tracking process explained earlier can be very useful for documenting the aggregation of data.

Spatial Data Scale

Spatial information systems are scale-blind. Data can be captured and stored at one scale and displayed at any other scale. Although the coordinate values are stored at the original scale, the spatial information system is blind to that scale and can present spatial information at any scale. A problem occurs with the accuracy of data displayed at a scale larger than the scale at which the data were captured.

The *multiple scale concept* defines levels of generalization for spatial data, as shown in Figure 12.14. Spatial data are captured and stored at a specific scale, such as 1:12,000 for geospatial data or 1:400 for structospatial data. These data can be generalized to a smaller scale, such as 1:25,000, 1:100,00, or 1:250,000 for geospatial data or 1:1200 for structospatial data. There could be several levels of generalization for any spatial data tier depending on the business needs.

Data layer generalization is the process of reducing the scale of a data layer extent from the scale at which the data were captured by a formal algorithm. This process is also known as "zooming out" and can occur with both geospatial data and structospatial data.

Example: The scale for surface water bodies may be reduced from 1:12,000 to 1:100,000 to gain a broader perspective for surface water bodies. The scale reduction, however, results in a loss of detail, and many smaller surface water bodies might not appear.

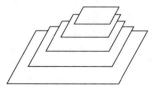

Figure 12.14   The multiple scale concept for spatial data.

> The scale of spatial data cannot be increased larger than the scale at which the data were captured.

Data layer specialization is the process of increasing the scale of a data layer extent. This process is also known as "zooming in" and can occur with both geospatial data and structospatial data. The scale, however, should not be larger than the scale at which the data were captured because it presents a false accuracy.

Example: Geospatial data are captured at 1:12,000 and then generalized to 1:100,000. Those data can be specialized to 1:12,000, but no larger because the apparent accuracy is better than the true accuracy.

Spatial data may be presented at a scale larger than the scale at which they were captured as long as the false accuracy inherent in the larger scale is known and documented.

Integrating spatial data could be difficult, particularly when older spatial data are less granular (smaller scale) than newer spatial data. One approach to integrating spatial data with different scales is to take newer spatial data to a smaller scale. Another approach is to compare data at different scales with the understanding that older spatial data may not be as accurate as newer spatial data.

INTEGRATING TABULAR AND SPATIAL DATA

With the increasing popularity of spatial data, interest in integrating tabular data with spatial data is increasing. The integration of tabular data and spatial data provides additional meaning to relatively meaningless boundaries.

Example: The boundaries of a school district are relatively meaningless without some data to display within those boundaries. If tabular data, such as average grades or race, are analyzed and displayed by school district, the boundaries have increased meaning.

The ability to easily integrate tabular data and spatial data makes massive quantities of tabular data readily available for spatial display.

Data Locating and Identifying Spatial Objects	Data Identifying and Describing Spatial Objects	Data Identifying but Not Describing Spatial Objects	Data Not Identifying or Describing Spatial Objects

Figure 12.15   Basic groups of data for spatial data referencing.

Example: On-line analytical processing of evaluational data produces population distributions for elementary school students that are displayed by school district. The trend in population distributions over time are displayed spatially.

Spatial Data Referencing

A *spatial data reference* is a data relation between tabular data and spatial data for the purpose of connecting and integrating spatial and tabular data. *Spatial data referencing* is the process of integrating tabular and spatial data through a spatial data reference. A spatial data reference is a data relation between tabular and spatial data; therefore, it can be modeled.

The concept of spatial data referencing is shown in Figure 12.15. Four groups of tabular and nontabular data are used in spatial data referencing. The first group contains spatial data that locate and identify spatial objects, but does not contain any data that describe spatial objects. The second group contains tabular data that identify and describe spatial objects, but does not contain any spatial data that locate spatial objects. The third group contains tabular data that identify, but do not describe, spatial objects. The fourth group contains tabular data that do not identify or describe spatial objects.

Three rows are added above these basic groups to show the relationship between spatial data and tabular data and between descriptive data and nondescriptive data, as shown in Figure 12.16. The top row shows the spatial data and the tabular data maintained in database management systems. The third row shows the descriptive data maintained in spatial information systems and nondescriptive data.[4]

---

[4]Most spatial information systems have the capability to store tabular data.

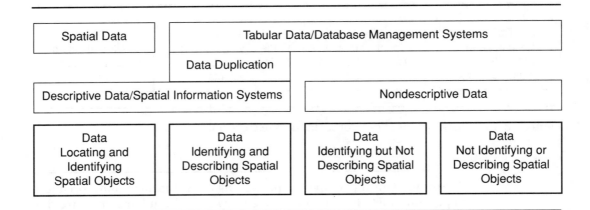

Figure 12.16   Potential duplication of tabular data.

The middle row shows the potential duplication of tabular data between database management systems and spatial information systems. These duplicate data must be properly maintained to prevent any discrepancy.

Another layer is added to the bottom of the diagram, as shown in Figure 12.17. The box on the left represents spatial objects. The boxes on the right represent the different types of spatial data referencing that can occur between tabular data and spatial data.

Descriptive Spatial Referencing

A *descriptive spatial reference* is a spatial data reference that occurs between a set of tabular data that identify and describe a spatial object and spatial data that locate and identify that object.

Example: The length, upper elevation, lower elevation, maximum flow, and minimum flow of a stream; the date of construction, capacity, and value of a school; and the size, land area, and population of a county are tabular data describing a geospatial object that can be referenced to that object.

A *descriptive geospatial reference* is a descriptive spatial reference for geospatial data.

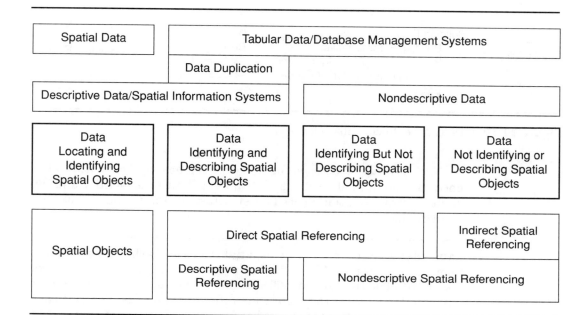

Figure 12.17   Spatial data referencing concept.

Example: Descriptive georeferencing is shown for school districts in Figure 12.18. The data layer is School District Spatial with School District Name as the unique identifier. The tabular data subject also contains the unique identifier and describes each School District. A descriptive geospatial reference occurs between the tabular data subject and the geospatial data layer using School District Name. The subject relation diagram for referencing is shown on the right of the diagram.

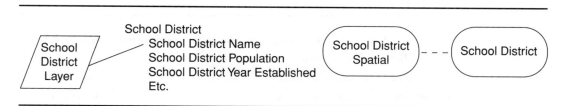

Figure 12.18   Descriptive geospatial referencing.

Figure 12.19   Descriptive structospatial referencing.

A *descriptive structospatial reference* is a descriptive spatial reference that occurs between a set of tabular data that identify and describe a structospatial object and structospatial data that locate and identify that object.

Example: A descriptive structospatial reference is shown for building floor data in Figure 12.19. The structospatial layer is Building Floor Spatial with Building Floor Identifier as the unique identifier. The tabular data subject contains the unique identifier and data that describe each Building Floor. A reference occurs between the tabular data subject and the structospatial data layer using Building Floor Identifier.

Nondescriptive Georeferencing

A *nondescriptive spatial reference* is a spatial data reference that occurs between a set of tabular data that either identify but do not describe spatial objects or do not identify or describe a spatial object and spatial data that locate and identify that object.

Example: Data about the analysis of water samples from a stream, data about students in a school, and data about customers are tabular data that do not describe a geospatial object, but can be referenced to a geospatial object.

A *nondescriptive geospatial reference* is a nondescriptive spatial reference for geospatial data.

Example: Nondescriptive geospatial reference for elementary students is shown in Figure 12.20. The geospatial data layer is still School District Spatial with School District Name as the unique identifier. The tabular data subject for Elementary Students does not describe the School

Figure 12.20   Nondescriptive geospatial referencing.

District, but it contains the unique identifier of School District Name. A reference occurs between the tabular data subject and the geospatial data layer using School District Name.

A *nondescriptive structospatial reference* is a nondescriptive spatial reference for structospatial data.

Example: A nondescriptive structospatial reference for construction projects is shown in Figure 12.21. Construction Project data do not describe the Building Floor Spatial, it contains the Building Floor Identifier. A reference is made between Construction Project and Building Floor Spatial.

Indirect Spatial Referencing

The preceding examples represent a *direct spatial reference* because the unique identifier for objects in the spatial data layers are stored in the corresponding tabular data subjects. A spatial reference can be made directly from the tabular data subject to the spatial data layer using the unique identifier.

An *indirect spatial reference* is a spatial data reference that occurs between a tabular data subject that does not identify or describe a spatial object and a spatial data layer that locates and identifies that spa-

Figure 12.21   Nondescriptive structospatial referencing.

368

tial object. The referencing occurs indirectly through another tabular data subject that contains the unique identifier for the spatial object.

Example: Data about the method of water sample analysis, data about the race of schoolchildren, and data about the population in a county are tabular data that do not describe a spatial object and can only be spatially referenced to that object indirectly through another tabular data subject.

An *indirect geospatial reference* is an indirect spatial reference for geospatial data.

Example: Indirect geospatial reference for the race of schoolchildren is shown in Figure 12.22. Race does not contain the identifier for School District, so a reference cannot be made directly between Race and School District. It must be made indirectly through Elementary Student, which contains the unique identifier School District Name. In other words, the Race is determined for each Elementary Student, which is summarized and displayed by School District.

An *indirect structospatial reference* is an indirect spatial reference for structospatial data.

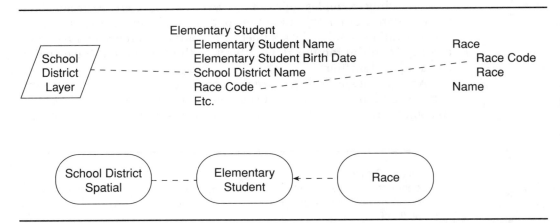

Figure 12.22   Indirect geospatial referencing.

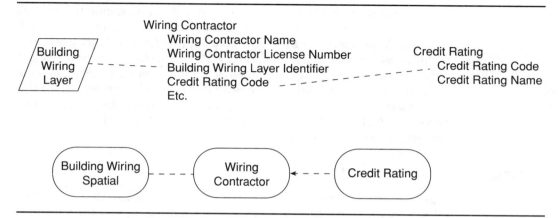

Figure 12.23   Indirect structoreferencing.

Example: Credit Rating for a Wiring Contractor and Building Wiring Spatial is shown in Figure 12.23.

SUMMARY

The proper management of spatial data is important for the proper integration of spatial data, the integration of spatial and tabular data, and the effective and efficient use of spatial data. The time, budget, and personnel constraints that organizations face today do not allow redundant or inconsistent data development or the unnecessary use of resources to collect and maintain data. All resources, including the spatial data resource, must be used effectively to support the business activities of an organization. An organization must plan ahead and build an integrated data resource that includes spatial data, expand that data resource as needed, and build in flexibility to meet changing needs.

Considerable spatial data already exist in many organizations; however, the existing data are not necessarily consistent across those organizations. To maximize the use of existing spatial data, a spatial data hierarchy should be developed and existing data layers should be aligned to that hierarchy. Even though the alignment could result in an additional effort for some organizations, the result would be spatial data that are more readily shared among organizations. Any new spatial data should be developed within the spatial data hierarchy.

Commonality is the theme when developing and managing spatial data because they are shared more than any other data in the data resource. The common data architecture provides the framework and techniques for developing common data, including common spatial data. Data commonality provides a synergy across organizations resulting in a shared data resource that has benefits greater than the sum of the individual databases. Organizations would be remiss in the proper utilization of their resources if they do not actively promote the development of common data.

QUESTIONS

The following questions are provided as a review of the chapter and to stimulate thought about developing and managing spatial data and integrating spatial data with tabular data.

1. What are geographic information systems?
2. Why should geographic information systems be renamed to spatial information systems?
3. What is the current situation with spatial data?
4. Why should spatial data be managed within the common data architecture?
5. What is the difference between geospatial data and structospatial data?
6. What is the difference between a data layer, a data layer extent, and a data layer coverage?
7. What is the difference between a primitive and a derived data layer?
8. What is a framework data layer?
9. What is the difference between specific and business data layers?
10. How are spatial data named and defined?
11. How are spatial data modeled?
12. How are the objects in a data layer uniquely identified?
13. Why are datums necessary for spatial data?
14. What are the problems with linear referencing systems?
15. How does a linear addressing system differ from a linear referencing system?
16. What is linear object segmentation?
17. How are spatial data tiers related to spatial data themes?
18. What is the difference between duplicate data layers and multiple data layer extents?
19. Why are time-variant spatial data becoming important?
20. How does the three-dimensional concept control spatial data aggregation?

21. How are spatial data and tabular data integrated?
22. What is the difference between descriptive and nondescriptive spatial referencing?
23. What is the difference between direct and indirect spatial referencing?
24. Why is it necessary to coordinate spatial data management among organizations?

CHAPTER 13

Distributing Data

> Improper data distribution will destroy the quality and usefulness of an organization's data resource.

Telecommunication networks are prominent in today's society and will continue to play an increasing role in the movement and storage of data. The development of worldwide networks, such as the Internet, wide area networks, metropolitan area networks, and local-area networks provides many options for the transmission and storage of data. The explosion of personal computers, many of which are connected to some type of telecommunication network, adds options for the development, storage, and transmission of data.

Most businesses could not survive today without some form of telecommunications network. The uncontrolled, unmanaged, undocumented movement and storage of data across many different data sites on mainframe computers and telecommunications networks could be a disaster for many businesses, however. An already disparate data resource, made more disparate by the rapid collection of additional data and the uncoordinated development of data warehouses and geographic information systems, could be fragmented beyond recovery if distributed in an unorganized manner.

Chapter 13 begins with an explanation of the concept for distributing data within a common data architecture. It presents the concepts of data origination, official data, and data replication and explains how distributed data are named, defined, and structured. This chapter describes the techniques for partitioning and distributing a data resource within a common data architecture. The chapter concludes with an explanation about how to maintain the quality of a distributed data resource.

DATA DISTRIBUTION CONCEPT

The data distribution concept includes a definition of data distribution and how it relates to data deployment, an explanation of the data distribution dilemma and how a common data architecture helps resolve that dilemma, and the identification of official data and their replication for distribution.

Data Distribution

Data distribution is one part of the overall deployment of a data resource to meet the business information demand. *Data deployment*, also known as *data logistics*, is the dynamic placement and maintenance of the data resource in appropriate products, such as database management systems, data warehouses, and geographic information systems, and at appropriate data sites on mainframe computers and across a telecommunications network in an optimum manner to meet the business information demand.

Data distribution is the placement and maintenance of replicated data at one or more data sites on a mainframe computer or across a telecommunications network. It is the part of developing and maintaining an integrated data resource that ensures data are properly managed when distributed across many different data sites. Data distribution is the deployment of data to data sites.

Data distribution is not the same as data dissemination. *Data dissemination* is the process of getting data from the data resource to a client, within or without the organization, through appropriate applications and telecommunication networks. Data are disseminated through client-server applications, electronic mail, and traditional business applications. Data dissemination is not the process of distributing the data resource across data sites.

Distributed database management is a rapidly evolving technology that distributes and maintains the data resource at a variety of different data sites. A *distributed database* is a collection of multiple logically related databases distributed over a telecommunications network. A *distributed database management system* is a software product that manages and maintains the distributed database and makes it transparent to clients. Data flow freely over any network, or combination of networks, using one or more network protocols. A *distributed database system* is a combination of distributed databases and distributed database management systems. Any database management system can interact with any other database management system across multiple system configurations to provide data to clients.

> Changing technology will change data distribution strategies.

Downsizing, upsizing, rightsizing, outsourcing, insourcing, and a variety of other scenarios prominent today or in the future involve the distribution of data. Data can be moved to and from mainframes, servers, and personal computers or between organizations in any of these scenarios. Data may be moved to many smaller computers to support distributed computing, and they might be moved to fewer larger computers in the future as bandwidths increase and larger volumes of data can be moved rapidly. Data may also be moved to larger, more central sites for integration and analysis.

Data Distribution Dilemma

A major problem today is the large quantities of disparate data that already exist and the need to distribute data to meet business needs. Disparate data are being produced faster than ever before with client-friendly tools, automated data capture techniques, and personal computers. Uncoordinated development of client-server applications, data warehouses, and geographic information systems further increases the disparity. Many organizations are not taking the initiative to stop the development of disparate data and often do not have the time or resources to refine the existing disparate data.

Another major problem most organizations face today is the need to distribute data to support business needs. Organizations are all too willing to grab any set of data and distribute those data to different data sites to support immediate business needs without regard for their quality or maintenance. The result is extensive fragmentation of an already disparate data resource.

> An organization may lose control of its data resource through the distribution of disparate data.

The conflict between the growing disparity of the data resource and the need to distribute and maintain consistent data to support business needs creates a dilemma. A *data distribution dilemma* exists when an organization has a growing data disparity, does not control that disparity or refine disparate data, and distributes disparate data to support individual business needs. An organization could lose complete control of its data resource for a long time if it allows the dilemma to exist.

An organization needs to gain control of its data resource before control is completely lost. The development of disparate data must be stopped, and the existing disparate data must be refined, properly distributed, and consistently maintained. A window of opportunity exists for most organizations to gain control before all control is completely lost. The window varies from one organization to the next, but it exists if an organization takes the initiative.

Common Data Architecture

Control of the data distribution can be gained through a common data architecture. All data are distributed and maintained with techniques based on understanding, modeling, and documenting data within a common data architecture. The emphasis today is on how data are distributed, the medium, particularly with client/server applications and distributed database management systems. There is little emphasis on what data are distributed, the message. Emphasis needs to be placed on what data are distributed and on increasing control over distributed data.

A common data architecture is the base for managing distributed data and resolving the data distribution dilemma.

A common data architecture provides the base for distributing and maintaining distributed data. The distribution of data must be designed and modeled within the common data architecture. A common data architecture that can be used consistently in a decentralized environment must be developed. Organizations must learn that distributing data involves more than moving data files to different data sites. Data distribution involves the evaluation of many different scenarios, alternatives, and criteria.

A common data architecture provides consistency across heterogeneous telecommunication networks and heterogeneous database management systems. It will be a long time, if ever, before the operating environment is homogenous. The operating environment will become more open with any-to-any networks, but it is not likely to become homogenous in the near future. The existence of a heterogeneous operating environment is not an excuse, however, to create a heterogeneous data resource. The common data architecture helps an organization develop a homogenous data resource that is properly distributed and maintained in a heterogeneous environment.

Official Data

Official data are data designated as the official record of reference or system of reference to be used for data replication. They are the official data from which all distributed data should be replicated. *Nonofficial data* are data that are not designated as official data.

Official data variations are the data characteristic variation that has been designated as official for short-term data sharing and long-term development of an integrated data resource, as defined in Chapter 9. They are designated during the data refining process and are identified with an asterisk (*) in front of the data characteristic variation name.

An *official data source* is a data characteristic designated as containing official data, as defined in Chapter 9. Official data sources are designated during data refining by reviewing all redundant sources of a data characteristic and designating one of those redundant sources as the official data source. A *nonofficial data source* is a data characteristic that contains nonofficial data.

An official data source is identified with a pound sign (#) in front of the data site name, the data subject name, or data occurrence group name, or the data characteristic name. If a data site contains data characteristics that are all official data sources, the data site name is prefixed with a pound sign.

Example: # Boston is the data site where all the data subjects and data characteristics are official data sources.

If the data site does not contain data subjects and data characteristics that are all designated as official data sources, it is not prefixed with a pound sign. If a data subject at that data site contains data characteristics that are all official data sources, the data subject name is prefixed with a pound sign.

Example: # Employee or # Western Equipment are data subjects containing data characteristics that are all official data sources.

If all the data characteristics in a data subject or data occurrence group are not official data, the data subject or data occurrence group name is not prefixed with a pound sign, but the appropriate data characteristics are prefixed with a pound sign.

Example: # Employee Height Inches and # Employee Hair Color are official data sources.

Replicating Data

Data are replicated so that they can be distributed to optimize performance and make data readily available to clients. Organizational goals for performance optimization and data availability often mandate the replication and distribution of data. Data are also replicated and distributed for backup and recovery purposes or for alternate access should a data site become unavailable.

Data need to be replicated before they are distributed to data sites. A *data replicate* is the set of data characteristics from a single data subject or data occurrence group that is copied from the official data source and placed at another data site. *Horizontal data replication* is the formal process of creating an exact copy of official data and placing that exact copy at one or more data sites.[1]

Example: Two copies of employee data from an official data source that are placed in two other data sites represent two data replicates.

Data replication creates exact copies of official data.

Data replication is not the same as data duplication. *Data duplication* is a term used to identify data that are captured, processed, or

---

[1]Remember that vertical data replication is the replication of data characteristics from a parent data subject to a subordinate data subject during denormalization.

stored redundantly. It results in unknown, uncontrolled, and unmanaged data redundancy. It is not orderly and creates additional disparate data. Data replication is a planned, known, and controlled data redundancy. Data replicates are knowingly created in an orderly manner from official data and are routinely maintained from those official data.

Data replicates must be created from an official data source. If data are not copied from the official data source, they are not data replicates. A basic concept behind developing an integrated data resource is limiting data redundancy by designating official data sources and using those official data sources for data replication. Data should not be replicated from nonofficial data; this situation is known as *chained data replication*. If data are replicated from nonofficial data, they are considered duplicated data, not replicated data.

Data must be replicated from official data sources and official data variations.

Distributed data must also be the official data variation. If the official data variations are not replicated and distributed, the concept of identifying official data variations for developing an integrated data resource is weakened. Another basic concept behind developing an integrated data resource is limiting the variability of data. Limit variability by designating official data variations and using those official data variations for data replication. If official data variations have not been designated, data should not be replicated and distributed. Replication of nonofficial data variations perpetuates the disparate data situation.

DISTRIBUTED DATA DESCRIPTION

The common data architecture provides techniques for uniquely identifying, precisely naming, and comprehensively defining distributed data.

Distributed Data Names

The data naming taxonomy provides unique data names for distributed data. Unique data site, data occurrence group, and data version names are particularly important for distributed data. Formal data names provide a way to control the distribution and maintenance of data, and ultimately make distributed data transparent to the client.

> The data naming taxonomy provides unique distributed data names.

The data site component of the data naming taxonomy provides a unique name for each data site. The unique data site name may contain the organization name, city name, hardware name, node name, or any other name that uniquely identifies a specific data site, as described in Chapter 5.

Example: Chicago, Dallas, and San Francisco might be data site names, and Purchasing, Marketing, and Manufacturing might be data site names.

The data occurrence group component of the data naming taxonomy provides a unique name for a specific set of data occurrences selected from a data subject.

Example: If employees eligible for retirement are extracted from Employee for distribution, that data occurrence group would be named Retirement Eligible Employee. If all vehicles powered by diesel engines were extracted from Vehicle, that data occurrence group would be named Diesel Powered Vehicle.

The data version component of the data naming taxonomy provides a unique name for each data version at a data site. It identifies whether the distributed data are synchronized with the official data from which they were replicated.

Example: The data version for the official data is <January 1994>, and the data version for distributed data is <December 1993>, which indicates the distributed data are not synchronized with the official data.

The data subject, data characteristic, and data characteristic variation components of the data naming taxonomy provide unique names for distributed data the same as they do for data that exist in one location.

Data replication products are improving steadily. As they become more formalized, they will use formal data names and will automatically document the distribution of data and the refreshing of distributed data. Until data distribution products use formal data names and automatically enhance the metadata warehouse, there is still a need to precisely identify and document the distribution of data. The automatic documentation of distributed data could be combined with data tracking processes to identify data lineage and the changes that occurred to the data at each data site.

Distributed data can have both an official (logical) name and an abbreviated (physical) name. The official data name is used during the design and modeling of data distribution, and the abbreviated data name is used during the movement and maintenance of the distributed data.

Distributed Data Definitions

Comprehensive data definitions are mandatory for distributed data, particularly for data sites, data occurrence groups, and data versions. The techniques for developing comprehensive data definitions presented in Chapter 5 apply to the development of distributed data definitions.

DISTRIBUTED DATA STRUCTURE

The common data architecture provides techniques for formally structuring distributed data. Development of a formal structure for distributed data provides a base for performing a variety of analyses, such as data volumes, performance and response time, capacity, backup and recovery, and the location of data sites. These analyses can be very detailed and depend on the specific operating environment and the organization's criteria for supporting business needs. They are not explained in this book.

> The common data architecture provides techniques for documenting the structure of distributed data.

The approach to structuring distributed data is to logically structure the data independent of the data sites, logically distribute data to the appropriate data sites based on business needs, and then denormalize the data based on the specific operating environment at each data site. The three data structures involved are the logical data structure, the distributed data structure, and the physical data structure. Chapter 14 explains the details for modeling distributed data within the new five-schema concept.

Logical Data Structure

The logical data structure shows the normalized structure of data in the integrated data resource using the official data name. It represents the full set of data subjects and data characteristics available in the integrated data resource. There is no indication of the data located at specific data sites. The logical structure is shown on a data subject structure the same as any other data.

Example: Figure 13.1 shows the logical data structure for Employee.

Distributed Data Structure

The distributed data structure is a logical data structure that shows the data located at specific data sites using the official data name. Distributed data are initially structured at the logical level using a distributed data structure that indicates the specific data subjects or data occurrence groups and the data characteristics located at each data site. Each data site usually contains a subset of data that support business needs.

The distributed data structure is shown on either a logical data distribution outline or a logical data distribution matrix. *The logical data distribution outline* shows the data subjects or data occurrence groups that appear at each data site and their data characteristics in an outline format. The data characteristics are nested within the data subjects or data occurrence groups, which are nested within the data sites. The data sites are listed alphabetically, the data subjects or data occurrence groups are listed alphabetically within each data site, and the data characteristics are listed alphabetically within each data subject or data occurrence group.

```
Employee
    Employee Birth Date CYMD
    Employee Body Build Description
    Employee Hair Color
    Employee Height Inches
    Employee Name Complete Inverted
    Employee Weight Pounds
```

Figure 13.1   Logical data structure for data to be distributed.

Example: The logical data distribution outline for employee data is shown in Figure 13.2. Notice that Employee Hair Color and Employee Weight Pounds are located in Boston but not in Seattle, and Employee Body Build Description is located in Seattle but not in Boston.

More than one data subject or data occurrence group may be distributed to a data site.

Example: The distribution of employee data, equipment data, and customer data for three data sites is shown in Figure 13.3. The data characteristics are left off the diagram for brevity. Notice that Dallas has all Employee data occurrences, but Boston and Seattle have Eastern Employee and Western Employee data occurrence groups respectively. Seattle has all Equipment data occurrences, but Dallas and Boston have Southern Equipment and Eastern Equipment data occurrence groups respectively. Boston has the Eastern Customer data occurrence group, Dallas has the Southern Customer data occurrence group, and Seattle has the Western Customer data occurrence group.

The *logical data distribution matrix* shows data subjects or data occurrence groups that appear at each data site and the data charac-

```
Boston
    Eastern Employee
        Employee Birth Date CYMD
        Employee Hair Color
        Employee Height Inches
        Employee Name Complete Inverted
        Employee Weight Pounds

Seattle
    Western Employee
        Employee Birth Date CYMD
        Employee Body Build Description
        Employee Hair Color
        Employee Name Complete Inverted
```

Figure 13.2   Logical data distribution outline for one data subject.

```
Boston
    Eastern Customer
    Eastern Employee
    Eastern Equipment
Dallas
    Employee
    Southern Customer
    Southern Equipment
Seattle
    Equipment
    Western Customer
    Western Employee
```

Figure 13.3   Logical data distribution outline with many data subjects.

teristics that appear in each data subject or data occurrence group in a matrix. The data sites are listed across the top of the matrix and the data subjects or data occurrence groups with their data characteristics are listed down the left side of the matrix. The data sites are in alphabetical order, the data subjects and data occurrences are in alphabetical order, and the data characteristics are in alphabetical order within their data subject or data occurrence group.

The logical data distribution matrix shows the distribution of data in less space. It is useful for determining the extent of data replication and adjusting the distribution of data between data sites.

Example: The logical data distribution matrix for the employee data shown in Figure 13.2 is shown in Figure 13.4.

Physical Data Structure

The physical data structure shows the data located at data sites using the abbreviated data name to meet product limitations. It is developed from a denormalization of the distributed data structure according to the specific operating environment at each data site. The physical data structure is shown on either a physical data distribution outline or a physical data distribution matrix.

The *physical data distribution outline* shows the data subjects or

Employee	Boston Eastern Employee	Dallas Employee	Seattle Western Employee
Employee Birth Date CYMD	X	X	X
Employee Body Build Description		X	X
Employee Hair Color	X	X	X
Employee Height Inches	X	X	
Employee Name Complete Inverted	X	X	X
Employee Weight Pounds	X	X	

Figure 13.4   Logical data distribution matrix for one data subject.

data occurrence groups located at each data site and the data characteristics in each data subject or data occurrence group in an outline format. The data characteristics are nested within the data subjects or data occurrence groups, which are nested within the data sites. Either the logical data site and data subject or data occurrence group names or the physical network node and data file names can be shown. The logical names are usually listed alphabetically, and the physical names may be listed alphabetically, geographically, or any other convenient way. The data item names are usually listed in the order they appear in the data file.

Example: The physical data distribution outline for the employee data shown in Figure 13.2 is shown in Figure 13.5.

The *physical data distribution matrix* shows data subjects or data occurrence groups that appear at each data site and the data characteristics that appear in each data subject or data occurrence group in a matrix. The data sites are listed across the top of the matrix, and the data subjects or data occurrence groups with their data characteristics are listed down the left side of the matrix.

Example: The physical data distribution matrix for the employee data shown in Figure 13.4 is shown in Figure 13.6.

```
Boston
        Eastern Employee
                Empl Brth Dt CYMD
                Empl Hair Colr
                Empl Ht In
                Empl Nm Cmpl Invtd
                Empl Wt Pnds
    Seattle
        Western Employee
                Empl Brth Dt CYMD
                Empl Bdy Bld Descptn
                Empl Hair Colr
                Empl Nm Cmpl Invtd
```

Figure 13.5   Physical data distribution outline.

Distributed Data Diagram

The distribution of data is documented on a *data distribution diagram*. The diagram represents the movement of data replicates. It does not represent data derivations, data translations, or data transformation. An oval represents a data site and a solid line with an arrow represents the movement of data between data sites. The arrow points in the direction of data movement.

> A data distribution diagram shows the movement of distributed data sets between data sites.

A *distributed data set* is one data subject or data occurrence group that is distributed. Each separate data subject or data occurrence group is a separate distributed data set and is shown with a different line on the data distribution diagram. If a data subject or data occurrence group is distributed to several data sites, the line may be split. A *single data replicate distribution* is the movement of one data replicate, as shown in the diagram at the top of Figure 13.7. A *multiple data replicate distribution* is the movement of two or more data replicates from the official data source to two or more data sites, as shown in the diagram at the bottom of Figure 13.7.

The data site name is placed in the symbol representing the data site and the distributed data set name is placed on the solid line between data sites. The distributed data set name shown on the data distribution diagram is a *short data replicate name* consisting of only the data subject or data occurrence group name. If the data subjects or data occurrence names are different, the name representing the data set being moved is shown on the data distribution diagram.

Example: The distribution of Eastern Employee and Western Employee data from the Dallas data site to the Boston and Seattle data sites is shown in Figure 13.8.

The *formal data replicate name* consists of the source data site name and the target data site name separated by a hyphen and followed by a colon, followed by the data subject or data occurrence group name.

Example: New York-Dallas: Employee and Seattle-Boston: Western Employee are formal data replicate names.

If the data subjects or data occurrence groups are different at the source data site and the target data site, the data subject or data occurrence name is shown for each data site.

	Boston Eastern Employee	Dallas Employee	Seattle Western Employee
Employee			
Empl Bth Dt CYMD	X	X	X
Empl Bdy Bld Descptn		X	X
Empl Hair Colr	X	X	X
Empl Ht In	X	X	
Empl Nm Cmplt Invtd	X	X	X
Empl Wt Pounds	X	X	

Figure 13.6   Physical data distribution matrix.

Example: If the Boston Employee data occurrences are replicated in Seattle Western Employee, the notation is Boston: Employee-Seattle: Western Employee.

The preceding data distribution diagrams above show only the movement of data replicates between data sites. A *data distribution process diagram* shows the movement of data replicates between data sites and the processes that move those data replicates. A *data distribution process* is a process that moves and maintains one or more data replicates. The data distribution process is indicated by a rectangle and the name of the process is shown inside the rectangle. The process definition explains the detail for moving and maintaining the data replicates, such as the timing and frequency for refresh. A separate data distribution process must be used for each separate data subject or data occurrence group.

Example: The diagram at the top of Figure 13.9 shows separate processes for moving and maintaining multiple data replicates. Separate

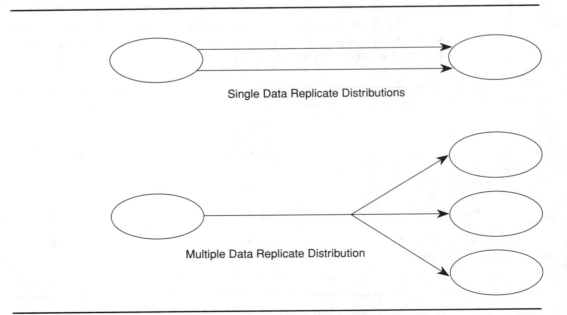

Single Data Replicate Distributions

Multiple Data Replicate Distribution

Figure 13.7   Single and multiple data set distribution.

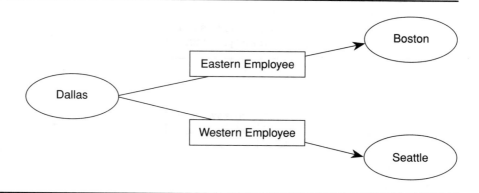

Figure 13.8   Distribution of employee data.

processes are used when the timing and frequency are different for multiple data replicates.

Example: The diagram at the bottom of Figure 13.9 shows one process for moving and maintaining multiple data replicates. A single process may be used when the timing and frequency are the same for multiple data replicates.

DATA PARTITIONING

When data replicates are distributed to different data sites, not all data are needed at all data sites, as shown by the examples above. *Data partitioning* is the formal process of determining which data subjects, data occurrence groups, and data characteristics are needed at each data site. It is an orderly process for deploying data to data sites that is done within the common data architecture.

Data fragmentation is an unorderly process of placing data at various data sites. It is not done within the common data architecture, is not well-managed or documented, and results in unknown, undocumented, redundant data. Fragmented data are sometimes referred to as *dispersed data*.

> Formal data partitioning prevents data fragmentation.

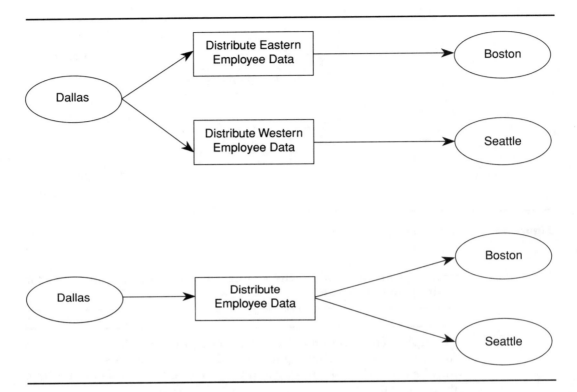

Figure 13.9   Data distribution process diagram.

Too much data fragmentation exists today. The pressure of getting data to clients to support immediate business needs at their data sites results in unknown sets of data all over the network. It perpetuates the disparate data problem. Formal data distribution prevents data fragmentation and helps an organization move toward an integrated data resource.

Data Subject Partitioning

Not all data subjects are needed at every data site. *Data subject partitioning* is the process of identifying the data subjects needed at each data site. The term *table partitioning* is also used to represent the identification of tables needed at each data sites. This term, however, is confusing to many people and is not used in this book.

Example: A particular data site may deal only with customers and customer orders. That data site needs data about the Customers,

Customer Orders, and Products. The data site does not need to have data about Employees, Vehicles, or Facilities.

> Data subject partitioning identifies data subjects that need to be distributed to each data site.

Data Occurrence Partitioning

Not all data occurrences in a data subject are needed at every data site. *Data occurrence partitioning* is the process of identifying the data occurrence groups needed at each data site. The term *horizontal partitioning* is also used to represent the identification of data occurrences from a data subject needed at each data site. The term originated from splitting a table horizontally by taking selected rows. This term, however, is confusing to many people and is not used in this book.

> Data occurrence partitioning identifies data occurrences for each data site.

A data subject hierarchy is useful for showing data occurrence partitioning.

Example: An organization has an eastern region office in Boston and a western region office in Seattle. Employees work either for the eastern region or the western region. A data subject hierarchy shows that Employees are either Eastern Employee or Western Employee, as shown in Figure 13.10. In this situation, the data subject hierarchy shows the data occurrence groups that are distributed to data sites.

A separate subject relation diagram is developed for each data site.

Example: The Dallas subject relation diagram, on the left side of Figure 13.11, shows all Employees, Southern Equipment and Southern Customers. The Boston subject relation diagram in the center shows the Eastern Employees, Eastern Equipment and Eastern Customers. The Seattle subject relation diagram on the right shows Western Employees, Equipment, and Western Customers.

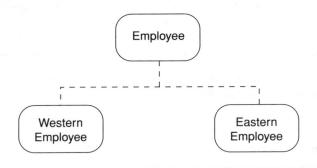

Figure 13.10   Data subject hierarchy for data occurrence partitioning.

Data Characteristic Partitioning

Not all data characteristics are needed at every data site. *Data characteristic partitioning* is the process of identifying the data characteristics from a data subject or a data occurrence group needed at each data site. The term *vertical partitioning* is also used to represent the identification of data characteristics needed at each data site. The term originated from splitting a table vertically by selecting certain columns. This term, however, is confusing to many people and is not used in this book.

> Data characteristic partitioning identifies data characteristics for each data site.

A distributed data structure outline or distributed data structure matrix shows the data characteristic partitioning.

Example: Figure 13.2 shows a distributed data structure outline for the Boston and Seattle data sites, and Figure 13.4 shows a distributed data structure matrix for the Boston, Dallas, and Seattle data sites.

A data site should not be labeled as containing a full set of data characteristics or a partial set of data characteristics because the data characteristics may change at any time. Data characteristics may be added or removed from the data resource, and data characteristics may be added or removed from a data site. Only the data characteristics available at a

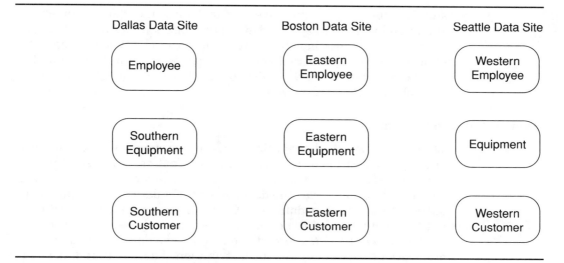

Figure 13.11   Subject relation diagram for data sites.

data site are listed without any designation as to whether they are a full set or a partial set. A distributed data structure matrix indicates whether or not any particular data site has all the data characteristics.[2]

Dual Data Partitioning

Dual data partitioning is when both data occurrence partitioning and data characteristic partitioning are done on the same data subject. Dual data partitioning is common in most data distributions.

Example: The previous examples show both data occurrence partitioning, such as the Eastern Employee and Western Employee, and data characteristic partitioning, such as Employee Height Inches and Employee Hair Color.

DISTRIBUTING DATA

When all the data distribution techniques are understood, the data to be distributed can be identified, distributed, and maintained. The first

[2]Brackett, 1990 referred to distributed and dispersed data meaning a full set of data and a subset of data, respectively. Those terms are no longer used.

step is determining what drives the distribution of data in an organization and what data are needed at each data site to support business needs. The data are then distributed appropriately. When the data distribution scheme is established, it must be constantly reviewed to determine whether the data distribution scheme should be changed to meet changing business needs.

Data Distribution Driver

The drivers for data distribution can be either a business need for data at a specific location or the availability of a data site at a specific location. In *business-driven data distribution*, the business need for data at a specific location drives the development of a data site and the distribution of data to that data site. Business-driven data distribution is independent of the existence of a telecommunications network. In *network-driven data distribution* the existence of a data site on a telecommunications network drives the distribution of data to that data site to support a business need at that data site.

> A combination of business needs and network configuration drives the distribution of data.

In reality, the distribution of data is determined by a combination of the business need for data at a specific location and the existence of a telecommunications network at that location. Business needs may promote development of a network, and the existence of a network may promote business needs. Together they determine the need to distribute data to a data site. The actual distribution and maintenance of data replicates should be transparent to the client. Ultimately, clients should go to the network to get the data they need without having any idea where those data are stored.

Distributing Tabular Data

Tabular data are distributed according to the techniques described previously. The important principle to remember when distributing tabular data is that the data must be refined before they are distributed. The redundancy and variability of disparate data must be identified, and official data sources and official data variations must be designated before data are formally replicated and distributed. Distributing unrefined tabular data perpetuates the disparate data situation, blocks development of an integrated data resource, and could result in disastrous business decisions.

> Disparate tabular data must be refined before they are distributed.

Distributing Evaluational Data

Evaluational data are also distributed to multiple data sites according to the techniques described previously. Evaluational data replication does not include any data transformation. Data transformation is done when operational data are moved into the evaluational database. Evaluational data are only distributed after they are in the evaluational database.

Evaluational data must be replicated from official data sources using official data variations just like operational data. Ideally, an evaluational database is developed from official data sources with official data variations, and there is no need to further designate official data. However, if an existing evaluational database contains disparate data, they must be refined before they can be distributed.

> Evaluational data may be distributed between data sites or within a data site.

Evaluational data may be partitioned to support specific business needs at data sites the same as operational data. Ideally, a central evaluational database should be maintained so that business analyses can be performed across different sets of evaluational data.

Example: Evaluational data for Equipment Summary may be distributed to Seattle, and evaluational data for Employee Summary may be distributed to Dallas.

Evaluational data can also be distributed at a particular data site. High-use evaluational data can be readily accessible on faster, more expensive hardware and lower use evaluational data can be archived to slower, less expensive hardware. The same techniques for partitioning evaluational data for distribution to data sites are used to partition evaluational data at a single data site. The process of determining which evaluational data should be readily available and which should be archived at a data site is based on the frequency of use and the cost of maintenance.

Distributing Spatial Data

As spatial data become more prominent, many different clients want access to spatial data to support their business needs. One alternative is to distribute spatial data to different data sites for local use. This alternative requires large storage and processing capability at those data sites. Another alternative is to maintain spatial data at a central site for access from distributed data sites. This alternative requires a telecommunication network capable of transmitting large volumes of spatial data to those data sites to provide the desired response time. Each organization must determine its options based on its needs and the capability of the telecommunications network.

Spatial data should be distributed to meet local business needs.

Spatial data are distributed using the techniques described previously. Spatial data, like tabular data and evaluational data, must be replicated from official data sources using official data variations. Ideally, a spatial information system is developed from official data sources with official data variations, and there is no need to further designate official data. If an existing spatial information system contains disparate data, those data must be refined before they can be distributed.

Spatial data may be partitioned the same as operational and evaluational data. Specific data layers may be designated for distribution to data sites.

Example: Only data layers containing demographic data may be distributed to a particular data site.

Specific spatial objects in a data layer may be selected for distribution to data sites through data occurrence partitioning.

Example: Only Grade Schools from the School Data Spatial that contains all schools are distributed to a particular data site.

A portion of a data layer extent may be selected for distribution to data sites through data occurrence partitioning.

Example: A data layer represents all the primary state highways in the entire state. Only the primary state highways within a particular county are selected and distributed to that county.

If spatial data have any associated tabular data, those tabular data must also be distributed to support the spatial data through data characteristic partitioning.

Example: A stream data layer is distributed to several data sites. The stream segments have associated water flow measurements and chemical analyses that are distributed along with the spatial data.

Distributing Metadata

Metadata need to be readily available to both business clients and technical personnel to properly maintain and fully utilize the data resource. One approach to making metadata available is to provide a central metadata warehouse for people to access. Another approach is to distribute metadata to data sites for local access.

> Metadata must be shared if they are to be used to share the data resource.

Metadata are distributed the same as any other tabular data using the techniques described previously. Metadata must be replicated from official data sources using official data variations. A central metadata warehouse should be maintained for all the metadata, and any metadata that are distributed should be replicated and distributed from that metadata warehouse. If there is not a central location containing official metadata, the disparate metadata must first be refined to identify official data sources and official data variations the same as data are refined. Then the metadata can be distributed from those official data sources using official data variations.

Metadata may be partitioned for distribution to data sites the same as any other data. Metadata partitioning may be done according to the data that are available at a data site, or the entire set of metadata may be distributed to each site. The decision depends on the metadata desired by the people at a data site. If clients only want to see metadata about the data available at their data site, then only those metadata need to be distributed. If clients want to see metadata about all the data that are available to them from the data resource, then all metadata need to be distributed. Having the ability to review all the metadata may prevent unnecessary data duplication and wasted resources.

Data Marts

The concept of a data mart was originally introduced as a subset of a data warehouse where data for a specific purpose or a major subject area were partitioned and made available for analysis. A *data mart* in an integrated data resource is a subset of the data resource, usually oriented to a specific purpose or major data subject, that may be distributed to support local business needs. The concept of a data mart can apply to any data whether they are operational data, evaluational data, spatial data, or metadata.

Example: Data about population trends, financial data, or customer orders could be used to build local data marts.

Data marts supply subsets of data for a specific purpose or subject area.

Analogy: The data mart concept is similar to a centralized supermarket and distributed mini-markets. An organization may have its entire data resource available on a central computer and distributed sets of data at different data sites to support local business needs. The data mart is like the mini-market that contains data to support local needs. Operational tabular data marts, evaluational tabular data marts, operational spatial data marts, evaluational spatial data marts, and metadata marts could be developed to meet specific needs.

Data marts are distributed data and must contain data from official data sources using official data variations. In some situations, such as data warehouses, the data may be adjusted to be optimally efficient at a particular data site. These adjustments for efficiency must be done within the common data architecture to ensure that all data are consistent and are part of the integrated data resource.

A metadata mart could ultimately be used to order the data desired from any convenient data mart. The metadata mart becomes a data catalog that clients can review to determine what data are available and then order the appropriate data to meet their business needs. Clients can select the data they need and indicate the data site where those data are to be placed. This capability requires a well-designed, integrated data resource and a robust metadata warehouse.

Data and accompanying metadata could ultimately be ordered automatically through a metadata mart.

If metadata are not readily available to clients, the metadata should be distributed with the data so they are readily available at the data site.

Example: If clients order data through a metadata mart for delivery to their data sites and the appropriate metadata are not readily available at those data sites, the appropriate metadata should accompany the data and be stored at the data sites.

The process of ordering data, and their accompanying metadata, automatically invokes data partitioning, data replication, and data distribution. *Automatic data partitioning* is the process of automatically partitioning data and metadata based on a client's request for data at a specific data site. *Automatic data replication* is the process of automatically creating data and metadata replicates based on a client's request for data at a specific data site. *Automatic data distribution* is the process of automatically distributing replicated data to data sites. All these processes require a well-designed and integrated data resource.

Redistributing Data

The distribution of data is only a temporary situation. With dynamic changes in the business environment, the client base, the data volume, the applications, and the telecommunication network, there is a constant need to evaluate and change the distribution of data. In organizations where development of information technology is evolving at a rapid pace, the redistribution of data may be dynamic, and data may be moved numerous times to a variety of different data sites.

Dynamic data distribution is the situation where distributed data need to be continually evaluated and adjusted to meet the business information demand in an optimum manner. In some situations, data distribution is active, and there are frequent changes to the data being distributed; in other situations, data distribution is stable, and there are few changes to the distributed data.

Data redistribution is the process of moving data replicates from one data site to another to meet business needs. It is a process that constantly balances data needs, data volumes, data usage, and the physical operating environment. An organization that distributes data should establish a program of dynamic data distribution and data redistribution to ensure that data are always properly distributed to meet business needs.

Data will be constantly redistributed as information technology evolves.

Data redistribution can be done automatically if an integrated data resource is properly developed within the common data architecture. *Automatic data redistribution* can be done with expert systems that evaluate the demand and the data volumes needed at each data site and keep track of the changes in data sites as the organization's telecommunications network evolves. Automatic data redistribution could also include adjustments based on unique client orders placed the network. If frequent requests were made from the same data site, data could automatically be distributed to that data site on a regular basis.

DISTRIBUTED DATA QUALITY

Maintaining high-quality data is a primary objective for an integrated data resource. The ability to distribute data to many different data sites adds another dimension to the maintenance of high-quality data. Data distribution is good because it provides data to many different data sites, promotes data sharing, and supports business autonomy. Data distribution, however, can result in data fragmentation and the perpetuation of disparate data, which lowers data quality. An organization needs to make sure that data are distributed within a common data architecture so that high-quality data are readily available to support business needs.

Data Origination

Data do not always originate at their official data source. They could originate at some other data site and be moved to an official data source.

Example: Environmental data could be captured at a field office and transmitted to the corporate office for editing and storage.

A *primary data site* is the data site where data originate. It is a data site where data are captured, created, or generated. A *secondary data site* is a data site where data may be moved after their origination. Both a primary and a secondary data site can contain official data.

> Primary data sites are the sites where data originate.

Primary and secondary data sites were originally defined as primary and secondary data sources, which were defined as organizations that captured and maintained data, and primary data sources were defined as the record of reference.[3] They are now termed primary and secondary data sites and a distinction is made between the data sites where data originate and the data sites where data are moved to after their origination and between the data sites that are the official source for data replication and distribution and the data sites that contain replicated data.

Data Tracking

As data become more readily available and are more frequently shared, it becomes increasingly important to track the movement of data. *Data tracking* is the process of tracking data from their origin to their ultimate destination, as explained in Chapter 8. It includes the movement of data from their origination to the official data sources and the distribution of data replicates to data sites. It shows where data originate, their original content and meaning (the data heritage), and any changes that occur as they move between data sites (the data lineage).

Data can be tracked between data sites, into and out of information systems, and between processes within information systems. Data tracking into, within, and out of information systems is relatively easy

---

[3]Brackett, 1994.

with data flow diagrams. Data tracking between data sites within an organization is more difficult and data tracking between organizations is often very difficult.

Data tracking documents the heritage and lineage of data.

Data tracking is documented on a *data tracking diagram* that is similar to a data distribution diagram. The data tracking diagram was named a major data flow diagram,[4] but the name was changed to emphasize the importance of tracking the heritage and lineage of data. It also emphasizes the change from just tracking the data moving between organizations to tracking data between all data sites, whether they are within or without the organization.

A data tracking diagram usually shows a network of data flowing between data sites. Data originate at one data site, move to another data site where they are modified or additional data are created, and may move to yet another data site for storage. They can then be distributed to a variety of other data sites to support client needs. If the movement of data is not properly tracked, the data quality and resulting business decisions could suffer dramatically.

Each organization must develop a data tracking diagram for their data.

A data tracking diagram shows any movement of data between data sites. The associated data structures for each data site indicate whether the data at that data site are the official data source for replication (a # prefix) and official data variations (an * prefix). The associated data structures for each data flow indicate whether the data in that data flow are official data variations.

Any organization that has data moving between data sites needs to develop a data tracking diagram and keep that diagram current. Organizations often spend more time tracking purchase orders, electrical wiring, employee expenses, customer buying trends, and a host of

---

[4]Brackett, 1994.

other things than they do tracking their data. Yet their data are the foundation supporting most of their business activities. The movement of data must be tracked to ensure that high-quality data are available to support business needs.

Both the ordering of data from a metadata mart and the automatic redistribution of data result in a change to the data resource and create a corresponding change to the metadata. The metadata must be kept current to understand all the data in the data resource and where those data are located. Anytime the data at a data site change, the metadata need to be updated to reflect that change, including changes in the data version.

Automatic data tracking and metadata updating with expert systems is possible if an integrated data resource is developed and data are distributed within the common data architecture. Automatic data tracking is part of an active metadata warehouse that shows the current status of all data in the data resource. Data analysts can monitor changes in the demand for data and the distribution of data and make more informed decisions about the integrated data resource.

Data Concurrency

Data concurrency is a big issue when data are distributed. Replicated data values must be consistent with the data values at the official data source to properly support an organization's business needs. *Data concurrency* means the replicated data values are synchronized with the corresponding data values at the official data source. When the data values at the official data source are updated, the replicated data values must also be updated so they are consistent with the official data source.

> Replicated data values must be consistent with the official data source.

Data replicates can be active or passive. An *active data replicate* is a data replicate that must have its data values consistent with those at the official data source.

Example: Replicated employee data must be consistent with the data values at the official data source.

A *static data replicate* is a data replicate that does not need to have its data values consistent with those at the official data source.

Example: The data supplied to another organization or another un-connected network cannot be easily updated.

Data synchronization is the process of identifying active data replicates and ensuring that data concurrency is maintained. Data synchronization is also known as *data version synchronization* or *data version concurrency* because all replicated data values are consistent with the same version as the official data. All data sites must have the same data version.

Data should be refreshed on a regular, known schedule.

Data refreshing is the process of updating active data replicates based on a regular, known schedule. The frequency and timing of data refreshing must be established to match business needs and must be known by clients. Ideally, data refreshing should be done immediately when the official data are updated, or as soon thereafter as possible. Immediate refresh is not always possible; data could be refreshed hourly, daily, or weekly at any prescribed time.

Replicated data should not be updated directly. Updates should be done to the official data source first and the replicated data should be refreshed from the official data source. All data editing should be done before or at the official data source so that source contains valid data. It is a poor practice to directly update replicated data because there is no way to ensure data concurrency. Data from a primary data site that is not an official data source should go to the official data source first and then be replicated to other data sites.

Replicated data should not be directly updated.

One important principle to remember with evaluational data is that primitive evaluational data are not refreshed when the operational data values change. Evaluational data replicates at different data sites will need to be refreshed when the official data values change.

Distributed Data Quality Principles

The quality of distributed data must be maintained to ensure consistent support to the business. Ten principles for maintaining high-quality data during data distribution ensure high-quality distributed data.

- All data distribution must be done within the common data architecture. The common data architecture provides a construct for integrating and distributing data. It provides a central data architecture that allows decentralized data use while ensuring consistency. Random data distribution outside a common data architecture results in a loss of control and directly affects data quality.
- All data must be refined before they are distributed. The redundancy and variability of data must be determined through a data refining process, and data replicates must be made from official data sources using only official data variations. The quality of disparate data must be documented and improved as much as possible during data refining before the data are distributed.
- The data integrity present at the official data source must be maintained in the replicated data unless a profound reason exists for not maintaining the data integrity.
- Replicated data must be synchronized with the official data source to ensure consistent support to the business. The frequency and timing of data refreshes must meet business needs within the resource limitations and must be known to clients using the data.
- Data updates must not be made directly to replicated data. Data updates must be made to the official data source and the replicated data must be refreshed according to a formal data refresh schedule. Making replicated data read-only is one way of ensuring that they are not updated directly by clients.
- A data tracking diagram must be developed and maintained to understand the heritage and lineage of all data. The data tracking diagram must document data from the time and place where they originate to their ultimate destinations. The data tracking diagram is used to ensure that data replicates have a common data heritage.
- Robust metadata must be maintained for all data, including distributed data, and must be readily available to clients. The metadata must include everything from names and definitions to data heritage and lineage. Official data sources and official data variations must be readily identified, as well as official data and replicated data.
- Data distribution needs to be constantly evaluated and adjusted to meet changing business needs and changing technology. If data

distribution is not adjusted to changes, people will not get the data they need and will begin developing their own data. This independent development of data perpetuates the disparate data situation and lowers data quality.

- The proper security must be maintained on distributed data. Unauthorized access, alteration, or destruction of data could affect data quality and the business decisions based on distributed data. Organizations must develop separate databases, build firewalls, or take other measures to keep their data secure. They should have extra protection, and backup, on their official data.
- The privacy of individuals and organizations must be maintained. Any data that are available for public viewing must not contain privileged data. Organizations need to make sure that readily available data, particularly data open to the public, do not contain privileged data.

SUMMARY

The need to distribute data is continually increasing. As more people acquire computers and become computer literate, as telecommunication networks become more prominent and powerful, and as business becomes more dynamic and decentralized, there is an increasing need to distribute data. The problem is that the need to distribute data quickly to meet business needs is presently greater than the need to control data disparity, resulting in increased data disparity. At the same time, the need to reduce data disparity is mandatory for data integration to support business analysis. Organizations are in the situation of actively perpetuating the problem that is directly affecting them.

The only solution is to refine, develop, and distribute all data within a common data architecture. Distributed data are uniquely identified and formally named using the data site, data occurrence group, and data version components of the data naming taxonomy. Logical data structures, distributed data structures, and physical data structures for distributed data are developed within the common data architecture to show what data are distributed. Distributed data diagrams show how data are distributed and maintained.

Data partitioning identifies the data subjects, data occurrence groups, and data characteristics needed at each data site to support business needs. Data replication makes exact replicates of official data for distribution. Data synchronization and data refreshing ensure that active data replicate values are consistent with the official data values. Data tracking documents the movement and alteration of data from their origination to their ultimate destination. All data updates are made from the data source, through the official data, to the replicated data to ensure consistency.

The identification of data to be distributed can be business-driven, network-driven, or driven by a combination of business needs and network capability. The distribution of data must be constantly reviewed and adjusted to ensure that it continues to meet changing business needs and changing network capabilities. Data quality must be maintained through the data distribution process to ensure that high-quality data are available to adequately support business needs. Robust metadata must be maintained and distributed so clients are aware of the data available to support their business needs.

Organizations must take the initiative to stop the development of disparate data, refine the disparate data that already exist, and formally distribute official data to consistently support business needs. They must properly manage the distribution of data within a common data architecture to ensure high-quality data. If organizations do not take the initiative, their data resource could fragment beyond recovery. The result could be inadequate support for business activities and disastrous business decisions.

QUESTIONS

The following questions are provided as a review of the material presented in the chapter and to stimulate thought about the distribution of data to support business needs:

1. What is the difference between data deployment and data distribution?
2. What is dynamic data distribution?
3. What is the data distribution dilemma?
4. What role does the common data architecture play in data distribution?
5. What are the important components of distributed data names?
6. What are the three data structures for distributed data?
7. What does the distributed data structure represent?
8. What is the difference between a logical data distribution outline and matrix?
9. What does a distributed data diagram represent?
10. What is the difference between the abbreviated and formal data replicate name?
11. What is a data distribution process diagram?
12. What are the different types of data partitioning?
13. How does data partitioning help prevent data fragmentation?

14. What is data replication?
15. How does data replication differ from data duplication?
16. What is an official data source?
17. What is the difference between primary and secondary data sites?
18. What is data tracking?
19. What is the difference between data concurrency, data synchronization, and data refreshing?
20. What is the driver for data distribution?
21. What is the most important principle for distributing tabular data?
22. What is the most important principle for distributing evaluational data?
23. Why should metadata be distributed?
24. Why is it necessary to be concerned about data redistribution?
25. What are the principles for maintaining high-quality data during data distribution?

## CHAPTER 14

Common Data Model

Common data modeling techniques support development of an integrated data resource.

An organization can develop and manage an integrated data resource using a common data model based on the techniques described in the previous chapters. All data in the data resource are integrated and distributed using a common data model. All data are identified, documented, and understood with a common data model. Data redundancy and variability are reduced through a common data model. A common data model produces a minimum set of consistent, integrated data to meet the business information demand.

The problem today is a poor perception of data modeling that often masks the true benefits of a good data model. Many different terms are used, and these terms are often confusing, conflicting, or used inappropriately. Different notations are used, making the data models difficult to interpret and understand. Data models are more elaborate than they need to be and frequently take far longer to develop than is reasonable. A common data model concept helps resolve most of these problems.

Chapter 14 begins with an explanation of the five-schema concept that is the foundation for developing a common data model and how that concept fits with the Framework for Information Systems. This chapter explains the concept of a common data model and the techniques of forward, reverse, and vertical data modeling. The chapter concludes with a description about how an integrated data resource is developed within a common data architecture using the common data model techniques.

THE DATA SCHEMA CONCEPT

The data schema concept is the foundation for developing data models. A *schema* is a diagrammatic representation of the structure or framework of something. *Data schema* are diagrammatic representations of the structure of data. They represent any set of data that is being captured, manipulated, stored, retrieved, transmitted, or displayed. The data sets described and used throughout this book for documenting the structure and movement of data within a common data architecture are data schema. The *data schema concept* provides a structure or framework for managing the integrated data resource.

The traditional two-schema concept for data files has evolved to a new five-schema concept to form the foundation for developing a common data model for the integrated data resource.

Two-Schema Concept

The initial two-schema concept for managing data was prominent during the flat-file days before the emergence of database management systems. The *two-schema concept* for managing data consisted of an internal schema and an external schema, as shown in Figure 14.1. The *internal schema* represented the structure of data stored in data files. The *external schema* represented the structure of data used by applications. If the external schema and internal schema matched, an application could easily store data in a data file or retrieve data from a data file.

The problem with the two-schema concept was that the external schema required by different applications did not match the single internal schema of the data files. The variety of different external schema needed to meet application needs could not be easily obtained from a single internal schema. The mismatch between the requirement for many different, dynamic external schema and single, relatively inflexible internal schema caused a conflict.

> The two-schema concept did not meet different data structures required by applications.

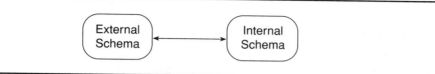

Figure 14.1   The two-schema concept for managing data.

Only two operational approaches existed with this two-schema conflict. The first approach was to perform excessive processing to assemble the different external schema for each application into a single internal schema. This approach was contrary to the objective of limiting processing on relatively expensive computers. The second approach was to store data in many different internal schema that closely matched the application needs. This second approach was usually chosen because it reduced processing time.

As more applications were developed, more data files were created and more redundant data were stored. New data files were developed by the extract-sort-merge process where the data to support new applications were extracted from existing data files, sorted in the proper order, and merged into a new data file to match the data structure needed by an application. Even though processing for a single application was faster, the storage of redundant data became a problem, a problem that is still prominent today.

Three-Schema Concept

The problems with the two-schema concept were solved with the *three-schema concept* for managing data that includes an internal schema, an external schema, and a new conceptual schema, as shown in Figure 14.2. The internal and external schema are the same as the two-schema concept. The *conceptual schema* represent a common structure of data that is the common denominator between the internal schema and external schema. Data normalization is a process to develop the conceptual schema from the external schema, and data denormalization is a process to develop the internal schema from the conceptual schema.

The conceptual schema provide independence between the use of data by applications and the storage of data in data files that is the foundation for database management systems. The data management responsibility moved from applications to the database management system. Database management systems converted the fixed internal schema to the dynamic external schema needed by each application through data views. An application used only the data items it needed

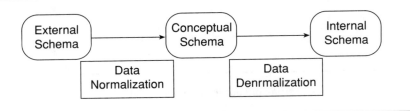

Figure 14.2   The three-schema concept for managing data.

rather than the entire data record. Data items could be added to the database without affecting existing applications.

The conceptual schema also led to conceptual data modeling. Traditionally, the data applications needed from the database became the external schema. These external schema were combined to form the conceptual schema, which were used to define the internal schema. As business clients became more involved in data modeling, there was confusion about what drove the definition of the external schema.

> Business clients could not apply conceptual modeling to the business.

The problem with the three-schema concept was that the external schema were developed from the perspective of the database, not from the perspective of the business client.[1] Business clients did not understand exactly what was being normalized during data modeling. They did not understand how the conceptual schema were developed from the data an application needed from the database. Business clients had trouble applying conceptual modeling to the business.

Four-Schema Concept

Problems with the three-schema concept are solved with the *four-schema concept* for managing the data resource.[2] The four-schema concept includes a physical schema, a logical schema, a data view schema, and a business schema, as shown in Figure 14.3.

---

[1]The origin of the term external was from a schema external to the database.
[2]The four-schema concept was developed and presented by the author in Brackett, 1990.

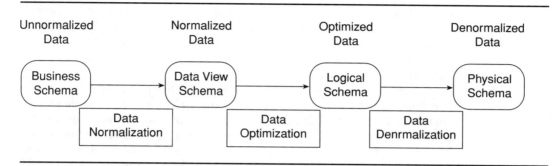

Figure 14.3   The four-schema concept for managing the data resource.

The *business schema* represents the structure of business transactions used by clients to conduct business in the real world. They are considered to be *unnormalized data*. The *data view schema* are the former external schema that represent the structure of data used by applications. They represent the data stored in and retrieved from the database by an application and are considered to be *normalized data*. The *logical schema* are the former conceptual schema that represent the logical structure of the data resource independent of how the data are stored or used. They represent a common view of all data in the data resource and are considered to be *optimized data*. The *physical schema* are the former internal schema that represent the physical structure of data in the database. They are considered to be *denormalized data*.

Data normalization is the process that develops normalized data views for each data subject from the unnormalized business schema. It makes the data easier to understand and ensures data independence between the application and the data resource. Data optimization is the process that combines the normalized data views by data subject to form the optimized logical schema.[3] It aggregates all the data views into a consistent subject data resource. Data denormalization is the process that develops the denormalized physical schema from the logical schema based on the specific operating environment. It adjusts data to a specific operating environment without compromising the subject data resource.

The business schema represent business transactions on the business side of the application. The business schema are normalized into

---

[3]Optimization as used here is logical optimization that occurs during logical data modeling. It is not the physical optimization that occurs during physical processing, such as query optimization.

data views representing data on the database side of an application. The data views are then optimized into a logical schema by aggregating all the data characteristics by data subject. The logical schema are then denormalized into physical schema representing the storage of data in a specific operating environment.

Terms in the four-schema concept were changed from those in the three-schema concept to reflect a formal information technology perspective rather than a database perspective and to be more meaningful to business clients. External has no meaning to business clients and was changed to data view representing a specific view of a data subject. Logical is more meaningful to business clients than conceptual and represents a logical view of the data resource independent of data use or storage. Internal was changed to physical because it represents the physical storage of data.

> The four-schema concept switched orientation from a database perspective to an information technology perspective.

The four-schema concept led to development of the common data architecture concept that supports development of a subject data resource from the organization's perspective of the real world. The four-schema concept helped business clients understand the use of unnormalized data in the business world and the conversion of those unnormalized data to data normalized by data subject. It allowed the data used to track or manage objects and events in the real world to drive the definition of data stored in the data resource.

The problem with the four-schema concept is the inability to properly model the distribution of data. The four-schema concept cannot handle the added complexity of data distribution. It has no way of showing the partitioning and replication of data involved in data distribution.

Five-Schema Concept

A new *five-schema concept* for designing and implementing the data resource was developed by the author to manage the added complexity of data distribution. A distribution schema was added between the logical schema and the physical schema, and a data deoptimization process was added to prepare the distribution schema, as shown in Figure 14.4.

The *distribution schema* represent the distribution of data to data sites and are considered to be *deoptimized data*. The distribution

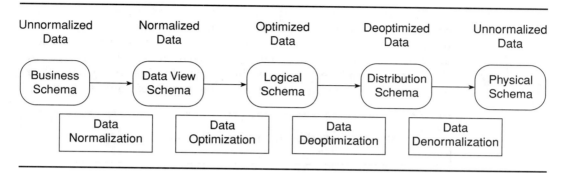

Figure 14.4   Five-schema concept for managing the data resource.

schema are logical data designated for partitioning, replication, and distribution to data sites. These schema are considered logical data because they have not yet been denormalized for a specific operating environment and they still have the official data name. They have the physical aspect of being designated for a particular data site, however.

> The five-schema concept includes a distribution schema for managing the complexity of data distribution.

The *data deoptimization* process prepares the distribution schema from the logical schema based on the data required at data sites to support business needs. The subsets of data needed at a data site are identified and partitioned from the logical schema. Data deoptimization is the counterpart of data optimization that replicates data for distribution and storage at multiple data sites.

Abstract Schema Concept

The five-schema concept contains the detail for developing and managing an integrated data resource. It represents the operational detail that includes all data subjects, data characteristics, and data relations in the data resource. It encompasses data from the business perspective for clients to the technical perspective for database analysts. The five-schema concept, however, does not cover abstractions of the detail that provide a more general view of the data resource. The *abstract schema concept* consists of two levels of abstract schema above the detailed schema, as shown in Figure 14.5.

The *strategic schema* are a high-level logical schema of the data resource. It provides an organization-wide view of the data resource with minimum detail. It includes only data subjects corresponding to objects and events in the real world that are tracked or managed by the organization, such as employees, vehicles, buildings, streams, and people. There are often many-to-many data relations between those data subjects.

The abstract schema show generalized views of the data resource.

The tactical schema are an intermediate schema between the strategic schema and the logical schema that provide more detail about the data resource than the strategic schema, but not all the detail necessary for developing the data resource. They show data subjects in the strategic schema, data subjects that directly support data subjects shown in the strategic schema, and data subjects added to resolve many-to-many data relations.

Framework for Information Systems

The Framework for Information Systems developed by John Zachman is a matrix consisting of six columns and six rows for developing information systems. The columns in the Framework represent the six basic

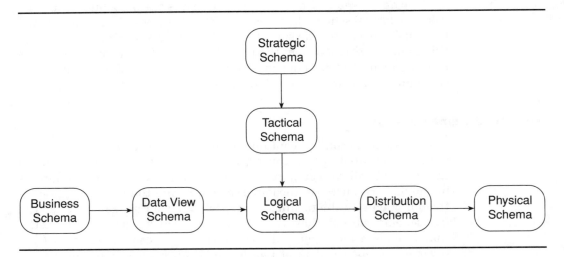

Figure 14.5   Abstract schema concept for the data resource.

What	How	Where	Who	When	Why
Data	Process	Network	People	Time	Rules

Figure 14.6   Columns in the Framework for Information Systems.

interrogatives of what, how, where, who, when, and why, which represent data, processes, network, people, time, and rules, respectively, as shown in Figure 14.6.

The rows in the Framework represent levels of abstraction from initial scope to an implemented system, as shown in Figure 14.7. The first row represents the scope of the information system, the second row represents the enterprise model, the third row represents the information system model, the fourth row represents the technology model, the fifth row represents the component detail, and the sixth row represents the functioning system. Progression down the rows represents transformations from more general models to more detailed specifications.

Five-Schema and the Framework

The five-schema concept fits very well in the data column of the Framework for Information Systems, as shown in Figure 14.8. The strategic schema are part of the enterprise model (second row) because it represents objects and events in the real world that an organization tracks or manages. The tactical schema are part of the information system model (third row) because it represents the major data subjects used to design an information system.

1	Scope
2	Enterprise Model
3	Information System Model
4	Technology Model
5	Components
6	Functioning System

Figure 14.7   Rows in the Framework for Information Systems.

1 Scope	
2 Enterprise Model	2 Strategic Schema
3 Information System Model	3 Tactical Schema
4 Technology Model	4a Business Schema 4b Data View Schema 4c Logical Schema 4d Distribution Schema 4e Physical Schema
5 Components	
6 Functioning System	

Figure 14.8   Fit between the five-schema concept and the Framework.

The detailed schema in the five-schema concept belong in the fourth row because they represent steps in development of the technology model. The business schema become row 4a, the data view schema become row 4b, the logical schema become row 4c, the distribution schema become row 4d, and the physical schema become row 4e.

> The five-schema concept and the abstract schema concept fit within the Framework for Information Systems.

Movement from the enterprise model to the information system model to the technology model represent a *vertical model transformation* within the Framework. More detail is added in the progression from defining the scope to implementing a functioning system. Movement within the technology model represents a *horizontal model transformation* within the Framework. The detail is transformed from data contained in business transactions in the real world to a common logical view of the data to physical data that support the functioning system.

COMMON DATA MODELING

Organizations are beginning to understand that planning and developing an integrated data resource to support dynamic business needs is important. An integrated data resource that crosses disciplines and organizational boundaries is the only way that consistent data can be readily available to all business activities. Organizations are realizing that a data resource integrated and deployed within a common data architecture is mandatory for survival in a dynamic business environment.

Common data modeling is the process of developing a model of the integrated data resource within a common data architecture. The process facilitates the integration of existing data and increases the awareness and understanding of those data. This process develops a plan for the distribution of data based on business needs and the physical operating environment. The process provides a model of the data resource in its current state and a model of the desired integrated data resource. Common data modeling helps an organization plan the data resource to survive changing business needs.

Data Modeling Perceptions

Some people believe that data modeling is no longer needed. They believe data can be quite adequately managed without any type of modeling. Just use the tools available today to build the data files and store the data wherever it is convenient. Data integration tools will take care of connecting databases and integrating data when they need to be integrated. Just let people develop their own data to meet the current business needs.

> There are many different perceptions of data modeling.

Other people believe data modeling is the center of the business. Developing an entity relation diagram is all that is needed for understanding the business and building a good data resource. Get with the client, build an E-R diagram, and automatically develop the database with schema generation tools. Nothing else is needed; the whole world can be controlled through an E-R diagram.

Still others are convinced that object modeling is the only way to go. Out with entities and in with objects. No need for architectures with objects because data and processes are encapsulated. But ever notice how similar the two models really are? They both start, or should start, by modeling the objects and events in the real world that an organization tracks or manages.

> Data modeling is a powerful tool for managing the data resource, if done properly.

Data modeling has had some bad times due to misuse, lack of performance, lack of relevance, high cost, long lead time, poor results, models that are not understandable, and a variety of other reasons. Rapid development techniques have not helped the situation because they tend to circumvent data modeling within a common data architecture. The result in many cases is the abandonment of data modeling and more rapid development of disparate data to meet current business needs.

Data Modeling Problems

Several problems exist with current data modeling techniques. One major problem is the many different notations used on data models. There is little commonality between techniques, and sometimes there is no commonality within a technique. The notations in each prominent data modeling technique have both strong and weak points, but none are robust enough to model an integrated data resource.

Many people change notations for change's sake, without any rationale or formality supporting the changes. They play with different notations for a standard tabular data model without extending the data model to include evaluational data, nontabular data, and data distribution. People spend too much time playing with notations and fancy symbols without attacking the real issues of data modeling.

> Data models are often too complicated and confuse business clients.

Logical data models are often too complicated and difficult to understand. Many data models are jargon that is incomprehensible to anyone other than the person who created the model. The problem is not with the data model itself, but with people who develop the data model. They make it more complicated than necessary. The model should be simple enough to understand, although it may be very detailed. The world is very detailed, and a data model that represents that world needs to be very detailed, but it must be readily understandable to people other than those who developed the model.

Quote: Einstein said, "We should endeavor to make everything as simple as possible, but no simpler."

A data model should present perspectives of the real world that the business clients can readily understand.

Another problem is the confusion between a business model and a data model. A business model shows the business world from the perspective of the organization developing the model. It shows the objects and events in the real world and the way an organization interacts with those objects and events. A data model shows the data resource supporting the way an organization wants to do business. A data model is not a data modeler's view of the business, nor is it a business model; it is a model of the data resource supporting the business.

The business model and the data model are two different models.

Too much time is often spent on developing data models, particularly data models at the information system level. There is no time to do data modeling for modeling's sake or to produce meaningless data models. An organization needs to get its data modeling done right one time and get on with using data to support the business. A common data model needs to be developed so the data models for a specific information system can draw from that common data model. Anything new that is not in the common data model is defined in data model for the information system and put into the common data model for the next information system.

Too much brute-force physical data modeling is done under the name of logical data modeling. Many information system projects are still starting with a database design based on specific data needs and a specific operating environment. They have a narrow scope, inconsistently truncated data names, confusing notations for primary and foreign keys, and limited data definitions. These physical data models are often given to business clients for review and approval. They confuse clients trying to relate the physical data to their business needs. This puts clients in a bind; they must either agree with the physical data model without fully understanding support for the business, or risk delaying the project while they try to understand if the model adequately supports their business.

Brute-force physical data models perpetuate disparate data.

This one-step approach to designing data files defeats the purpose of developing a consistent data model for the integrated data resource. It can bring data files up more quickly, but it perpetuates the creation of disparate data. After-the-fact integration of independently developed physical data models, known as *canonical synthesis*, does not create a common data model. Brute-force physical data modeling is part of the disparate data cycle that needs to be broken.

Many excuses exist for not modeling data, such as it is not necessary with CASE tools, it takes too long and there is not enough time, or the benefits are not understood. People need to understand the techniques for developing comprehensible data models and the benefits of a good data model.

Common Data Architecture

The common data architecture provides the framework for developing a common data model. It helps solve the problems described previously by supporting the architecture-driven development of data models. A common data architecture is the enabler for reusing the integrated data resource to support many different and changing information systems. Tools then become the support for developing data models within a common data architecture.

The common data architecture provides notations that are consistent across all models in the information technology infrastructure. The notations are based on semiotic theory consisting of syntax, semantics, and pragmatics.[4] A consistent syntax means all notations must have formal rules for how they are used that is consistent across all models in the infrastructure. Consistent semantics means that all notations must have a formal, denotative meaning that is consistent across the infrastructure. Consistent pragmatics means that all notations must have a practical use. These consistent notations provide a common language for expressing the real world as perceived by an organization.

---

[4]Semiotic theory is explained in detail in Brackett, 1990 and Brackett, 1994.

> Reality cannot be communicated without a common language.

Analogy: The common data architecture represents the universe of data in the data resource, much the same as *Webster's Dictionary* represents the universe of words in the English language. Only a few of those data are used by any information system or application, and only a few of the words in a dictionary are used in any book or article. Each information system or application uses a subset of the total data resource; a book or article uses a subset of words in the English language.

The common data architecture contains the detail about all data in the data resource. Anyone developing a new information system, large or small, should check with the common data architecture to see whether the data are already defined. If they are, those definitions should be drawn down to the information system to ensure consistency. If the data are not defined, they should be defined and placed back in the common data architecture for the benefit of others.

> The common data architecture represents the universe of data.

Not having a common data architecture usually results in long lead times. Even brute-force physical data modeling takes time, but drawing data definitions from the common data architecture shortens the lead time. Lack of a common data architecture also results in high development costs and high maintenance because effort is spent to develop disparate data and additional effort is spent to maintain and integrate those disparate data. Data files developed without a common data architecture run the risk of having high redundancy and variability, resulting in low reliability and flexibility.

An organization cannot develop an integrated data resource by trial and error. A trial-and-error approach only works when considerable time is available, and no critical dependencies exist. In most cases, there is not much time to play around with a trial-and-error approach on an integrated data resource because the business is depending on that data resource for its survival. An organization needs to get on with developing one common data architecture and building its applications and databases within that common data architecture.

Common Data Modeling Concept

Changes need to be made to traditional data modeling so it produces a more understandable and useful integrated data resource. Data modeling must be more relevant to business clients and have client involvement. It must be an integral part of any rapid development or joint development method and be cost-effective in the short term without losing sight of a long-term vision. Data modeling must promote use of the data resource beyond the initial ideas and business needs because clients have different uses for data from a good data model.

A *common data model* is a comprehensive model for developing and maintaining an integrated data resource. It is based on the five-schema concept and the abstract schema concept. It includes a strategic overview of the integrated data resource, the tactical steps to achieve an integrated data resource, and the operational detail to support specific data needs. A common data model encompasses data from the business perspective for clients to the technical perspective for database analysts. It includes all the data megatypes, such as tabular, spatial, image, text, and voice.

> A common data model is a model for developing an organization's integrated data resource.

A common data model provides the vision of an integrated data resource and the incremental steps for achieving that common vision. It provides a model of the integrated data resource that matches an organization's business needs and drives development of an integrated data resource. It provides a base for integrating and deploying all data needed to meet the business information demand. It provides a way to align past data and to develop new data within a common data architecture. A common data model gives organizations a consistent way to manage their data and to reuse those data in different information systems.

Forward Data Modeling

The normal progression of data modeling is from the business environment to the physical database, as shown in Figure 14.9. *Forward data modeling* is data modeling from the business schema to the data view schema to the logical schema to the distribution schema to the physical schema. It is a progression that transforms one data schema to the next through formal processes.

Forward data normalization is a process that transforms the business schema to the data view schema. The business schema are taken apart, and data views are developed for each data subject represented in the business schema. Data normalization is a necessary step to ensure that the data resource is developed by data subjects within the common data architecture. It is the first step for properly defining data to reduce redundancy and variability and to increase understanding.

> Forward data modeling is moving from the business to the physical database.

Forward data optimization is a process that transforms the data view schema to the logical schema. All the data characteristics for each data subject are combined to form a complete set of data characteristics for each data subject. The data must be normalized before they can be properly optimized. *Forward data deoptimization* is a process that transforms the logical schema to the distribution schema. The data are partitioned based on the data needed at each data site. The data must be properly optimized before they can be deoptimized for distribution.

Forward data denormalization is a process that transforms the distribution schema to the physical schema or the logical schema to the physical schema if there is no data distribution. The data are adjusted to be optimally efficient in a specific operating environment without compromising the logical schema. This step is important for operational efficiency. Going directly from unnormalized business schema to denormalized data is the brute-force physical approach described pre-

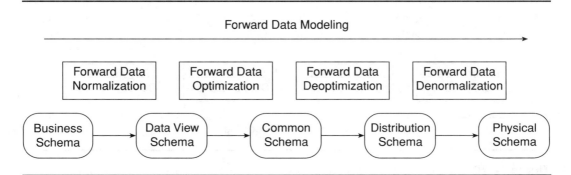

Figure 14.9   Forward data modeling.

viously that results in the data redundancy and variability that are common today.

Reverse Data Modeling

Reverse data modeling is data modeling from the physical schema to the distribution schema to the logical schema to the data view schema to the business schema, as shown in Figure 14.10. Each step transforms one schema to a schema earlier in the sequence.

Reverse data denormalization is a process that transforms the physical schema to the distribution schema. It undoes the database to its distributed schema or to the logical schema if there is no data distribution. *Reverse data deoptimization* is a process that transforms the distribution schema to the logical schema. This process can be done during dynamic data distribution where data are redistributed to other data sites. *Reverse data optimization* is a process that transforms the logical schema to the data view schema. This process is done in database management systems to prepare data views for applications. *Reverse data normalization* is a process that transforms the data view schema to the business schema. This process is done in applications to prepare business transactions from data views or prepare data views from business transactions.

> Reverse data modeling progresses from the physical database to the business schema.

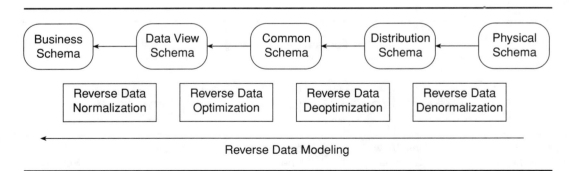

Figure 14.10   Reverse data modeling.

These terms were developed to avoid any confusion between the techniques of forward and reverse engineering and to specifically define the process being performed. Too often the terms forward engineering and reverse engineering are used without any reference to their location in the five-schema concept, which often causes confusion. These new terms eliminate any confusion.

Vertical Data Modeling

Vertical data modeling is the process of moving through the logical, tactical, and strategic data schema, as shown in Figure 14.11. Transforming a general schema to a more detailed schema is a specialization process, and transforming a detailed schema to a more general schema is a generalization process.

Strategic schema identification is the process of developing the strategic schema from an organization's perspective of the business world. Data subjects are defined based on objects and events in the business world that are tracked or managed by an organization. *Tactical schema specialization* is the process of developing the tactical schema from the strategic schema. It is done by identifying the data subjects that directly support the data subjects shown in the strategic schema and resolving the many-to-many data relations. *Logical schema specialization* is the process of developing the logical schema from the tactical schema. It is done by identifying all the data subjects.

> Vertical data modeling is moving between detail and abstractions of the data resource.

Tactical schema generalization is the process of developing the tactical schema from the logical schema. The process is done by removing the data subjects that represent the detail that is not important for a broader view of the data resource. This process is the reverse of the logical schema specialization process. *Strategic schema generalization* is the process of developing the strategic schema from the tactical schema. The process is done by removing all data subjects that do not represent objects or events in the real world that are tracked or managed by the organization. This process is the reverse of the tactical schema specialization process.

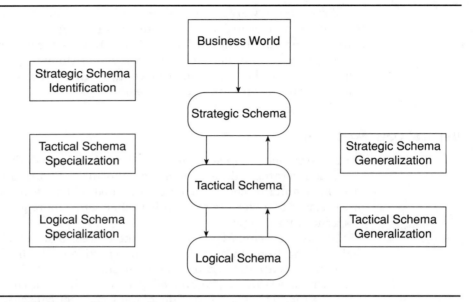

Figure 14.11   Vertical data modeling.

Common Data Modeling Method

The forward, reverse, and vertical data modeling processes can be combined into one *common data modeling method,* as shown on the diagram in Figure 14.12. The 13 data modeling processes, represented by the arrows on the diagram, form the common data modeling method. The method provides an easy way to move between the unnormalized business transactions and a denormalized database and between the real world and detailed data resource design within the common data architecture.

Basic Data Modeling Components

A common data model is developed from a small set of basic components, such as one-to-many data relations, many-to-many data relations, and data subject hierarchies. These basic components are developed from the types of data subjects and data relations described in Chapter 6. Figure 14.13 shows the basic data modeling components. They can be combined in a variety of ways to develop a common data model of the integrated data resource.

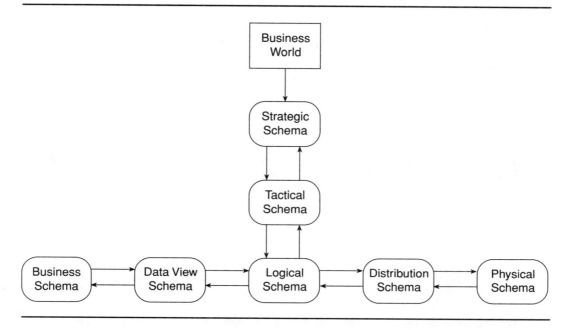

Figure 14.12   Common data modeling method.

The first row in the diagram contains components that show a relationship between data occurrences in two different data subjects. A many-to-many data relation between data subjects is resolved with the addition of a new data subject, as shown in the component at the right of the second row.

The second row in the diagram contains components that show a relationship between data occurrences within the same data subject. They are commonly known as recursive data relations. A many-to-many data relation to the same data subject is also resolved with the addition of a new data subject, as shown in the component at the right of the second row.

The third row in the diagram contains components that show a relationship between parents and subordinates. Data subject hierarchies show mutually exclusive relationships between a parent data subject and multiple subordinate data subjects. Mutually exclusive parents show mutually exclusive relationships between multiple parent data subjects and a subordinate data subject. Data categories show mutually inclusive relationships between a parent data subject and multiple subordinate data subjects.

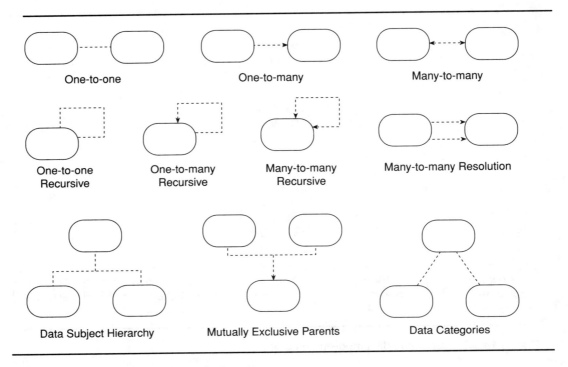

Figure 14.13   Data modeling components.

AN INTEGRATED DATA RESOURCE

An integrated data resource must be stable to support dynamic business needs. The more dynamic the business, the more stable the data resource must be. A data resource must also be common across the organization. The more diverse the organization is, the more common the data resource must be. An integrated data resource is easy to build and maintain with the common data modeling method.

> The data modeling process can go any direction in the common data modeling method.

The common data modeling method covers all possible scenarios encountered in data modeling. The modeling process can go any direction through the data modeling method. A few of the prominent modeling processes are described in the following sections.

Modeling Logical Schema

The modeling process can start with the strategic schema, develop the tactical schema, and then develop the logical schema. It can also go from the business schema through the data view schema to the logical schema at the detail level. The intersection of vertical data modeling above the detail level and forward data modeling to the logical schema at the detail level produce a fully normalized model of the data resource that represents the real world.

> The complete logical schema is an intersection of vertical and forward data modeling.

The modeling process can also go from the logical schema through tactical schema to strategic schema for broader views of the data resource. This sequence is used when the logical schema are changed, and the tactical schema and strategic schema need to be enhanced to reflect those changes.

Developing New Data

Ideally, all new data, including tabular and nontabular data, are defined within the common data architecture using the techniques described in the previous chapters. The modeling process uses forward data modeling from the business schema to the data view schema to the logical schema to the distribution schema to the physical schema. The modeling process can go directly from the logical schema to the physical schema if there is no data distribution, or it can go through the distribution schema if the data are distributed. This is the normal sequence for developing new data.

> The normal sequence for developing new data is the complete forward data modeling process.

If for some reason new data cannot be developed with the normal forward data modeling sequence, they can be developed using part of the sequence and adjusted later.

Example: A project that has a critical deadline may not be able to follow the normal sequence. Data files can be developed and cross-referenced to the common data architecture at a later date using the data refining techniques.

This common data model retrofitting should be the exception, however, because it requires extra effort to bring the system in line with the integrated data resource. In most cases, if an organization does not have the time to develop an information system right initially, it will not have the time to do it right later.

Refining Disparate Data

Disparate data, including both tabular and nontabular disparate data, are refined to the common data architecture using the techniques described in Chapter 9, as shown in Figure 14.14. *Unstructured physical schema* represent data files that are not aligned with the common data architecture. *Semi-structured logical schema* represent logical schema that are not aligned with the common data architecture. *Structured logical schema* represent logical schema aligned with the common data architecture. *Structured physical schema* represent physical schema aligned with the common data architecture.

Unstructured physical schema and semi-structured logical schema

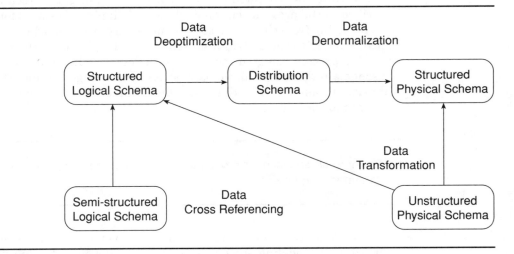

Figure 14.14   Data refining with the common data modeling method.

are cross-referenced to the structured logical schema. The structured physical schema are developed from the structured logical schema, using the distribution schema if necessary. The unstructured physical database is converted to a structured physical database through the data transformation process.

Developing Evaluational Data

New evaluational data, including tabular and nontabular evaluational data, are developed the same as any other new data using the full forward data modeling process and the techniques described in Chapter 10. Generally, an *evaluational subject relation diagram* representing evaluational data subjects and any operational data subjects that contribute to those evaluational data subjects is developed separate from an *operational subject relation diagram* representing operational data subjects. Corresponding *evaluational data subject structures* and *operational data subject structures* are developed to show the structure of evaluational data and operational data.

Evaluational data must be normalized, or renormalized, in the logical data model so they appear in the common data architecture. This normalization may make the logical data structure appear strange because data are replicated from a parent data subject to a subordinate data subject. This approach, however, ensures that all operational and evaluational data are included in the common data model.

The designation of a data focus that represents the fact table for evaluational data analysis and a summary data subject that represents the results of the evaluational data analysis helps clarify the situation.

Example: Insurance Claim is designated as the data focus for evaluational data analysis. It contains all the unnormalized data characteristics necessary for performing that analysis. Insurance Claim Summary contains the data characteristics representing the results of the evaluational data analysis. Insurance Claim Summary 1, 2, and so on, contain the specific results of an evaluational data analysis.

Distributing Data

Tabular and nontabular data are distributed and redistributed using techniques described in Chapter 13. Data distribution is defined by forward data modeling from the logical schema to the distribution schema to the physical schema, as shown in Figure 14.15. Data redistribution is defined by reverse data modeling from the physical schema to the dis-

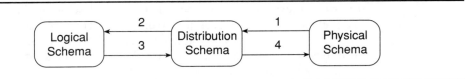

Figure 14.15   Distributing and redistributing data.

tribution schema to the logical schema, and then forward data modeling with a new distribution schema to a new physical schema as shown by the sequence numbers.

If there are heterogeneous operating environments for the distributed data, there is a data denormalization for each operating environment followed by data replication. If there are homogenous operating environments for distributed data, there is one denormalization and several data replications. This sequence is the normal modeling sequence for developing a common database and distributing data.

This sequence only works when the physical schema are aligned with the common data architecture. If the physical schema are not aligned with the common data architecture, the data refining process must be used before the data can be redistributed. It is a poor practice to distribute and redistribute physical data that are not aligned with the common data architecture.

Changing Operating Environments

Operating environments frequently change causing a change to the physical schema. The physical schema are adjusted by reverse data modeling from the physical schema to the logical schema and then forward data modeling to a new physical schema. The data distribution schema are usually not involved unless there is a change to the distribution of data at the same time the operating environment changes. When the new physical schema are defined, the data can be physically converted from the old operating environment to the new operating environment, as shown in Figure 14.16.

This sequence only works when the physical schema are aligned with the common data architecture. If the physical schema are not aligned with the common data architecture, the data refining process must be used before the data can be redistributed. It is a poor practice to change operating environments when the physical schema not aligned with the common data architecture. An organization should take the opportunity to align its data with the common data architecture when changing operating environments.

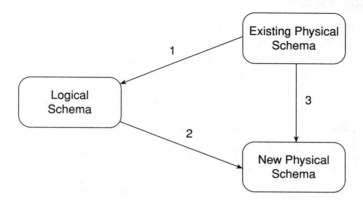

Figure 14.16   Changing operating environments.

Integrating Data

All data, including tabular and nontabular data and operational and evaluational data, are integrated using the common data modeling method. Disparate data are integrated by aligning them with the common data architecture through the data refining process. Common tabular and nontabular data are integrated by modeling them together within the common data modeling method.

Example: Purchase Order and Purchase Order Image and Timber Stand and Timber Stand Spatial are modeled as shown in Figure 14.17.

Nontabular data can be modeled as separate data subjects, as shown in the diagram in Figure 14.17. They can also be modeled as data characteristics within a data subject.

Example: A purchase order image can be included as a data characteristic for Purchase Order Image within the Purchase Order data subject.

Data merging is not the same as data integration. *Data merging* is the process of moving a set of data from one database and adding it to another database. The data from several databases can be merged into a single database. Data merging can involve some form of data conversion, but it does not include data refining. Just because data are merged in an open system environment it does not mean they are aligned with the common data architecture and integrated into an integrated data resource.

Data Model Interfaces

When an integrated data resource is being developed, there is often a need to connect major segments of the data resource. In some situations, however, the major segments may not yet be implemented or may be under development. This situation should not be allowed to prevent the development of an integrated data resource. The best approach to resolving this situation is to use interface data subjects.

Interface data subjects allow independent development of segments of an integrated data resource.

An *interface data subject* is a data subject that is created temporarily to support an information system until the permanent data subject can be designed and implemented. The interface data subject is named by qualifying the permanent data subject with a suffix representing the information system using the interface data subject. When the permanent data subject is available, the data from the interface data subject are moved to the permanent data subject, the information system is connected to the permanent data subject, and the interface data subject is removed.

The interface data subject contains only the data characteristics from the permanent data subject that are necessary to support the new information system. Those data characteristics are named according to the permanent data subject, not according to the interface data subject, to ensure an easy switch from the interface data subject to the permanent data subject when it is developed.

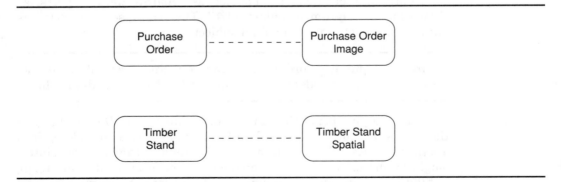

Figure 14.17   Modeling tabular and nontabular data.

Example: An integrated data subject for Business Client is being designed to contain all the information about all business clients for an organization, but it is not yet available. A new information system is being implemented to track all outside requests to the organization. The new information system should use the new integrated Business Client data subject; however, it cannot be delayed until Business Client is implemented.

To resolve this situation, an interface data subject, Business Client Request, is defined to contain the data characteristics from Business Client that are necessary to support the request tracking system, as shown at the top of Figure 14.18. When Business Client is available, Business Client Request will be removed and the connections will be made to Business Client, as shown at the bottom of Figure 14.18.

The data characteristics in Business Client Request are prefixed with Business Client, not Business Client Request so that when the connection is made to Business Client the information system will be able to access the data without alteration.

Data Subject Hierarchies

The general trend of an integrated data resource, particularly one developed on a relational database management system, is to create fewer, larger data subjects with more data subject types. A data subject hierarchy is very useful for showing the relationships between parent and subordinate data subjects. It is also useful for showing which data subjects in that hierarchy will become data files.

Example: A data subject hierarchy is developed to show the relationships between different types of wells, as shown in Figure 14.19. The

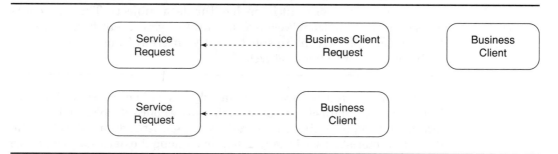

Figure 14.18   Interface data subject example.

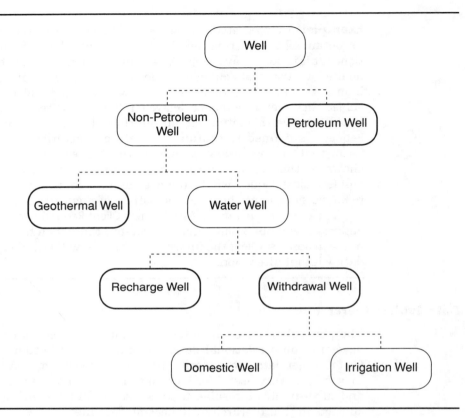

Figure 14.19   Data subject hierarchy with data file designations.

data subjects that will become data files are shown with bold lines. The determination, in this situation, was made based on the data characteristics that were present in each of the data subjects. The data characteristics for Petroleum Wells are substantially different from those for Geothermal Wells, which are substantially different from those in either Recharge Wells or Withdrawal Wells.

The determination of which data subjects will become data files can be based on the data characteristics that are applicable to each data subject or on the processing that could occur against a data subject. If the data characteristics are largely disjointed among the data subjects, those data subjects could become separate data files. If the data characteristics are largely similar among data subjects, the data subjects should be part of the same data file. If there are a large number of data occurrences and the processing against the data subjects is relatively separate, the data subjects could become separate data files. The final determination is up to each organization and its particular processing environment.

The data characteristics are usually named according to the data subject that will become a data file or a parent data subject. If there is a high probability that the data files may be combined, the data characteristics should be named according to a parent data subject. If there is a high probability that the data files will not be combined, the data characteristics should be named according to the data subject that becomes the data file.

Example: In the preceding diagram , the data characteristics in Petroleum Well and Geothermal Well would be prefixed with Petroleum Well and Geothermal Well respectively because they are largely disjointed sets of data characteristics and there is a low probability that they would ever be combined. The data characteristics in Recharge Well and Withdrawal Well are not totally disjointed and there is a chance that the two could be combined into one data file in the future. The data characteristics, therefore, are prefixed with Water Well rather than Recharge Well or Withdrawal Well.

Common Person

An individual performs many roles in the real world, such as employee, patient, driver, student, welfare recipient, or business owner. When an organization tracks or manages individuals, it sees them only within its perspective, such as a patient. It does not see individuals in any other roles. The result is development of databases that identify and track individuals in a variety of different ways, such as social security number, driver's license number, and patient identification. Even within the same discipline, an individual may be tracked different ways, such as different patient identifiers in different hospitals and clinics.

The question often faced is how to combine different data for the same individual. Is that individual always a Person or are there different types of people, such as Patient, Student, and Driver? The best approach to integrating data about individuals is to consider Person a real data subject and make all manifestations of a Person the first level of data subject types, as shown in Figure 14.20. Notice that the first level of data subject types represents broad groupings of individuals, such as Health Care Person, Employment Person, and Justice Person.

Each broad data grouping can be further subdivided.

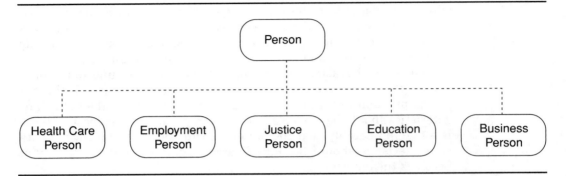

Figure 14.20   Data subject hierarchy for Person.

Example: An Employment Person can be an Employee, Candidate, or Retiree, as shown in Figure 14.21. The data subject hierarchy can continue to more detailed levels, such as dividing Employee into Faculty, Staff Employee, and Classified Employee. Similar hierarchies could be developed for health care, such as patient, doctor, and nurse; for education, such as student, teacher, and aide; for the justice system, such as judge, suspect, witness, and attorney; and for business, such as officer, owner, and shareholder.

All data characteristics about a person are defined in the Person data subject and prefixed with Person, such as Person Name Complete Normal and Person Birth Date CYMD. These data characteristics are fundamental

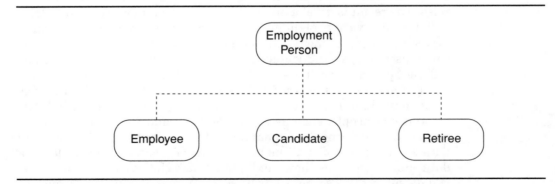

Figure 14.21   Data subject hierarchy for Employment Person.

data about a person. Data characteristics in the data subject types could be prefixed with Person or with the name of the data subject type, such as Employee Name Complete Normal, Student Name Complete Normal, and Driver Name Complete Normal. In the latter situation, a reference is made to the corresponding data characteristic in Person to inherit that data definition.

Example: The definition for Student Name Complete Normal is *the person name complete normal for a student.*

> Integration of common person data begins with a comprehensive data subject hierarchy.

The tendency to name all data subject types Person should be avoided because Person represents all people. An individual may exist in many different data subject types, but few individuals exist in all data subject types. Similarly, a data subject type does not include all individuals. It is better to use meaningful data subject type names to indicate the specific set of individuals being referenced.

When a data subject hierarchy is developed for Person, the primary key or keys for each data subject type are identified and used to integrate the data. In most cases, a single primary key does not exist and a set of primary keys must be used to integrate the data about an individual. Ultimately, a common person identifier may be used, such as DNA print, but until that common identifier is established, a set of different identifiers must be used.

Grouped Code Tables

Many people group code tables that are closely related into a single data file. A data subject is defined to contain the individual coded data values, and their corresponding names and definitions. It usually contains the common word *Type*. Another parent data subject is defined to identify the code table containing each of those codes. It usually contains the common word *Group*. A third data subject may need to be defined to resolve the many-to-many relation between the data subject containing the coded data values and the data subject those coded data values qualify.

Example: The features of Land Parcels, such as topography, size, view, and so on, can be qualified by many different code tables. These code tables can be grouped into one table for Land Parcel Feature Type, as shown in Figure 14.22. The individual code tables represented by Land Parcel Feature Type are shown in Land Parcel Feature Group. Land Parcel Feature resolves the many-to-many data relation between Land Parcel and Land Parcel Feature Type by showing each feature that exists on each land parcel.

Archive and History Data

Data that are out of date are often discarded without any consideration for their historical benefit for finding trends and patterns or making projections. Operational data that are out of date should be saved before they are updated if there is any potential benefit to the organization. Data can be saved in two ways.

The first way to save data is by archiving the entire data record with a corresponding date when there is no longer any operational use for that data record. The date can be either the beginning date of the data value, the ending date of the value, or both a beginning and ending date. Archived data are usually stored off-line or on some medium other than where the current operational data are stored.

The common word *Archive* is appended to the data subject name to indicate that the data subject contains archived data. No data relation exists between the data subject containing the current data and the data subject containing the archived data because the record exists either in the active data subject or the archive data subject. The data characteristics in the archive data subject retain the prefix of the original parent data subject.

Example: Land parcels are bought and sold on a regular basis. Only the current owner of a land parcel is important for valuation and taxation. Previous owner information is archived off-line as part of the legal record for a land parcel. Figure 14.23 shows Land Parcel and Land Parcel Archive.

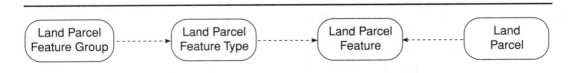

Figure 14.22   Grouping of code tables.

Figure 14.23   Saving archived data.

The second way to save data is through a history file containing only the data items that have been changed and a corresponding date. Whenever a change is pending to any value in a data record, that data item, or possibly the entire data record, is saved with a date. The date can be either the beginning date of the data value, the ending date of the data value, or both a beginning and ending date. History data are usually stored on-line so they are readily available for review.

The common word *History* is used in the data subject name to indicate that the data subject contains historical data. There is a one-to-many data relation between the data subject containing the current data and the data subject containing the historical data because the current record exists in the active data subject and many updated records can exist in the history data subject. The data characteristics in the history data subject retain the prefix of the original parent data subject.

Example: The data about business clients change frequently, such as their phone numbers, business addresses, home addresses, and possibly their names. Before any change is made, the old data value is saved to a history file with the appropriate date or dates. The history file can be viewed to determine the sequence of changes to a business client's data. Figure 14.24 shows Business Client and Business Client History. The one-to-many data relation indicates there are many history occurrences for a single business client occurrence.

Historical data may be archived at some point in time when there is no longer any reason for them to remain online for ready access. This

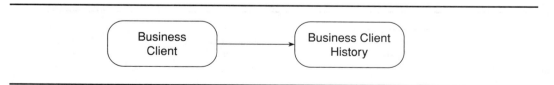

Figure 14.24   Saving historical data.

usually occurs after a set period of time or when the object or event represented by the data subject is no longer active and there is no need to keep the data online.

Example: The Business Client History data are moved to Business Client Archive after two years or six months after the business client is no longer an active client, as shown in Figure 14.25.

SUMMARY

Comprehensive data modeling is mandatory for developing, maintaining, and using an integrated data resource to meet the business information demand. Developing any data resource, particularly an integrated data resource, without robust data modeling techniques is nearly impossible. The problem is that data modeling has been abused to the extent that many organizations are not interested in modeling their data and proceed to build physical databases to meet their current needs, resulting in the rapid explosion of disparate data.

One of the fundamental problems with data modeling is the traditional three-schema concept. The three-schema concept defined an internal schema for data files, an external schema for applications, and a conceptual schema to resolve the dissimilarity between the internal and external schema. The four-schema concept added a business schema representing data use in the real world and changed the terms to be more meaningful to clients. The five-schema concept added a distribution schema to model the distribution of data.

The five-schema concept represents detailed schema for modeling the integrated data resource. It handles the complexity of an integrated data resource that is prominent in most organizations today. It includes data used in the real world, data views exchanged between applications and the database, a complete set of logical data, sets of data distributed to various data sites, and data in the database.

Two abstract schema above the detail represent broader views of the data resource for planning how the data resource supports business

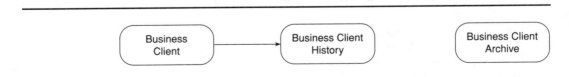

Figure 14.25   Moving historical data to an archive.

needs. The detailed schema fit within the data column of the technology model in the Framework for Information Systems. The tactical schema fit within the data column of the information system model of the Framework. The strategic schema fit within the data column of the enterprise model of the Framework.

The five-schema and the abstract schema concepts represent both functional and technical views of the data resource. Most buildings have a functional view, such as how the building will be used, and a technical view, such as the load diagrams. Building occupants are interested in having 110 volt electrical outlets at convenient locations, not in the wire gauge, insulation thickness, and circuit breaker loads. They are interested in hot and cold running water, and proper temperatures, not in the plumbing for delivering water and disposing waste water or the temperature control system.

The same situation is true for the data resource. Clients are interested in a functional view of the data resource as it pertains to their use of the data to support business needs. The technical staff is interested in a technical view for maintaining the data resource.

The common data modeling method pulls these two views together into a comprehensive method for developing and maintaining an integrated data resource. It resolves many of the technical and cultural problems with data modeling by providing forward, reverse, and vertical data modeling processes. It puts the five-schema concept, the abstract-schema concept, and the common data architecture techniques into a common data modeling method.

There are many scenarios for using the common data modeling method to build and maintain an integrated data resource. New tabular and nontabular data are integrated with the common data modeling method, and disparate tabular and nontabular data are refined to the common data architecture using the common data modeling method. Operational and evaluational data are modeled with the common data modeling method. Data are integrated, distributed, and redistributed to different operating environments using the common data modeling method.

Common data modeling helps an organization build an integrated data resource with minimum redundancy and variability. It provides a method to build a common data architecture that supports data distribution and coordinates decentralized application development. An organization can design new data properly from the beginning while correcting their existing disparate data. Common data modeling ensures high-quality data that are easily identifiable and readily available to support the business information demand.

Common data modeling within a common data architecture provides a way to discover and reuse the data that already exist in the data resource without affecting the operation of existing applications. It provides a way to view all data in the data resource and understand how those data represent the real world. It provides the way for an organization to survive on its disparate data while creating an integrated data resource.

QUESTIONS

The following questions are provided as a review of the chapter and to stimulate thought about how common data modeling helps build an integrated data resource within a common data architecture.

1. What is a data schema?
2. Why was the two-schema concept inadequate for properly modeling and managing the data resource?
3. Why was the three-schema concept inadequate for properly modeling and managing the data resource?
4. What benefits did the four-schema concept provide?
5. Why were terms changed in the four-schema concept?
6. What benefits does the five-schema concept provide?
7. What is the purpose of the abstract schema?
8. How are the five-schema concept and the abstract schema concept aligned with the Framework for Information Systems?
9. What are the perceptions and problems with data modeling today?
10. What is common data modeling?
11. How does the common data architecture support common data modeling?
12. How does common data modeling help build and maintain an integrated data resource?
13. What processes are involved in forward data modeling?
14. What processes are involved in reverse data modeling?
15. How does vertical data modeling enhance common data modeling?
16. How are the logical schema developed to represent the integrated data resource?
17. How is common data modeling used to refine disparate data?
18. How is common data modeling used to change operating environments?
19. How is common data modeling used to integrate tabular and nontabular data?
20. What are the benefits of common data modeling?

## CHAPTER 15

Resolving
the Dilemma

The future belongs to organizations that seize the opportunity to resolve the data dilemma and build an integrated data resource.

The future belongs to those who seize opportunities. Organizations wishing to gain or retain a competitive advantage and survive in a dynamic business environment must seize the opportunity to create an integrated data resource. They must take the initiative to resolve the data dilemma and organize their data to support current and future business information demand. Organizations must be proactive at developing and maintaining a stable data resource that supports changing business activities.

The future is both promising and scary. It is promising in the sense that many opportunities exist for forward-thinking organizations to be successful. It is scary in the sense that many unknowns and uncertainties exist. There are few absolute certainties in the world today.

Organizations need to prepare themselves to take the opportunities and face the uncertainties by developing an initiative to pull their data together. They need to transform all data into an integrated data resource and deploy those data to products and data sites that directly support the business information demand. Organizations need to face the data dilemma head-on, just like they face any other major challenge.

Chapter 15 begins with a description of prominent data issues faced by organizations today. It reviews the problem with legacy systems and how legacy systems can be dismantled and rebuilt using a common activity architecture patterned after the common data architecture. The chapter concludes by outlining an initiative for resolving the data dilemma and creating an integrated data resource that supports business survival.

DATA ISSUES

The last several chapters described techniques for building an integrated data resource, managing evaluational data, transforming data to an integrated data resource, managing spatial data, distributing data to a variety of data sites, and developing a common data model. These techniques are mandatory for managing the major complexities of an integrated data resource. Several other techniques are available to manage unique issues.

Increasing Data Disparity

Data disparity is increasing rapidly! Organizations usually concentrate on people, processes, and technology, but not on data. They spend considerable effort on total quality improvement, business process improvement, quality control, business process redesign/reengineering, integrated offices, and other process improvement activities. They also spend considerable effort on applying new technology to the business, such as data warehouses, geographic information systems, client/server networks, kiosks, and telecommunications. Organizations do not spend enough time on understanding and controlling their data.

Organizations spend considerable effort on self-directed work teams, empowering the employee, developing flatter organizations, creating virtual organizations, distributing workforces, telecommuting, and a variety of other organizational structures. They are moving to self-managed teams and on to self-managed individuals. Although these approaches usually benefit the organization, they require an integrated data resource to provide consistency and stability.

> A stable data resource supports decentralized actions.

A few organizations have a limited interest in their data resource. Some believe there is no data problem or the data problem is solved. Others do not even know they have a problem. They concentrate on platform issues, such as communications and access to individual databases, but not on transforming data into an integrated data resource. They achieve current success at an individual database and information system level; however, they court disaster in the future.

Most data management techniques concentrate on new data at the information system level. These techniques perpetuate disparate data by not aligning all data within a common data architecture. The quantities of evaluational data, current spatial data, and historical spatial data are increasing exponentially. Client/server technology and cooperative processing provide many benefits for decentralized organizations, but they are also creating the next wave of legacy systems and disparate databases. Document imaging system, textual information management systems, and object-oriented technology are also creating a new wave of legacy systems. Organizations must be proactive at stopping the creation of disparate data and creating an integrated data resource.

Knowledge Loss

Data and information are often confused, as explained in Chapter 4. Data are the individual facts about the real world that are stored in a data resource. Information is a set of data that is relevant to a person at a point in time; it is data in context that has meaning and purpose. *Knowledge* is information that is retained with an understanding about the significance of that information. It is knowing something gained by experience, study, familiarity, association, awareness, or comprehension.

One reason for increasing data disparity is a loss of knowledge about the data resource. Both individual and institutional knowledge about the data resource are being lost on a daily basis. People are not capable of knowing and understanding the entire data resource. Organizations are too dynamic to retain any significant knowledge about their data resource. People frequently change jobs, change organizations, and retire taking the knowledge with them. The result is a loss of knowledge about the data resource, and new information systems and databases are developed without knowing what data already exist.

> An integrated data resource supported by a comprehensive metadata warehouse is the institutional memory for an organization.

The only way to prevent loss of knowledge about the data resource is to develop and maintain a comprehensive metadata warehouse. Data architects and data engineers build and maintain the metadata warehouse to document the integrated data resource. Information analysts and information engineers use the metadata warehouse to find data needed to build and maintain information systems. Business clients use the metadata warehouse to find data they need to support business needs.

Millennium Date Problem

The problem with existing date formats and the rapidly approaching year 2000 is known as the *millennium date problem*. Five major problems exist with the dates in applications and databases. First, most dates in existing databases and applications do not contain a century identifier. They contain year, month, and day; year and month; or year. Seldom do they contain the century. Second, the format of dates varies widely, such as year/month/day, month/day/year, and day/month/year. Third, the location of all dates in existing databases is unknown. Fourth, the location of application code using dates is unknown. Fifth, all the uses of each date in a database are unknown.

> The extent of the millennium date problem and its impact are largely unknown in most organizations.

The millennium date problem will not arrive in the year 2000; it is here today. Contracts, loans, and licenses are being issued that extend beyond 2000. The criminal justice system already sets dates beyond the year 2000. Plans and major construction projects extend beyond the year 2000. The millennium date problem is a time bomb that is already ticking and may have gone off in some organizations. The shock wave is yet to come.

Another major problem with dates is that the great majority of date routines are written in COBOL, yet qualified COBOL programmers are scarce. Many COBOL programmers have reached retirement age or are moving on to more advanced application development techniques. This news is devastating for organizations because they need COBOL programmers to correct date routines. This is good news, however, for former COBOL programmers looking for contract opportunities.

The only way out of the millennium date problem is to change both database dates and application date routines to include the century. By inventorying all databases to find the location and format of dates, inventorying all applications to find the location of date routines, and documenting the database dates maintained or used by each application. When all database dates and date routines are identified, changes can be made in a controlled manner.

Changing only date routines or only database dates is disastrous because the impact of uncoordinated changes is unknown. Independently changing database dates or date routines could cause applications to process data incorrectly or to abort; therefore, database date changes and date routine changes must be closely coordinated.

> Database date changes and application date routine changes must be closely coordinated.

The millennium date problem should be a wake-up call about the disparate data situation. It should alert organizations to the fact that they do not have control of their data resource. The location, format, content, and meaning of their data are unknown. The uses of data and the impact of changing data are unknown. There is no consistency across the data resource, or there is complete independence of data and applications. The millennium date problem should be a major incentive for organizations to immediately move toward an integrated data resource.

Client Data Access

There is an evolving trend toward clients accessing data directly, such as people accessing licensing or travel data through kiosks, business clients accessing the database with ad hoc query routines, or customers reviewing and ordering products through phones or interactive television. This direct client access to data mandates that data be understood, integrated, and consistent.

The traditional approach for client access to data is shown in Figure 15.1. A client typically goes to an information system to obtain the data. They are constrained by the capabilities of that information system. Even worse, clients go to some organization, or organizational unit, which in turn goes to an information system to obtain the data.

The ideal situation for client access is a common interface that interacts with an integrated data resource, as shown in Figure 15.2. A comprehensive metadata warehouse supports the common interface and helps the clients find the data they need. Major information systems still maintain the integrated data resource.

Several intermediate steps can exist between the traditional client access and the ideal client access, such as the one shown in Figure 15.3. A client can go to an interim interface that accesses translation routines to different databases. The interim interface is supported by a

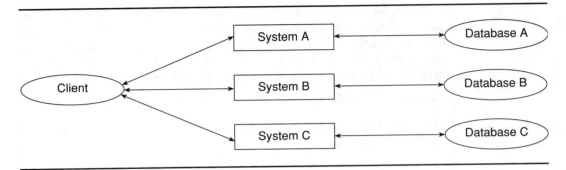

Figure 15.1   Traditional client access to data.

metadata warehouse, and the databases are maintained by major information systems. The translation routines give the client the appearance of accessing integrated data.

Many different scenarios exist for the interim steps to an integrated data resource. The key to direct client access is a comprehensive metadata warehouse that documents the status and contents of the data resource, helps clients find the data they need, and translates the data for client use.

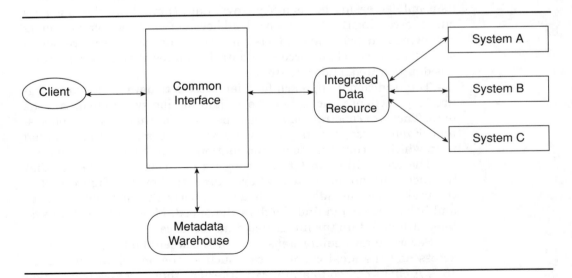

Figure 15.2   Ideal client access to data.

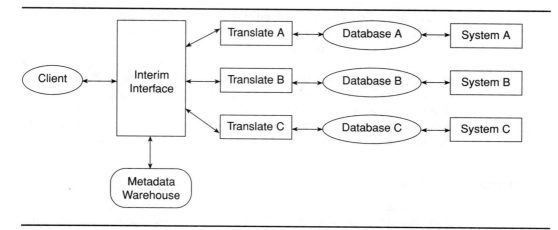

Figure 15.3   Interim steps for client access to data.

Acquired Applications

Many organizations are faced with the decision whether to build or to acquire their applications, known as the *application build-acquire dilemma*. Acquired applications could be purchased from a vendor or acquired from another organization. Acquiring applications is usually less costly, but the applications may not be aligned with the way an organization does business or with the integrated data resource. Building applications is usually more costly, but the applications are more aligned with the way an organization does business and with their integrated data resource.

The proactive approach to implementing an application is to develop a logical model of the desired information system, including both processes and data, based on business needs. That model is then used to review all the alternatives, including building and acquiring the application. The decision to build or acquire is based on how closely the business needs are met, the cost of acquisition and maintenance, the proprietary nature of the application code, and a variety of other criteria.

The reactive approach to implementing an application is to acquire and implement an application, commit to using that application, and then determine its functional capabilities. The result of a reactive approach could be an instant legacy system.

Unplanned purchase of applications could result in instant legacy systems.

If an application is acquired with the reactive approach, the database supporting the application should be immediately cross-referenced to the integrated data resource. The cross-reference serves three purposes. First, it identifies any data variations from the integrated data resources and ensures the proper data variations are used. Second, it identifies any data translations that need to occur to align the application's database with the integrated data resource. Third, it allows data definitions in the integrated data resource to be applied to the application so that proper data are entered.

Conflicting Data Standards

Data standards are becoming a real problem. Many different organizations develop independent data standards for the same data resulting in disparate data standards. Data standards often are physically oriented, have minimal definitions based on use, and use a format that is difficult to understand and apply. Clients required to use the data standards are seldom involved in developing data standards. The situation creates a dilemma as to which data standard to use. It is an emotional and often political situation that is promoting hostility rather than progress. There appears to be no way to stop the development of disparate data standards, at least in the near future.

Conflicting standards mean there is no standard!

The problem with many data standards is that they are not developed within a common data architecture. The ideal approach is to develop all data standards within a common data architecture. In addition, data standards should be developed as a logical data model rather than a physical data model. The implementation of data standards is determined by the specific operating environment, which cannot be easily explained in the data standard. Data standards should also be developed with a team consisting of business experts, domain experts, and data experts.

Data standards should be developed within a common data architecture with a team of business, domain, and data experts.

Until the ideal is achieved, disparate data standards are best managed by cross-referencing them to a common data architecture in order to understand their content and meaning. When disparate data standards are understood within a common context, the appropriate data characteristics are selected and designated as official data variations. Designating selected data characteristics as official data variations avoids the problem of creating yet another data standard and allows data to be translated to any data standard for sharing.

Standards and Guidelines

Standards are appropriate for the platform resource segment of the information technology infrastructure. There need to be more standards so that hardware and system software applications can interconnect and be more compatible. Platform resource standards would benefit all organizations and make the implementation of information technology to support business needs less complicated.

Standards may not be quite as appropriate for the data resource segment of the information technology infrastructure. Standards imply mandates, compliance, enforcement, and possibly punishment (perish the thought). Perhaps the development of data guidelines is a better approach. Guidelines imply involvement, consensus, and acceptance. A simple, but very important, principle for managing an integrated data resource within a common data architecture is as follows:

Involvement leads to commitment, which leads to acceptance, which leads to success.

When any link in that chain is broken, the success of an integrated data resource is at risk.

Another important aspect of guidelines is that they are not rigid and can be readily changed as technology evolves. The formal route of making, adjusting, and adopting standards by some authoritative body may take too long and may lag behind technology. When people want to take advantage of new technology, they will deviate from standards. Guidelines, however, can change more rapidly as technology evolves. Combining consensus and evolution into workable guidelines is an excellent approach to developing an integrated data resource.

Guidelines may be more appropriate than standards for managing an integrated data resource.

One bad aspect of standards and guidelines is their limit on finding new applications of technology to support business strategies. Although standards and guidelines are needed to provide consistency and gain workforce productivity, they can limit the use of new technology to improve business processes or transform the business. Being too rigid limits the discovery of new ways to provide better service. An excellent approach is to allow a small group of people investigate the use of new technology independent of existing standards and guidelines. When a new technology is found that is applicable to the business, guidelines can be put into place to provide consistency and increase productivity.

Standards for the products used by clients to access and analyze the data are not as important if an integrated data resource exists. An attempt to develop standards for these end-client products is often done in the name of data standardization. Although there may be other reasons for standardizing data access and manipulation products, such as support, training, and upgrades, standardizing the data resource should not be the reason.

Rapid Development

Rapid application development and joint application development methods are both good and bad. They are good in the sense that knowledgeable people are brought together to design and develop information systems that meet their information needs. The synergy of these teams produces excellent information systems. They are also good because information systems are developed incrementally and begin supporting business activities without a lengthy development. Rapid development methods, however, are bad because they often perpetuate disparate data. They tend to ignore the common data architecture because it "takes too long." It is easier to look at a narrow scope, develop an independent data model for that scope, generate the database, and put the information system in production.

> An integrated data resource and comprehensive metadata warehouse helps rapid application development.

It is just as easy, and possibly faster, to rapidly develop applications within a common data architecture. Data that are already defined in the common data architecture are drawn into the information system design. New data are defined and placed in the common data architecture for the next project. Data that already exist in the integrated data resource support the new information system. New data are added to the integrated data resource as defined in the common data architecture.

In some situations, it may be necessary to allow a noncritical database to be developed outside the common data architecture. The database can be developed and then cross-referenced to the common data architecture at a later date. Although this approach is not recommended and should be kept to a minimum, it allows development of a noncritical database without utilizing resources that could be better applied to development of more critical databases within the common data architecture. Every effort should be made, however, to align a noncritical database with the integrated data resource.

Multiple Common Data Architectures

The situation may arise where multiple common data architectures are developed, either within an organization or across several organizations. These multiple common data architectures could be closely aligned with each other, or they could be quite different from each other. The problem that arises is how to integrate these multiple common data architectures.

> Multiple common data architectures are integrated by cross-referencing them to a new integrated common data architecture.

The best approach is to treat each contributing common data architecture as a data product and cross-reference it to a new integrated common data architecture. The cross-reference may be as simple as a cross-reference between data subject and data characteristic names, or it may be as detailed as identifying data variability and designating official data variations. Regardless of the similarity or diversity of multiple common data architectures, they are integrated through cross-references to a new common data architecture.

LEGACY SYSTEMS

Legacy systems are disparate processes supporting business activities. They are largely undocumented, have highly variable routines, and often perform redundant processing. They are difficult to understand and nearly impossible to change, and the impact of major changes is largely unknown. In many respects, legacy systems are more disparate than the data resource.

> Disparate legacy systems prevent implementation of critical business improvements.

Legacy systems are an anchor around an organization's neck. They use valuable staff resources because they are difficult to maintain. They prevent changes to the business processes because the processes are directly dependent on the legacy systems. Legacy systems frequently prevent the implementation of otherwise successful business transformation and business improvement efforts because they are extremely difficult to change.

Legacy systems need to be constructively dismantled and rebuilt as flexible information systems with interchangeable parts. Individual parts are easily changed to meet changing business needs. The problem with constructive dismantling is the substantial knowledge required about the system's construction and operation. Constructive dismantling of legacy systems requires a thorough understanding of the data, logic, calculations, and business rules. The massive amount of detail within and between legacy systems is often overwhelming.

Stabilizing Variables

Control of legacy systems cannot be achieved with a direct approach. The direct approach only makes the situation worse because there is no common context within which legacy systems can be dismantled and flexible information systems can be built. There is no disciplined way to understand the content and meaning of legacy systems.

> There are too many variables for an organization to successfully manage at one time.

The primary reason why legacy systems cannot be controlled directly is the existence of too many variables for an organization to deal with at one time. The disparate data resource is a variable, the rapidly evolving platform resource is a variable, changing business activities are a variable, and the dynamic business environment is a variable. A method is needed to stabilize the variables so legacy systems can be constructively dismantled and rebuilt.

The best approach is to stabilize the variables within the information technology infrastructure. The data resource is stabilized first, followed by the platform resource, and then the business activities. When these components are stabilized, the legacy systems can be constructively dismantled and rebuilt.

The information technology infrastructure provides the framework for stabilizing variables.

The data resource is stabilized first because it is the most stable component of the information technology infrastructure. The data resource is stabilized by building an integrated data resource within a common data architecture as explained throughout this book.

The platform resource cannot be stabilized to the extent the data resource is stabilized because of rapidly evolving technology. It must be recognized that technology will continue at the vendor's pace. There is little an organization can do to speed up or slow down the evolution of platform technology. The platform technology can only be tracked and implemented in a consistent and judicious manner through a common platform architecture.

The business activities can be stabilized within a common activity architecture that is patterned after the common data architecture. The *common activity architecture* is the common context for understanding the content and meaning of all business activities. It provides the foundation for integrating disparate business activities the same as the common data architecture is the foundation for integrating disparate data. A common activity architecture also provides the foundation for refining business activity, developing common activity models, and improving business activities. Like disparate data, disparate business activities must be resolved one at a time. This task requires considerable thought and analysis supported by appropriate tools.

Legacy systems are dismantled and rebuilt within a set of common architectures.

When the data resource, the platform resource, and the business activities are stabilized within a set of common architectures, the legacy systems can be dismantled within those common architectures. The data in legacy systems are aligned with the common data architecture, the business processes are aligned with the common activity architecture, and the technology processing is aligned with the common platform architecture. The legacy systems are then rebuilt as flexible information systems with exchangeable parts within the common architectures.

Business Improvement

The information technology infrastructure and its common architectures support business transformation and business process improvement. Business transformation is the process of determining what lines of business an organization wants, or is required, to perform. Business process improvement is the process of determining how those lines of business will be performed. Both are ongoing processes.

The front-end approach to business improvement views business activities and the platform resource as the drivers. Decisions are made about the current and future lines of business, the business activities that support those lines of business, and the technology that supports those business activities. The data supporting the business activities are a secondary concern in the front-end approach and are often ignored, which leads to disparate data.

The back-end approach to business improvement views data as a stable data resource that supports changing business activities and information systems. Emphasis is placed on developing a data resource and aligning the data supporting information systems to that data resource. The back-end approach is the traditional data-focused data administration approach.

> The new data resource manager must be prepared to support front-end initiatives with an integrated data resource.

The new approach to data resource management must recognize that the data resource is driven by front-end initiatives. Data resource management has a supporting role to business improvement and information system development, even though it is critical to business success. The new data resource manager must have the skills and techniques readily available and take the opportunities to develop an integrated data resource. This situation is different than having the data drive the development of information systems. The switch from data administration to data resource management emphasizes the support role for the data resource.

Data are behind the scenes and are not readily visible until there is a problem developing the appropriate information. It is difficult to get emphasis on data when other variables are more important to the business.

RESOLUTION INITIATIVE

Numerous concepts and techniques are presented in this book and previous books by the author for understanding the current data situation, building an integrated data resource, resolving the data dilemma, and sharing data. These concepts and techniques can be combined into a few simple steps to create an initiative that resolves the data dilemma, transforms data into an integrated data resource, and deploys those data to meet the business information demand.

Recognition

The first step to resolve the data dilemma is to recognize that a problem exists and determine to resolve that problem. An organization must go through the shock of realizing that it has disparate data that are not meeting its needs. It must realize that the data resource needs to be controlled and managed to support changing business activities in a dynamic business world.

Organizations often make the excuse that it is too difficult to rebuild their data resource while it supports the business.

Analogy: An analogy is the difficulty of maintaining a car while traveling nonstop across the country. It is more difficult to try rebuilding a car while traveling nonstop across the country, but it is not impossible.

An integrated data resource can be built while supporting the business using the concepts and techniques presented here. Organizations need to find a way, not an excuse.

> When the pain of not meeting business needs exceeds the pain of controlling data, an organization will develop an integrated data resource.

In some situations, the starting point for resolving the data dilemma is resolving a perception problem. Creating an integrated data resource is intangible. People cannot visualize the benefits of developing an integrated data resource. There is a perception that if a process does not produce code, it does not provide any benefits to an organization. Building an integrated data resource is often perceived as an esoteric process where "the rubber meets the sky," and a few data administration units have not helped the perception. This perception needs to be overcome by selling the disadvantages of disparate data and the benefits of an integrated data resource.

> An integrated data resource reduces the business risks to an organization.

One approach to selling the advantages of an integrated data resource is disaster reduction and disaster avoidance. Disparate data create a risk for an organization by being large and costly to maintain and by not being able to support rapidly changing business initiatives. That risk could lead to a disaster if an organization misses opportunities or fails to fully utilize an opportunity. Developing an integrated data resource can prevent a disaster or reduce the impact of a disaster by reducing the risk.

Vision

The next step after recognizing the data dilemma is to develop a vivid vision of what the future will be like with an integrated data resource. A good vision includes scenarios about how the integrated data resource will support constantly changing business needs. The scenarios should be specific to the organization's business and should make people say, "Yes, that is what I want."

> It's the eleventh-hour—do you know where your data are?

A good vision explains how an integrated data resource with minimum data redundancy and data variability is developed within a common data architecture. The vision describes how common data modeling describes the integrated data resource. The vision also describes how a robust metadata warehouse documents the integrated data resource, promotes data sharing within and without an organization, and helps clients find and properly use data to support their business needs.

A good vision includes all the data megatypes, not just current tabular data. Support for future business needs requires the integration of all types of data and the analysis of historical data for trends, projections, and alternatives. The integrated data resource must include tabular and nontabular data, operational and evaluational data, distributed and centralized data, internal and external data, automated and nonautomated data, and hard and soft data.

> A good vision paints a vivid picture of the desired data resource.

A good vision describes an architectural approach to resolving disparate data and supporting the constructive dismantling of legacy systems. The vision explains the information technology infrastructure and how things fit within that infrastructure. It emphasizes commonality within an integrated infrastructure. A good vision helps people think globally and act locally.

A good vision explains the tangible and intangible benefits of an integrated data resource. It shows how development of an integrated data resource is incrementally cost effective while achieving the long-term goal. It explains the savings-times-three approach of using data templates. The vision describes how to reduce or avoid data disasters by identifying and using the data properly.

> A good vision explains how to successfully cross the disparate data chasm.

A good vision explains how to bridge the broad chasm of disparate data with a common data architecture. Broad chasms cannot be crossed incrementally, nor can they be crossed in one quantum leap. The common data architecture is a virtual bridge to cross the disparate data chasm.

Orientation

The third step to resolve the data dilemma is developing the proper business survival orientation for achieving the integrated data resource vision. An integrated data resource must support business activities, help resolve business issues, and lead to more informed business decisions. It must cross multiple jurisdictions and disciplines because nothing is isolated today. An integrated data resource helps people learn about the business, understand the business, and operate the business successfully. Information is today's business weapon, and analysis is tomorrow's business weapon. Learning about the data supporting information and analysis helps a business become successful.

> People do not mind changing; they mind being changed.

A good orientation is people-focused. Teams of business experts, domain experts, data experts, and stake holders develop an integrated data resource. The real incentive for building an integrated data resource is to get people interacting and sharing their problems, techniques, visions, options, and solutions. The real benefits are achieved through cooperation, coordination, and partnerships. A win-win situation is created by using from-above and from-below approaches that include all organizational levels from executives setting directions to workers on the firing line. A people-focused orientation puts people first and helps them adapt to changing business needs and changing technology.

Quote: Voltaire said, "No problem can stand the assault of sustained thinking."

A good orientation uses acceptable terms that are readily understood. Many terms in use today are used inappropriately. The information technology discipline tends to grab terms, wear them out with overuse and hype, and then discard them and go on to other terms. Soft, well-defined, meaningful terms should be used to draw people into development of an integrated data resource. Harsh, irritating terms should be avoided.

> Tools do not understand data; people understand data.

A good orientation is not tool-driven. There are many tools available today and considerable hype about the use of tools to solve disparate data problems. Tools, however, cannot solve the disparate data problem and build an integrated data resource because tools cannot understand the problem. Only people can understand the problem, and tools support people. There is a over-reliance on tools because organizations are looking for the silver bullet. There are no silver bullets, and there will not be any silver bullets to develop an integrated data resource. An integrated data resource cannot be developed automatically.

Analogy: A housewife went into a department store one day and found a new zippo-zappo on sale that "cut a housewife's work in half." She immediately ran to the counter and bought two.

Strategy

The fourth step to resolve the data dilemma is to develop a strategy for building an integrated data resource. There is no one starting point for resolving disparate data or building an integrated data resource. The starting point varies for each organization, based on its specific business issues. The key to developing a good strategy is to develop an infrastructure and then develop an integrated data resource within that infrastructure. Once the integrated data resource is started, it will evolve with the needs of the organization.

A good strategy increases the awareness of existing data and where those data are located. Data awareness is increased through data surveys that identify broad groupings of data and the organizations that maintain those data and through data inventories that identify specific data files and data items. A good strategy also increases the understanding of existing data through cross-references to a common data architecture.

> A good strategy increases the awareness and understanding of existing data.

A good strategy includes the development of a robust metadata warehouse. A metadata warehouse helps increase data awareness and understanding by documenting the existence of data, what those data mean within a common data architecture, where those data are located, and who to contact for additional information about those data. A metadata warehouse evolves with the development of an integrated data resource.

A good strategy is based on priorities driven by identifying critical business functions and building an integrated data resource to support those critical functions. A two-dimensional priority scheme is often established. Horizontal prioritization involves selecting the subject areas that provide support to critical business functions. The subject areas that provide support to critical business functions become the highest priority for developing the integrated data resource. Vertical prioritization involves selecting specific data subjects in a subject area that support critical business functions. Only the data subjects that support critical business functions should become high priority.

Evaluation

The last step for resolving the data dilemma is constant evaluation of the progress toward developing an integrated data resource. An organization must constantly evaluate its progress toward developing an integrated data resource and how well that integrated data resource supports the business. It must review the lessons learned during development of an integrated data resource and adjust the approach for continued development. The priorities must be constantly adjusted to meet changing business needs.

SUMMARY

Organizations must prepare themselves to face rapid changes and uncertainties and structure themselves for success. They must control increasing data resource disparity, platform resource disparity, and business activity disparity to be prepared for change. They must increase the awareness and understanding of their data resource with a comprehensive metadata warehouse that prevents the loss of institutional knowledge. Organizations must heed the millennium date problem as a wake-up call to the disastrous impact of not having control of their data resource.

Widely disparate data need to be transformed into an integrated data resource to provide better service. Citizens and customers both need to be treated on a personal basis. The public sector should look at citizens as a total person by combining health care, welfare, unemployment, job market and training, and judicial data into an integrated data resource. They should be oriented to making citizens productive members of society rather than treating them through independent business functions. The private sector should look at its customers as people by analyzing buying patterns, providing better options. and advising them about those options. It needs to recognize customers by name when contact is made.

Promoting client access to integrated data will ease the workload for an overworked information technology staff. Clients will be data-enabled to find the data needed to support their business needs. Clients will become programmers just like they became telephone operators with the implementation of dial telephones. They will no longer need a programmer to find data anymore than they need an operator to place a telephone call.

Application acquisition is a prominent trend today, but it can increase the data disparity if not properly integrated into the data resource. Conflicting data standards can also increase disparity and cause confusion if not properly integrated into the data resource. A common data architecture ensures that acquired applications and data standards are properly integrated. It also supports rapid development efforts and the integration of multiple common data architectures.

Creating an integrated data resource stabilizes the data resource variable. The common data architecture is a pattern for developing a common platform architecture to stabilize the platform resource and a common activity architecture to stabilize business activities. These common architectures are used to understand the content and meaning of legacy systems and to dismantle legacy systems and build new information systems with exchangeable parts. The common architectures reduce the variables an organization must manage so that they can focus on business improvement and business transformation.

An initiative to resolve the data dilemma begins with a recognition of the data dilemma and a determination to resolve that dilemma. A vivid vision of the future is created to focus people on the benefits of developing an integrated data resource to resolve the data dilemma. Development of a vivid vision must include creative ideas from a wide variety of people. The visionaries must be retained through implementation to ensure the vision is achieved. One major problem with implementing an integrated data resource is that visionaries back out, or are pushed out, too soon.

An orientation to people is important for successful resolution of the data dilemma because it is people who create disparity. People must be involved in the techniques for stopping disparity and creating an integrated data resource. Generally, people do not resist using new technology; they resist being changed by new technology. People need to understand that there are no silver bullets for resolving the data dilemma. It takes considerable effort stop the disparity and create common data.

A good data strategy for taking control of the data resource requires patience and understanding. The task is difficult and challenging, but not impossible. The situation will get worse before it gets better; however, the benefits more than pay for the effort if an integrated data resource is developed based on critical business functions.

The benefits will vary from project to project and from year to year. The secret is that there are no failures, only successes and lessons learned.

Seize the opportunity! Develop an integrated data resource that supports business survival!

QUESTIONS

The following questions are provided as a review of the chapter and to stimulate thought about how to resolve the data dilemma and how to use an integrated data resource to support control of legacy systems:

1. Why is the future both promising and scary?
2. Why is data disparity still increasing today?
3. Why is knowledge about the data resource lost over time?
4. How can the knowledge loss be prevented?
5. How can widely disparate data about individuals be integrated?
6. Why is the millennium date problem so important?
7. How can the millennium date problem be resolved?
8. How can client access to common data be improved?
9. How can acquired applications be successfully implemented into an organization?
10. How are conflicting data standards properly managed?
11. Why are guidelines often better than standards for managing data?
12. How can an integrated data resource support rapid development efforts?
13. How can multiple common data architectures be integrated?
14. Why is it so difficult to maintain and change legacy systems?
15. Why are organizations faced with managing many different variables?
16. How can an organization successfully manage multiple variables?
17. How can legacy systems be successfully controlled?
18. How does a stable data resource support business improvement?
19. What constitutes a good approach to resolving the data dilemma?
20. Why is it necessary to have a good vision for resolving the data dilemma?
21. Why should teams of people be formed to solve the data dilemma?
22. Why is it necessary to increase the awareness and understanding of the data resource?
23. Why should development of an integrated data resource be constantly evaluated?
24. Why should an organization be concerned about resolving the data dilemma?

Glossary

abstract schema concept A concept that consists of two levels of abstract schema above the detailed schema. *See strategic schema, tactical schema.*

active data replicate A data replicate that must have data values consistent with those at the official data source. *See static data replicate.*

active data warehouse A data warehouse that searches for trends and patterns in evaluational data. It is an active process that searches an evaluational database for trends, patterns, and exceptions.

active derived data Data derived from contributing data characteristics that still exist and whose values can change. Active derived data must be rederived when the contributing data values change or when new contributing data values appear. *See static derived data.*

active documentation The process of automatically capturing and storing the algorithm for creating a summary data subject. This self-documenting process for evaluational data that automatically provides useful metadata without business analyst or data analyst involvement. *See intuitive data warehouse.*

active metadata warehouse A *metadata warehouse* that is automatically updated when new data enter the data resource. *See passive metadata warehouse.*

actual data value An actual measurement, value, or description of a trait or feature of a data subject. *See coded data value.*

aggregation Used in the broad sense to mean aggregating data horizontally, vertically, and chronologically. *See integration.*

alternate foreign key A *foreign key* that matches an *alternate primary key*.

alternate primary key A *primary key* whose value is unique for all data occurrences in the common data structure, but has not been designated as the *official primary key*.

anchor point A starting point for determining the accumulated distance along a linear object. *See linear addressing system, linear referencing system*.

application build-acquire dilemma The *dilemma* an organization faces about whether to build or to acquire its applications.

arbitrary event A random frequency established to capture data for a continuous event. *See data currentness*.

arbitrary primary key A *primary key* whose value is created and assigned by an information system. It is also known as a *system assigned primary key*.

area seen area The portion of the landscape that can be seen from another area on the landscape. *See seen area*.

automatic data distribution The process of automatically distributing replicated data to *data sites*.

automatic data partitioning The process of automatically partitioning data and metadata based on a client's request for data at a specific *data site*.

automatic data redistribution The automatic redistribution of distributed data if the data are properly developed within the common data architecture.

automatic data replication The process of automatically creating data and metadata replicates based on a client's request for data at a specific *data site*.

business activities A component of *information technology infrastructure* that represent all business activities in an organization, whether they are automated or manual. They utilize the data resource and the platform resource to perform specific processes and tasks.

business data layer Any *derived data layer* resulting from an aggregation of *framework data layers* or *specific data layers* to meet specific business needs.

business-driven An approach to identifying the data needed to support business activities, acquiring or capturing those data, and maintaining them in a data resource that is readily available. *See business survival-driven*.

business-driven approach The process of identifying the data needed to support business activities, acquiring or capturing those data, and maintaining them in the data resource. *See business survival orientation*.

business-driven data distribution The situation where the business need for data at a specific location drives the development of a data site and the distribution of data to that data site. Business-driven data distribution is independent of the existence of a telecommunications network. *See network-driven data distribution.*

business experts People that thoroughly understand the business and the data supporting the business. They know the specific business rules and processes unique to the organization or organizations within the scope of the *common metadata. See domain experts data experts.*

business foreign key *The foreign key* that matches the *business primary key.*

business improvement The process of adjusting an organization's business activities to support its desired lines of business. *See business transformation.*

business information demand An organization's continuously increasing, constantly changing need for current, accurate information, often on short notice, to support its business activities.

business primary key A meaningful *primary key* that is usually assigned by business clients and is visible to business clients. It is used to uniquely identify and manage objects in the real world and to properly normalize data into data subjects. *See physical primary key.*

business question approach An approach to developing an *evaluational database* where the basic business questions to be answered are identified and used to define the data perspectives to answer those questions. *See primary key approach.*

business schema A *schema* that represents the structure of business transactions used by clients in the real world. It is considered to be *unnormalized data.*

business survival-driven An approach to identifying the data needed to support both current and future business needs, acquiring or capturing those data, and maintaining them in an integrated data resource so they are readily available. *See business-driven.*

business survival orientation The process of identifying the data needed to support both current and future business needs, acquiring or capturing those data, and maintaining them in an integrated data resource so they are readily available to information systems. *See business-driven approach.*

business tier A tier in the *four-tier concept* that consists of data layers that are a combination of data layers from the thematic and/or subthematic tiers to meet business needs. There are relatively few thematic and subthematic data layers, but there can be many extractions and combinations of those data layers to meet business needs. The data layers in the business tier may be permanent or temporary depending on the continued business needs.

business transformation The process of deciding what lines of business an organization wants to pursue and making the appropriate adjustments to pursue those lines of business. *See business improvement.*

business-driven data distribution The situation where the business need for data at a specific location drives the development of a data site and the distribution of data to that data site. It is independent of the existence of a telecommunications network. *See network-driven data distribution.*

candidate primary key Any *primary key* that has been identified in disparate data, but has not been reviewed for validity or range of uniqueness and has not been designated as any other type of primary key.

candidate tier A tier in the *four-tier concept* that consists of temporary *data layers* that are used for entering and adjusting data, determining what data to combine into a *subthematic data layer*, or determining how to combine data to form a subthematic data layer. It is a candidate for building subthematic data layers.

canonical synthesis After-the-fact integration of independently developed physical data models that does not create a *common data model.*

cardinality The number of *data occurrences* allowed on either side of a *data relation*. In the common data architecture, cardinality is documented with data integrity, not with the data structure.

categorical levels of data classification Abstract levels of data classification above the working level that provide a broader perspective of data. There are several types of categorical levels, including data classification schemes, data themes, data segments, and data clusters. *See data classification scheme, working levels of data classification.*

chained data replication The replication of *nonofficial data* to another nonofficial data. If data are replicated from nonofficial data, they are considered *duplicated data*, not replicated data.

characteristic list An alphabetical list of data characteristics in a *subject structure chart.*

chronological data aggregation The historical continuity of data between different time periods. *See horizontal data aggregation, vertical data aggregation.*

chronological data layer aggregation The aggregation of *data layers* chronologically to provide a history of changes.

class word A word used in *data naming conventions* to provide a standard structure and format for data values by using standard words to represent classes of data, such as integer, string, date, and name. They increase the meaning of a data name compared to traditional data names. *See common word, data naming vocabulary.*

clearinghouse keywords Any business words or terms that references *clearinghouse topics.*

clearinghouse topics Core topics used to reference *clearinghouse items.*

closed recursive data relation The same as a *one-to-one recursive data relation* because it forms a closed loop between two data occurrences.

coarse granularity *See highly summarized data.*

code table A set of coded data values that are closely related. Each set of closely related coded data values is defined as a separate code table in the common data structure. *See code table data subject, data code set.*

code table data subject A data subject containing a *code table.*

collection time The time data were actually collected about the event. *See distribution time, entry time, event time, identification time, temporal data.*

combined data A concatenation of individual facts. *See elemental data.*

combined data product unit A *data product unit* that contains two or more data characteristics that should not be combined.

common activity architecture The common context for understanding the content and meaning of all business activities. It provides the foundation for integrating disparate business activities the same as the common data architecture is the foundation for integrating disparate data. It also provides the foundation for business activity refining, common business activity modeling, and business activity improvement.

common data architecture A formal, comprehensive data architecture that provides a common context within which an integrated data resource is developed so that it adequately supports the business information demand. *See generic data architecture.*

common data characteristic variation word A *common word* for *data characteristic variations.*

common data characteristic word A *common word* for *data characteristics.*

common data model A comprehensive model that represents the universe of data available to an organization that have been identified and defined within the common data architecture. It represents the objects and events in the real world that are of interest to the organization, is subject-oriented, and includes all perspectives of the real world. *See logical data model, physical data model.*

common data modeling The process of developing a model of the integrated data resource within a common data architecture. The process facilitates the integration of existing data and increases the awareness and understanding of those data. It is a process to plan the distribution of data based on business needs and the physical operating environment.

common data modeling method A method that combines *forward data modeling, reverse data modeling,* and *vertical data modeling.* The method provides an easy way to move between unnormalized business transactions and a denormalized database and between the real world and detailed data resource design within the common data architecture.

common data site word A *common word* for *data sites.*

common data structure The structure of data within the common data architecture that provides a full understanding of all the disparate data structures and multiple perspectives of the real world represented by those data structures. *See logical data structure, physical data structure.*

common data subject word A *common word* for *data subjects.*

common metadata Metadata developed within the common data architecture to provide all the detail necessary to thoroughly understand the data resource and how it can be improved to meet the business information demand.

common meta-metadata The architecture component of the common data architecture consisting of formal data names, comprehensive data definitions, common data structure, and consistent data quality. The common meta-metadata provide the framework for the development of *common metadata.*

common word A word in the *data naming vocabulary* that has a consistent meaning wherever it is used. *See class word.*

comprehensive data definition A formal data definition that provides a complete, meaningful, easily read, readily understood definition explaining the content and meaning of data.

computer-aided data engineering A new class of tools to support data engineering and the resolution of disparate data.

conceptual schema A *schema* that represents a common structure of data that is the common denominator between the *internal schema* and *external schema.*

conditional data integrity value matrix A matrix for documenting *conditional data value integrity.*

conditional data structure integrity Specifies the *cardinality* for data relations.

conditional data structure integrity rule A rule for documenting data relation *cardinality.*

conditional data structure integrity table A table for documenting *conditional data structure integrity*.

conditional data value integrity *Data integrity* that specifies whether the values in data characteristics are required, optional, or prevented under certain conditions.

conditional data value integrity rule A rule for documenting *conditional data value integrity*.

conditional data value integrity table A table for documenting *conditional data value integrity*.

connotative meaning The idea or notion suggested by a data definition. The connotative meaning is what a person interprets from the definition in addition to what is explicitly stated. *See denotative meaning.*

consistent data quality The state of a data resource where the quality of existing data is thoroughly understood and the desired quality of the data resource is known. It is a state where disparate data quality is known, and the existing data quality is being adjusted to the level desired to meet the current and future *business information demand. See disparate data quality.*

contextless data *Data* that are nearly useless; they are noise.

critical data layer A *data layer* for emergency preparedness and response that are designated within the spatial data thematic hierarchy and usually become a high-priority for development.

data The individual facts with specific meaning at a point in time or for a period of time. Data include the atomic level, known as *primitive data*, and *derived data. See information.*

data access The process of entering a database to store or retrieve data.

data accuracy The component of *data integrity* that deals with how well data stored in the data resource represent the real world. It includes a definition of the current data accuracy and the adjustment in data accuracy to meet the business needs.

data aggregation A type of *data derivation* where a data value is derived from the aggregation of two or more contributing data characteristics in different data occurrences within the same data subject.

data architecture The science and method of designing and constructing an integrated data resource that is business-driven, based on real world objects and events as perceived by the organization, and implemented into appropriate operating environments. The overall structure of a data resource that provides a consistent foundation across organizational boundaries to provide easily identifiable, readily available, high-quality data to support the *business information demand.*

data architecture The component of the *data resource framework* that contains all activities, and the products of those activities, related to the identification, naming, definition, structuring, quality, and documentation of the data resource for an organization.

data area The second level in a *data classification scheme* representing a subdivision of a data discipline. It is also known as a data subject area.

data attribute Represents a *data characteristic variation* that is used in a *logical data model*.

data attribute group Represents the use of a *data characteristic group* in a *logical data model*.

data availability component A component of the *data resource framework* that contains all activities related to making data available while properly protecting and securing these data.

data availability inventory A detailed inventory that identifies the existence of data subjects and data characteristics and obtains detailed information about them. *See data resource inventory.*

data availability survey A high-level determination of data that are currently available to the organization. *See data resource survey.*

data awareness The knowledge about all the data that are available to the organization and where those data are located. *See data understanding.*

data certification levels Levels of data quality criteria for evaluating *data quality* and *data quality improvement*, such as high quality data, moderate quality data, and low quality data. *See data quality certification.*

data characteristic An individual characteristic that describes a data subject. It is developed, directly through measurement or indirectly through derivation, from a feature of an object or event. Each data subject is described by a set of data characteristics.

data characteristic contraction The removal of one or more data characteristics from an *evaluational database*. It is the opposite of *data characteristic extension*. *See evaluational data contraction.*

data characteristic cross-reference A *data cross-reference* between a *data product unit* and a *data characteristic variation*.

data characteristic cross-reference list A list that shows *data characteristic cross-references*.

data characteristic expansion The addition of more derived data characteristics to an evaluational database within the existing scope of the *evaluational database*. *See evaluational data expansion.*

data characteristic group A set of related *data characteristics* that are commonly grouped together.

data characteristic length variation list A list that shows data characteristic length variations.

data characteristic matrix A matrix showing the data characteristics that are valid for each *summary data subject*.

data characteristic name The unique name of a *data characteristic* within a *data subject* in a common data architecture. The data characteristic name consists of the data subject name followed by the *feature name*.

data characteristic partitioning The process of identifying the data characteristics from a data subject or a data occurrence group needed at each data site. Also known as *vertical partitioning*.

data characteristic retention rule A rule that specifies what is done when a data characteristic value is updated or deleted. It specifies the procedure to preserve the historical significance of data characteristic values. *See data occurrence retention rule, data retention integrity.*

data characteristic substitution name The name of a data characteristic that represents the substitution of a specific data characteristic variation.

data characteristic translation scheme A *data translation* scheme that translates data values between variations of the same data characteristics. Data characteristic translation schemes are developed only for format and value variations, not for meaning, content, or accuracy variations.

data characteristic variation A variation in the content or meaning of a *data characteristic*. Each data characteristic in the common data model has one or more variations in content and/or meaning. *See data attribute.*

data characteristic variation list A list that shows *data characteristic variations* under their parent *data characteristics*.

data characteristic variation name The unique name of a *data characteristic variation*. The data characteristic variation component of the data naming taxonomy uniquely identifies each content and meaning variation of a data characteristic by adding a variation name after the data characteristic name.

data class The lowest level in a *data classification scheme* representing a subdivision of a *data group*. It contains data subjects from the *working level of data classification*.

data classification scheme A scheme for classifying data that progresses from general levels to specific levels. The data classification scheme includes *working levels of data classification* and *categorical levels of data classification*. *See data cluster, data segment, data theme.*

data clearinghouse component A component of the *metadata warehouse* that provides a mechanism for collecting, classifying, and distributing information about data sources, unpublished documents, and projects related to the data resource.

data cluster A temporary group of data subjects for a specific purpose. It can be any useful combination of data subjects for any specific purpose that cannot be met by any of the other categorical levels. *See data classification scheme, data theme, data segment.*

data code An *actual data value* that has been encoded in some way.

data code cross-reference A *data cross-reference* between a *data product code* and a *data code.*

data code cross-reference list A list that shows the *data code values* that correspond to the *data product code values.*

data code matrix A matrix that contains all the *data code sets* for one set of data properties. It identifies the variability between the data code values and data code names for a data code set.

data code name The formal name of the *data code value* that uniquely identifies a *data code* within the common data architecture, not just within the data subject.

data code set A set of *data codes* within a code table data subject that are closely related. Either the data codes, the corresponding names, or both are different.

data code set name The unique name of a *data code set* within a *data subject* in the common data architecture.

data code translation scheme A *data translation scheme* that translates data between *data code sets.*

data code value The formal data value representing an *actual data value. See data code name.*

data code variation The same data property that is represented by more than one *data code value.*

data collection frequency The frequency at which data are collected from the world. *See data currentness, data instance, data volatility.*

data completeness An indication of whether or not all the data necessary to meet the current and future business information demand are available in the data resource. It deals with determining the data needed to meet the *business information demand* and ensuring those data are captured and maintained in the data resource so they are available when needed. *See data quality, data resource inventory, data resource survey.*

data concurrency The situation where the replicated data values at are synchronized with the corresponding data values at the *official data source.* When the data values at the official data source are updated, the replicated data values must also be updated so they are consistent with the official data source.

data conversion The process of changing data from one physical environment to another. This process makes any changes necessary to move data from one electronic medium or database product to another.

data cross-reference A link between disparate data names and common data names. The primary cross-reference is between data product units and data characteristic variations. Cross-reference may be made between data product entities and data subjects, and between data product codes and data codes. *See data refining.*

data currentness A measure of how relevant a data value is compared to the real world or how out-of-date the data value has become. Data currentness depends on the *data instance*, the *data volatility*, and the *data collection frequency. See event frequency.*

data denormalization The process of developing the *internal schema* from the *conceptual schema.*

data deoptimization A process that prepares the *distribution schema* from the *logical schema* based on the data required at data sites to support business needs. It is the counterpart of *data optimization.*

data deployment The dynamic placement and maintenance of the data resource in appropriate products and at appropriate data sites on mainframe computers and across a telecommunications network in an optimum manner to meet the *business information demand.* Also known as data logistics.

data derivation The process of creating a data value from one or more contributing data values through a *data derivation algorithm. See data aggregation, data generation, derived data, multiple contributor data derivation, single contributor data derivation.*

data derivation diagram A diagram that specifies the data characteristics contributing to the derived data characteristic.

data derivation integrity A subset of *data integrity* that specifies criteria for data derivation and for derived data maintenance. The specification includes the contributing data characteristics, the data derivation procedure, and the timing for data derivation.

data derivation procedure An algorithm, equation, logical expression, or matrix that specifies the method of deriving data.

data description activity An activity of the *data architecture component* that ensures the formal naming and comprehensive definition of all data in an integrated data resource.

data dictionary This component of the *metadata warehouse* is an alphabetical list of the formal data names and comprehensive data definitions for data sites, data subjects, data characteristics, data characteristic variations, data codes, and data versions within the common data architecture.

data dilemma The situation where a critical need for current, accurate data, often on short notice, to meet the business information demand is being compromised by the active development of large quantities of disparate data.

data dimension A representation of a single set of objects or events in the real world.

data directory A component of the *metadata warehouse* that contains information about organizations that maintain data, contacts in those organizations, how data can be acquired from the organizations, and other general information about data access and availability, and terms and conditions for accessing data.

data discipline The highest level in a *data classification scheme* representing a broad collection of data.

data discovery The process of identifying all the data that exist in an organization's data resource and learning the content and meaning of those data. It is the realization that considerable quantities of data are available. Data discovery is a process that reveals the value of the *hidden data resource*.

data dissemination The process of getting data from the data resource to a client, within or without the organization, through appropriate applications and telecommunication networks. Data are disseminated through client/server applications, electronic mail, and traditional business applications.

data distribution The placement and maintenance of replicated data at one or more data sites on a mainframe computer or across a telecommunications network. This part of developing and maintaining an integrated data resource that ensures data are properly managed when distributed across many different data sites. Data distribution is one type of data deployment, which is the transfer of data to data sites.

data distribution diagram A diagram that shows the distribution of data. The diagram represents the movement of data replicates. It does not represent data derivations, data translations, or data transformation.

data distribution dilemma A *dilemma* that exists when an organization has a growing data disparity, does not control that disparity or refine disparate data, and distributes disparate data to support individual business needs.

data distribution process A process that moves and maintains one or more *data replicates*.

data distribution process diagram A diagram that shows the movement of *data replicates* between *data sites* and the processes that move those data replicates.

data documentation activity An activity of the *data architecture component* that ensures current, complete, ongoing documentation of the entire data resource.

data domain A data subject that contains data integrity values or data integrity rules. It is a named set of data integrity values or data integrity rules defining the values that a data characteristic can contain under specific conditions. *See data rule domain, data value domain.*

data domain integrity A *data value domain* must have a data domain for each of the data characteristics in that domain. This is an important part of the consistent data quality for an integrated data resource.

data duplication A term used to identify data that are captured, processed, or stored redundantly. It results in unknown, uncontrolled, and unmanaged data redundancy. It is not orderly and creates additional disparate data. *See data replication.*

data engineering The discipline that designs, builds, and maintains the *data resource library.* It is a structured process for developing both the formal data resource and the integrated data resource in the data resource library and the metadata warehouse that documents the data resource library. *See information engineering.*

data entity Represents a data subject from the *common data model* that is used in the *logical data model.*

data experts People that thoroughly understand the development of an integrated data resource. They know how data are managed from the real world, through logical design to physical implementation. *See business experts and domain experts.*

data exploration The process of routinely searching *evaluational data* for patterns, trends, and exceptions. Data exploration usually starts with an incomplete definition of the search criteria and an unknown volume of data. As patterns, trends, and exceptions are discovered, the search criteria are refined and the volume of data may be changed. *See data mining.*

data file A representation of a *data entity* from the *logical data model* that is implemented with a *physical data model.* It is a physical file of data that exists in a database management system, as a computer file outside a database management system, or as a manual file outside a computer that represents a data entity.

data focus The central *multiple dimension data subject* in a *data perspective.* It is also known as a fact table. *See data perspective.*

data fragmentation An unorderly process of placing data at various data sites. It is not done within the common data architecture, is not well-managed or documented, and results in unknown, undocumented, redundant data. *See data partitioning, fragmented data.*

data generalization The process of creating successive layers of summary data in an *evaluational database.* It is a process of zooming out to get a broader view of a problem, trend, or situation. It is also known as rolling-up data. *See data specialization.*

data generation A type of *data derivation* where a data value is derived from a *data derivation procedure* without a contributing data characteristic.

data glossary A component of the *metadata warehouse* that contains an alphabetical listing of definitions for words, terms, and abbreviations used in data definitions in the common data architecture. It may also contain definitions for business words, terms, and abbreviations that are not used in data definitions.

data group The third level in a *data classification scheme* representing a subdivision of a *data area*.

data harvesting *See data mining.*

data heritage The content and meaning of the data at the time of their origination and as they move from their origin to their current data sites. It is a statement of how the content and meaning were altered during their life cycle. *See data lineage, heritage, lineage.*

data instance The point in time or the period of time for which the data value accurately represents the real world. Within the common data architecture, data instance is not the same as a data occurrence. Data instance is not the same as a *data occurrence* in the common data architecture. *See data currentness, data collection frequency, data occurrence, data volatility.*

data integrity The formal definition of comprehensive rules and the consistent application of those rules to assure high integrity data. It consists of techniques to determine how well data are maintained in the data resource and to ensure that the data resource contains data that have high integrity. Data integrity includes techniques for *data value integrity*, *data structure integrity*, *data retention integrity*, and *data derivation integrity*.

data integrity component A component of the *metadata warehouse* that contains the data integrity documentation for data subjects and data characteristics in the common data architecture.

data integrity rule A statement that defines the actual data values or coded data values that are allowed. *See data integrity value.*

data integrity value An actual data value or a coded data value that is allowed. *See data integrity rule.*

data inventory analysis A process that compares data needs from the data needs inventory with the data available from the data availability inventory to determine what data subject and data characteristics exist and what data subjects and data characteristics need to be acquired. *See data resource inventory.*

data item Represents a *data attribute* from the *logical data model* that is implemented with a *physical data model*. It is an individual field in a data record.

data item group Represents a data attribute group from a logical data model that is implemented with a physical data model. It is a set of related data items that are stored, processed, and displayed together.

data key A set of one or more *data characteristics* that have a special meaning and use in addition to describing a feature or trait of a data subject. Data keys are important for uniquely identifying *data occurrences* in each data subject and for navigating through the data resource.

data layer A separate and distinct set of related *spatial data* that are stored and maintained in a *spatial database*. It represents a particular theme or topic of interest in the real world and is equivalent to a data subject.

data layer aggregation The process of combining *data layers* to get a more enhanced data layer. Data layers are aggregated vertically within or between spatial data tiers to form a more enhanced data layer. *See chronological data layer aggregation, horizontal data layer aggregation, vertical data layer aggregation.*

data layer coverage The portion of a *data layer* extent for which data are captured and stored in a *spatial database*. It is always within the data layer extent. *See data layer extent, data layer exclusion.*

data layer exclusion The portion of a *data layer extent* for which data are not captured and stored. It is the reverse of a *data layer coverage.*

data layer extent The outer boundary, or limits, of a *data layer*. *See data layer coverage.*

data layer generalization The process of reducing the scale of a *data layer extent* from the scale at which the data were captured by a formal algorithm. It is also known as *zooming out* and can occur with both *geospatial data* and *structospatial data*. *See data layer specialization.*

data layer specialization The process of increasing the scale of a *data layer extent*. It is also known as *zooming in* and can occur with both *geospatial data* and *structospatial data*. *See data layer generalization.*

data layer templates A pattern for developing *data layers*.

data lineage The process to track the descent of data values from their origin to their current data site. It includes determining where the data values originated, where they were stored, and how they were altered or modified. It is a history of where data values originated and how they were altered or modified to their present form. *See data heritage, heritage, lineage.*

data lineage diagram A diagram of the flow of data sets from their origin to their current data sites. It shows where the data originated, the flow of data sets between data sites within organization or across organizations, and the data sites where the data are currently located.

data logistics *See data deployment.*

data management component A component of the *data resource framework* that contains all activities related to management of the data resource.

data mart A subset of the data resource, usually oriented to a specific purpose or major data subject, that may be distributed to support business needs. The concept of a data mart can apply to any data whether they are *operational data, evaluational data, spatial data,* or *metadata.*

data megaclasses Broad groupings of data forms that are developed and maintained differently. *See data megagroups, data megatype, nontabular data, tabular data.*

data megagroups Broad groupings of data representing both the granularity of data and the time frame which data represent. *See data megaclasses, data megatype.*

data megatype A broad grouping of data forms within the common data architecture. *See data type.*

data merging The process of moving a set of data from one database to and adding it to another database. The data from several databases may be merged into a single database. Data merging can involve some form of *data conversion,* but it does not include *data refining.*

data mining The process of and utilizing the results of data exploration to adjust or enhance business strategies. It builds on the patterns, trends, and exceptions found through data exploration to support the business. It is also known as data harvesting. *See data exploration.*

data name A label for a data site, data subject, data characteristic, data characteristic variation, or data code.

data name abbreviation The shortening of the *formal data name* to meet a product length restriction. *See formal data name abbreviation, informal data name abbreviation.*

data name abbreviation algorithm A formal algorithm for abbreviating *formal data names* using an established set of *data name word abbreviations.*

data name homonym A situation that occurs when two or more different data characteristics have the same data name. *See data name synonym.*

data name synonym A situation that occurs when the same data characteristic has two or more different data names. *See data name homonym.*

data naming convention A convention established to resolve problems with *Traditional data names*. Many of these conventions are in use today, such as the *Of Language, entity - attribute - class, role - type - class, prime - descriptor - class, entity - adjective - class, entity - attribute - class word, entity - description - class, entity keyword - minor keyword - type keyword*, and *entity keyword - descriptor - domain*.

data naming lexicon A component of the *metadata warehouse* that contains the vocabulary that supports the data naming taxonomy. It contains the common words prominent sets of abbreviations for the words used in data names.

data naming taxonomy A rigorous system for uniquely naming data units consistently within the common data architecture. It provides a common language for naming data.

data naming vocabulary A set of *common words* that are used consistently for forming data names in each component of the data naming taxonomy. *See class word.*

data needs inventory Identifies data subjects and data characteristics needed to support an organization's business activities. *See data resource inventory.*

data needs survey A high-level determination of the data an organization needs to meet the *business information demand*. *See data resource survey.*

data normalization A process to develop the *conceptual schema* from the *external schema*.

data occurrence A logical record that represents one existence of an object or one occurrence of an event in the real world. It is used in both the *common data model* and the *logical data model*.

data occurrence contraction The removal of a set of data occurrences from an *evaluational database*. It is the opposite of *data occurrence extension*. *See evaluational data contraction.*

data occurrence expansion The addition of more data occurrences to an *evaluational database*. *See evaluational data expansion.*

data occurrence group A set of related *data occurrences* in a *logical data model* that meet a specific set of criteria.

data occurrence partitioning The process of identifying the data occurrence groups needed at each data site. Also known as *horizontal partitioning*.

data occurrence retention rule Specifies exactly how long a *data occurrence* is retained and what is done before a data occurrence is deleted. It specifies the procedure to preserve the historical significance of the data occurrence and the data characteristic values in that data occurrence. *See data characteristic retention rule, data retention integrity.*

data occurrence selection name The unique name of a selection of *data occurrences* from a *data subject*.

data optimization A process that prepares the *logical schema* from the *data view schema*. It is the counterpart of *data deoptimization*.

data origin The location where a data value originated, whether it was collected, created, measured, generated, derived, modified, or aggregated. *See data tracking*.

data partitioning The formal process of determining which data subjects, data occurrence groups, and data characteristics are needed at each data site. It is an orderly process for allocating data to data sites that is done within the common data architecture. *See data fragmentation*.

data perspective A set of related data subjects in the *evaluational database* consisting of a central *multiple dimension data subject* surrounded by several single dimension data subjects that qualify the central data subject. *See data focus*.

data product A major, independent piece of documentation of any type that contains the names and/or definitions of *disparate data*, such as a dictionary, a database, a major project, or a major information system.

data product code A *data code* that exists in a *data product unit*.

data product group A major grouping of data within a *data product*, such as a data entity, data file, a data record, a data record type, a screen, a report, a document, or a program.

data product reference A component of the *metadata warehouse* that contains documentation about data products, including data names and definitions, data structure, data accuracy and integrity, and cross-references to the common data architecture.

data product unit An individual element of data in a *data product group*, such as a data attribute, a field in a record, or an element on a screen, or data in a program.

data quality Indicates how well data in the data resource meet the *business information demand*. Data quality includes *data integrity*, *data accuracy*, and *data completeness*. *See disparate data quality*.

data quality activity An activity in the *data architecture component* that ensures the maintenance of high-quality data in an integrated data resource.

data quality certification A process to determine the specific level of *data quality*. *See data certification levels*.

data quality improvement The process of improving *data quality* to the level desired to support the *business information demand*. *See prospective data quality improvement, retrospective data quality improvement*.

data quality process Documents and improves *data quality* by using both the deductive and inductive techniques. It is a systematic process of examining the data resource to determine its level of data quality and ensuring that the data quality is adjusted to the level necessary to support the business information demand. *See data quality improvement.*

data recasting The process of altering the structure of operational data so that they have a consistent structure for the entire time period represented in the *evaluational database.* It provides historical continuity.

data record A data occurrence from the *logical data model* that is implemented with a *physical data model.* It is a physical grouping of *data items* that are stored or retrieved from a *data file.*

data record group A *data occurrence group* from the *logical data model* that is implemented with a *physical data model.* It is a set of related data records in a data *file.*

data redistribution The process of moving *data replicates* from one *data site* to another to meet business needs. It is a process that constantly balances data needs, data volumes, data usage, and the physical operating environment.

data refining A process that refines *disparate data* within a common context to increase the awareness and understanding of the data, remove data variability and redundancy, and develop an integrated data resource. Disparate data are the raw material and an integrated data resource is the final product. *See refining, semantic data refining.*

data refreshing The process of updating *active data replicates* based on a regular, known schedule. The frequency and timing of data refreshing must be established to match business needs and must be known by clients.

data relation An association between *data occurrences* in different data subjects or within the same data subject. It provides the connection between data subjects for building the common data structure. A data relation within the common data architecture is an association only, does not have names, and does not contain any data characteristics. *See recursive data relation.*

data relation diagram A term that was used to represent data subjects and their relations. The term now refers to a set of three diagrams representing the three types of data models. *See entity relation diagram, file relation diagram, subject relation diagram.*

data replicate A set of data copied from a data site and placed at another data site during data replication. A set of data characteristics from a single data subject or data occurrence group that is copied from the official data source and placed at another data site. Data replicates are not the same as *redundant data*. *See horizontal data replication*.

data replication A formal process of creating exact copies of a set of data from the data site containing the *official data source* and placing those data in at other data sites.

data resource A component of *information technology infrastructure* that represents all the data available to an organization, whether they are automated or nonautomated.

data resource challenge An organization's determination to resolve the data dilemma by breaking the disparate data cycle and transforming data into an integrated data resource that meets the *business information demand*.

data resource enhancement The process of constantly changing data values in the data resource to reflect changes in the real world. *See data resource expansion, data resource extension*.

data resource expansion Vertical enlargement of the data resource to encompass detailed data not previously included within the current scope. *See data resource enhancement, data resource extension*.

data resource extension Horizontal enlargement of the data resource to encompass business areas not previously included. *See data resource enhancement, data resource expansion*.

data resource framework An information technology framework that represents a discipline for the complete development and maintenance of an integrated data resource. It consists of three components for *data management, data architecture*, and *data availability*.

data resource initiative An initiative that provides the incentive for developing an integrated data resource.

data resource inventory A detailed determination of the organization's data needs and the data available to the organization based on data subjects and data characteristics. *See data completeness, data resource survey*.

data resource library A library of data for an organization that contains both the *formal data resource* and the *integrated data resource*.

data resource survey A high-level determination of an organization's data needs and the data available to the organization based on a higher level data classification scheme. *See data completeness, data resource inventory*.

data restructuring The process to restructure the source data to the target data during *data transformation*. *See evaluational data restructuring, logical data restructuring, physical data restructuring*.

data retention integrity A subset of *data integrity* that specifies criteria for preventing the loss of critical data through updates or deletion. It considers the future value of data to determine what data should be retained and how they should be retained. It looks to the future to determine the unknown or hidden usefulness of the data.

data rule domain A *data domain* that contains data integrity rules. The data integrity rules may also have begin and end dates defining the timeframe for which data values are valid. *See data value domain.*

data schema A diagrammatic representation of the structure of data. It represents any set of data that is being captured, manipulated, stored, retrieved, transmitted, or displayed.

data schema concept A concept that provides a structure or framework for managing the integrated data resource. *See two-schema concept, three-schema concept, four-schema concept, five-schema concept.*

data segment A set of *data subjects* that are closely related by a high frequency of *data relations* between the data subjects in the set. There is a low frequency of data relations between the data subjects in different data segments. *See data classification scheme, data cluster, data theme.*

data set A unique set of related *data characteristics* used for a specific purpose. A data set can be used for many purposes, such as a set of data characteristics defining a data subject, a set of data characteristics extracted from a data subject, a set of data characteristics being moved between data sites, or a set of data characteristics in a report or on a screen. A data set is the basic tool for managing data within the common data architecture. *See nested data set, single data set.*

data sharing The process of understanding the content and meaning of data, identifying and selecting the appropriate data to meet business needs, and sharing those data according to the *data sharing concept. See data access.*

data sharing concept A concept where *official data variations* are shared over a data sharing medium, such as a network, tape, diskette, or other medium. If the data source does not maintain the official data variation, it must translate its nonofficial data variation to an official data variation by accepted data translation schemes prior to sharing. If the data target does not use the official data variation, it must translate the official data variation to its nonofficial data variation by accepted data translation schemes. *See traditional data sharing.*

data sharing medium The mechanism by which data are shared; it is the *how* of data sharing.

data sharing message The actual data being shared; it is the *what* of data sharing.

data site Any specific location where data are stored. A data site may be manual storage, such as a filing cabinet, or electronic storage, such as a data file or a database management system, and it may be on a mainframe computer or anywhere on a telecommunications network.

data site name The unique name of a specific *data site* within a common data architecture.

data source A specific data site where data are stored and can be obtained. Any source of data from a specific organization, such as a database or data file. A data source may include nonautomated data, but it does not include unpublished documents containing data. *See primary data source, secondary data source.*

data specialization The process of viewing data in more detail, often known as *drilling down*. It is a process of zooming in to get a more detailed view of a problem, trend, or situation. *See data generalization.*

data structure A representation of the arrangement, relationship, and contents of data subjects, data entities, and data files in the *common data architecture*. It includes all logical and physical data within the common data architecture. *See disparate data structure, common data structure.*

data structure activity An activity in the *data architecture component* that ensures the proper logical and physical structure of data in an integrated data resource.

data structure component A component of the *metadata warehouse* that contains the structure of data within the common data architecture.

data structure integrity A subset of *data integrity* that specifies the integrity for *data relations*.

data structure integrity diagram A diagram that documents *data structure integrity*.

data structure integrity matrix A matrix that documents *data structure integrity*.

data structure integrity table A table that documents *data structure integrity*.

data subject A person, place, thing, event, or concept about which an organization captures, maintains, and uses data. It is developed from an organization's perspective of an object or event in the real world. *See data entity.*

data subject area *See data area.*

data subject contraction The removal of one or more summary data subjects from an *evaluational database* because they no longer need to be maintained for analysis. It is the opposite of *data subject extension. See evaluational data contraction.*

data subject cross-reference A data cross-reference between a *data product group* and a *data subject* when there is a one-to-one relationship between the data product group and the data subject and all data product units belong to that data subject.

data subject expansion The creation and maintenance of more derived summary data subjects in the *evaluational database* within its existing scope. *See evaluational data expansion.*

data subject hierarchy A hierarchical structure of data subjects with branched one-to-one data relations. It represents mutually exclusive situations between data subjects at each level in the hierarchy. In the common data structure, each supertype and subtype is considered a data subject regardless of its level in the hierarchy; therefore, the hierarchical structure is referred to as a data subject hierarchy.

data subject matrix A matrix that shows which data characteristics are valid for each data subject type.

data subject name The unique name of a *data subject* within the common data architecture that indicates both the meaning and structure of the data subject.

data subject partitioning The process of identifying the data subjects needed at each data site.

data subject type A breakdown of a *true data subject* that either has no data characteristics of its own or has data characteristics that inherit their names and definitions directly from a true data subject. *See virtual data subject.*

data suitability The part of *data completeness* that indicates how suitable data are for a specific purpose. It varies with the specific data uses.

data summarization The process of summarizing primitive evaluational data or derived evaluational data to create more generalized derived evaluational data. *See data generalization.*

data survey analysis A process that compares the data needs survey with the data availability survey to identify data that already exist and data that need to be acquired. *See data resource survey.*

data synchronization The process of identifying *active data replicates* and ensuring that data concurrency is maintained. Also known as *data version synchronization* or *data version concurrency* because all replicated data values are consistent with the same version as the official data.

data themes The specific groupings of *data subjects* for a specific purpose. They are identified within some scope, such as a major project, and are based on the way people view the grouping of data subjects for that project. Data themes are usually temporary and can easily change. *See data classification scheme, data cluster, data segment.*

data thesaurus A component of the *metadata warehouse* that contains a set of data name synonyms to help people locate the particular data they need. It provides a reference between similar names or business terms and the common data names.

data tracking The process of tracking data from their *data origin* to their current data site. *See data source.*

data tracking diagram A diagram that documents *data tracking*. It is similar to a *data distribution diagram.*

data transformation The formal process of transforming data in the data resource within a common data architecture. It includes transforming disparate data to an integrated data resource, transforming data within the integrated data resource, and transforming disparate data. It includes transforming operational, historical, and evaluational data within a common data architecture.

data translation scheme A translation between data characteristic variations when those *data characteristic variations* represent measurements or format variations. Data translation schemes are not the same as *data derivation algorithms.*

data translation scheme component A component of the *metadata warehouse* that contains the data translation schemes between common data characteristic variations when those data characteristic variations represent measurements or format variations.

data type The form of a *data value*, such as date, number, string, floating point, packed, and double precision. *See data megatype.*

data understanding The process of learning the full content and meaning of the data and what those data represent in the real world. *See data awareness.*

data value The individual facts and figures contained in data characteristics, *data characteristic variations*, *data attributes*, and *data items*. *See actual data value, coded data value.*

data value domain A *data domain* that contains a set of data integrity values. It can contain a list of values that may be continuous or disjointed, or a list of value combinations for several related data characteristics. *See data rule domain.*

data value integrity A subset of *data integrity* that specifies the allowable values for each data characteristic and each relation between data characteristics within the common data architecture. Data value integrity is specified as *data integrity values* or *data integrity rules.*

data version A set of data values that represent the real world a specific point in time. An enhancement to a set of data in the data resource. Data versions occur when a set of data is either enhanced with different values, with new data occurrences, or with the removal of data occurrences.

data version concurrency *See data synchronization.*

data version name The unique name of a *data version* within a common data architecture. The data version name is placed in carets at the end of the data name. *See modification identifier, version identifier.*

data version synchronization *See data synchronization.*

data view schema *Schema* that represent the structure of data used by applications. They represent the data stored in and retrieved from the database by an application and are considered to be *normalized data*. It replaces the former external schema.

data visualization The process of creating and presenting a chart from a set of data based on a set of attributes. It deals with understanding patterns, trends, and relationships in historical data, and providing visual information to the decision maker.

data volatility How quickly the data representing the real world become inaccurate, which is dependent or how quickly the real world changes. It is the rate at which data cease to accurately represent the real world. *See data collection frequency, data currentness, data instance.*

data warehouse A subject oriented, integrated, time-variant, nonvolatile collection of data in support of management's decision making process. A repository of consistent historical data that can be easily accessed and manipulated for decision support. *See integrated evaluational data.*

datum A base for calculating or measuring. Sea level is a traditional datum for measuring elevations, and latitude/longitude are a traditional datum for locating objects on the Earth's surface.

decision support database A database that contains historical and summary data to support on-line analytical processing. *See operational database, evaluational database.*

decision support processing *See on-line analytical processing.*

deductive data quality A general-to-specific process where the desired data quality criteria are first developed and then applied either to existing data to determine the level of compliance or to new data to ensure they meet the desired criteria. *See data quality improvement, inductive data quality process.*

demographic A term derived from *demos* meaning population and *graphein* meaning to write or describe. Literally it means describing populations.

demographic data Any data that locate, identify, or describe populations. Demographic data can be related to the Earth the same as geographic data.

demos A term meaning population.

denormalized data Data that have been through data denormalization. The data in the *physical schema* and *internal schema*.

denotative meaning The explicit meaning in a data definition. *See connotative meaning.*

deoptimized data Data that have been through *data deoptimization* for distribution to various data sites. The data in the *distribution schema.*

dependency conflict A problem that can occur with a structural *data naming taxonomy* when one organization tracks many occurrences of a data subject and another organization tracks only one occurrence of a data subject. *See key conflict, type conflict.*

deployment Used in the broad sense to mean placing data and metadata in a product at one or more data sites where they can most appropriately support the business activities. *See data deployment.*

derived data *Data* that are derived from other data through a *data derivation procedure*, not by the measurement or observation of an object or event. *See active derived data, primitive data, static derived data.*

derived data layer A *data layer* built by combining two or more *primitive data layers* or derived data layers to meet a specific business need. A derived data layer represents two or more sets of objects or events in the world.

derived data maintenance The process for ensuring that *active derived data* are properly rederived when their contributing data characteristics values change or when new contributing data characteristics appear.

derived data maintenance criteria Criteria that specify the frequency and timing for rederiving active derived data, such as immediately, daily at midnight, and monthly on the first workday of the month.

descriptive geospatial reference A *descriptive spatial reference* for *geospatial data.*

descriptive spatial reference A *spatial data reference* that occurs between a set of *tabular data* that identify and describe a *spatial object* and *spatial data* that locate and identify that object.

descriptive structospatial reference A *descriptive spatial data reference* that occurs between a set of *tabular data* that identify and describe a *structospatial object* and *structospatial data* that locate and identify that object.

desired data quality criteria The desired criteria needed to support the *business information demand. See existing data quality criteria.*

detailed primary key matrix A matrix showing primary key characteristics by qualifying data subject. *See simple primary key matrix.*

dilemma A situation that requires a choice between two or more options that are, or appear to be, unfavorable or mutually exclusive. It is a situation that seems to defy any resolution.

direct spatial reference A *spatial data reference* made directly between *tabular data* and *spatial data* because the unique identifier for objects in the *spatial data layers* are stored in the corresponding tabular data subjects. A spatial reference can be made directly from the tabular data subject to the spatial data layer using the unique identifier. *See indirect spatial reference.*

disparate data Data that are essentially not alike, or are distinctly different in kind, quality, or character. They are unequal and cannot be readily integrated to adequately meet the business information demand. Disparate data are *heterogeneous data.*

disparate databases Databases or database management systems that are not electronically or operationally compatible. Disparate databases are known as *heterogeneous databases.*

disparate data codes Data codes that appear in *disparate data* and are often undefined and inconsistent. They cause severe problems with the proper management and use of the data resource.

disparate data cycle A self-perpetuating cycle where disparate data are continuing to be produced at an ever-increasing rate because people either do not know about existing data or do not want to use existing data.

disparate data quality The state of a data resource where the data quality is essentially not alike, or is distinctly different in kind, quality, or character. It is a state where the data quality is not known and does not meet the *business information demand. See consistent data quality.*

disparate data shock This is the realization that the *data dilemma* really exists and is severely affecting an organization's ability to be responsive to changes in the business environment. It is the panic that an organization has about the sad state of its data resource.

disparate data standards The situation where many different organizations develop independent data standards for the same data. Data standards often are physically oriented, have minimal definitions based on use, and use a format that is difficult to understand and apply.

disparate data structure One of a variety of different *data structures* exist that are based on different perspectives of the real world, different application support requirements, and different operating environments. *See common data structure.*

disparate evaluational data Evaluational data developed from either disparate operational data or disparate historical data without any data refining or any attempt to resolve the data disparity.

disparate historical data The *disparate operational data* that have been archived either as individual data values or as full records.

They have been saved or archived in their disparate form, but they are time-variant because they represent the operational values at different points in time. *See disparate evaluational data.*

disparate metadata Metadata that are essentially not alike, or are distinctly different in kind, quality, or character. They often do not exist, or if they do exist, they are incomplete, out-of-date, poorly written, and difficult to understand. They are scattered through many documents and are often difficult to locate. *See massively disparate metadata.*

disparate metadata cycle A self-perpetuating cycle where disparate metadata are being produced faster than ever before. *See disparate data cycle.*

disparate operational data The current-value operational data that support daily business transactions. They are the disparate data, including both tabular and nontabular data, that most organizations currently use to support their daily business operations. *See disparate evaluational data, disparate historical data.*

dispersed data Same as *fragmented data.*

distributed database A collection of multiple, logically related databases that is provided to data sites.

distributed database management system A software product that manages and maintains the *distributed database* and makes it transparent to clients. Data flow freely over any network or combination of networks by using one or more network protocols.

distributed database system A combination of *distributed databases* and *distributed database management systems*. Any database management system can interact with any other database management system across multiple system configurations to provide data to clients.

distributed data set A *data set* from one data subject or data occurrence group that is distributed. *See multiple data replicate, single data replicate.*

distribution schema A *schema* that represents the distribution of data to *data sites*. It is considered to be *deoptimized data*. It is logical data designated for partitioning, replication, and distribution to data sites.

distribution time The time data were distributed to a data site. *See collection time, entry time, event time, identification time, temporal data.*

domain experts People that thoroughly understand a particular discipline, such as finance, engineering, or water resources. They know the discipline involved in the common metadata. *See business experts and data experts.*

drilling down The process of viewing data in more detail. *See data specialization.*

dual database concept A concept that consists of an *operational database* and a *decision support database* resolves the conflict between two data formalities.

dual data partitioning The situation where both *data occurrence partitioning* and *data characteristic partitioning* are done on the same data subject. Dual data partitioning is common in most data distributions.

dual primary keys A concept that involves development of both a *business primary key* that is business-oriented and a *physical primary key* that is system-oriented. The business primary key and physical primary key are variations of the official primary key.

duplicate data layers Exist when the same spatial data layer extent is maintained redundantly by different organizations.

dynamic data analysis The analysis of data values that are constantly changing, such as those in an *operational database. See single dimension processing, static data analysis.*

dynamic data distribution The situation where distributed data need to be continually evaluated and adjusted to meet the *business information demand* in an optimum manner.

elemental data The individual facts that cannot be subdivided and retain any meaning. *See combined data.*

enhanced data extraction The ongoing process that extracts snapshots of *operational data* on a regular basis for enhancing the *evaluational database. See evaluational data extraction, initial data extraction.*

entity relation diagram A *data relation diagram* that represents the arrangement and relationship of *data entities* for the *logical data structure.* It is also known as an E-R diagram.

entity structure chart A chart that shows the existence and structure of data attributes and data entities in the common data structure. It directly supports the *entity relation diagram* to provide a complete representation of the logical data structure. *See file structure chart, subject structure chart.*

entity type hierarchy Traditional name for a *data subject hierarchy.*

entry time The time a transaction was entered into the data resource. *See collection time, distribution time, event time, identification time, temporal data.*

E-R diagram *See entity relation diagram.*

evaluational data Data used in decision support processing to evaluate trends, projections, and alternatives. They are usually historical, are derived from the *operational data*, and contain many levels of summarization above the operational data.

evaluational data addition The process of adding new data to an *evaluational database.*

evaluational database A database that contains *evaluational data*.

evaluational data contraction The removal of data subjects, data occurrences, or data characteristics from an *evaluational database*. It is the opposite of *evaluational data expansion*. *See data characteristic contraction, data occurrence contraction, data subject contraction*.

evaluational data enhancement The addition of a new set of primitive data occurrences to the *evaluational database* within its existing scope.

evaluational data expansion The addition of more derived data subjects, data occurrences, and data characteristics within the existing scope of the *evaluational database*. *See data characteristic expansion, data occurrence expansion, data subject expansion*.

evaluational data extension The increase in the scope of an *evaluational database* into new business areas.

evaluational data rederivation The process of automatically rederiving summary data when there is a version or modification change to any of their contributors.

evaluational data reduction The removal of a set of primitive data occurrences from the *evaluational database*. It is the opposite of *evaluational data enhancement*.

evaluational data removal The process of removing unnecessary or unused data from an *evaluational database*.

evaluational data restructuring The process that ensures that all the data necessary for multiple dimension analysis are in multiple dimension data subjects. *See data restructuring*.

evaluational data retraction The removal of primitive and derived evaluational data subjects from an *evaluational database* resulting from a reduction in scope. It is the opposite of *evaluational data extension*.

evaluational data subject A *single dimension data subject* or a *multiple dimension data subject* supporting business analysis. *See operational data subject*.

evaluational data subject structure A *data subject structure* that shows the structure of *evaluational data*. *See operational data subject structure*.

evaluational metadata *Metadata* about *evaluational data*. *See operational metadata*.

evaluational subject relation diagram A *subject relation diagram* representing *evaluational data subjects* and any *operational data subjects* that contribute to those evaluational data subjects. *See operational subject relation diagram*.

event A happening in the real world. *See object*.

event frequency The frequency at which an event occurs or an object changes in the real world. *See arbitrary event, data collection frequency, data currentness.*

event time The time an event happened in the real world. *See collection time, distribution time, entry time, event time, identification time, temporal data.*

existing data quality criteria The criteria documenting the data quality that currently exists in the data resource. *See data quality improvement, desired data quality criteria.*

expanded business perspective An overall perspective of the real world that includes all the individual perspectives by many different organizations in many different disciplines. *See extended business perspective.*

extended business perspective A perspective of the real world that includes both how the real world changes over time and how an organization's perspective of that real world changes over time. It is a chronological perspective that includes the past, present, and future. *See expanded business perspective.*

extended data product definition A data product definition that includes the definition as it appears in the original documentation, followed by any additional information gained during data refining. The additional information should contain a date, the name of the person extending the definition, and the source of the extended definition.

extent of interest The outer boundary of an area that is of interest to an organization for a specific business purpose. It may be part of a *data layer extent*, a complete data layer extent, or multiple data layer extents.

external schema A *schema* representing the structure of data used by applications. *See internal schema.*

fact table *See data focus.*

feature name The part of the *data characteristic name* that represents the feature of a data subject.

file relation diagram A *data relation diagram* that represents the arrangement and relationship of data files for the *physical data model*. It represents that denormalized model and is used to develop the physical database.

file structure chart A chart that shows the existence and structure of data items within data files in the common data structure. It directly supports the file relation diagram to provide a complete representation of the physical data structure. *See entity structure chart.*

fine granularity *See lightly summarized data.*

five-schema concept A new concept for managing the data resource including the added complexity of data distribution. A *distribution schema* was added between the *logical schema* and the *physical schema,* and a *data deoptimization* process was added to prepare the distribution schema.

focus data subject The central multiple dimension data subject that is developed during the transformation of operational data to evaluational data. It contains the most detailed nonvolatile data in the evaluational database. It is the lowest level for drilling down in an *evaluational database. See summary data subject.*

foredata A new term developed from *fore,* meaning beforehand, up front, at or near the front. Foredata are all data about the objects and events, including both praedata and paradata. Foredata are the upfront data that an organization sees about objects and events. *See metadata.*

foreign key The *primary key* of a parent data subject that is placed in a subordinate data subject. Its value identifies the *data occurrence* in the parent data subject that is the parent of the data occurrence in the subordinate data subject.

formal data name A data label that is developed from a formal data naming taxonomy. It is unique for that unit of data within the common data architecture. It is fully spelled out, is not codified or abbreviated, does not contain special symbols, and is not subject to any length restrictions. *See traditional data name.*

formal data name abbreviation A *data name* that has been consistently abbreviated by a formal algorithm according to an established set of data name word abbreviations. *See informal data name abbreviation.*

formal data replicate name The distributed data set name consisting of the source data site name and the target data site name separated by a hyphen and followed by a colon followed by the data subject or data occurrence group name. *See short data replicate name.*

formal data resource An interim step between disparate data and an integrated data resource where disparate data are identified and defined within a common context. The data awareness and understanding is increased, and the data variability and redundancy are identified but not resolved. The accuracy is known but has not been adjusted to the desired level. *See data resource library, integrated data resource.*

forward data denormalization A process that transforms the *distribution schema* to the *physical schema* or the *logical schema* to the *physical schema* if there is no data distribution. The data are adjusted to be optimally efficient in a specific operating environment without compromising the logical schema. *See reverse data denormalization.*

forward data deoptimization A process that transforms the *logical schema* to the *distribution schema*. The data are partitioned based on the data needed at each data site. *See reverse data deoptimization.*

forward data modeling Movement from the *business schema* to the *data view schema* to the *logical schema* to the *distribution schema* to the *physical schema*. It is a progression that transforms one data schema to the next through formal processes. *See reverse data modeling.*

forward data normalization A process that transforms the *business schema* to the *data view schema*. The business schema are taken apart and data views are developed for each data subject represented in the business schema. *See reverse data normalization.*

forward data optimization A process that transforms the *data view schema* to the *logical schema*. *See reverse data optimization.*

four-schema concept A concept that resolves problems with the *three-schema concept*. It includes a *physical schema*, a *logical schema*, a *data view schema*, and a *business schema*.

four-tier concept A concept for *spatial data* that contains four *spatial data tiers*. *See business tier, candidate tier, subthematic tier, thematic tier.*

framework data layer A *primitive data layer* that is basic to many other map and business data layers. It is based on a spatial reference system and provides the base for developing detail data layers and business data layers.

framework for information systems A framework developed by John Zachman consisting of a matrix containing six columns and six rows for developing information systems. The columns in the Framework represent the six basic interrogatives of *what, how, where, who, when*, and *why*, representing *data, processes, network, people, time*, and *rules* respectively.

generic data architecture A standard architecture for a specific purpose, such as purchase orders or student registration. It is an attempt to get organizations to do similar business functions in a similar manner. *See common data architecture.*

geo A term meaning Earth.

geocoding The process of designating primary keys for geospatial objects and maintaining those unique identifiers in both the geospatial data layers and related tabular data subjects so that the tabular and spatial data can be related.

geodatum A *datum* for aligning objects on, above, or below the Earth's surface.

geographic A term derived from *geo* meaning Earth and *graphein* meaning to write or describe. Literally it means describing the Earth.

geographic data Any data that locate, identify, or describe objects on the Earth.

geographic information system An organized collection of computer hardware, software, geographic data, and personnel designed to efficiently capture, store, update, manipulate, analyze, and display all forms of geographically referenced information. *See spatial information systems.*

geolinear referencing system A *linear referencing system* for *geospatial linear objects.*

georeferencing The process of accurately placing geospatial objects on, above, or below the surface of the Earth according to a spatial reference system.

geospatial A term derived from *geo* meaning Earth and *spatium* meaning of, relating to, involving, or having the nature of space. Literally, it means spatial locations on, above, or below the surface of the Earth.

geospatial data Any data that represent the geographic location and identifying characteristics of a *geospatial object*. They place objects on, above, or below the surface of the Earth and uniquely identify those objects.

geospatial database Any database containing *geospatial data.*

geospatial data hierarchy A *spatial data hierarchy* for *geospatial data.*

geospatial data layer A *data layer* that contains *geospatial data.*

geospatial object Any natural feature, constructed feature, or boundary on, above, or below the Earth's surface. The object may be a point, a line, an area, or a three-dimensional object.

geospatial reference system A *spatial reference system* that provides the control for accurately placing spatial objects and events on, above, or below the surface of the Earth.

graphein A term meaning to write or describe.

hard data The historical facts and figures about operating the business. *See soft data.*

heritage Something transmitted by or acquired from a predecessor, or something possessed as a result of one's natural selection or birth. *See data heritage, data lineage, lineage.*

heterogeneous data *See disparate data.*

heterogeneous databases *See disparate databases.*

hidden data resource The large quantities of data maintained by an organization that are largely unknown, unavailable, and unused because people are either not aware of the data or do not understand the data. *See data discovery.*

highly summarized data *Evaluational data* that are summarized by removing many data characteristics from the primary key of the data focus. Highly summarized data have coarse granularity.

horizontal data aggregation The edge-matching of data between different sets of data. *See chronological data aggregation, vertical data aggregation.*

horizontal data layer aggregation The edge connection of two or more *data layer extents*, usually from different organizations, for the same data layer to provide an expanded data layer for a specific extent of interest.

horizontal data replication The formal process of creating an exact copy of *official data* and placing that exact copy at one or more *data sites*. *See data replication.*

horizontal model transformation Movement within the technology model of the *framework for information systems*. The detail is transformed from data contained in business transactions in the real world, to a common logical view of the data, to physical data that support the functioning system. *See vertical model transformation.*

horizontal partitioning Same as *data occurrence partitioning*.

identification time The time an organization found out about the event. *See collection time, distribution time, entry time, event time, temporal data.*

indirect geospatial reference An *indirect spatial reference* for *geospatial data*.

indirect spatial reference A *spatial data reference* that occurs between a *tabular data* subject that does not identify or describe a *spatial object* and a *geospatial data layer* that locates and identifies that geospatial object. *See direct spatial reference.*

indirect structospatial reference An *indirect spatial reference* for *structospatial data*.

inductive data quality process A specific-to-general process where the existing data are analyzed and existing data quality criteria are developed from those existing data. *See data quality improvement, deductive data quality process.*

informal data name abbreviation A *data name* that has not been consistently abbreviated by a formal algorithm or an established set of data name word abbreviations. *See formal data name abbreviation.*

information A collection of data that is relevant to one or more recipients at a point in time. It must be meaningful and useful to the recipient at a specific time for a specific purpose. Information is data in context, data that have meaning, relevance, and purpose. *See data.*

information engineering The discipline for identifying information needs and developing information systems that produce *messages* that provide information to a recipient. It is a manufacturing process that uses data as the raw material to construct and transmit a message to a recipient. Information engineering is a filtering process that reduces masses of data to a message that provides *information*. *See data engineering.*

information engineering objective An objective to get the right data, to the right people, in the right place, at the right time, in the right form, and at the right cost, so they can make the right decisions and take the right actions.

information systems A component of *information technology infrastructure* that represents the implementation of business activities, using the data resource, and residing on the platform resource.

information technology frameworks Four frameworks within the information technology infrastructure for *business activities*, the *data resource*, the *platform resource*, and *information systems*. The four frameworks have similar constructs, although the details are different.

information technology infrastructure An infrastructure for the information technology discipline that provides the resources necessary for an organization to meet its current and future business information demand. It consists of the *data resource*, the *platform resource, business activities*, and *information systems*.

infrastructure An underlying foundation or framework for a system or an organization. It generally refers to the basic installations and facilities for community development or military operations.

initial data extraction The process that first extracts the operational data to build the evaluational database. It is a one-time process that starts the *evaluational database. See enhanced data extraction.*

integration Used here in the broad sense to mean the transformation of disparate data into an integrated data resource. *See aggregation.*

integrated data resource A data resource where all data are integrated within a common context and are appropriately deployed for maximum use in supporting the business information demand. *See data resource library, formal data resource.*

integrated evaluational data Subject-oriented, integrated, time-variant, nonvolatile collection of data to support management's decision making process. Also known as *data warehouses. See disparate evaluational data.*

integrated historical data *Integrated operational data* that have either been archived as individual data values or as full records from integrated operational data or are disparate operational or disparate historical data that have been transformed to the integrated data resource. *See disparate historical data.*

integrated operational data Subject-oriented, integrated, time-current, volatile collection of data that support an organization's daily business activities. They are also known as operational data stores. *See disparate operational data.*

intelligent primary key A *primary key* whose value has meaning in the real world. It contains a fact that is meaningful with respect to the business. *See nonintelligent primary key.*

interface data subject A *data subject* that is created temporarily to support an information system until the permanent data subject can be designed and implemented.

internal schema A *schema* representing the structure of data stored in data files. *See external schema.*

intuitive data warehouse A *data warehouse* that tracks the analysis performed on evaluational data, adds or suggests the addition of permanent data subjects or queries based on frequency of use, and deletes or suggests the deletion of summary data subjects and queries based on a lack of use.

invalid primary key A set of data characteristics that do not meet the criteria for a primary key. *See valid primary key.*

irregular data product unit A *data product unit* that does not have a consistent content or format.

key conflict A problem that can occur with a structural *data naming taxonomy* when different sets of data characteristics form the primary key. *See key conflict, type conflict.*

knowledge Information that is retained with an understanding about the significance of that information. It is knowing something gained by experience, study, familiarity, association, awareness, or comprehension.

legacy data Another term for *disparate data* because they support legacy systems.

lightly summarized data Evaluational data that are summarized by removing one, or a few, data characteristic from the primary key of the *data focus*. Lightly summarized data have fine granularity.

limited foreign key A *foreign key* that matches a *limited primary key*.

limited primary key A *primary key* whose uniqueness is limited to a subset of the data occurrences within the scope of the common data architecture.

line seen area The portion of the landscape that can be seen from a linear feature on the landscape. *See seen area.*

lineage The direct descent from an ancestor, or the descendants of a common ancestor that is regarded as the founder of the line. *See data heritage, data lineage, heritage.*

linear addressing system A technique for establishing addresses along linear objects that do not change over time. It is a fixed addressing system that does not change if the linear object changes. *See linear referencing system.*

linear object segmentation A technique where an object or event can be located on segments of a linear object or across segment boundaries of adjacent linear objects. Multiple objects or events with different boundaries can be co-located on one or more connecting linear objects.

linear referencing disparity The situation where the distance according to a *linear referencing system* changes when the length of a linear object changes.

linear referencing system A technique for measuring the length along a linear object. It applies to both *geospatial linear objects* and *structospatial linear objects*. *See anchor point, linear addressing system.*

logical data distribution matrix A matrix that shows data subjects or data occurrence groups that appear at each data site and the data characteristics that appear in each data subject or data occurrence group. *See physical data distribution matrix.*

logical data distribution outline An outline that shows the data subjects or data occurrence groups that appear at each data site and their data characteristics. *See physical data distribution outline.*

logical data model A data model that represents the normalized design of data needed to support an information system. Data are drawn from the *common data model* and normalized to support the design of a specific information system. *See physical data model.*

logical data restructuring The restructuring of data from the logical data model of the source data to the logical data model of the target data. *See data restructuring.*

logical data structure The structure of data in the *logical data model*. It is a subset of the *common data structure* that supports a single information system and usually represents a single real world perspective. It contains data entities and data attributes needed in the information system. *See physical data structure.*

logical schema A *schema* that represents a common view of all data in the data resource. It is considered to be *optimized data*. It replaces the former *conceptual schema*.

logical schema specialization The process of developing the *logical schema* from the *tactical schema*.

many-to-many data relation A *data relation* that exists when a data occurrence in one data subject is related to more than one data occurrence in a second data subject, and each data occurrence in that second data subject is related to more than one data occurrence in the first data subject. A many-to-many data relation is shown by a dashed line with an arrowhead on each end.

many-to-many recursive data relation A *data relation* that exists when each data occurrence in a data subject is related to many other data occurrences in that data subject.

massively disparate data The existence of large quantities of *disparate data* within a large organization or across many organizations involved in similar business activities.

massively disparate metadata Disparate metadata scattered across many different organizations. *See disparate data.*

message A communication containing a collection of data in some order and format. If that message is relevant to the recipient, it contains *information*. If the message is not relevant to the recipient, it does not contain information and is useless or less than fully useful.

meta A later stage, situated behind, or transcending.

metadata Traditionally, metadata were *data about the data.* In the common data architecture metadata are all data describing the *foredata*, including *meta-praedata* and the *meta-paradata*. They are data that come after or behind the foredata and support the foredata. *See evaluational metadata, operational metadata.*

metadata demand An organization's need for complete, accurate data about its data resource that is easily understandable and readily available to anyone using the data resource.

metadata dilemma The situation where an organization has a critical need for readily available high-quality metadata to fully utilize the data resource, yet is actively creating and collecting new data without maintaining adequate metadata. *See data dilemma.*

metadata shock The realization that existing metadata do not, will not, and cannot provide readily available high-quality metadata about the data resource. It is the sudden realization that the metadata dilemma really exists and is severely limiting use of the data resource. Metadata shock is the panic an organization feels when it realizes the disparate metadata situation is getting worse rather than better. *See disparate data shock.*

metadata warehouse A database that contains the common metadata and client-friendly search routines to help people fully understand and utilize the data resource. It contains common metadata about the data resource in a single organization or an integrated data resources that cross multiple disciplines and multiple jurisdictions. It contains a history of the data resource, what the data initially represented, and what they represent now.

meta-metadata Data that provide the descriptions of *meta-praedata* and *meta-paradata*. They are the data that provide the framework for the developing high-quality metadata.

meta-paradata Data that define *paradata*.

meta-praedata Data that define *praedata*.

millennium date problem The problem with existing date formats and the rapidly approaching year 2000.

modification identifier The part of the data version component of the *data naming taxonomy* that uniquely identifies a change to one or more data values within an existing set of data, not the addition of a new set of data. *See version identifier.*

multiple contributor data derivation A type of *data derivation* where a data value is derived from two or more contributing data characteristics and a data derivation procedure.

multiple data layer extents Exist when different organizations maintain multiple extents of the same spatial data theme. If different organizations design and maintain their data layer extents differently, it is very difficult to edge-match those data layers without some type of conversion or adjustment.

multiple data product unit A *data product unit* that contains several values in the same data product unit.

multiple data replicate distribution The movement of two or more *data replicates* from the official data source to two or more data sites. *See single data replicate distribution.*

multiple dimension analysis *See multiple dimension processing.*

multiple dimension data subject A *data subject* that represents two or more dimensions. *See single dimension data subject.*

multiple dimension processing On-line analytical processing for decision support that uses a combination of single dimension and multiple dimension data subjects. It is also referred to as static data analysis because the data values do not change. It is also known as multiple dimensional analysis.

multiple primary keys The situation where disparate data contain more than one *primary key* for a data subject.

multiple scale concept A concept that defines levels of generalization for *spatial data*. *See data layer generalization, data layer specialization.*

nested data set The situation where two data sets are nested in a one-to-many relationship. The outer data set represents the parent data subject and the inner, or nested, data set represents the subordinate data subject. *See single data set.*

network-driven data distribution The situation where the existence of a data site on a telecommunications network drives the distribution of data to that data site to support a business need. *See business-driven data distribution.*

nondescriptive geospatial reference A *nondescriptive spatial data reference* for *geospatial data.*

nondescriptive spatial reference A *spatial data reference* that occurs between a set of *tabular data* that either identify but do not describe *spatial objects* or do not identify or describe a spatial object and spatial data that locate and identify that object.

nondescriptive structospatial reference A *nondescriptive spatial data reference* for *structospatial data.*

nonintelligent primary key A *primary key* whose value does not contain a fact and has no meaning in the real world. It is meaningless with respect to the business. *See intelligent primary key.*

nonofficial data Data that are not designated as *official data.*

nonofficial data source Any data site where data that are not the record of reference are stored. It is a data site where redundant data are located that should not be used for data extraction to develop an integrated data resource or to replicate to other data sites. A data characteristic that contains nonofficial data. *See official data source, primary data source, secondary data source.*

nonofficial data variation A *data variation* that was not designated as an *official data variation.*

nontabular data Any data that are not generally maintained in traditional databases or typically displayed in tabular form, such as spatial, textual, voice, image (photo, digitized image, remote sensed image, or digital ortho-photography), and video. *See tabular data.*

normalized data Data that have been through *data normalization.* The data in the data view schema and the external schema.

object A person, place, thing, or concept in the real world. *See event.*

obsolete foreign key A *foreign key* that matches an *obsolete primary key.*

obsolete primary key A *primary key* that no longer uniquely identifies each data occurrence in a data subject within the common data structure. It is no longer used because it has lost its uniqueness or is not appropriate for some reason.

official data Data designated as the official record of reference or system of reference to be used for *data replication.* They are the official data from which all distributed data should be replicated. *See nonofficial data.*

official data characteristic variation A *data characteristic variation* that has been designated by the consensus of knowledgeable people.

official data characteristic variation table A table showing *official data characteristic variations*.

official data code set A set of *data codes* that has been designated as official by a consensus of knowledgeable people.

official data derivation algorithm A *data derivation algorithm* documenting the derivation of a data characteristic that has been designated as official by a consensus of knowledgeable people.

official data domain A *data domain* in the common data architecture that has been designated as official by a consensus of knowledgeable people for maintaining data quality.

official data integration table A table created from the *official data source table* and the *official data characteristic variation table*.

official data retention rule A *data retention rule* that has been designated as official by a consensus of knowledgeable people.

official data source Any data site where the official data, the record of reference, are stored. When there are redundant data, it is the data site that contains the official source of data for extraction to develop an integrated data resource or to replicate to other data sites. A data characteristic designated as containing official data. *See nonofficial data source, primary data source, secondary data source.*

official data source table A table showing all the data product units corresponding to each data characteristic within the data integration scope. It is a table of redundant data product units used for designating the official data value source.

official data variation A *data variation* that has been accepted by a consensus of knowledgeable people for short-term data sharing and long-term development of an integrated data resource.

official foreign key The *foreign key* that matches the *official primary key* in a parent data subject.

official primary key A *primary key* that is designated as the dominant, outstanding, preferred primary key for a data subject in the integrated data resource. Its value is unique for all data occurrences within the scope of the common data architecture. It has been designated as official by a consensus of knowledgeable people.

official word abbreviations A set of word abbreviations that is applied consistently to all data names according to a formal *data name abbreviation algorithm*. *See unofficial word abbreviations.*

one-to-many data relation A data relation that exists when a data occurrence in a parent data subject is related to more than one data occurrence in a subordinate data subject, but each data occurrence in that subordinate data subject is related to only one data occurrence in the parent data subject.

one-to-many recursive data relation A *data relation* that exists when a data occurrence within a data subject is related to two or more other data occurrences in that data subject. A one-to-many recursive data relation is shown as a one-to-many data relation from the data subject to itself.

one-to-one data relation A *data relation* that exists when a data occurrence in one data subject is related to only one data occurrence in a second data subject, and that data occurrence in the second data subject is related to only one data occurrence in the first data subject.

one-to-one recursive data relation A *data relation* that exists when a data occurrence within a data subject is related to only one other data occurrence in that data subject. A one-to-one recursive data relation is shown as a one-to-one data relation from the data subject to itself.

on-line analytical processing Processing that supports the analysis of business trends and projections. It is also known as decision support processing and OLAP.

on-line transaction processing Processing that supports the daily business operations. Also known as operational processing and OLTP.

open recursive data relation Same as a *one-to-many recursive data relation* because the relationships can be navigated either up or down without coming back to the original data occurrence.

operational data Data used in the operational processing of business transactions that support day-to-day business operations. They are detailed, largely primitive data necessary to keep the organization operating. *See evaluational data.*

operational data stores See *integrated operational data.*

operational data subject A *single dimension data subject* supporting business operations. *See evaluational data subject.*

operational data subject structure A *data subject structure* that shows the structure of *operational data*. *See evaluational data subject structure.*

operational database A database that contains current, detailed data to support on-line transaction processing. It contains *operational data*. *See decision support database, evaluational database.*

operational metadata *Metadata* about *operational data*. *See evaluational metadata.*

operational processing See *on-line transaction processing.*

operational subject relation diagram A *subject relation diagram* representing *operational data subjects*. *See evaluational subject relation diagram.*

optimized data Data that have been through *data optimization*. The data in the *logical schema* and *conceptual schema*.

paradata Data that describe the quality of the *praedata*. A new term developed from *para*, meaning beside, near, alongside, or assisting.

passive metadata warehouse A *metadata warehouse* that depends on people for updates when new data enter the data resource. *See active metadata warehouse.*

permanent data subject A *data subject* that remains in the *evaluational database* permanently. *See temporary data subject, transient data subject.*

physical data distribution matrix A matrix that shows data subjects or data occurrence groups that appear at each data site and the data characteristics that appear in each data subject or data occurrence group. *See logical data distribution matrix.*

physical data distribution outline An outline that shows the data subjects or data occurrence groups located at each data site and the data characteristics in each data subject or data occurrence group. *See logical data distribution outline.*

physical data model A data model that represents the denormalized physical implementation of data that support an information system. The *logical data model* is denormalized to a physical data model according to specific criteria that do not compromise the logical data model but allow the database to operate efficiently in a specific operating environment. *See common data model.*

physical data restructuring The denormalization of the data from the logical data model to the physical operating environment represented by the physical data model. *See data restructuring.*

physical data structure The structure of data in the *physical data model*. It represents the physical implementation of a *logical data structure* for an information system in a specific operating environment. It contains data files and data items that support the information system.

physical foreign key The *foreign key* that matches the *physical primary key*.

physical primary key An arbitrarily assigned, permanent, *nonintelligent primary key* that may or may not be visible to the client. It is usually assigned by the database management system, is smaller than an intelligent key, and requires less processing. It is used for physical control of records and operational efficiency in a database management system. *See business primary key, surrogate key, system assigned primary key.*

physical schema The *schema* that represents the physical structure of data in the database. It is considered to be *denormalized data*. It replaces the former *internal schema*.

platform resource A component of *information technology infrastructure* that represents the hardware and system software at an organization's disposal.

point seen area The portion of the landscape that be seen from a specific point on the landscape. *See seen area.*

praedata Data that directly present features about objects and events. A new term developed from the Latin *praesentare*, meaning to present.

preferred-future approach An approach that helps an organization define and incrementally develop an integrated data resource through a vision that describes what that integrated data resource will be like when it is developed.

primary data site The *data site* where data originate. It is a data site where data are captured, created, or generated. *See secondary data site.*

primary data source The first data site where the original data are stored after their origination. *See data origin, official data source, nonofficial data source, secondary data source.*

primary data value integrity rules A shell of *data value integrity rules* around the integrated data resource. These primary data value integrity rules are developed through the definition of business rules to ensure that the data adequately support the business information demand.

primary key A set of one or more *data characteristics* whose value uniquely identifies each data occurrence in a data subject. A primary key is also known as a unique identifier. *See invalid primary key, range of uniqueness, valid primary key.*

primary key approach An approach to developing an *evaluational database* using a matrix of primary key data characteristics for all data subjects identified by the business questions to determine the data perspectives. *See business question approach.*

primitive data *Data* that are obtained by measurement or observation of an object or event in the real world. *See derived data.*

primitive data layer A *data layer* that represents one set of objects or events in the real world. *See derived data layer.*

primitive evaluational data The lowest level of detail desired in the *evaluational database*. They are the primitive level of data for *multiple dimension analysis* even though they are derived from operational data.

proactive updates Updates made to the data resource today that will not become effective until some future date. Proactive updates require at least an entry date and an effective date. *See retroactive updates, temporal data.*

prospective data quality improvement The process of improving only the quality of new data coming into the data resource, but generally ignoring improvement of data quality for data already in the data resource. *See retrospective data quality improvement.*

qualifying data subject A single dimension data subject that qualifies a *data focus*.

range of uniqueness The range of data occurrences for which values of the *primary key* provide uniqueness.

recursive data relation A *data relation* between data occurrences in the same data subject. A recursive data relation may be one-to-one, one-to-many, or many-to-many, the same as data relations between data subjects. *See one-to-one recursive data relation, one-to-many recursive data relation, and many-to-many recursive data relation.*

redundant data The situation where the same data characteristic exists at two or more data sites. Redundant data are created, stored, and maintained independent of each other and are often unknown to the organization.

redundant data diagram A diagram that specifies the data characteristics representing the *official data source* and the redundant data characteristics that should be maintained from that official data source.

redundant data integrity The process of identifying, documenting, and maintaining redundant data until the redundancy can be eliminated or reduced to a manageable level.

redundant data maintenance The process of maintaining consistent values in each existence of a redundant data characteristic.

redundant data table A table that specifies the data characteristics in the *official data source* and the redundant data characteristics that are maintained from the official data source.

referential integrity The part of *data structure integrity* that ensures a parent data occurrence exists for each subordinate data occurrence. A subordinate data occurrence cannot be added if there is no parent data occurrence, and a parent data occurrence cannot be deleted if subordinate data occurrences still exist.

refining A process that removes impurities from crude or impure material to form useful products, such as refining crude oil. *See data refining.*

retroactive updates Updates made to the data resource today that were effective at some past date. Retroactive updates require at least an entry date and an effective date. *See proactive updates, temporal data.*

retrospective data quality improvement The process of improving the quality of data that already exist in the data resource. *See prospective data quality improvement.*

reverse data denormalization A process that transforms the *physical schema* to the *distribution schema*. It undoes the database to its distributed schema or to the logical schema if there is no data distribution. *See forward data denormalization.*

reverse data deoptimization A process that transforms the *distribution schema* to the *logical schema*. *See forward data deoptimization.*

reverse data modeling Movement from the *physical schema* to the *distribution schema* to the *logical schema* to the *data view schema* to the *business schema*. *See forward data modeling.*

reverse data normalization A process that transforms the *data view schema* to the *business schema*. *See forward data normalization.*

reverse data optimization A process that transforms the *logical schema* to the *data view schema*. *See forward data optimization.*

rolling-up data *See data generalization.*

schema A diagrammatic representation of the structure or framework of something. *See data schema.*

secondary data site A *data site* where data may be moved after their origination. *See primary data site.*

secondary data source Any data site where data acquired from another data site are stored without alteration or modification. The data for a secondary data source may come from a primary data source or another secondary data source. If data are altered or modified in any way at a data site, that data site becomes a primary data source for those new data. *See official data source, nonofficial data source, primary data source.*

seen area An area of the landscape that is visible and can be seen from another area of the landscape. *See area seen area, line seen area, point seen area.*

semantic data refining The process of cross-referencing *disparate data* to the common data architecture to understand their content and meaning without changing the data or impacting the day-to-day operation information systems. It is a nondestructive, no-impact process that increases data awareness and understanding, and reduces the variability and redundancy through cross-references. *See data refining, refining.*

semi-structured disparate data *Disparate data* that are at least partially structured by some method, but are not equivalent to the common data architecture. They conform to some type of naming, definition, structure, and quality criteria, but not to those of the common data architecture. *See unstructured disparate data.*

semi-structured logical schema The *logical schema* that are not aligned with the common data architecture.

short data replicate name The distributed data set name shown on the *data distribution diagram* consisting of only the data subject or data occurrence group name. *See formal data replicate name.*

simple primary key matrix A matrix showing the primary key characteristics for all *summary data subjects* in a *data perspective. See detailed primary key matrix.*

single contributor data derivation A type of *data derivation* where a data value is derived from one contributing data characteristic and a data derivation procedure.

single data replicate distribution The movement of one *data replicate* between data sites. *See multiple data replicate distribution.*

single data set A set of *data characteristics* belonging to one data subject. *See nested data set.*

single dimension data subject A *data subject* that represents one data dimension.

single dimension processing On-line transaction processing that uses single dimension data subjects in an operational database. It is also referred to as *dynamic data analysis* because the data values are constantly changing to reflect changes in the real world.

soft data The opinions, comments, explanations, observations, and evaluations about the business. Soft data enhance the value of the *hard data* and support more informed decisions.

spatial A general term including both *geospatial* and *structospatial.*

spatial data A type of nontabular data with a spatial component that allows them to be precisely located on some base, such as the Earth. Sometimes referred to as aspatial data. Includes both *geospatial data* and *structospatial data. See tabular data.*

spatial database Any database that contains *geospatial data* or *structospatial data.*

spatial data hierarchy A *data subject hierarchy* for defining spatial data themes and subthemes that includes both current and future spatial data needs. *See geospatial data hierarchy, structospatial data hierarchy.*

spatial data reference A *data relation* between *tabular data* and *spatial data* for the purpose of connecting and integrating spatial and tabular data.

spatial data referencing The process of integrating *tabular data* and *spatial data* through a *spatial data reference.*

spatial data tier A set of *data layers* representing a particular level of spatial data aggregation. *See four-tier concept.*

spatial evaluational database A database for the analysis of trends and projections using *spatial data. See tabular evaluational database.*

spatial information systems A new term for *geographic information systems* that can capture, store, manipulate, and display all types of two-dimensional, three-dimensional, and time-variant spatial data.

spatial reference system Provides the horizontal (x and y), and sometimes vertical (z), control necessary for accurately positioning spatial objects and events. A spatial reference system also provides control for combining the data between two or more data layers. *See geospatial reference system, structospatial reference system.*

spatium A term meaning of, related to, involving, or having the nature of space.

specific data layer Any *primitive data layer*, other than a framework data layer, that is of interest to an organization. It has a more specific, limited interest than a *framework data layer*. A specific data layer can be based on either a *spatial reference system* or a framework data layer.

static data analysis The analysis of data values that do not change, such as those in an *evaluational database*. *See dynamic data analysis.*

static data replicate A *data replicate* that does not need to have its data values consistent with those at the *official data source*. *See active data replicate.*

static derived data Data derived from contributing data characteristics that no longer exist or whose values will never change. There is no need to rederive static derived data. *See active derived data.*

strategic schema The high-level *logical schema* of the data resource. It provides an organization-wide view of the data resource with minimum detail and includes only data subjects corresponding to objects in the real world that are tracked or managed by the organization. *See tactical schema.*

strategic schema generalization The process of developing the *strategic schema* from the *tactical schema*.

strategic schema identification The process of developing the *strategic schema* from an organization's perspective of the real world. Data subjects are defined based on objects and events in the real world that are tracked or managed by an organization.

structocoding The process of designating primary keys for structospatial objects and maintaining those unique identifiers in both the structospatial data layers and related tabular data subjects so that the tabular and spatial data can be related.

structodatum A *datum* for aligning objects in, on, or around a structure.

structographic A term derived from *structus* meaning structure and *graphein* meaning to write or describe. Literally, it means describing a structure.

structographic data Any data that locate, identify, or describe objects on, in, or around a *structure*.

structolinear referencing system A *linear referencing system* for *structospatial linear objects*.

structoreferencing The process of accurately placing structospatial objects in, on, or about a structure according to a spatial reference system. The term is developed from *structus* meaning structure and *referre* meaning to carry back.

structospatial A term derived form *structus* meaning structure and *spatium* meaning of, relating to, involving, or having the nature of space. Literally it means spatial locations on, in, or around a structure.

structospatial data Any data that represent the location and identifying characteristics of *structospatial objects*. They place structospatial objects on, in, or around a *structure* and uniquely identify those objects.

structospatial database Any database containing *structospatial data*.

structospatial data hierarchy A *spatial data hierarchy* for *structospatial data*.

structospatial data layer A *data layer* that contains *structospatial data*.

structospatial object Any feature or boundary on, in, or around a *structure*. The object may be a point, a line, an area, or a three-dimensional object.

structospatial reference system A *spatial reference system* that provides the control for accurately placing spatial objects and events on, in, or around a structure.

structure An object with elements arranged in a definite pattern or organization that bear a relationship to each other.

structured logical schema Schema that represent *logical schema* aligned with the common data architecture.

structured physical schema Schema that represent *physical schema* aligned with the common data architecture.

structus A term meaning structure.

subthematic tier A tier in the *four-tier concept* that consists of primitive *data layers* that collectively contribute to a major data theme in a fully enhanced thematic data layer.

subject-oriented data resource A data resource that is organized by data subjects based on the identification and definition of objects and events in the world that are of interest to an organization.

subject relation diagram A *data relation diagram* that shows the arrangement and relationship of data subjects in the *common data structure*. Limited detail is shown on a subject relation diagram so that it is technically correct as well as culturally acceptable. A subject relation diagram is traditionally known as an *entity relation diagram* or *E-R diagram*.

subject structure chart A chart that shows the existence and structure of *data characteristics* within *data subjects* in the common data structure. It directly supports the *subject relation diagram* to provide a complete representation of the common data structure. *See entity structure chart, file structure chart.*

subthematic tier A tier in the four-schema concept that consists of *primitive data layers* that collectively contribute to a major data theme in a fully enhanced thematic data layer. There are usually one or more permanent data layers in a subthematic tier, but there may be none if there is a single layer in the *thematic tier.*

summary data subject The central multiple dimension data subject containing the summary data resulting from multiple dimension analysis. It contains the derived evaluational data that are developed from either the primitive evaluational data or other derived evaluational data during multiple dimension analysis. *See focus data subject.*

surrogate primary key A *physical primary key* that is not visible to clients.

system-assigned primary key A *primary key* whose value is created and assigned by a database management system. *See intelligent primary key, nonintelligent primary key, surrogate key.*

table partitioning The process of identifying the tables needed at each *data site. See data subject partitioning.*

tabular data The traditional data that are maintained in a traditional database and are displayed in tabular form. *See nontabular data, spatial data.*

tabular evaluational databases An evaluational database containing tabular data. *See spatial evaluational database.*

tactical schema The intermediate *schema* between the *strategic schema* and the *logical schema* that provide more detail about the data resource than the strategic schema, but do not contain all the detail necessary for developing the data resource.

tactical schema generalization The process of developing the *tactical schema* from the *logical schema.*

tactical schema specialization The process of developing the *tactical schema* from the *strategic schema.* It is done by identifying the data subjects that directly support the data subjects shown in the strategic schema and resolving the many-to-many data relations.

temporal Related to, concerned with, or limited by time. It is derived from *tempus,* meaning time.

temporal data Any data that represent a point in time or a time interval. They are data with a time component. *See collection time, distribution time, entry time, event time, identification time.*

temporal database A database that has the capability to store temporal data and manage data based on those temporal data. It can recreate data values for past or future dates based on the temporal data values. These databases are also known as *time-relational databases*.

temporary summary data subject A *data subject* that remains in the *evaluational database* for a shorter period of time. *See permanent data subject, transient data subject.*

thematic tier A tier in the *four-tier concept* that consists of primitive or *derived data layers* that represent a major data theme, such as transportation, land use, surface water, or waste water infrastructure. Data layers in the thematic tier may include a control data layer, a framework data layer, or a map data layer. Data layers in the thematic tier are usually permanent, but may be temporary or nonexistent, depending on the use and importance of data layers in the subthematic tier.

three-dimensional data layer aggregation *Vertical data aggregation, horizontal data aggregation*, and *chronological data aggregation* that form a network of aggregations.

three-schema concept A concept for managing data that includes an *internal schema*, an *external schema*, and a *conceptual schema*.

time interval A single time for a data occurrence or data characteristic. *See temporal data.*

time point A begin and end time for a data occurrence or data characteristic. *See temporal data.*

time relational database *See temporal database.*

time-variant spatial data The situation where multiple versions of a spatial *data layer extent* are maintained over a period of time.

traditional data name A data name that usually does not have any structure and often has little or no meaning, resulting in many data name homonyms and *data name synonyms*. *See formal data name.* Traditional data names were usually abbreviations due to physical limitations and are not consistent across programs or data files.

traditional data sharing The situation where individual physical files and independent translation schemes are only useful as long as the source and target databases retain the same content and structure. *See data sharing concept.*

transient data subject A *data subject* that is created for a particular analysis and deleted. It is not maintained beyond a specific analysis. *See permanent data subject, temporary data subject.*

true data subject A *data subject* that contains one or more data characteristics that describe the data subject. *See data subject type and virtual data subject.*

two-schema concept A concept for managing data consisting of an *internal schema* and an *external schema*.

type conflict A problem that can occur with a structural *data naming taxonomy* when there are dissimilar structures. An object or concept may be a data subject to one organization and a data characteristic to another organization. *See dependency conflict, key conflict.*

unique identifier *See primary key.*

unnormalized data The data in the *business schema* that are structured for use in the real world. Data that are not normalized.

unofficial word abbreviations A set of word abbreviations that are not applied consistently to all data names according to a formal data name abbreviation algorithm. *See official word abbreviations.*

unstructured disparate data *Disparate data* that do not conform to any type of naming, definition, structure, or quality criteria and have no similarity to the common data architecture. *See semi-structured disparate data.*

unstructured logical schema A *schema* representing *logical schema* that are not aligned with the common data architecture.

unstructured physical schema A *schema* representing data files that are not aligned with the common data architecture.

valid primary key A set of data characteristics that meet the criteria for being a primary key. *See invalid primary key.*

variable data product unit A *data product unit* that contains different data attributes under different situations.

version identifier The part of the *data version component* of the data naming taxonomy that uniquely identifies a new set of evaluational data resulting from the addition of data to an *evaluational database* or the removal of data from an evaluational database. *See modification identifier.*

vertical data aggregation The summarization of data to higher levels of generalization. *See chronological data aggregation, horizontal data aggregation.*

vertical data layer aggregation The combination of two or more *data layers* to form a more enhanced data layer. Aggregation may occur with either *geospatial data layers* or *structospatial data layers*.

vertical data layer aggregation diagram A diagram showing the vertical aggregation of *data layers*.

vertical data modeling The process of moving through the *logical schema*, *tactical schema*, and *strategic schema*. Transforming a general schema to a more detailed schema is a specialization process, and transforming a detailed schema to a more general schema is a generalization process.

vertical data replication The replication of data values from a parent data subject to subordinate data subjects for more efficient processing. It usually occurs in *evaluational data,* but may occur in *operational data* under special circumstances.

vertical model transformation Movement from the enterprise model to the information system model to the technology model represented within the *framework for information systems.* More detail is added in the progression from defining the scope to implementing a functioning system. *See horizontal model transformation.*

vertical partitioning Same as *data characteristic partitioning.*

virtual data subject A *data subject* that represents a broad classification of subordinate data subjects. It has no data characteristics of its own. *See data subject type, true data subject.*

word abbreviation set A formal set of established word or word phrase abbreviations that is used to shorten a data name. Abbreviations for word phrases should be limited to word phrases that are in common use.

working levels of data classification The lower three levels of data classification consisting of data subjects, data characteristics, and data characteristic variations. They represent the operational level of data classification. These three levels are used for building the common data architecture and developing an integrated data resource. *See data classification scheme, categorical levels of data classification.*

Common Words

Common words are an extension of the class word concept used in data naming conventions. Examples of common words for data sites, data subjects, data characteristics, data characteristic variations, and data versions are listed in this appendix. These lists can be expanded as necessary during development of an integrated data resource.

COMMON DATA SITE WORDS

Common data site words are used to provide consistent meaning for data sites. The specific words are generally unique to the organization or organizations developing an integrated data architecture. They are developed as formal data names are defined.

COMMON DATA SUBJECT WORDS

Common data subject words are used to provide consistent meaning for data subjects, data occurrence selections, and data code sets. A few of the more prominent common data subject words are defined in the following list. The set can be expanded as formal data names are defined.

Account A data subject for tracking and managing monies, such as Customer Account.

Activity A data subject for actions or transactions that are pending, such as Customer Account Activity. Generally, a subordinate data subject.

Archive A data subject for data records that cease to be of interest for current operations, such as Employee Archive. The entire data record is moved to the archive data subject when it is no longer needed for current operations.

Authority A data subject for approval or delegation, such as Expenditure Authority.

Authorization A data subject showing approval or delegation, such as Employee Account Authorization.

Budget A data subject for planned monetary or effort expenditure, such as Yearly Budget.

Category A data subject representing a classification or grouping of objects, usually higher than Class or Group, such as Equipment Category. The hierarchy should be common for the organization, such as Category, Group, Class.

Class A data subject representing a class of objects, such as Facility Class. The hierarchy should be common for the organization, such as Category, Group, Class.

Detail A data subject containing details about a parent data subject, such as Customer Account Activity Detail.

Exemption A data subject containing an exclusion or different situation, such as Tuition Exemption.

Expense A data subject for monies expended, such as Equipment Expense.

Focus A data subject representing a data focus in an evaluational database, such as Vehicle Trip Focus.

Group A data subject representing a specific grouping of objects, such as Building Group. The hierarchy should be common for the organization, such as Category, Group, Class.

History A data subject for historical information, such as Customer Account History. It contains either the individual data values that were changed or all the data values.

Image A data subject containing graphic images of documents in an imaging system, such as Purchase Order Image. Generally not used for remote sensing or satellite imaging.

Income A data subject for income data, such as Client Income.

Integrity A data subject containing integrity rules for a corresponding data subject, such as Employee Integrity.

Inventory A data subject for tracking and managing objects, such as Part Inventory.

Item A data subject of individual objects that are part of another object, such as Purchase Order Item.

Month A data subject representing data for a month, such as Employee Month.

Project A data subject for grouping events, tasks, people, monies, and so on, such as Service Project.

Photo A data subject containing photographic images, such as Land Parcel Photo.

Quarter A data subject representing data for a quarter, such as Equipment Maintenance Quarter.

Rate A data subject representing monetary or other rates, such as Service Rate.

Revenue A data subject for income or monies received, such as Sales Revenue.

Spatial A data subject representing a specific layer of data in a geographic information system (GIS) consisting of lines, points, and polygons, such as Soil Spatial.

Status A data subject representing the status of objects, such as Project Status.

Summary A data subject of summary data above a detailed operational level, such as Employee Leave Summary. Usually used in an executive information system (EIS).

Suspense A data subject for items held for a specific purpose or action, usually pending resolution of a problem, such as Account Activity Suspense.

Text A data subject containing textual information that can be searched in a variety of ways for words, phrases, content, meaning, conclusions, and so on, such as Contract Text. Usually used in a text information management system (TIMS).

Type A data subject representing types of objects, such as Equipment Type.

Validation A data subject for verification or proof of a combination of objects, such as Equipment Part Validation.

Video A data subject containing video clips, such as Saltwater Bulkhead Video.

Voice A data subject containing voice data, such as Voice Message.

Week A data subject representing data for a week, such as Project Week.

Year A data subject representing data for a year, such as Equipment Year.

COMMON DATA CHARACTERISTIC WORDS

Common data characteristic words are used to provide consistent meaning for data characteristics and data characteristic substitutions. A few of the more prominent common data characteristic words are defined in the following list. The set can be expanded as formal data names are defined.

Altitude The distance above or below a specific datum (reference point), such as sea level.

Amount A monetary quantity in some type of currency, such as dollars. Not a count or a capacity.

Area A two-dimensional measurement of an object. Not a region, district, or other geographical area.

Balance The quantity or amount remaining, such as dollars in an account or parts in an inventory.

Capacity The maximum content of an object. Similar to Volume. Not used for monetary quantities.

Centuries A time interval, elapsed time, or duration in centuries. Not a point in time.

Code Alphabetic or numeric coded data values that indicate the existence of a code table data subject. Should not be used if data values are not coded.

Comment A textual comment about an object. Similar to Description, Explanation, Remark, and Text.

Constant A numerical value that does not change over time or circumstances and is used in one or more calculations. Not the same as a Literal.

Count The quantity of objects that exist or have occurred. Not the same as Amount or Number.

Date A point in time.

Day A number representing a point in time.

Days A time interval, elapsed time, or duration in days.

Depth A one-dimensional measurement below a specified plane, such as below the ground. Not the same as Altitude.

Description A textual description of an object. Similar to Comment, Explanation, Remark, and Text.

Distance A one-dimensional measurement between two points.

Duration A time interval or duration representing an elapsed time or the length of time an event lasted.

Explanation A textual explanation about an object. Similar to Comment, Description, Remark, and Text.

Flag An indication that some event has happened or should happen. A binary situation, such as on/off, true/false, 0/1, or yes/no. Similar to Indicator.

Height A one-dimensional measurement above a specified plane, such as a person's height. Not the same as Altitude.

Hour A number representing a point in time. Must have an associated date for meaning.

Hours The time interval, elapsed time, or duration in hours.

Identifier A unique alphanumeric identification of an object. Generally, not just a number.

Image An image stored as a data characteristic.

Indicator An indication of two possible conditions. A binary situation, such as on/off, true/false, 0/1, or yes/no. Similar to Flag.

Label A textual phrase that provides a distinctive designation for an object. Similar to Name and Title.

Length A one-dimensional measurement of an object.

Literal An alpha or alphanumeric value that does not change over time or circumstances. Not the same as a Constant.

Minute A number representing a point in time. Must have an associated hour and date to be meaningful.

Minutes A time interval, elapsed time, or duration in minutes.

Month A number representing a point in time.

Months A time interval, elapsed time, or duration in months.

Name A textual phrase that provides a distinctive designation for an object. Similar to Label and Title.

Number A number that identifies an object. Not an Amount, Capacity, Code, or Quantity.

Percent A number that represents a ratio between two objects, based on 100.

Photo A photo stored as a data characteristic.

Price A monetary amount charged for an object.

Quantity The capacity or count of something other than money. Not a Value, Amount, or Number.

Quarter A number representing a point in time.

Quarters A time interval, elapsed time, or duration in quarters.

Ratio A number that represents a ratio between two objects. Not the same as Percent.

Remark A textual remark about an object. Similar to Comment, Description, Explanation, and Text.

Second A number representing a point in time. Must have an associated date, hour, and minute to be meaningful

Seconds A time interval, elapsed time, or duration in seconds.

Sequence A string showing the sequence of a set of objects. Usually used with another common word, such as Number or Character.

Size A number indicating the extent of an object.

Status A textual remark about the status of an object.

Text A free-form string of text, usually unstructured or unformatted. Similar to Comment, Description, Explanation, and Remark. It may be implied in other common words like Description or Explanation.

Title A textual phrase that provides a distinctive designation for an object. Similar to Label and Name.

Value A monetary quantity that indicates the worth of something in some type of currency. Not the same as Amount.

Video Video data stored as a data characteristic.

Voice Voice data stored as a data characteristic.

Volume The capacity of an object. Similar to Capacity.

Week A number representing a point in time.

Weeks A time interval, elapsed time, or duration, in weeks,

Width A one-dimensional measurement of the breadth of an object.

Year A number representing a point in time.

Years A time interval, elapsed time, or duration in years.

COMMON DATA CHARACTERISTIC VARIATION WORDS

Common data characteristic variation words are used to provide consistent meaning for data characteristic variations. A few of the more prominent common data characteristic variation words are defined in the following list. The set can be expanded as formal data names are defined.

Acres, Square Feet, Hectares, and so on for variations to areas.

Complete, Abbreviated, Short, Long for different lengths of names, titles, or labels.

Cubic Inches, Gallons, Yards, and so on for variations in volumes.

Dollars, Yen, and so on for variations to monetary data characteristics, such as Amount, Price, and Value.

Estimated, Measured, Actual, and so on for variations in method of determining values.

Inches, Feet, Miles, Meters, and so on for variations in lengths, distances, heights, widths. and other measurements.

Irregular Indicates a data characteristic whose contents have no consistent format or meaning; that is, it varies from one data characteristic to another.

Multiple Indicates that the contents may have multiple values, such as several dates or several people's names.

Normal, Inverted Indicates different sequences within a data characteristic.

Variable Indicates a data characteristic that contains different data characteristics depending on the circumstances.

COMMON DATA VERSION WORDS

Common data version words are used to provide consistent meaning for data versions. A few of the more prominent common data version words are defined in the following list. The set can be expanded as formal data names are defined.

First Quarter The first quarter's data.
Fourth Quarter The fourth quarter's data.
Modification The modification number that follows a version, such as Version 5.6.
Second Quarter The second quarter's data.
Third Quarter The third quarter's data.
Version A version number, such as Version 5.
Year A year number, such as 1996.

COMMON DATA DEFINITION WORDS

Common data definition words are used to provide consistent meaning within data definitions. A few of the more prominent common data definition words are defined in the following list. The set can be expanded as comprehensive data definitions are developed.

Code Table Used with a data subject definition to indicate that it contains a set of data codes, such as *A code table data subject* . . . .
Combined Indicates that a data characteristic is formed from a combination of two or more single data characteristics, such as *A combined data characteristic consisting of.* . . .
Maximum Indicates that a data characteristic format has a maximum number of positions, but that all do not need to be used, such as *A maximum 32-character name.* . . . If Maximum is not used, it implies that all positions must be filled.
Parent Used with a data subject definition to indicate that it is a parent of a subtype, such as *It is the parent of.* . . .
Subtype Used with a data subject definition to indicate that it is a subtype of a parent data subject, such as *It is a subtype of.* . . .
Virtual Used with a data subject definition to indicate a virtual data subject, such as *A virtual data subject.* . . .

Short Data Names

Data names can be shortened through the use of shorthand notations. The following sections describe several of the prominent shorthand notations for data names.

PARENT ELIMINATION NOTATION

The parent elimination notation is a short data name that developed by eliminating the parent data unit name and indicating that elimination with the punctuation.

Example: The data site name Dallas can be eliminated from the data subject name for a set of data subjects listed under that site, as shown in Figure B.1. The colon before the data subject name indicates that Dallas must be inserted to make the formal data name.

Similarly, the data subject name Employee can be eliminated from the data characteristic name for a set of data characteristics listed

Dallas	Employee	Employee Birth Date
:Employee	.Name Complete	,CYMD
:Equipment	.Birth Date CYMD	,YMD

Figure B.1   Parent elimination notation.

under that data subject. The period before the data characteristic name indicates that Employee must be inserted to make the formal data name. The data characteristic name Employee Birth Date can be eliminated from the data characteristic variation name for a set of data characteristic variations listed under that data characteristic. The comma before the data characteristic variation name indicates that Employee Birth Date must be inserted to make the formal data name.

SUBORDINATE INCLUSION NOTATION

The subordinate inclusion notation is a short data name that represents the inclusion of the full set of subordinate data units with a symbol in parenthesis. These symbols are explained in the following list:

All data subjects at a data site are represented with an *s* in parenthesis after the data site name, such as Boston (s). Any reference to Boston (s) means all data subjects at the Boston data site.

All data characteristics for a data subject are represented with a *c* in parenthesis after the data subject name, such as Employee (c). Any reference to Employee (c) means all data characteristics for the Employee data subject.

All data characteristic variations for a data characteristic are represented with a *v* in parenthesis after the data characteristic name, such as Employee Birth Date (v). Any reference to Employee Birth Date (v) means all data characteristic variations for Employee Birth Date.

All codes for a data characteristic or data characteristic variation are represented with an *a* in parenthesis after the data characteristic or data characteristic variation name, such as Education Level Code (a). Any reference to Education Level Code (a) means all coded data values for Education Level Code.

SUBORDINATE SUBSTITUTION NOTATION

The subordinate substitution notation is a short data name that represents the substitution of a fundamental data characteristic variation by placing the fundamental data characteristic name in parenthesis.

Example: The substitution of a specific date variation is represented by placing the word Date in parenthesis, such as Employee Birth (Date). This notation means that any form of date, such as Date CYMD, Date YMD, or Date MDY can be substituted for Date.

PARENT SUBSTITUTION NOTATION

The parent substitution notation is a short data name that represents the substitution of a parent data unit name. The parent data name is represented by a letter in parenthesis preceding the subordinate data name, as explained in the following list:

An *l* in parentheses represents the substitution of any data site name (*l* represents *location*) for a data subject name, such as (l):Employee. This notation means the Employee data subject at any site.

An *s* in parenthesis represents the substitution of any data subject name for a data characteristic, such as such as (s).Birth Date CYMD. This notation is not frequently used, but it can be useful in some situations.

A *c* in parenthesis represents the substitution of any data characteristic for a data characteristic variation, such as (c) Date CYMD. This notation also has limited use.

SUMMARY DATA SUBJECT NOTATION

The summary data subject notation is a short data name that represents a set of summary data subjects by placing an *n* in parenthesis after the summary data subject name. Summary data subjects are usually grouped into sets representing a specific collection of related summary data subjects. The summary data subject set is uniquely identified with a summary data subject set name, such as Employee Summary. Each individual summary data subject in that set is uniquely identified with number, such as Employee Summary 1, Employee Summary 2, and so on. A summary data subject substitution is shown with the letter '*n*' inside the parenthesis representing the number of the summary data subject and following the summary data subject set name.

Example: Employee Summary (n) represents a set of summary data subjects including Employee Summary 1, Employee Summary 2, Employee Summary 3, and so on.

PROGRAM NAME NOTATION

The program name notation is a short data name that represents a data characteristic or data characteristic variation in a program. Data name abbreviation schemes often produce data names that are difficult to use in programs, in SQL statements, and in headings on reports or screens. A short, convenient data name that is meaningful and consistent is created by dropping the data subject or data file name and any words that are implied by common usage. The words in a program name notation are usually unabbreviated or use commonly known abbreviations. At the program level, people usually know what the data subject or data file represents and do not need that name.

Example: Employee Name Complete Normal could be shortened to Name Complete if the common use was a name in the normal form or to Name Complete Normal if the form were uncertain.

Example: Employee Birth Date CYMD could be shortened to Birth Date if the normal form were CYMD.

The use of short data names in programs or column headings is not a license to create random data names like those that currently exist in disparate data. The short data names must be consistent and must be based on common usage within an organization. They should also be cross-referenced to the common data architecture so there is no doubt about what the short data name represents.

Data Definition Examples

DATA SITES

Brushwood County Mainframe Employee

The Employee database located on the mainframe computer in the Brushwood County Courthouse.

Frost County Personnel Employee

The Employee database located at and maintained by the Personnel Department of Frost County.

Frost County Port Commission Employee

The Employee database located at and maintained by the Port Commission of Frost County.

Frost County Public Works Employee

The Employee database located at and maintained by the Public Works Department of Frost County.

DATA OCCURRENCE GROUPS

Disabled Employee

An Employee that is certified as disabled by the procedures established by the Governor's Commission on Disabilities.

Managerial Employee

An Employee that is in a managerial job classification as specified by the Merit System Rules.

Pilot-Certified Employee

An Employee that is certified as a pilot by the Federal Aeronautics Administration.

Retirement Eligible Employee

An Employee that is eligible for retirement under the Merit System Rules.

DATA SUBJECTS

Employee

Any person who works for another in exchange for financial compensation. A State Employee is any person employed by the State and receives compensation from the State. A State Employee is normally required to follow Merit System Rules, unless the position held is specified as being exempt from such rules.

Latitude Longitude

A Geographic Location coordinate representation for points on the surface of the Earth. Latitude and longitude are expressed in angles as degrees, minutes, and seconds, or as radians. Latitude is the angle above or below the Earth's equator. Longitude is the angle East or West of the Prime Meridian in Greenwich, England.

When latitude and longitude are expressed together, latitude is given first, followed by longitude. Each value is expressed from high order (degrees) to low order (seconds). When a decimal fraction is used, the lower order units are not expressed.

Transit Point

A Transit Point is a specific geographic location that can be used either as a Passenger Stop, as a Time Point, or both. It contains all the location data about Passenger Stops and Time Points. Transit Point Style Type indicates the style of the Transit Point.

Transit Point Style Type

A code table containing a set of codes designating the type of the Transit Point with respect to its style.

Transit Route

A Transit Route is a specific sequence of many Transit Points that are grouped together with a common identifier. It has a beginning and an ending Transit Point, and may include deadheads at the beginning or the ending of the route. Each Transit Route has a linear reference from an anchor point that is at the start of the route where passengers may board. Transit Route Bounding Type indicates whether the route is inbound or outbound. Transit Route Use Type indicates whether the route is available to carry passengers.

DATA CHARACTERISTICS

Employee Birth Date

The date that an Employee was born as shown on his or her Birth Certificate or other legal document.

Latitude Complete

A combined data characteristic consisting of Latitude Degrees, Latitude Minutes, and Latitude Seconds.

Latitude Degrees

The two-digit degrees of latitude from 00 through 90 above or below the Earth's equator. A corresponding Hemisphere Latitude Code is required for hemisphere identification.

Latitude Degrees Decimal

The six-digit degrees of latitude in degrees and decimal fractions of degrees from 00 through 90. Latitude Minutes and Latitude Seconds are not recorded. A corresponding Hemisphere Latitude Code is required for hemisphere identification.

Latitude Minutes

The 2-digit minutes of latitude from 00 through 59.

Latitude Radians

The radians of latitude above or below the Earth's equator represented by a decimal number not to exceed one-half of pi. The number of significant digits is defined as necessary. Latitudes south of the equator are identified with a minus sign (–) and latitudes north of the equator are identified with a plus sign (+) or a blank.

Transit Point Cross Street Distance

The distance from the head of the Transit Point to the curb or pavement edge of the cross street.

Transit Point Cross Street Name

The complete name of the cross street nearest to the Transit Point, such as S 12th Ave. or Jones Way S.W.

Transit Point Curb Paint Length

The length of the painted curb at the Transit Point.

Transit Point Length

The distance of the Transit Point.

Transit Point Location Description

The narrative description of the location of a Transit Point, such as "On 12 Ave S.W. mid block between Division Street and Central Street."

Transit Point Location Name

The complete name of a Transit Point, such as the "512 Park and Ride" or the "South Center Mall."

DATA CHARACTERISTIC VARIATIONS

Employee Birth Date CYMD

The Date CYMD that Employees were born as shown on their Birth Certificates or other legal document.

Employee Birth Date MDY

The Date MDY that Employees were born as shown on their Birth Certificates or other legal document.

Employee Birth Date M/D/Y

The Date M/D/Y that Employees were born as shown on their Birth Certificates or other legal document.

Transit Point Cross Street Distance Feet

The distance in feet from the head of the Transit Point to the curb or pavement edge of the cross street.

Transit Point Cross Street Distance Meters

The distance in meters from the head of the Transit Point to the curb or pavement edge of the cross street.

Transit Point Curb Paint Length Feet

The length in feet of the painted curb at the Transit Point.

Transit Point Curb Paint Length Meters

The length in meters of the painted curb at the Transit Point.

Transit Point Length Feet

The distance in feet of the Transit Point.

Transit Point Length Meters

The distance in meters of the Transit Point.

DATA CODES

Water Right Use Consumption Type

C   Consumptive

Where there is a definite diversion of water from a surface water source and, neglecting transportation losses, the full amount of the diversion is not returned directly to the original source body or any other surface water body by means of a definite surface water course, channel, or pipe.

Where there is a definite diversion of water from a surface water source for a consumptive-type use, such as irrigation or domestic supply.

All withdrawals shall be considered consumptive unless the full amount is returned to the source aquifer. Heat pump use will be consumptive if the water is not returned to the source aquifer, but is returned to some other aquifer. If the water is discharged to a surface drainage system, the use is also consumptive.

Where there is a definite diversion of water from a reservoir for a consumptive-type use, such as irrigation or domestic supply.

V   Reservoir Variable Level

Where a reservoir stores water for a nonconsumptive type of use, such as hydroelectric power generation, and where a nearly constant volume of stored water is not maintained in the reservoir under normal operating conditions. This definition includes run-of-the-river hydroplants.

F   Reservoir Fixed Level

Where a reservoir is normally filled once for a nonconsumptive type of use, such as fish propagation or beautification, and where a nearly constant volume of stored water is maintained in the reservoir under normal operating conditions for that use. In most cases, outflow from the reservoir is approximately equal to inflow.

P   Partially Consumptive

Where the full amount of diversion from a surface water source, neglecting transportation losses, is returned to the same surface water source at a point further than 25 feet downstream from the point of diversion.

DATA VERSIONS

1990 Calendar

The data are current through the end of calendar year 1990.

1990 Federal Fiscal

The data are current through the end of the federal fiscal year 1990.

1990 State Fiscal

The data are current through the end of the state fiscal year 1990.

1994 3rd Calendar Quarter

The data are current through the end of the third quarter (September 30th) of 1994.

1994 3rd Federal Fiscal Quarter

The data are current through the end of the third quarter (June 30th) of 1994.

1994 3rd State Fiscal Quarter

The data are current through the end of the third quarter (March 31st) of 1994.

Metadata Explanation

Metadata have traditionally been defined as data about the data. This traditional definition was useful until the need for increased data awareness and understanding, the resolution of data disparity, and the need for an integrated data resource became important. As organizations began looking at what data were available, how those data present a view of the real world, the quality of those data, and the metadata defining those data, it became clear that the traditional definition of metadata is not sufficient.

> The traditional definition of metadata is no longer sufficient.

Are data about the quality of data representing the real world considered data or metadata? In other words, there are data about the depth of wells and the populations of cities, and there are data about the accuracy of the well depth measurement and the population determination. Are the data about accuracy of data considered data or metadata?

Is the description of the data entities and data attributes for a new information system considered data or metadata? These descriptions are clearly metadata for the project team. However, those descriptions are data to the data dictionary that stores those descriptions. The data dictionary itself has metadata, such as the metadata about data entities, data attributes, and primary keys. Which are data and which are metadata?

The resolution is not easy; however, it is not impossible if a new perspective is taken regarding data and metadata. The first tier in Figure D.1 shows the objects and events that an organization is tracking in the real world. The objects and events are any person, place, thing, event, or concept that are commonly used for developing a business model or a logical data model. The data about the features of those objects and events are commonly referred to as data. The data defining the data about those objects and events are commonly known as metadata.

The second tier in Figure D.1 shows the situation in more detail. This tier has the same objects and events in the real world. The *praedata* are data that present the real world to the organization or the business client. Praedata is a new term developed from the Latin *praesentare*, meaning to present. Praedata directly present features about objects and events.

Example: John Smith, Swift River, 12/23/1992, and $125.83 are praedata.

Paradata are data that describe the quality of the praedata. Paradata is also a new term developed from *para*, meaning beside, near, alongside, or assisting. Paradata represent the quality of praedata. They include anything about the praedata quality, but do not include anything about the definition or structure of the praedata.

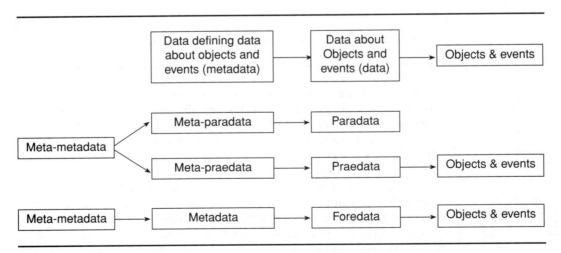

Figure D.1   Diagram of data and metadata types.

Example: *Only people employed by the state, rivers in the northern region*, and *to the nearest 10 feet* are paradata.

Meta-praedata and meta-paradata are both new terms and were developed by prefixing praedata and paradata with *meta*, meaning a later stage, situated behind, or transcending. *Meta-praedata* are data that define the praedata.

Example: The definitions of Stream Name Complete, Person Birth Date CYMD, and Well Depth Feet are meta-praedata.

Meta-paradata are data that define the paradata.

Example: The definitions of Well Depth Measurement Accuracy and Timber Layer Coverage are meta-paradata.

These two sets of data, collectively, are referred to as *metadata*. *Meta-metadata* are data that provide the descriptions of meta-praedata and meta-paradata.

Example: The definitions of data entity, data attribute, and data file are meta-metadata.

A new perspective of metadata helps resolve the metadata dilemma.

The third tier in Figure D.1 shows the current terms based on the definitions in the second tier. This tier has the same objects and events in the real world. Foredata are the data about the objects and events, including both praedata and paradata. They are the up front data that people see about objects and events. *Foredata* is a new term developed from *fore*, meaning beforehand, up front, at or near the front.

Metadata are the data describing the foredata, including meta-praedata and the meta-paradata. The metadata come after or behind the foredata. They are data supporting the foredata. The metadata include the meta-praedata and the meta-paradata.

Cross-Reference Example

The example on the following pages is a set of data quality metadata extracted from a larger set of metadata standards pertaining to geospatial metadata.

ORIGINAL DATA DEFINITIONS

The data definitions from the original geospatial metadata standards document are listed below.

Data Quality Information

2   Data Quality Information—A general assessment of the quality of the data set. (Recommendations on information to be reported and tests to be performed are found in "Spatial Data Quality," which is Chapter 3 of Part 1 in Department of Commerce, 1992, *Spatial Data Transfer Standard (SDTS)* (Federal Information Processing Standard 173): Washington, Department of Commerce, National Institute of Standards and Technology.)
Type:compound

Data Quality Information =
   Attribute Accuracy =
   0{Attribute Accuracy}1 +
   Logical Consistency Report +
   Completeness Report +
   0{Positional Accuracy}1 +
   Lineage +
   (Cloud Cover)

Attribute Accuracy =
    Attribute Accuracy Report +
(1 {Quantitative Attribute Accuracy Assessment} n)

Quantitative Attribute Accuracy Assessment =
    Attribute Accuracy Value +
    Attribute Accuracy Explanation

Positional Accuracy =
    0 (Horizontal Positional Accuracy}1 +
    0{Vertical Positional Accuracy}1

Horizontal Positional Accuracy =
    Horizontal Positional Accuracy Report +
    (1{Quantitative Horizontal Positional Accuracy Assessment}n)

Quantitative Horizontal Positional Accuracy Assessment =
    Horizontal Positional Accuracy Value +
    Horizontal Positional Accuracy Explanation

Vertical Positional Accuracy =
    Vertical Positional Accuracy Report +
    (1{Quantitative Vertical Positional Accuracy Assessment}n)

Quantitative Vertical Positional Accuracy Assessment =
    Vertical Positional Accuracy Value +
    Vertical Positional Accuracy Explanation

Lineage =
    0{Source Information}n +
    1{Process Step}n

Source Information =
    Source Citation +
    0{Source Scale Denominator}1 +
    Type of Source Media +
    Source Time Period of Content +
    Source Citation Abbreviation +
    Source Contribution

Source Citation =
    Citation Information
    Source Time Period of Content =

Time Period Information +
Source Currentness Reference

Process Step =
Process Description +
0{Source Used Citation Abbreviation}n +
Process Date +
(Process Time) +
0{Source Produced Citation Abbreviation}n +
(Process Contact)

Process Contact =
Contact Information

2.1   Attribute Accuracy An assessment of the accuracy of the identification of entities and assignment of attribute values in the data set.
Type: compound

2.1.1   Attribute Accuracy Report An explanation of the accuracy of the identification of the entities and assignments of values in the data set and a description of the tests used.
Type: text
Domain: free text

2.1.2   Quantitative Attribute Accuracy Assessment A value assigned to summarize the accuracy of the identification of the entities and assignments of values in the data set and the identification of the test that yielded the value.
Type: compound

2.1.2.1   Attribute Accuracy Value An estimate of the accuracy of the identification of the entities and assignments of attribute values in the data set.
Type: text
Domain: "unknown" free text

2.1.2.2   Attribute Accuracy Explanation The identification of the test that yielded the Attribute Accuracy Value.
Type: text
Domain: free text

2.2   Logical Consistency Report An explanation of the fidelity of the relationships in the data set and the tests used.
Type: text
Domain: free text

2.3   Completeness Report Information about omissions, selection criteria, generalization, definitions used, and other rules used to derive the data set.
Type: text
Domain: free text

2.4   Positional Accuracy An assessment of the accuracy of the positions of spatial objects.
Type: compound

2.4.1   Horizontal Positional Accuracy An estimate of accuracy of the horizontal positions of the spatial objects.
Type: compound

2.4.1.1   Horizontal Positional Accuracy Report An explanation of the accuracy of the horizontal coordinate measurements and a description of the tests used.
Type: text
Domain: free text

2.4.1.2   Quantitative Horizontal Positional Accuracy Assessment Numeric value assigned to summarize the accuracy of the horizontal coordinate measurements and the identification of the tests that yielded the value.
Type: compound

2.4.1.2.1   Horizontal Positional Accuracy Value An estimate of the accuracy of the horizontal coordinate measurements in the data set expressed in (ground) meters.
Type: real
Domain: free real

2.4.1.2.2   Horizontal Positional Accuracy Explanation The identification of the test that yielded the Horizontal Positional Accuracy Value.
Type: text
Domain: free text

2.4.2   Vertical Positional Accuracy An estimate of accuracy of the vertical positions in the data set.
Type: compound

2.4.2.1   Vertical Positional Accuracy Report An explanation of the accuracy of the vertical coordinate measurements and a description of the tests used.
Type: text
Domain: free text

2.4.2.2   Quantitative Vertical Positional Accuracy Assessment   Numeric value assigned to summarize the accuracy of vertical coordinate measurements and the identification of the test that yielded the value.
Type: compound

2.4.2.2.1   Vertical Positional Accuracy Value   An estimate of the accuracy of the vertical coordinate measurement in the data set expressed in (ground) meters.
Type: real
Domain: free real

2.4.2.2.2   Vertical Positional Accuracy Explanation   The identification of the test that yielded the Vertical Positional Accuracy Value.
Type: text
Domain: free text

2.5   Lineage   Information about the events, parameters, and source data that constructed the data set and information about the responsible parties.
Type: compound

2.5.1   Source Information   List of sources and a short discussion of the information contributed by each.
Type: compound

2.5.1.1   Source Citation   Reference for a source data set.
Type: compound

2.5.1.2   Source Scale Denominator   The denominator of the representative fraction on a map (for example, on a 1:24,000-scale map, the Source Scale Denominator is 24000).
Type: integer
Domain: Source Scale Denominator >I

2.5.1.3   Type of Source Media   The medium of the source data set.
Type: text
Domain: "paper" "stable-base" "material" "microfiche" "microfilm" "audio-cassette" "chart" "filmstrip" "transparency" "videocassette" "videodisc" "videotape" "physical" "model" "computer program" "disc" "cartridge tape" "magnetic tape" "on-line" "CD-ROM" "electronic bulletin board" "electronic mail system" free text

2.5.1.4   Source Time Period of Content   Time period(s) for which the source data set corresponds to the ground.
Type: compound

2.5.1.4.1   Source Currentness Reference The basis on which the source time period of content information of the source data set is determined.
Type: text
Domain: 'ground condition' 'publication date' free text

2.5.1.5   Source Citation Abbreviation Short-form alias for the source citation.
Type: text
Domain: free text

2.5.1.6   Source Contribution Brief statement identifying the information contributed by the source to the data set.
Type: text
Domain: free text

2.5.2   Process Step Information about a single event.
Type: compound

2.5.2.1   Process Description An explanation of the event and related parameters or tolerances.
Type: text
Domain: free text

2.5.2.2   Source Used Citation Abbreviation The Source Citation Abbreviation of a data set used in the processing step.
Type: text
Domain: Source Citation Abbreviations from the Source Information entries for the data set.

2.5.2.3   Process Date The date when the event was completed.
Type: date
Domain: "unknown" "not complete" free date

2.5.2.4   Process Time The time when the event was completed.
Type: time
Domain: free time

2.5.2.5   Source Produced Citation Abbreviation The Source Citation Abbreviation of an intermediate data set that is significant in the opinion of the data producer, is generated in the processing step, and is used in later processing steps.

Type: text
Domain: Source Citation Abbreviations from the Source Information entries for the data set.

2.5.2.6   Process Contact The party responsible for the processing step information.
Type: compound

2.6   Cloud Cover Area of a data set obstructed by clouds, expressed as a percentage of the spatial extent.
Type: integer
Domain: 0 < Cloud Cover < = 100 "Unknown"

CROSS-REFERENCES

The cross-references between the data names in the geospatial metadata standards and the common data architecture are listed below.

Cross-References by Common Data Name

Geospatial Dataset Attribute Accuracy Description	Attribute Accuracy Report
Geospatial Dataset Attribute Accuracy Estimate	Attribute Accuracy Value
Geospatial Dataset Attribute Accuracy Explanation	Attribute Accuracy Explanation
Geospatial Dataset Cloud Cover Percent	Cloud Cover
Geospatial Dataset Horizontal Accuracy Description	Horixontal Positional Accuracy Report
Geospatial Dataset Horizontal Accuracy Esitmate Meters	Horizontal Positional Accuracy Value
Geospatial Dataset Horizontal Accuracy Explanation	Horizontal Positional Accuracy Explanation
Geospatial Dataset Process Date Variable	Process Date
Geospatial Dataset Process Description	Process Description
Geospatial Dataset Process Produced Ciation Abbreviation	Source Produced Citation Abbreviation
Geospatial Dataset Process Time Variable	Process Time
Geospatial Dataset Process Used Citation Abbreviation	Source Used Citation Abbreviation

Geospatial Dataset Source Object Vertical Count	Vertical Count
Geospatial Dataset Source Citation Abbreviation	Source Citation Abbreviation
Geospatial Dataset Source Contribution Description	Source Contribution
Geospatial Dataset Source Currentness Reference Name	Source Currentness Reference
Geospatial Dataset Source Media Type Name	Type of Source Media
Geospatial Dataset Source Scale Denominator	Source Scale Denominator
Geospatial Dataset Vertical Accuracy Description	Vertical Positional Accuracy Report
Geospatial Dataset Vertical Accuracy Explanation	Vertical Positional Accuracy Explanation
Geospatial Dataset Vertical Accuracy Value Meters	Vertical Positional Accuracy Value

Cross-References by Product Data Name

Attribute Accuracy Report	Geospatial Dataset Attribute Accuracy Description
Attribute Accuracy Explanation	Geospatial Dataset Attribute Accuracy Explanation
Attribute Accuracy Value	Geospatial Dataset Attribute Accuracy Estimate
Cloud Cover	Geospatial Dataset Cloud Cover Percent
Horixontal Positional Accuracy Report	Geospatial Dataset Horizontal Accuracy Description
Horizontal Positional Accuracy Explanation	Geospatial Dataset Horizontal Accuracy Explanation
Horizontal Positional Accuracy Value	Geospatial Dataset Horizontal Accuracy Estimate Meters
Process Date	Geospatial Dataset Process Date Variable
Process Description	Geospatial Dataset Process Description
Process Time	Geospatial Dataset Process Time Variable
Source Citation Abbreviation	Geospatial Dataset Source Citation Abbreviation
Source Contribution	Geospatial Dataset Source Contribution Description
Source Currentness Reference	Geospatial Dataset Source Currentness Reference Name
Source Produced Citation Abbreviation	Geospatial Dataset Process Produced Ciation Abbreviation
Source Scale Denominator	Geospatial Dataset Source Scale Denominator

Source Used Citation Abbreviation	Geospatial Dataset Process Used Citation Abbreviation
Type of Source Media	Geospatial Dataset Source Media Type Name
Vertical Count	Geospatial Dataset Source Object Vertical Count
Vertical Positional Accuracy Explanation	Geospatial Dataset Vertical Accuracy Explanation
Vertical Positional Accuracy Report	Geospatial Dataset Vertical Accuracy Description
Vertical Positional Accuracy Value	Geospatial Dataset Vertical Accuracy Value Meters

SUBJECT RELATION DIAGRAM

The subject relation diagram for the data quality metadata is shown in Figure E.1.

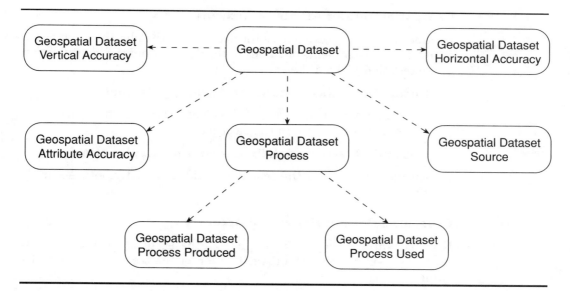

Figure E.1   Subject relation diagram for metadata.

DATA DEFINITIONS

The common data definitions, which were extracted from the original metadata standards document, are listed below by their common data name.

Geospatial Dataset

Data about the content, quality, condition, and other characteristics of a data set.

Geospatial Dataset Attribute Accuracy Description

An explanation of the accuracy of the identification of the entities and assignments of values in the data set and a description of the tests used.

Geospatial Dataset Cloud Cover Percent

Area of a data set obstructed by clouds, expressed as a percentage of the spatial extent.

Geospatial Dataset Horizontal Accuracy Description

An explanation of the accuracy of the horizontal coordinate measurements and a description of the tests used.

Geospatial Dataset Attribute Accuracy

A value assigned to summarize the accuracy of the identification of the entities and assignments of values in the data set and the identification of the test that yielded the value.

Geospatial Dataset Attribute Accuracy Estimate

An estimate of the accuracy of the identification of the entities and assignments of values in the data set.

Geospatial Dataset Attribute Accuracy Explanation

An identification of the test that yielded the Attribute Accuracy Value.

Geospatial Dataset Horizontal Accuracy

Numeric value assigned to summarize the accuracy of the horizontal measurements and the identification of the test that yielded the value.

Geospatial Dataset Horizontal Accuracy Estimate Meters

An estimate of the accuracy of the horizontal coordinate measurements in the data set expressed in (ground) meters.

Geospatial Dataset Horizontal Accuracy Explanation

The identification of the test that yielded the Horizontal Positional Accuracy Value.

Geospatial Dataset Process

Information about a single event.

Geospatial Dataset Process Date Variable

The date when the event was completed.

Geospatial Dataset Process Description

An explanation of the event and related parameters or tolerances.

Geospatial Dataset Process Time Variable

The time when the event was completed.

Geospatial Dataset Process Produced

(none)

Geospatial Dataset Process Produced Citation Abbreviation

The Source Citation Abbreviation of an intermediate data set that is significant in the opinion of the data producer, is generated in the processing step, and is used in later processing steps.

Geospatial Dataset Process Used

(none)

Geospatial Dataset Process Used Citation Abbreviation

The Source Citation Abbreviation of a data set used in the processing steps.

Geospatial Dataset Source

List of sources and a short discussion of the information contained by each.

Geospatial Dataset Source Citation Abbreviation

Short-form alias for the source citation.

Geospatial Dataset Source Contribution Description

Brief statement identifying the information contributed by the source to the data set.

Geospatial Dataset Source Currentness Reference Name

The basis on which the source time period of content information of the source data set is determined.

Geospatial Dataset Source Scale Denominator

The denominator of the representative fraction on a map (for example, on a 1:24,000-scale map, the Source Scale Denominator is 24000).

Geospatial Dataset Vertical Accuracy

Numeric value assigned to summarize the accuracy of vertical coordinate measurements and the identification of the test that yielded the value.

Geospatial Dataset Vertical Accuracy Explanation

The identification of the test that yielded the Vertical Positional Accuracy Value.

Geospatial Dataset Vertical Accuracy Value Meters

An estimate of the accuracy of the vertical coordinate measurement in the data set expressed in (ground) meters.

Evaluation Data Example

The example on the following pages was extracted from a larger set of evaluational data for health care claims. These pages show an operational subject relation diagram, an evaluational subject relation diagram, the primary key matrix for the summary data subjects, and the data characteristic matrix for the summary data subjects.

OPERATIONAL SUBJECT RELATION DIAGRAM

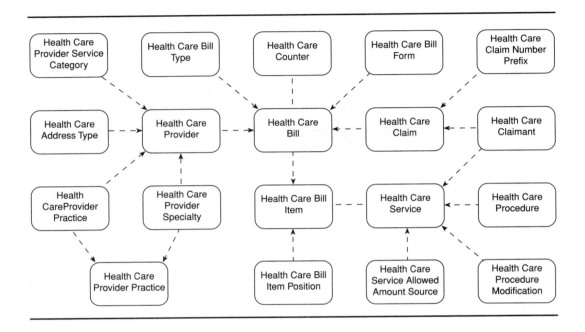

EVALUATION SUBJECT RELATION DIAGRAM

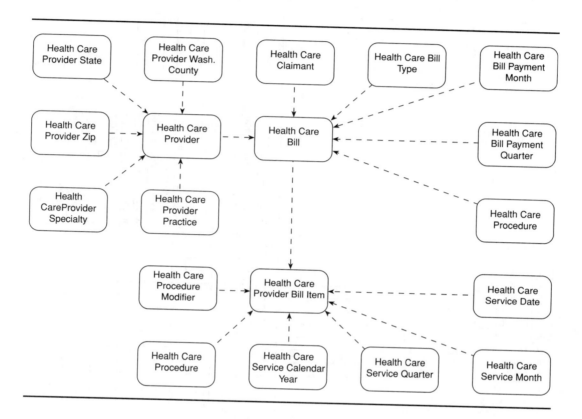

PRIMARY KEY MATRIX

#	Health Care Claim Summary (n)	HC Claimant Identifier	HC Service Type Code	HC Service Begin Date CYMD	HC Bill Type Code	HC Provider Identifier	HC Provider Practice Code	HC Provider Specialty Code	HC Procedure Group Identifier	HC Procedure Code	HC Procedure Modifier Code	HC Service Begin Month Number Calendar Year	HC Service Begin Quarter Number Calender Year	HC Service Begin Calendar Year Number	HC Payment Month Number Calendar Year	HC Bill Payment Quarter Number Calendar Year	HC Bill Payment Date Calendar Year	HC Provider Address Zip Code Complete	HC Provider Address Washington County Code	HC Provider Address State Name Postal Abbreviation
1	(no selection)																			
2	Claimant	X																		
3	Service Unit Count		X																	
4	Service Date			X																
5	Provider					X														
6	Provider, Service Month					X						X								
7	Provider, Service Quarter					X							X							
8	Provider, Service Calendar Year					X								X						
9	Provider, Payment Month					X									X					
10	Provider, Payment Quarter					X										X				
11	Provider, Payment Calendar Year					X											X			
12	Provider Type						X													
13	Provider Type, Service Month						X					X								
14	Provider Type, Service Quarter						X						X							
15	Provider Type, Service Calendar Year						X							X						
16	Provider Type, Payment Month						X								X					
17	Provider Type, Payment Quarter						X									X				
18	Provider Type, Payment Calendar Year						X										X			
19	Claimant, Provider Type	X					X													
20	Service Unit Count, Provider Type		X				X													
21	Service Date, Provider Type			X			X													
22	Provider Type, Provider Specialty						X	X												
23	Provider Type, Provider Specialty, Service Month						X	X				X								
24	Provider Type, Provider Specialty, Service Quarter						X	X					X							
25	Provider Type, Provider Specialty, Service Calendar Year						X	X						X						
26	Provider Type, Provider Speciality, Payment Month						X	X							X					
27	Provider Type, Provider Specialty, Payment Quarter						X	X								X				
28	Provider Type, Provider Specialty, Payment Calendar Year						X	X									X			
29	Claimant, Provider Type, Provider Specialty	X					X	X												
30	Service Unit Count, Provider Type, Provider Specialty		X				X	X												
31	Service Date, Provider Type, Provider Specialty			X			X	X												
32	Service Type		X																	
33	Service Type, Calendar Year		X											X						

PRIMARY KEY MATRIX *(cont.)*

	Health Care Claim Summary (n)	HC Claimant Identifier	HC Service Type Code	HC Service Begin Date CYMD	HC Bill Type Code	HC Provider Identifier	HC Provider Practice Code	HC Provider Specialty Code	HC Procedure Group Identifier	HC Procedure Code	HC Procedure Modifier Code	HC Service Begin Month Number Calendar Year	HC Service Begin Quarter Number Calendar Year	HC Service Begin Calendar Year Number	HC Payment Month Number Calendar Year	HC Bill Payment Quarter Number Calendar Year	HC Bill Payment Date Calendar Year	HC Provider Address Zip Code Complete	HC Provider Address Washington County Code	HC Provider Address State Name Postal Abbreviation
34	Bill Type				X															
35	Procedure and/or Modifier									X	X									
36	Provider Type, Provider Modifier						X				X									
37	Procedure, Provider Type, Payment Quarter						X				X					X				
38	Procedure Group, Service Calendar Year								X					X						
39	Procedure Group, Payment Calendar Year								X								X			
40	Procedure Group, Procedure Modifier, Service Calendar Year								X		X			X						
41	Procedure Group, Procedure Modifier, Payment Calendar Year								X		X						X			
42	Provider Zip Code																	X		
43	Provider Specialty, Provider Zip Code							X										X		
44	Washington County																		X	
45	Provider Specialty, Washington County							X											X	
46	Claimant, Washington County	X																	X	
47	Service Unit Count, Washington County																		X	
48	Service Date, Washington County																		X	
49	Claimant, Washington County, Provider Type	X					X												X	
50	Service Unit Count, Washington Country, Provider Type						X												X	
51	Service Date, Washington Country, Provider Type			X																
52	Claimant	X																		
53	Claimant, Provider Specialty, Provider Zip Code	X						X												
54	Claimant, Provider Specialty, Washington County	X						X												
55	State																			X
56	Claimant, State																			X
57	Service Unit Count, State	X																		X
58	Service Date, State			X																X
59	Claimant, State, Provider Type	X					X													X
60	Service Unit Count, State, Provider Type						X													X
61	Service Date, State, Provider Type			X			X													X
62	State, Provider Type						X													X
63	Washington County, Provider Type						X													X
64	Provider, Provider Type, Provider Specialty					X	X	X												

DATA CHARACTERISTIC MATRIX

#	Health Care Claim Summary (n)	.Average Amount Billed	.Average Amount Paid	.Percent of Total Amount Paid	.Total Amount Billed Change Percent	.Total Amount Billed	.Total Amount Billed Change	.Total Amount Billed Comparison Claimant to Group	.Total Amount Billed percent of Total Expenditure	.Total Amount Billed to Paid Change	.Total Amount Paid	.Total Amount Paid Change	.Total Amount Paid Change Percent	.Total Amount Paid Comparison Claimant to Group	.Total Amount Paid per Claimant	.Total Amount Paid Percent of Total Expenditure	.Total Bill Count	.Total Bill Count Change Percent	.Total Claim Count	.Total Claim Count Change Percent	.Total Claimant Count	.Total Claimant Count Change Percent	.Total Service Unit Count	.Total Service Unit Count Change	.Total Service Unit Count Change Percent	.Total Service Unit Count Comparison Claimant to Group	.Total Visit Count
1	(no selection)	X	X	X	X	X	X	X	X	X	X	X	X	X	X	X	X	X	X	X	X	X	X	X	X	X	X
2	Claimant	X	X	X	X	X	X	X	X	X	X	X	X	X	X												
3	Service Unit Count	X	X	X	X	X	X	X	X	X	X	X	X	X	X												
4	Service Date	X	X	X	X	X	X	X	X	X	X	X	X	X	X												
5	Provider	X	X	X	X	X	X	X	X	X	X	X	X	X	X												
6	Provider, Service Month	X	X	X	X	X	X	X	X	X	X	X	X	X	X	X	X	X	X	X	X	X					
7	Provider, Service Quarter	X	X	X	X	X	X	X	X	X	X	X	X	X	X	X	X	X	X	X							
8	Provider, Service Calendar Year	X	X	X	X	X	X	X	X	X	X	X	X	X	X	X	X	X	X	X							
9	Provider, Payment Month	X	X	X	X	X	X	X	X	X	X	X	X	X	X	X	X	X	X	X							
10	Provider, Payment Quarter	X	X	X	X	X	X	X	X	X	X	X	X	X	X	X	X	X	X	X							
11	Provider, Payment Calendar Year	X	X	X	X	X	X	X	X	X	X	X	X	X	X	X	X	X	X	X							
12	Provider Type	X	X	X	X	X	X	X	X	X	X	X	X	X	X	X	X	X	X	X	X	X					
13	Provider Type, Service Month	X	X	X	X	X	X	X	X	X	X	X	X	X	X	X	X	X	X	X							
14	Provider Type, Service Quarter	X	X	X	X	X	X	X	X	X	X	X	X	X	X	X	X	X	X	X							
15	Provider Type, Service Calendar Year	X	X	X	X	X	X	X	X	X	X	X	X	X	X	X	X	X	X	X							
16	Provider Type, Payment Month	X	X	X	X	X	X	X	X	X	X	X	X	X	X	X	X	X	X	X							
17	Provider Type, Payment Quarter	X	X	X	X	X	X	X	X	X	X	X	X	X	X	X	X	X	X	X							
18	Provider Type, Payment Calendar Year	X	X	X	X	X	X	X	X	X	X	X	X	X	X	X	X	X	X	X							
19	Claimant, Provider Type	X	X	X	X	X	X	X	X	X	X	X	X	X	X												
20	Service Unit Count, Provider Type	X	X	X	X	X	X	X	X	X	X	X	X	X	X												
21	Service Date, Provider Type	X	X	X	X	X	X	X	X	X	X	X	X	X	X												
22	Provider Type, Provider Specialty	X	X	X	X	X	X	X	X	X	X	X	X	X	X	X	X	X	X	X	X	X	X	X	X	X	X
23	Provider Type, Provider Specialty, Service Month	X	X	X	X	X	X	X	X	X	X	X	X	X	X	X	X	X	X	X							
24	Provider Type, Provider Specialty, Service Quarter	X	X	X	X	X	X	X	X	X	X	X	X	X	X	X	X	X	X	X							
25	Provider Type, Provider Specialty, Service Calendar Year	X	X	X	X	X	X	X	X	X	X	X	X	X	X	X	X	X	X	X							

DATA CHARACTERISTIC MATRIX *(cont.)*

	Health Care Claim Summary (n)	Average Amount Billed	Average Amount Paid	Percent of Total Amount Paid	Total Amount Billed Change Percent	Total Amount Billed	Total Amount Billed Change	Total Amount Billed Comparison Claimant to Group	Total Amount Billed percent of Total Expenditure	Total Amount Billed to Paid Change	Total Amount Paid	Total Amount Paid Change	Total Amount Paid Change Percent	Total Amount Paid Comparison Claimant to Group	Total Amount Paid per Claimant	Total Amount Paid Percent of Total Expenditure	Total Bill Count	Total Bill Count Change Percent	Total Claim Count	Total Claim Count Change Percent	Total Claimant Count	Total Claimant Count Change Percent	Total Service Unit Count	Total Service Unit Count Change	Total Service Unit Count Change Percent	Total Service Unit Count Comparison Claimant to Group	Total Visit Count
26	Provider Type, Provider Speciality, Payment Month	X	X	X	X	X	X	X	X	X	X	X	X	X	X	X	X	X	X	X	X						
27	Provider Type, Provider Specialty, Payment Quarter	X	X	X	X	X	X	X	X	X	X	X	X	X	X	X	X	X	X	X	X						
28	Provider Type, Provider Specialty, Payment Calendar Year	X	X	X	X	X	X	X	X	X	X	X	X	X	X	X	X	X	X	X	X						
29	Claimant, Provider Type, Provider Specialty	X	X	X	X	X	X	X	X	X	X	X	X	X	X												
30	Service Unit Count, Provider Type, Provider Specialty	X	X	X	X	X	X	X	X	X	X	X	X	X	X												
31	Service Date, Provider Type, Provider Specialty	X	X	X	X	X	X	X	X	X	X	X	X	X	X												
32	Service Type	X	X	X	X	X	X	X	X	X	X	X	X	X	X												
33	Service Type, Calendar Year	X	X	X	X	X	X	X	X	X	X	X	X	X	X												
34	Bill Type	X	X	X	X	X	X	X	X	X	X	X	X	X	X												
35	Procedure and/or Modifier	X	X	X	X	X	X	X	X	X	X	X	X	X	X												
36	Provider Type, Provider Modifier	X	X	X	X	X	X	X	X	X	X	X	X	X	X												
37	Procedure, Provider Type, Payment Quarter	X	X	X	X	X	X	X	X	X	X	X	X	X	X												
38	Procedure Group, Service Calendar Year	X	X	X	X	X	X	X	X	X	X	X	X	X	X												
39	Procedure Group, Payment Calendar Year	X	X	X	X	X	X	X	X	X	X	X	X	X	X												
40	Procedure Group, Procedure Modifier, Service Calendar Year	X	X	X	X	X	X	X	X	X	X	X	X	X	X												
41	Procedure Group, Procedure Modifier, Payment Calendar Year	X	X	X	X	X	X	X	X	X	X	X	X	X	X												
42	Provider Zip Code	X	X	X	X	X	X	X	X	X	X	X	X	X	X												
43	Provider Specialty, Provider Zip Code	X	X	X	X	X	X	X	X	X	X	X	X	X	X												
44	Washington County	X	X	X	X	X	X	X	X	X	X	X	X	X	X	X	X	X	X	X	X	X	X	X	X	X	X
45	Provider Specialty, Washington County	X	X	X	X	X	X	X	X	X	X	X	X	X	X												

DATA CHARACTERISTIC MATRIX *(cont.)*

#	Health Care Claim Summary (n)	.Average Amount Billed	.Average Amount Paid	.Percent of Total Amount Paid	.Total Amount Billed Change Percent	.Total Amount Billed	.Total Amount Billed Change	.Total Amount Billed Comparison Claimant to Group	.Total Amount Billed percent of Total Expenditure	.Total Amount Billed to Paid Change	.Total Amount Paid	.Total Amount Paid Change	.Total Amount Paid Change Percent	.Total Amount Paid Comparison Claimant to Group	.Total Amount Paid per Claimant	.Total Amount Paid Percent of Total Expenditure	.Total Bill Count	.Total Bill Count Change Percent	.Total Claim Count	.Total Claim Count Change Percent	.Total Claimant Count	.Total Claimant Count Change Percent	.Total Service Unit Count	.Total Service Unit Count Change	.Total Service Unit Count Change Percent	.Total Service Unit Count Comparison Claimant to Group	.Total Visit Count
46	Claimant, Washington County	X	X	X	X	X	X	X	X	X	X	X	X	X	X	X											
47	Service Unit Count, Washington County	X	X	X	X	X	X	X	X	X	X	X	X	X	X	X											
48	Service Date, Washington County	X	X	X	X	X	X	X	X	X	X	X	X	X	X	X											
49	Claimant, Washington County, Provider Type	X	X	X	X	X	X	X	X	X	X	X	X	X	X	X											
50	Service Unit Count, Washington Country, Provider Type	X	X	X	X	X	X	X	X	X	X	X	X	X	X	X											
51	Service Date, Washington Country, Provider Type	X	X	X	X	X	X	X	X	X	X	X	X	X	X	X											
52	Claimant	X	X	X	X	X	X	X	X	X	X	X	X	X	X	X											
53	Claimant, Provider Specialty, Provider Zip Code	X	X	X	X	X	X	X	X	X	X	X	X	X	X	X											
54	Claimant, Provider Specialty, Washington County	X	X	X	X	X	X	X	X	X	X	X	X	X	X	X											
55	State	X	X	X	X	X	X	X	X	X	X	X	X	X	X	X	X	X	X	X	X	X	X	X	X	X	
56	Claimant, State	X	X	X	X	X	X	X	X	X	X	X	X	X	X	X											
57	Service Unit Count, State	X	X	X	X	X	X	X	X	X	X	X	X	X	X	X											
58	Service Date, State	X	X	X	X	X	X	X	X	X	X	X	X	X	X	X											
59	Claimant, State, Provider Type	X	X	X	X	X	X	X	X	X	X	X	X	X	X	X											
60	Service Unit Count, State, Provider Type	X	X	X	X	X	X	X	X	X	X	X	X	X	X	X											
61	Service Date, State, Provider Type	X	X	X	X	X	X	X	X	X	X	X	X	X	X	X											
62	State, Provider Type																X	X	X	X	X	X	X	X	X	X	X
63	Washington County, Provider Type																X	X	X	X	X	X	X	X	X	X	X
64	Provider, Provider Type, Provider Specialty																										X

Bibliography

Bateson, Gregory. *Steps to an Ecology of Mind.* New York: Ballantine Books, Inc. 1972.

Brackett, M. H. *Developing Data Structured Information Systems.* Topeka, KS: Ken Orr and Associates, Inc., 1983.

——. *Developing Data Structured Databases.* Englewood Cliffs, NJ: Prentice-Hall, 1987.

——. *Practical Data Design.* Englewood Cliffs, NJ: Prentice-Hall, 1990.

——. *Data Sharing Using a Common Data Architecture.* New York, NY: John Wiley & Sons, Inc, 1994.

Collins, Jim C., Porras, Jerry I. *Built to Last: Successful Habits of Visionary Companies.* New York: Harper Business, 1992.

Conner, Daryl R. *Managing at the Speed of Change: How Resilient Managers Succeed and Prosper While Others Fail.* New York: Villard Books, 1993.

Covey, Steven R. *The 7 Habits of Highly Effective People.* New York: Simon and Schuster, 1989.

Davenport, Thomas H. *Process Innovation: Reengineering Work Through Information Technology.* Boston: Harvard Business School Press, 1993.

Deming, W. Edwards. *Out of the Crisis.* Cambridge: Massachusetts Institute of Technology, 1986.

Hammer, Michael and Champy, James. *Reengineering the Corporation: A Manifest for Business Revolution.* New York: Harper Business, 1993.

——. *Beyond Reengineering.* Harper Collins, 1995.

————. *The Reengineering Revolution: A Handbook.* New York: Harper Business, 1995.

Imparto, Nicholas. *Jumping the Curve: Innovation and Strategic Choice in an Age of Transition.* San Francisco: Jossey-Bass Publishers, 1994.

Inmon, W.H. *Building the Data Warehouse.* New York: QED, 1990

Inmon, W.H. and Hackathorn, R.D. *Using the Data Warehouse.* New York: John Wiley & Sons, 1994.

Juran, Douglas J.M. *Juran on Planning for Quality.* New York: Free Press, 1986.

Khoshatian, Setrig. *Object-Oriented Databases.* New York: John Wiley & Sons, 1993.

Lewis, David, and Greene, James. *Thinking Better.* New York: Rawson, Wade Publishers, Inc., 1982

Osborne, D., and Gaebler, T. *Reinventing Government.* New York: Plume, 1993

Pagels, Heinz. *The Cosmic Code.* New York: Bantam Books, 1983.

————. *Perfect Symmetry.* New York: Bantam Books, 1986.

————. *The Dreams of Reason.* New York: Simon and Schuster, 1988.

Ross, Ronald G. *Data Dictionaries and Data Administration: Concepts and Practices for Data Resource Management.* New York: McGraw-Hill, 1984.

————. *Entity Modeling: Techniques and Application.* Boston: Database Research Group, 1987.

Sowa, J.F. *Conceptual Structures: Information Processing in Mind and Machine.* Reading, MA: Addison-Wesley, 1984.

Stoll, Clifford. *Silicon Snake Oil: Second Thoughts on the Information Highway.* New York: Doubleday, 1995.

Strabel, Paul. *Breakpoints: How Managers Exploit Radical Barriers to Change.* Boston: Harvard Business School Press, 1992.

Toynbee, Arnold J. *Surviving the Future.* NY: Oxford University Press, 1971.

von Oech, Roger. *A Whack on the Side of the Head.* New York: Warner Books, 1983

Waterman, Robert H. Jr. *The Renewal Factor: How Best to Get and Keep Competitive Advantage.* New York: Bantam Books, 1989.

Wurman, Richard S. *Information Anxiety.* New York: Doubleday, 1989.

Youngblood, Mark D. *Eating the Chocolate Elephant.* Richardson, TX: Micrografx, Inc., 1994.

Zachman, J.A. "A Framework for Information Systems Architecture," *IBM Systems Journal* 26, no. 3 (1987): 276–292.

Index